To Brian

The

NEW

ENCYCLOPEDIA

for the

younger generation

With Love from Grandma

xxx

Xmas
1963

SPRING BOOKS

The NEW

SPRING BOOKS • WESTBOOK HOUSE • FULHAM BROADWAY • LONDON

ENCYCLOPEDIA

for the younger generation

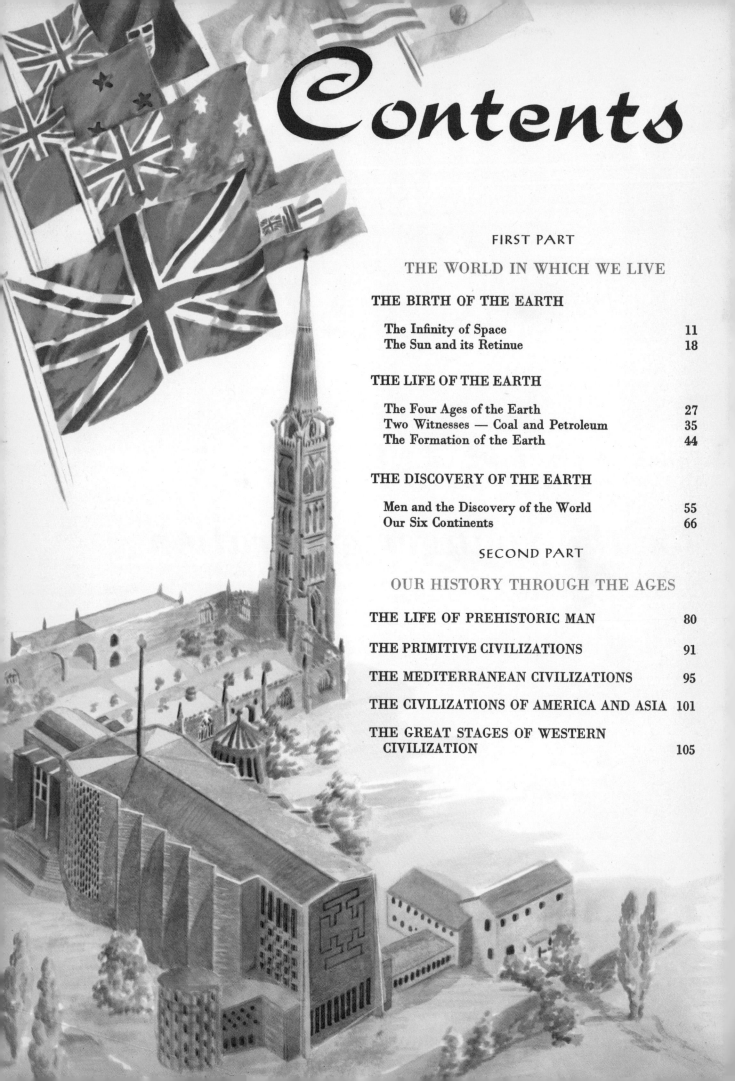

Contents

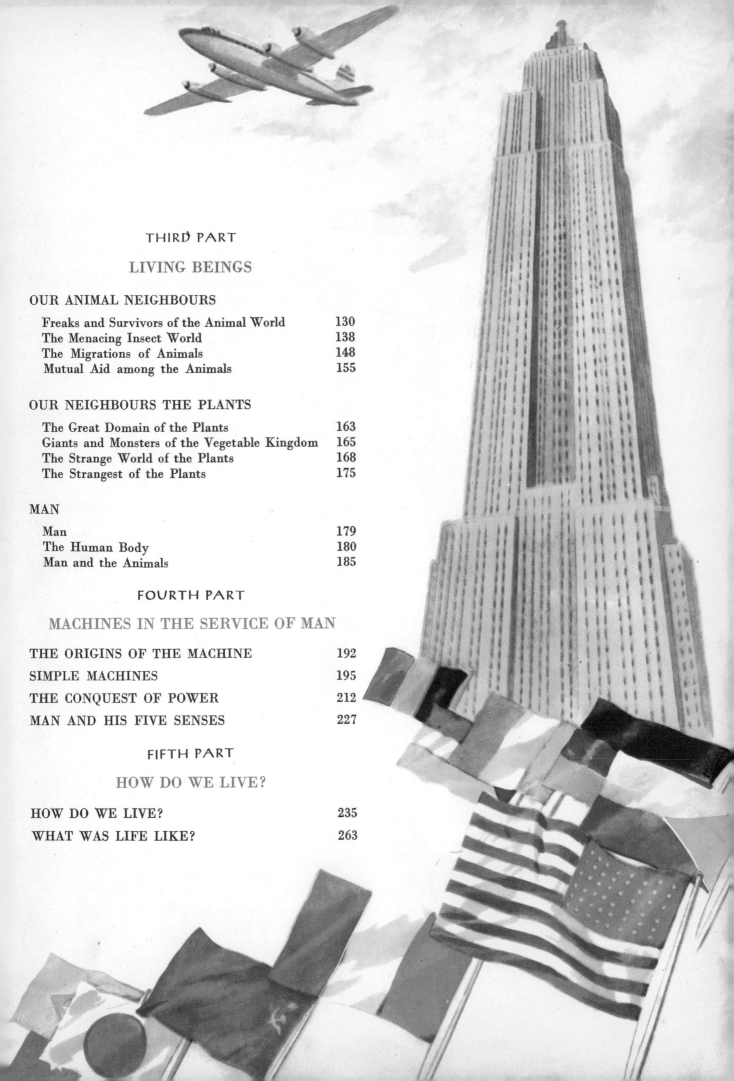

INTRODUCTION

There have been many encyclopedias for young people but it is doubtful whether there has yet been one as colourful and at the same time as informative as this volume.

To collect in one book a series of brief entries on all the subjects with which schoolchildren ought to be familiar, and thus produce a handy reference volume, is not difficult: it has been done many times before. But such books, however well presented, remain little more than text-books that a boy or girl consults without pleasure.

This encyclopedia is different. Instead of brief paragraphs alphabetically arranged, it consists of readable narrative, fascinating in itself and invaluable for the knowledge it imparts. The index provides a quick guide to specific references, but the book can be *read* for sheer enjoyment. It is a treasure-house of information, full of strange, picturesque facts as well as all essential background material. The boy or girl who has questions to ask about our world and its inhabitants, past and present, will find the answers here, attractively presented.

Great care has been taken to ensure that the vivid writing and lavish illustrations are consistent with the orthodox sciences and the most modern research; but, believing that a rigorous factual approach can sometimes become too dry, the editors have not hesitated to make use of examples or illustrations likely to strike the imagination, awaken the memory and compel attention.

Few books have been as skilfully designed as this one; few books have provided as much pleasure or been referred to as often. The editors keep it under constant revision, ensuring that the results of modern developments and new discoveries are incorporated in each successive impression.

The New Encyclopedia for the Younger Generation

*Translated and adapted into English by Maurice Michael
from L'Encyclopédie Larousse des Enfants
by René Guillot, published by © Augé, Gillon,
Hollier-Larousse, Moreau et Cie, the Librairie Larousse, 1956
Printed in Czechoslovakia from lithographs made in France and England*

© GOLDEN PLEASURE BOOKS LTD
Revised edition 1958
Second impression 1963
T 1062

FIRST PART

*the world
in which
we live*

THE BIRTH OF THE EARTH

The Infinity of Space

WHAT is this Earth on which we live in the immensity of space, with its fathomless night, its billions of twinkling stars and billions of suns which are just as big as or even bigger than ours?

By the standards of the universe the globe of our Earth is no more than a mere particle of dust — just a speck of dust circling another glowing speck, our Sun, amidst a vast cloud of sparkling dust.

Our Earth, which escorts the Sun and belongs to its retinue of planets, also takes its part in the dance of the heavenly bodies. The hub around which this dance revolves is still a mystery to us. The universe, which engulfs us with its shimmering milky belt, seems itself to rotate round our tiny speck of dust.

When the goddess Juno was suckling Jupiter's son Hercules in Olympus, a few drops of the milk spilt from the lips of the babe — such was the poetic way in which the ancients tried to explain the origin of the Milky Way, that gaseous band which on clear nights we see spanning our horizon.

It is called a galaxy and in fact surrounds the whole Earth, whose inhabitants, however, can see only part of it: a different part at the same hour of night as the seasons change. On a moonless night in London, for instance, it may look like a glittering arc widening at first and growing brighter around the constellation of Cygnus (the Swan), until it finally splits up into two arms and then drops below the horizon. Above Buenos Aires, in the splendour of the southern sky, the Milky Way forms a similar arc with the Southern Cross sparkling at its zenith.

This galaxy of the Milky Way is our universe, in which we travel through space on our speck of dust, the Earth.

The Sun, which carries the Earth along on its course, is in its turn only an unimportant star among billions of others. And just like these others it is being propelled along at a dizzy speed with the whole giant eddy of stars. Everything is in motion in the vastness of the heavens, and the stars which look immobile and, as it were, fixed to their magnificent heavenly vault are travelling through space at speeds of up to 400 miles per second!

Our galaxy has such huge dimensions that it is difficult to imagine. Where it is widest, the light from a little star travelling with us in the outer circle of the Milky Way takes 100,000 years to pass along the diameter of the galaxy.

Our galaxy is shaped like a disc swollen at the centre. From the Earth we see few stars outside the main axis where the conglomeration of them gives the powdery appearance we call the Milky Way.

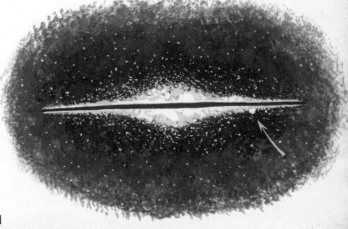

We know that light travels at a speed of 186,000 miles per second. In a thunderstorm we can see the lightning some time before we hear the clap of thunder, because light is nearly a million times faster than sound.

But when we try to imagine and to measure those vast spaces which the light of the stars takes millions of years to cross, ordinary figures are no longer any use for working out the distances between the stars. Therefore, astronomers had to find a different unit of measurement . . . an astronomic one! It is not a mile, or a million miles, but a light year. This is the distance light travels in a year, which means 365 days of 24 hours, or 24 times 3,600 seconds each day, at a speed of 186,000 miles per second.

Therefore, a light year equals

$$186,000 \text{ miles} \times 3,600 \times 24 \times 365$$
$$= 5,865,696,000,000 \text{ miles}.$$

These figures seem a bit frightening, but now we have a measure by which we can work out the diameter of the Milky Way, which, according to what we have found, must be 100,000 light years. We can express in figures those seemingly incalculable distances which separate the various galaxies from each other in space. Those galaxies are other universes, for there *are* other universes beyond the Milky Way, which is our own universe. And now we can start playing with our astronomical figures. Those galaxies are so far away from us that to photograph them takes 7 hours' exposure with a huge telescopic camera 30 feet long and 6 feet in diameter.

The great nebula in Andromeda, for instance, is

The University of Chicago has the longest astronomical telescope in the world. It is over 60 feet long, and its marvellous rotation axes allow the astronomer to scrutinize the sky in all directions. With it you can see nebulae millions of light years away from our planet.

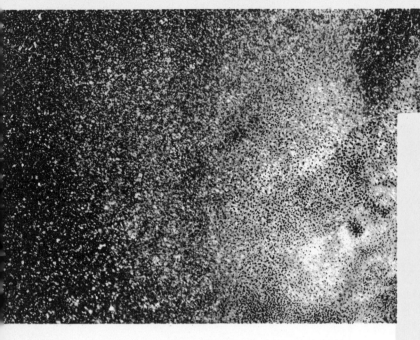

The teeming stars of the Milky Way as seen through a telescope, and the photograph of another galaxy – in Ursa Major (The Great Bear) – seen from the front. A galaxy can appear as a disc or a spiral, and in other shapes too.

another universe which seems very like our own. This nebula is comparatively near to us, so that we can see it with the naked eye, and yet it is about 1,800,000 light years distant from the Earth!

Everything is in motion in infinite space, where stars and worlds follow their eternal course at terrific speeds.

We believed we had found a unit, the light year, by which we could measure Space. But now these universes of stars whose light takes millions of years to reach us make us think of other universes still further away.

Even with light years we can never hope to express the measurements of something which is immeasurable because it is infinite.

Let us take a number, 25, for instance, and multiply it by 10, by 100, by 1,000, and eventually by a figure with an interminable sequence of noughts:

1 000 000 000 000 000 000 000 000 000 000 000 . . . etc. What we get is: 250, 2,500, 25,000 and 25,000,000, 000,000,000,000,000,000,000,000,000,000 . . . etc. As we can keep on adding noughts as long as we want to, we get a figure which never ends, a figure which becomes *infinitely* great.

Because of the tremendous distances that separate them from us, some stars may have been extinct for a long time, and yet their light is still reaching us. The people living under Ethelred I and, later, the subjects of Henry VIII could see the same stars twinkling in their sky as we do today, though some of these were already extinct in their time. And between those two reigns, that is within approximately 700 years, the light from these extinct stars had travelled the fabulous distance of one thousand billion miles.

If, after an explosion, for instance, the star Rigel in the constellation Orion were to disappear, our descendants would not notice it for another 540 years, which means they would find out towards the year 2500.

Let's go off together on an interstellar trip. But we are not going to use any of those rockets which, no doubt, one day in the near future will carry the first travellers from the Earth to the Moon; that kind of vehicle is still too slow for us. Let's suppose that our spaceship travels at least as fast as light. At the end of a day's journey, after 24 hours at the rate of 186,000 miles per second, we shall have travelled 16,000 million miles. We should reach that point in space well in advance of a jet airliner which, at a speed of 600 miles per hour, would take 3,000 years to cover the same distance.

Let's stop and take a look round: the starlit sky looks much the same as we saw it the night before. Here is Ursa Minor and there Ursa Major (with the 'Plough'), and a little further on the lovely constellation of Orion. But what is that new star down there, brighter and bigger than all the others? What looks like a bright star is, in fact, our Sun.

Now where are we going? As short a distance as possible. We shall try to reach the star nearest our Earth, which is Alpha Centauri in the constellation of Centaurus. How long then will it take us at our fantastic speed to get there? Four years and a hundred days!

And yet we cover 16,000 million miles a day. Work it out yourselves. Find out how many seconds there are in a little more than four years, and then multiply that number by 186,000.

If we figure out the whole thing on the scale of a grain of wheat representing our sun, from that grain we should have to cover 125 miles in order to reach another grain representing Alpha Centauri.

This gives one some idea of the vast empty space in which the stars are moving, and shows how little chance there is of their colliding.

But the immensity of numbers is something very relative. They seem to us enormous because we are comparing them with human life on Earth — with the measures of man, whose step covers but one yard. Here is an example of how deceptive numbers can be: at the end of his short life a man, at the rate of a mile or two a day, will have gone through the motion of putting one foot in front of the other more than 100 million times!

Do not let big numbers impress you. The grains in a field of wheat amount to millions, the same as the stars in the sky. A tiny grain of wheat is a world in itself. The grain 'wheat', the grain 'Earth', the grain 'Sun', and all the grains of stars scattered in the sky are but minute specks of dust in the infinite universe.

No one will ever know the exact number of all the stars in our galaxy. Nor will it ever be possible to give each one a name. In order to recognize them, we have grouped them into constellations in the sky, 'signs' to which we have given descriptive names, such as the Plough, Leo, Virgo, Pegasus, Cygnus, Orion, Canis Major (to which belongs Sirius, one of the most brilliant stars of our winter skies, which is relatively close to our

Four thousand years before our era the astronomers of Chaldea picked out twelve constellations from the others because, during a month, the sun rose at the spot where one of them had just risen and then disappeared with the end of night. This cycle is repeated interminably, and its inevitability profoundly impressed the Ancients. Thus each month of the year had a sign associated with it: the Ram, the Bull, the Twins, the Crab, the Lion, the Virgin, the Scales, the Scorpion, the Archer, the Sea Goat, the Water-bearer, and the Fish. The predominance of animals in the list has caused it to be named the zodiac (circle of animals). The Ancients believed in the good or evil influence of the constellation under which they were born. Even today some people are inclined to share this belief.

Earth) and the constellation of Auriga (the Charioteer) with a giant star, Capella, which is so large that our Sun is a dwarf beside it.

These constellations are groups of stars which look to us as if they were all the same distance from us; yet some of them are much further away than others.

At first sight the skyscrapers of New York look to anyone arriving by night just like such an enormous constellation, a series of glittering dots which seem to be fixed to a huge black wall. They belong, however, to buildings at greatly varying distances from the beholder. Some lights shine brighter than others because their bulbs are stronger, but they might well be further away than those with only a faint glimmer.

Although, fifty centuries ago, the constellations presented to the astronomers of Egypt and Assyria more or less the same appearances as they do today, we have in the meantime learnt that stars do change, though very slowly. We can be sure that prehistoric man, living in the Northern Hemisphere 100,000 years ago, did not see,

A 200-watt bulb 1,000 yards away has the same apparent brilliance as a pocket torch 100 yards distant. Thus the apparent brilliance of a star depends on its distance from the viewer and its intrinsic brilliance. If this latter can be estimated, you can deduce the star's distance away by its apparent brilliance.

for instance, the Plough as we do today. The astronomers have succeeded in working out the deviation of every star in that group, and determined not only what the Plough must have looked like 100,000 years ago, but also the shape it will have in another 100,000 years from now.

In the beautiful calm of the night sky, in the serene infinity which gives no inkling of their dizzy speed, the stars — probably the same as those seen by the first inhabitants of the Earth — are always present. If we look through a telescope, they show different colours, as though the jewels of an enormous necklace had been strewn all over the sky. The stars are blue and red and white, and shine like sapphires, rubies, turquoises, and diamonds.

Most of the stars seem to rise in the east and to set in the west, just as the sun does. Across the immense distance they look as if attached to a vast revolving sphere which describes a circle of 24 hours around us. But this movement is in fact an optical illusion. It is the Earth which makes a full turn around itself in a day, so that first the vault of the night sky is gradually revealed before our eyes, then we are carried past the sun which shines on us, and finally we are swung back into the night. During the day when the Sun floods the sky with its fire, we can no longer see the stars, but they are there all the same, pursuing their courses.

But those stars which are relatively close to the point (called the 'pole') where the axis of the Earth pierces the heavenly sphere seem to describe smaller and smaller circles round that pole just above the horizon. A single star makes an exception and, apparently, scarcely moves at all: the Pole Star. It can be seen almost exactly due north. Its 'immobility' has for centuries helped mariners to get their bearings.

But it has not always been like this, because the axis around which the Earth rotates, and therefore the pole, is also changing. In 12,000 years' time, Vega will be our pole star, marking the north.

Let us once more look at the sky, our universe, the Milky Way into which billions of suns like our own are born, and let us think of the immensity of the cosmos

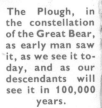

The Plough, in the constellation of the Great Bear, as early man saw it, as we see it to-day, and as our descendants will see it in 100,000 years.

that has room for millions of galaxies, for other universes, other 'islands of light', which in our telescopes appear as so many tufts of wool.

Finally, let us try to imagine all those innumerable suns somewhere in distant space which are, perhaps, shining on other 'earths' like ours.

It is not impossible that on these 'earths', these unknown planets far away in space, there are intelligent beings who will never see our Earth or our Sun, but who can see in their sky the silvery band of our Milky Way, our little field of stars lost in the vast expanse of worlds.

Is it not amazing to think that these 'men', if they exist, these inhabitants of far-distant planets, who live in our times, should be the same as we are — wonderstruck spectators of the magic pageantry of the universe?

15

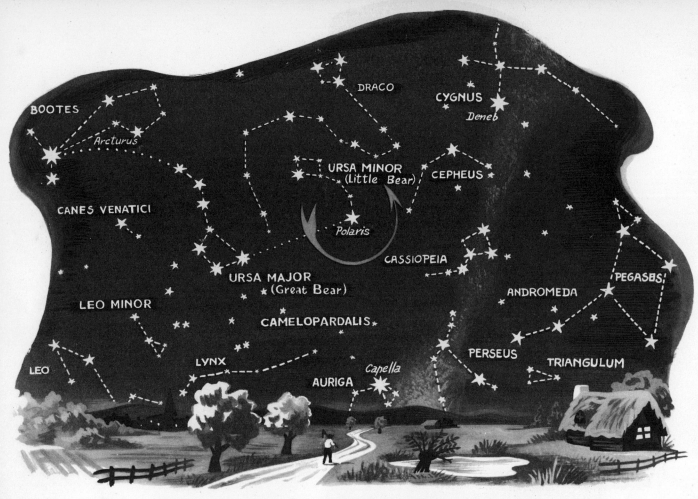

The appearance of the starry vault changes constantly from one season to another. These four studies show the sky at about eleven o'clock in the evening: above, in midsummer, facing north; below, facing south.

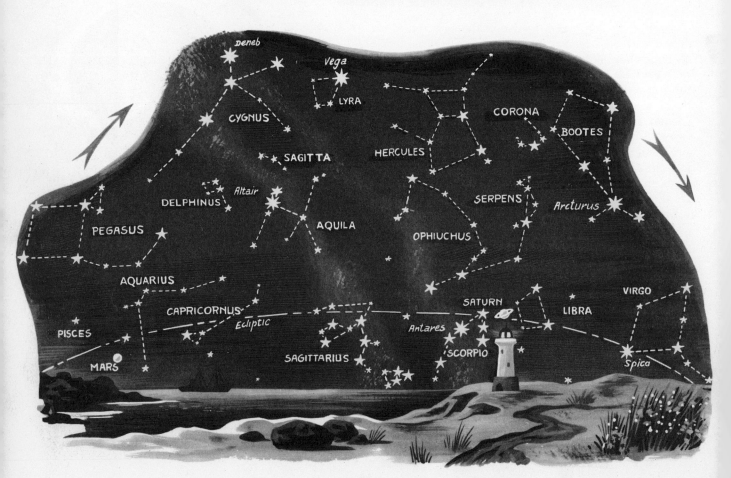

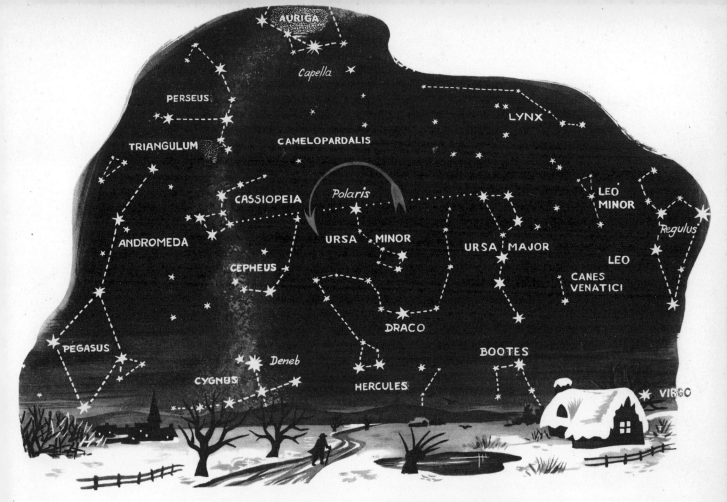

Here is the same area of the heavens observed in early January: above, facing north; below, facing south. The stars at the top of these four diagrams are those which are to be found directly above the observer.

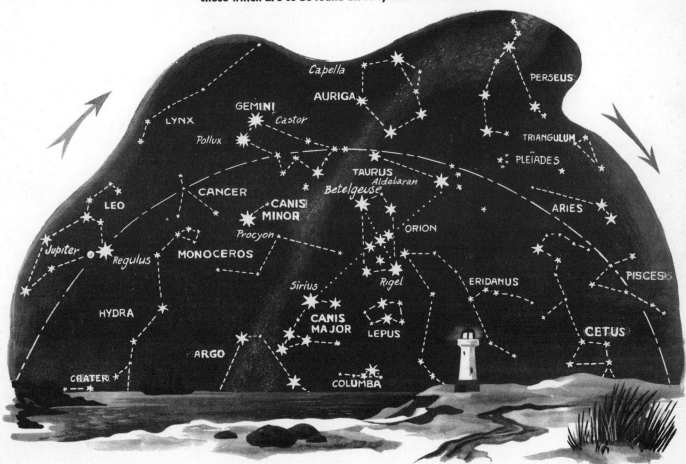

17

THE SUN AND ITS RETINUE

To gain some idea of the universe and its worlds, it is necessary to look at the sky through a giant telescope in an observatory. I would like to take you to Mount Palomar Observatory in California, which has the most powerful telescope in the world, piercing the sky for millions of miles, but Herstmonceux is so much easier to get at that I had better take you there instead.

Even though it is daylight when we arrive, we can still ask to see a star, because our own Sun is a star like any other, seeming so large owing to its nearness. Let's take advantage of our visit to observe the Sun carefully. A screen of smoked glass placed in front of the telescope will enable us to look at the Sun's surface. We can see a continually moving formation of grains, called rice-grains by astronomers. They can be seen at such a great distance because each one is at least 450 miles wide and 600 long.

In this moving mass we can also observe dark rents, which are sunspots. They are much bigger than the rice-grains and could almost be seen without a telescope, if we held a smoked glass in front of our eyes so as not to be blinded by the unbearable glare of the Sun. It is said that only the eagle can look straight into the Sun.

There are other details to be seen, but we must go to a mountain observatory free of the Earth's misty atmosphere, then we shall be able to see the luminous corona surrounding the Sun by means of a special fitting on the telescope.

If we are very lucky we shall be able to see the colossal flames which leap up like eruptions to a distance of 450,000 miles, almost twice the distance between the Earth and the Moon, but it is very difficult to catch them in the instrument. In any case we shall only be able to see one at a time. We can imagine the Sun as a Catherine-wheel, a flower of spinning fire flinging streamers of flame into space.

We shall be able to see the patterns made by the stars particularly well at night: the clouds of stars in the Milky Way that start in the bright constellation of Cygnus, the crescent moon which moves out of the range of the telescope unless we follow it like a sportsman following a flying partridge with his gun, and far, far away in space the fluffy spirals of the nebulae.

We will probably not be able to see any of the comets which appear from time to time in the sky and shoot across it like rockets, streaming their great tails in their wake.

This tail which sweeps the sky and makes a luminous train many millions of miles long is like a cloud of stardust weighing almost nothing. If the Earth or the Moon happened to be in the path of a comet, they would pass through its tail without danger, like a balloon going through a cloud. This happened in 1910, when Halley's Comet, the most famous, passed close to the Earth. It will reappear again in 1986, for it turns round the sun in 76 years. Grant's Comet completes its cycle in 164 years. Some comets, however, will never appear again, probably having collided with another heavenly body on their path. Others will not be visible on the Earth again for thousands of years.

This is because their orbit, or the curve that they, like the planets and the Earth, describe round the Sun, is an elongated ellipse.

You may have seen a gardener outline an elliptical flower-bed by means of two sticks and a piece of string stretched between them with a piece of wood. The two sticks are the two 'foci' of the ellipse, and if the string is always the same length, the further apart they are, the flatter is the ellipse. A circle is an ellipse where the two foci become one.

In our solar system, the foci of the planets' ellipses are quite close to each other; the Sun is at one focus, but there is a second mysterious, invisible one where even the telescope can see nothing. Indian sages were intrigued by the problem and found an answer to it. Since the Sun, source of heat and life on our planet, is at one focus, these sages invented a second, invisible sun, source of the forces of love and friendship in the whole universe.

Today we are less inclined to accept such views on the universe! We prefer to base our beliefs on what we can observe through the telescope.

In the thirteenth century Roger Bacon studied the effects of mirrors and lenses, and wrote about the magnifying properties of convex glass — that is, glass which curves upwards in a shallow dome. He found that distant objects looked larger when different lenses were used.

Most experts claim that the telescope proper was invented in Holland in 1608, and there is plenty of documentary evidence for this. The story goes that Hans Lippershey of Middelburg, a maker of spectacles, found two children playing in his shop with two lenses. They showed him that when one looked through both the lenses at once, adjusting their relative positions, the nearby church tower seemed to come much closer. Lippershey fixed the two lenses in a tube . . . and thus invented the telescope.

This early instrument was speedily developed and improved. The most famous experimenter in those early days was the Italian, Galileo, who studied the movements of the planets and also observed spots on the Sun.

Progress now was rapid. To study the stars, it was clear that a telescope simply held to the eye was far from adequate: the mounting of the instrument was an important factor. It had to be capable of vertical and horizontal movement, and of exact adjustment in order to follow any object moving across the field of vision.

Today scientists look forward to the time when we can build observation stations on artificial satellites far beyond the Earth's atmosphere. For there is still one major problem that has not yet been overcome—the problem of carrying out accurate astronomical observations free from the distorting optical effects of our atmosphere.

On a fine summer night, without using field-glasses or a telescope, you can see a shower of shooting stars falling from the sky. They are no bigger than a pin-head, and suddenly light up and go out again immediately.

These shooting stars are not minute suns with their own light, but imperceptible fragments called meteorites travelling through space on an elliptical course. They spin like stones through the darkness of space, and suddenly they pass close to the Earth, which is surrounded by a layer of air 75 miles thick. When they pass through this layer of air they are heated by the friction and become like red-hot iron filings. These 'stars' light up and go out again in the time it takes to make a wish.

There are other, bigger bodies called meteorites which come from outer space and travel across our skies in the same way, flare up and disappear as rapidly as the rest, but being larger do not vaporise in the air; they crash to the Earth.

Some of these meteorites are travelling so fast that they do considerable damage. They are sometimes huge — one of them flattened the Siberian forest for 30 miles around. Fortunately the meteorites which fall in large numbers on the Earth and, when they have cooled off, look rather like rusty iron sponges, are not nearly as big

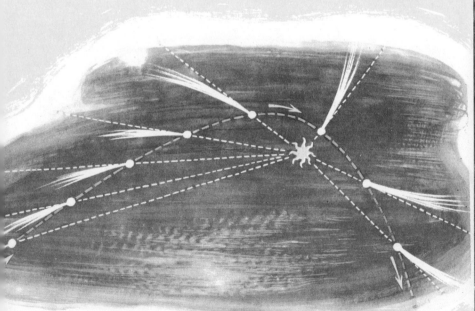

The tails of comets are made up of fine, impalpable particles. Because of the repulsion of the radiation of the sun, the tail of a comet is always pointed into space in the direction opposite the sun. On the right: a photograph of Halley's comet taken in May 1910. Its tail was over 70 million miles long.

as that. The majority of them weigh only one ounce or even less, but they fall continuously. They are found in the snow on mountains, in gutters and reservoirs, and on pavements. You would never guess how many fall on the Earth in a day — 8,000 million; but because of their small size, their total weight per day is not more than 100 tons.

They are like a shower of stones from heaven, but it would take 2,000 million years to cover Earth in a layer two inches thick. No one has ever been known to have been killed by a meteorite. Does that not make the Earth, that grain of dust in the universe, seem suddenly comparatively huge?

Comets and meteorites are rather eccentric members of the solar system. They appear and disappear in a tremendous flare of light, and the Ancients considered their appearance, particularly that of comets, as a sign of the anger of the gods. They saw them as imaginary snakes and swords, and waited terror-stricken for the punishment of their sins and the end of the world.

However, apart from these freaks, the solar system is peopled with more ordinary bodies which never stop turning round the Sun. Let us examine them one by one, starting at their centre. To reach the Sun, we will again take our rocket which moves at the speed of light. It will take only 8 minutes to cover the 93,000,000 miles from the Earth to the Sun.

Suppose, however, we go up in a jet airliner which travels over sea and land at 500 m.p.h. It would take more than 22 years, and a 10-year-old boy setting off in the aeroplane would be 32 years old when he arrived!

If the SUN is a tiny speck in the universe like all the other stars in the vastness of space, it is colossal when measured in relation to the solar system of which it is the centre. The diameter of the Sun is 100 times the diameter of the Earth (8,075 miles) and if we wanted to go round the Sun in our jet airliner it would take more than 6 months. If the Sun were to leave its course and try to pass between the Earth and the Moon without touching them, it would not be able to do so. It would cannon into them like billiard balls, because the Sun's diameter is nearly four times the distance from the Earth to the Moon.

Like Apollo in his chariot, the Sun, source of energy and light, holds its sway over the planets which revolve round it and follow it in its course through the Milky Way. It is a fiery ball and, like all the other stars, a gigantic furnace with a temperature, at the centre, of more than 15,000,000° C. It is like an atomic power-station radiating light and heat, released in the transformation of hydrogen into helium.

How much does it consume? In one second it uses more energy than all the power-stations on earth could produce in 200,000 years. This energy represents the heat which would be released in one year by a piece of coal 150 times bigger than the Earth.

You can imagine how, at the beginning of time, the first men trembled with fear when the Sun set and night fell. That is why, on all the continents of the Earth, our ancestors worshipped the Sun. Now we know only by legend of the sacred rites by which primitive tribes sought to make the sun god return to life with the dawn.

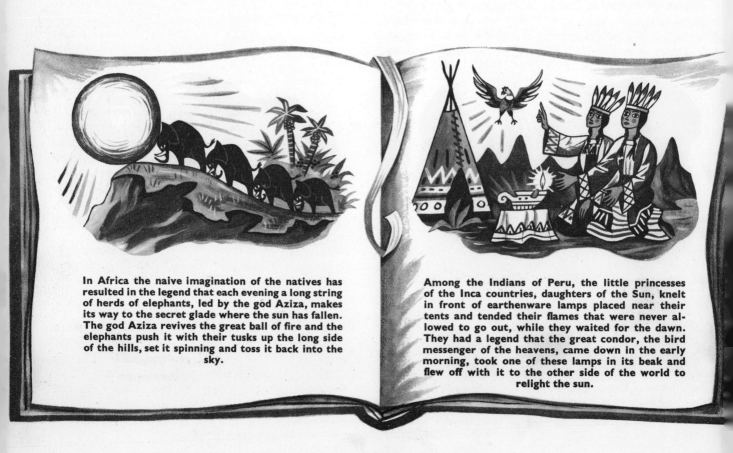

In Africa the naive imagination of the natives has resulted in the legend that each evening a long string of herds of elephants, led by the god Aziza, makes its way to the secret glade where the sun has fallen. The god Aziza revives the great ball of fire and the elephants push it with their tusks up the long side of the hills, set it spinning and toss it back into the sky.

Among the Indians of Peru, the little princesses of the Inca countries, daughters of the Sun, knelt in front of earthenware lamps placed near their tents and tended their flames that were never allowed to go out, while they waited for the dawn. They had a legend that the great condor, the bird messenger of the heavens, came down in the early morning, took one of these lamps in its beak and flew off with it to the other side of the world to relight the sun.

MARS · MERCURY · VENUS

SATURN

EARTH

JUPITER

There are now nine known principal planets, without counting the little ones included in the vast number of planets revolving round the sun. In order, starting from the sun, they are :
MERCURY, VENUS, EARTH, MARS, JUPITER, SATURN, URANUS, NEPTUNE and PLUTO.

Let's leave the Sun now, whose surface temperature of 6,000° C. is not very attractive.

To give you an idea of the respective sizes of the Sun and its planets, and of the distances between them, we will represent the Sun by one of those big beach balls measuring about 3 feet.

MERCURY, the smallest of the planets, would be a grain of millet 46 yards from the ball. It is 100 times smaller than the Earth and so near the Sun that it is perpetually scorched. To us Mercury appears full, half or as a crescent. Like all the planets it turns on its own axis and also revolves round the Sun. It takes a little less than 3 months to complete its revolution.

Tidal friction has slowed down the rotation of Mercury, so that it has become a world of extremes: the zone which faces the Sun is perpetually hot, while the other side must have an extremely low minimum temperature. The sun rises and sets on the twilight zone in between — but even that is almost certainly a barren, inhospitable area, and the lack of atmosphere would make human life there impossible.

VENUS is about the same size as the Earth; it will be represented by a pea 93 yards from the ball. It revolves round the Sun in 225 days. It is a mysterious planet which has not revealed its secrets, any more than has Mars. We still do not know if it is inhabited, whether beings can live and breathe as we do on this other 'earth' which spins between us and the Sun. Some scientists believe that, because of the scarcity of oxygen in its atmosphere and its lack of water, the planet must be like a rocky desert. Others consider that Venus is going through a time of upheavals, of floods and deluges, similar to those of the Carboniferous period on the Earth. If so, luxuriant mosses and giant lichens would flourish on the surface of Venus as though in a hot-house. Whatever may be the answer, if life is possible on the planet, climatic conditions suggest that it would have nothing in common with the life we know on Earth.

In 1790 one observer claimed to detect mountainous irregularities; another has identified some apparent bright areas as polar ice caps. But the impenetrable clouds make most such speculations unreliable. In spite of her mystery, Venus is normally the brightest object in the heavens, and her phases can be studied through binoculars.

MARS, whose diameter is half that of the Earth, is represented by a small marble 181 yards from the ball. Mars turns on itself in about one day, so that its days and nights are roughly as long as ours. It completes its course in a little less than 2 years, and the seasons are therefore almost twice as long as on Earth. The Earth has one satellite, the Moon; Mars has two.

URANUS

Mars has always intrigued men more than any other planet. Long before those machines said to be invented by the Martians to visit the Earth were named 'flying saucers', the early astronomers had wondered if there were organic life on Mars. Mars is the best known of all the planets in our solar system. Most of the time it is further from us than Venus, but at certain times we get a closer view of it and can study it in some detail. In this way we know that Mars is surrounded by an atmosphere thinner than, but like, the Earth's. It was only a step from there to imagining that there were not only plants and animals on Mars, but also beings as intelligent as we are, if not superior; this supposition was lent colour when people thought that they could make out a complete system of irrigation canals and changes in colour in the Martian springtime which were due to the growth of crops. This fine theory excited the imagination of scientists and writers alike, and continues to stir the daydreams of young people, but it is now abandoned by most astronomers.

NEPTUNE

Mars is a cold planet. In winter the temperature falls to minus 148° F. Eskimos perhaps could stand that climate; but there is very little water in the atmosphere, in fact 5 per cent of the quantity in the Earth's atmosphere, and without water life is scarcely possible.

The planet has two ice caps whose thaw, which takes only fifteen days, can be observed, but it does not seem possible that the water from this thaw would be sufficient to fill seas and canals. Moreover, the canals, which should have appeared more and more clearly as the instruments for observing them have improved, look less and less like canals the more powerful the telescopes through which they are viewed.

Can we still hope to go in a rocket in the near future to see if there are any Martians on Mars? Although it seems doubtful that the human body could withstand such different conditions of velocity and gravity, we can continue to respect our dreams of doing so. However, let's suppose for a moment that the planet will soon be a suburb of the Earth which could be reached in 50 hours. On arrival we would be pleasantly surprised to find that we were three times stronger than on earth, since one pound is the equivalent of six ounces on Mars, a reassuring discovery for explorers approaching an unfamiliar land for the first time.

JUPITER, represented by a tennis ball 600 yards from the beach ball, is surrounded by twelve satellites which revolve round it, and marked by the mysterious Great Red Spot, 30,000 miles long. This spot is probably a gigantic chemical storm raging in the planet's frigid atmosphere.

Jupiter is 1,300 times bigger than the Earth, but its mass is only 320 times that of the Earth. Nevertheless, it is so enormous that it weighs twice as much as all the other planets put together. A person transported to it would have the unpleasant sensation of weighing 30 stone and would collapse under his own weight.

SATURN, the biggest of the planets after Jupiter, would be a golf ball half a mile from the beach ball. It appears in the sky surrounded by its shining silver ring and crowned by a scattering of little satellites. The volume of Saturn is 745 times greater than that of the Earth, but its mass is less than 100 times greater, so that Saturn would float like a cork on a vast imaginary sea. Jupiter takes 12 years to run its course, and Saturn takes 29 years.

URANUS, represented by an apricot one mile from the beach ball, describes its ellipse in the circus of planets in 84 years, at 1,860,000,000 miles from the Sun.

NEPTUNE, represented by another apricot more than one and a half miles from the ball, turns round the Sun in 164 years, and has attracted only two satellites. The discovery of this planet, of which little is known, is a memorable date in astronomical history. Astronomers had noticed disturbances in the movement of Uranus. An unknown body in outer space was making its presence felt by pulling on Uranus, which had itself been discovered because it affected Saturn's motion. Le Verrier, a French astronomer, succeeded, after long calculations, in finding out when and where the new planet would appear. He wrote to Galle the astronomer of the Berlin Observatory telling him in what part of the sky he might observe the unknown planet. On 23 September 1846, Galle saw, in that quarter of the sky indicated by Le Verrier, the 'new' planet, Neptune.

Lastly PLUTO, the latest discovery, an icy planet which spins round 3,720,000,000 miles from the Sun, and is barely as big as Mercury, may be represented by a grain of sand 2 miles from the ball.

* * * * * * * * * *

If other planets in our solar system were inhabited like the EARTH, life would be ruled there too by the division of day and night, for seven planets out of the nine spin round, offering part of their surface to the Sun's rays which, by the movement of rotation, is gradually covered in shadow. The Earth turns on its axis in 24 hours, which for us constitutes a whole day, but, apart from Mars, which rotates at about the same speed, the bigger planets like Jupiter and Saturn turn much more quickly. On Jupiter and Saturn day and night last only 4 or 5 hours each.

The planets have seasons too, like the Earth, but think how long they must be on Uranus or Neptune! While the Earth completes its cycle in one year, which gives us four seasons, Uranus and Neptune take 84 and 164 years respectively to turn round the Sun!

If the planets' orbits were a strict circle they would always remain at the same distance from the Sun, but because of the flattened, elliptical paths they follow, this is not so. The seasons vary according to the distance

At the summer solstice (June 21st) the sun rises high above the horizon, rising in the north-east and setting in the north-west. It shines for a long time and its rays fall almost perpendicularly. That is why it is hot.

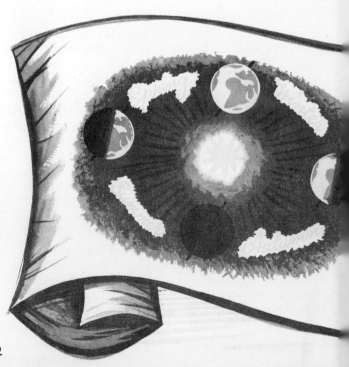

between the Sun and the Earth. The Earth is closest to the Sun when it is winter in the Northern Hemisphere. That is rather surprising to us, but not to someone living in the Southern Hemisphere, where it is very hot in December. His calendar may be the same as ours, but December, January and February are still the summer months for him.

The phenomenon of the seasons is due to the inclination of the Earth's axis and the angle at which the Sun's rays fall, according to the different seasons of the year. In winter, the Sun's rays are very low in the Northern Hemisphere and give less heat than in summer, when they fall almost perpendicularly. In the Southern Hemisphere where it is summer, the two factors, i.e., the minimum distance from the Sun and the perpendicular angle of the Sun's rays, combine instead of being separate. That is why the southern summer is so hot.

Inversely, when it is summer in the Northern Hemisphere, it is winter in the Southern, and again the factors are separated in the north and combined in the south, when the Earth is furthest from the Sun and the rays of the Sun lowest. Winter is therefore very severe in the Southern Hemisphere and the polar ice cap is much bigger at the South than at the North Pole.

The inclination of the Earth, however, becomes less and less important as you approach the Equator from either hemisphere. Between the two Tropics, Cancer and Capricorn, it is always very hot, and there is very little difference in the length of day and night. The low

The earth will never experience a sudden halt or a sudden acceleration in its rotation. If the earth were to stop turning, everything would be flung off it into space.

angle of the Sun's rays at the poles is the reason for the perpetual cold there.

We rotate with the Earth in 24 hours and are carried round the Sun in $365\frac{1}{4}$ days; we travel along our course at nearly $18\frac{1}{2}$ miles per second. The Sun leads us and all the other planets through the Milky Way, in the direction of the star Vega. What do we notice of all this fantastic motion?

We do not notice that the Earth is spinning like a top in space, where everything appears to be motionless, except, of course, the Sun and the Moon. When you go up in an aeroplane, you can see the Earth's surface gradually spread out beneath its wings like a map, and you seem to have stopped moving.

The Earth has neither top nor bottom. No one is hanging head downwards. On the other side of the world, at the antipodes, any whale or porpoise of fish sticking its head out of the water will see the sky as well. Why a fish? Because the Earth always balances a continent with an ocean. There are many more seas than islands on the Earth, and the continents are only big islands. Like us, our porpoise or whale at the antipodes will see the Sun rise in the morning and the moon in the evening in a sky full of apparently motionless stars.

At the winter solstice (December 21st) the sun does not rise so high. It rises in the south-east and sets in the south-west. It shines for a short time, and its rays fall at a low angle. That is why it is cold in winter. It rises in the east and sets in the west only at the equinoxes (March 22nd and September 22nd). In the Southern Hemisphere, of course, it does the opposite, but because of the inclination of the earth the southern summer is hotter than northern summer and the southern winter is colder than the northern winter.

THE MOON

The distance from the Earth to the Moon is not fixed. In a year it varies in stages from 226,000 to 252,000 miles. An interplanetary rocket has covered this distance recently in about forty hours.

The MOON is the body closest to the Earth. It is 238,000 miles away — a relatively small distance, and one that plenty of people cover in the course of their lives. Its diameter is a quarter that of the Earth. It revolves round the Earth once in every 29½ days. Though man has been watching and studying the Moon for thousands of years, he has never seen more than one half of it, for the Moon turns on its own axis in exactly the same time as it takes to turn round the Earth, the effect being the same as though it never moved at all. But it has not always been like this.

The Moon also spun on its own in the days of its youth, until Earth brought it into line with itself. This is a very common phenomenon. The Moon is close to the Earth, as Venus and Mercury are to the Sun.

The 'pull' that produces our tides by acting on the seas of the Earth also affected the two latter planets and the Moon at a time when they were still plastic, having a braking effect on their motion and slightly deforming their spherical shape. As a result of this braking, these three bodies have adopted a speed of rotation equal to that of their revolution.

When the Moon passes between the Sun and us, it disappears from sight, for the whole of the face turned towards us is then in shadow. The Moon is now 'New'. It continues on its round, and gradually it becomes possible to make out an illuminated part of its surface, growing night by night, on which — for the Moon — it is day. The Moon then appears like a crescent in the sky, growing until we can see one entire half. Then, when the Earth is between the Moon and the Sun, the whole face of our satellite is lit up before us: this is the 'Full Moon', a great yellow disc in the sky.

Every 28 days the process begins anew, and always the Moon goes through the same phases.

One can easily imagine the sight that will greet the first travellers to it when they alight from their rocket.

The stars are shining with unaccustomed brilliance in a sky that is as black as pitch, and yet it is broad daylight. The Earth, in its first quarter, is a giant crescent.

It is the atmosphere that makes the sky of Earth seem blue, extinguishes the twinkling of the stars and gives the Sun its yellow colour; but the Moon has no atmosphere.

A Sun of dazzling white, sending out streamers of flame, surrounded by pink protuberances and a huge silver corona, sheds a harsh light on the ground, which is like a desert with nothing to relieve its appalling monotony. In the distance the chain of mountains called 'the Apennines' sends its peaks soaring up to 16,000 feet; yet in the fierce light the detail can be seen with great distinctness.

The rocket having landed in the Sea of Rains, the travellers are a considerable distance from the foothills of the giant crater of Archimedes. However, as on this planet one of Earth's pounds weighs no more than a few ounces, such a distance is no obstacle. Strides of 30 feet cost no more effort there than normal walking.

The long lunar day that lasts 14 of Earth's days is drawing to a close. The ground that has been subjected to temperatures of more than 100° C. is shortly to experience the cold of night — anything up to minus 200° C.

There can be no life on the Moon. No one there goes out for a walk by 'earthlight'. No sounds break the silence of that desert, since sound waves cannot travel in a vacuum.

However, it is possible that that inhospitable land contains hidden riches, and insatiable man wants them.

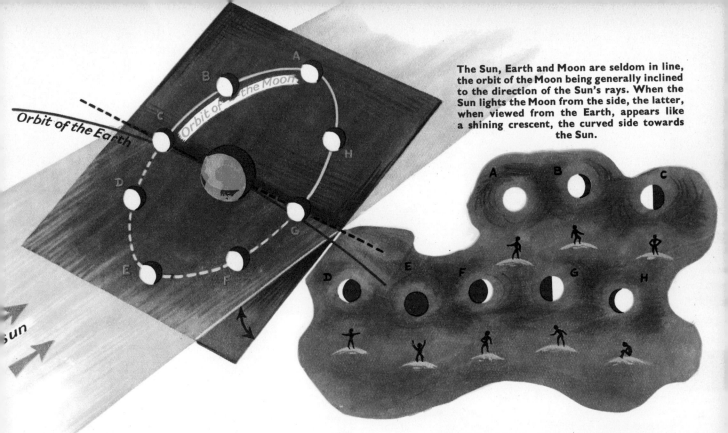

The Sun, Earth and Moon are seldom in line, the orbit of the Moon being generally inclined to the direction of the Sun's rays. When the Sun lights the Moon from the side, the latter, when viewed from the Earth, appears like a shining crescent, the curved side towards the Sun.

When the Moon is in the same direction as the Sun, this makes it invisible: that is the new moon. When it is in the opposite direction, the whole of it is seen: that is the full moon.

Does he know that Earth is threatened with the same fate as that of its satellite? But there is no need to worry. That danger will not confront him or his immediate descendants, and he will have had plenty of time to build his rockets and explore the Moon and its deposits, if he can manage it.

The astronomers discovered the danger with which Earth is threatened when they measured the duration of Earth's rotation on its own axis to one-thousandth of a second. They discovered that having made Mercury and Venus (much closer to it than the Earth) fall into step with it, the Sun was in the process of doing the same with our Earth, whose speed of rotation was slowing down day by day. Only very slightly, of course, yet sufficient to have caused an increase of 3 hours 20 minutes altogether since the beginning of the Christian era. It is calculated that in 5,000 million years Earth will have stopped rotating on its own axis. It will still be revolving round the Sun, as the Moon does around the

If you were transported to the Moon, the Earth would then be your 'moon', only thirteen times larger and more luminous.

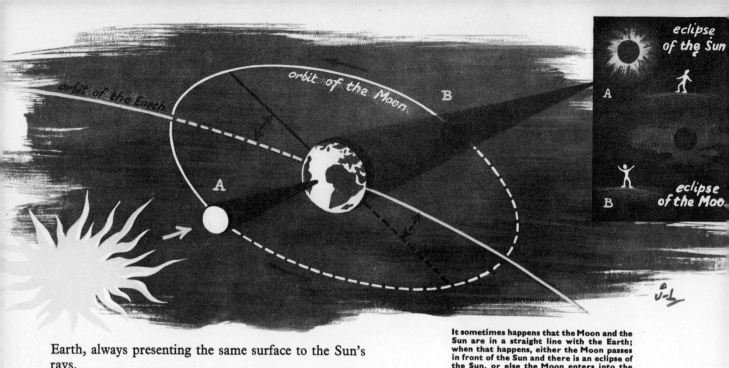

It sometimes happens that the Moon and the Sun are in a straight line with the Earth; when that happens, either the Moon passes in front of the Sun and there is an eclipse of the Sun, or else the Moon enters into the cone of the Earth's shadow and there is an eclipse of the Moon. These eclipses can be partial or total.

Earth, always presenting the same surface to the Sun's rays.

Earth will then be a dead planet, like its neighbour, unless it has previously run into another heavenly body and been destroyed, though such an accident scarcely seems possible in view of the immense extent of interstellar space. The chances of it happening are as great as of two aeroplanes, circling alone above the Earth, running into each other.

The combined pull of the Moon and Sun determines the ebb and flow of the tides. Enclosed seas, like the Caspian, Black Sea and Mediterranean, have no tides. In such confined spaces the moving waters cannot get up the impetus that the vastness of the oceans allows.

The tides are stronger at those times when the Sun adds its attraction to that of the Moon — that is, at the Full Moon and the New Moon. These are the spring tides, the opposite of which are the neap tides.

Both of these pulls are greatest at the time of the autumnal and vernal equinoxes. The tides are greatest, too, when the Moon is at the closest point of its journey round the Earth. The chance coincidence of all three can, produce exceptionally high tides that will break down dykes and flood the hinterland, if it is flat, as happened with part of East Anglia and the Dutch coast in the disaster of 1952.

When the Sun and the Moon play hide and seek in the heavens, they cause eclipses. Passing between the Earth and the Sun, the Moon can hide the latter either wholly or in part. This we call a total or partial eclipse of the Sun. The Moon is eclipsed when the Earth passes between it and the Sun, so that the Moon is in the shadow that Earth casts far behind it.

Eclipses, being, like comets, extraordinary lapses in the otherwise regular, mechanical functioning of the stars, were always regarded with fear and awe by primitive peoples, who saw in them a struggle between the Sun, source of life, and the Moon, source of evil and death, and were naturally anxious about the outcome.

To the Ancient Egyptians an eclipse was Apapi, the great serpent who dwelt at the bottom of the heavenly Nile, swallowing the sun-boat in which Ra was travelling to inspect his empire. However, Apapi was always conquered by the defenders of Ra and flung back into the depths.

In Africa, legend has it that the victor never enjoys his victory long. If it is the Sun that has swallowed the Moon, its belly becomes so cold that it has to vomit up the Moon. If the Moon has swallowed the Sun, it is so hot that it cannot keep it down. The combat of Sun and Moon is always accompanied by wild beatings of tom-toms and shouts of encouragement from the natives, until things revert to normal.

Is it surprising that in times long past man, viewing the star-studded vault of the heavens, should have thought that Earth was at the centre, and that there was only one sun, that which illuminated the Earth, and only one moon, that which he saw at night? In those days people had no knowledge of the laws of universal attraction, nor of the prodigious number of worlds. They could not conceive that Earth could support itself in equilibrium in space, and so they invented the old legends of Earth being supported on the shoulders of the giant Atlas. The Chinese made the Earth rest on the heads of four elephants; the Hindus said that it stood on the back of a fish swimming in the ether.

There is nothing astonishing in the naivety of the Ancients concerning the marvellous secrets of the universe. We too can dream when gazing at the immensity of the unknown heavens, as, perhaps, beyond the infinity of night, on other revolving planets other beings are dreaming as they contemplate their star-studded universe. Other beings — who knows? Other people inhabiting an unknown stellar city thousands of light years away from our tiny, grandiose universe.

THE LIFE OF THE EARTH

ITS FOUR AGES

A RECONSTRUCTION in colour of the different transformations the Earth underwent in its early Ages would make a wonderful film, and one day some enterprising producer will certainly make it. It would give a series of pictures of the life of our planet and of the animals and plants of prehistoric times.

The researches of the 'paleontologists', the people who have discovered the skeletons of prehistoric monsters and reconstructed them, working out their shape from fossils found in the ground, make such a film possible. It would be easy to make lots of animal figures, with joints like puppets, copying the skeletons and fossils in the Natural History Museum and the drawings made by the paleontologists. These models would represent the fauna that inhabited the Earth millions of years ago. The wonderful techniques of the cinema would be able to do the rest and would bring to life in their right settings those prehistoric monsters which, for all we know, may still survive on Venus.

Imagination is not enough. Only a real picture can help us to visualize the chaos of the world's beginnings, the birth of the Earth, the emergence of the continents and, over millions of years more, the gradual development and disappearance of animal and vegetable species through the various ages of the world's history.

But how, you may ask, can one distinguish the different ages of the Earth from each other? Quite simply, by removing the leaves of the geologists' amazing calendar one by one. But first let me explain about this calendar, which is one that you go through the opposite way, from last to first.

The geologists' calendar

In the course of time, folds and subsidences of the Earth's crust have buried in the depths of land and sea the remains of the animals and plants that were living when those cataclysms took place. Above the first layer thus formed, the deepest, a second was laid, then a third. These are called *sedimentary strata*.

The name comes from what has been deposited, having been conveyed there by water, as alluvium or *sediment* in the hollows of valleys, in the trenches of the sea bed, or on the bottoms of lakes. At the same time volcanoes were spitting out molten matter, *lava*, and this flowed, then solidified and formed the eruptive strata, such as basalt. Granite formed inside the Earth's crust.

It is easy to distinguish these strata, for they are of different colours; you can see them, one upon the other, in the wall of an old quarry or where a well is being dug.

If you search through the sedimentary strata you will find, pressed as though between the leaves of a calendar or book, things called *fossils*; these are the remains of animals and plants that were engulfed thousands and thousands of years ago. The relics of the first age are right at the bottom. They were buried first and covered by other sediment.

Geologists study the ground and the formation of rocks, and you are being a geologist without knowing it when you get a bucket of coal from the cellar. On a piece of that coal, brought up perhaps from nearly 2,000 feet down in the ground, you may see a serrated imprint like that of a leaf dried between the pages of the enormous calendar that is the rock.

Is it a flower? A fern?

No: it is a piece of the wing of a giant dragonfly that had a wing-span as large as that of a model glider. The body of the dragonfly left its imprint on the coal which was formed in the depths of the Earth from the forests of tree-ferns that were engulfed at that time.

The geologists have given names to these layers. That of coal, for instance, marks the Carboniferous Period, which was one of the periods of the Paleozoic Era.

The film we suggested would bring to life before our eyes the great eras of our world — its four ages. Let us call the primary era that of 'The Struggle between Water and Fire'; the secondary era, 'The Advent of the Rains and Beasts'; the tertiary era, 'The Advance of the Trees', and the quaternary era 'The March of the Glaciers and Man'.

The names by which these four ages are known to geologists are, in the same order as above: Paleozoic, Mesozoic, Tertiary and Quaternary.

THE STRUGGLE BETWEEN WATER AND FIRE

Now let us pretend that we are watching that film. It is night. Slowly the screen begins to glow with a strange dull light, that of the beginning of the world and of the reign of fire. In space is a ball, the Earth, lit by an enormous oval sun, its light an intense electric blue.

Lightning flashes and spurting flames light up the screen; waterspouts swirl, and we watch scenes from the gigantic struggle between the fires and waters of our planet. Earth is swept and covered by seething seas, on which the storm-winds whip up enormous waves. In the midst of the waters appear craters that spew out flames and a shower of red-hot ashes that rain down into the boiling water.

Thousands of years pass. The fires in the centre of the Earth burst open and blister our watery world. See, near the poles, islands of lava appear, cleaving the boiling waters; they are submerged, but they emerge again.

That is the birth of the land, which now emerges out of the waters. These are mere scattered islands that scarcely indicate where Greenland, Canada, Great Britain, Australia, Africa and Brazil are going to be.

Further thousands of years pass. Nature seems to be hesitating: shall she animate the plants, uproot them and from the vegetable kingdom create the animal? If so, shall she use those giant mushrooms that have circumferences of 100 feet? Or the huge ferns, straight and erect like asparagus, yet taller than poplars? Or those water-lilies, one leaf of which lying on the slime of the swamp would support an antelope?

The first animals seem still to be clinging to the rock by roots. Look at the swaying of the branches of that live bush which is an animal. It is a coral, and builds pink cities at the bottom of the sea. We shall now see the first signs of movement, of life, in the depths of the tepid waters: worms coiling, molluscs, soft and shapeless, on which a shell like a snail's will grow, or arms resembling snakes, like those on the head of the octopus.

Gradually Nature perfects her marine monsters, clothing them in a carapace, armour to contain their flabby bodies.

Already we have come a long way from the animal-plants.

The landscapes of ocean, the deep trenches, show enormous creatures swarming among the rocks: these are the early crustaceans, resembling crabs, lobsters and crayfish.

This knight of the waters we see advancing, weighed down by his armour ... is he an ancestor of the king-crabs we can still find today on the coasts of North America? Is he a knight in armour or a deep-sea diver in his suit? He protects himself with a broad shield, a buckler in the sides of which are two portholes, two eyes with cut facets.

It is the waters that are finally victorious in the struggle between fire and water of the chaotic Primary Era. Nature now begins to people the air and the islands with articulate creatures that fly, like those dragonflies the size of one of our gulls; elastic creatures that bound like giant grasshoppers, creatures that have a thousand feet to climb with, like the scolopendra.

All these creatures have flaccid bodies, without bones or skeleton, and they adapt themselves as well as they can; one acquires two shells to live between, like the oyster, another encloses itself in a carapace.

Now here are the first of the vertebrates appearing. First the marine monsters that have fish's backbones, yet are not fish. Then the batrachians which breathe in water, monstrous frogs and enormous lizards. And the reptiles that breathe in the air.

These shapeless creatures become fossilized. Of the milliards of molluscs that peopled the waters, there remains only the rock made from their shells.

EARTH is about to know a new form of life with the coming of the rains and the beasts during the Secondary Period.

Here is our Sun. It is still oval, but is not so big now. It has aged. The crust of our terrestrial sphere has cooled. It is still wrinkled and cracked, and now you can make out new mountain ranges. The mountainous skeleton of the continents has emerged out of the water, while the incessant torrential rains have uprooted the forests and filled the lakes and valleys.

Earth is covered with swamps, glades of hot mud in the tangle of greenery of a new, virgin, dense forest — a forest of giant grasses inhabited by monsters.

Day breaks and reveals a fantastic, nightmare landscape. The great reeds part and an enormous, misshapen creature appears: it is the diplodocus! Laboriously it moves its 20-ton body that is 80 feet long, threshing the mire with a tail as long again as its supple neck that coils like a snake. Behind it, a whole herd of others emerge out of the swamps. Their immense necks stretch out, thrust forward and tear up the pulpy plants.

These gigantic herbivores with their ridiculously small mouths will crop several tons of those grasses, never stopping as long as the daylight lasts.

Around these monsters is the seething mass of the reptiles, knotting and unknotting themselves. Through the muddy water come some dinosaurs, gigantic lizards, swimming with their heads above water as they make for the shore.

The moving forest opens to admit these huge herds which crush the giant rushes and tree-ferns. They move forward, on and on, devouring the forest as they go. These are the pilgrims of the rain, who follow in its track. Thousands of years later the great mammoths will still be marching along behind the rains, as even now the herds of elephants do in the equatorial forests of Africa and Asia.

OF THE RAINS AND THE BEASTS

Now the burning bush and the forest crushed by the deluges of the early ages reveal the secrets of their fauna. Terrifying they look, yet these huge herbivores were quite inoffensive: the brontosaurus, a squatter edition of the diplodocus, the iguanodon, and that extraordinary monster with two feet, the thespesius, which resembled a monstrous goose.

Here, on four great feet, is a stegosaurus leading its herd into the tangle of lianas. It has two brains, the larger of which is used to direct its hind legs.

All these giants of the Secondary Era, even the triceratops, helmeted like a medieval warrior and with horns on its forehead, had no other means of defence than the plates of their armour and the darts of the prickly crest articulated to their spines.

All at once the grazing brontosauri raise their heads, twist their necks. Seized with sudden panic, they trample, jostle and knock each other over as they roll, rather than run, towards the swamp which is their refuge. Fighting is easier in the water, which helps to support their vast weight.

But too late! The giant grasses part and a savage horde hurls itself upon the terrified monsters. These bounding carnivores are not beasts of prey, but lizards, ceratosauri and tyrannosauri. They are huge and covered with scales. They run upright, like humans, on their hind legs, and use their tails as levers for jumping and hurling themselves forward in enormous bounds. They fling themselves upon the herd of brontosauri, brandishing their forefeet, which are armed with formidable claws. They open their vast jaws like a crocodile's and snap — a dreadful sound.

It is a savage combat. The defenceless brontosauri are being wiped out. Their tiny heads at the end of their long necks are crushed between the jaws of the attackers. With tooth and claw the assailants rip up the live flesh of the great monsters.

All at once the attackers are compelled to stop the carnage. They stand erect, jaws dripping blood, to await the onslaught of a herd of triceratops charging with lowered heads and horns couched. On they come in a veritable avalanche of tumbling, trampling, pounding, crushing bodies. In the horror of the slaughter and spurting mud you can make out nothing but vast shapes, one of which occasionally collapses as it is ripped open by a giant horn. Necks twist and swing, jaws open, thrust and tear.

Evening falls on the glade. The last survivors are still fighting, more dead than alive. In the darkening sky above the morass of death slowly circle the birds of prey, the pteranodons, giant bats with the jaws of a crocodile. Then, with a swish of a thousand wings, this black eddy alights, and the scene of carnage is hidden by the great bodies of these vultures. With claws and horrible saw-edged beaks they attack the mountains of flesh lying there.

Scarcely has darkness blotted out the desolate swamp than, in the distance, the heavens light up. The dull hammering sound you hear, like that of a herd of great animals charging through the bush, is the noise of the rain, of a tornado. A prolonged clap of thunder sounds the charge with a shattering tattoo. Lightning cleaves the night. Through the rents torn by its fire, the rain makes its assault upon the earth.

Now let us take a trip to the bottom of the sea. Nature has peopled the waters with monsters strangely like those which inhabit the air and the marshy forests. All three elements are the realm of the giant lizard: the lizard bat that flies with stiff creaking wings like sheets of metal, the crocodilian one that stands erect and can climb, the great saurian with jaws like a saw-blade that swims in the depths of the sea.

And all these creatures lay eggs. All these monsters were hatched out of shells, some hard, some soft.

Out of the eddying waters rise crocodile-fish, the mosasauri, looking rather like the sea-serpent of legend. In the deep, as on land, fierce battles are fought between these shapeless monsters, ichthyosauri and plesiosauri, creatures that are neither fish nor serpent, but armoured with scales and armed with barbed points and a narwhal's or unicorn's horn on their foreheads.

There between the rocks you can see the coils of a serpent emerging from the carapace of a giant turtle whose flesh it has been eating. Torpedo-fish cleave through the seething mass of the octopi. Cuttle-fish let their soft arms trail in the current like streamers of sea-wrack. They look inanimate, like plants, but that is just to enable them better to surprise their prey.

What tricks has Nature taught these monsters? There, attached to the rock by a long, flexible stalk, is a live flower swaying and opening in the waves. This is the encrinus. Is it a flower or an animal? Its calyx is as large as a baby's cot and its corolla is attached to the heart of the flower which is an animal's gullet. Suddenly, like a buoy at the end of its cable, the live flower leaps, stretching to the full the stalk that anchors it. The greedy thing has snapped up a silver fish, over which its jaws close their twining tentacles.

Again thousands of years pass, and Earth is much older now. The end of the Secondary Era sees the last of those monstrous dragons the flying lizards, giant daughters of the rains. Nature leaves nothing to remind us of these misshapen giants, whose remains have long since been buried in the strata of earth, beneath layers of peat formed by the forests that have been engulfed.

Secretly Nature is preparing other miracles of life. She is perfecting the mechanism of really small creatures: the grasshopper, the earwig, the dung-beetle, the locust. Soon she will launch a new swarm of insects.

Till now, the Earth has seen only the smoking, torrential rains and the hordes of beasts scarcely grouped into clans, fighting each other for a piece of forest to devour.

Now the rains are no longer so tremendous. They are about to link their comings and goings with the seasons, for the seasons have come into being. The world is green — the green of the swamp, of the rains and giant forests. All the colours of the rainbow are about to come to Earth. Nature, continuing her selection between plant and beast, is about to produce flowers and bees as well.

After these savage beginnings, Nature is going to create the world's first flower gardens, and these teach the insects to build the first city, the hive — grouped round their queen, an industrious little people are going to seek the secret of happiness in work and peace.

Thousands of years have yet to pass before man will make his appearance on Earth, where the law of the survival of the fittest still prevails; but already with termites in the ground and bees in the air, Nature is trying to organize life into societies.

She makes her first experiments with colonies of insects, teaching those tiny creatures to live together in the great brotherhood of work.

THE ADVANCE OF THE
TREES

FROM now on the pictures of life on the Earth will hold no more terrifying surprises for us.

During its third age, the Tertiary Era, Earth gradually assumes the appearance it has today. Huge folds are forced up in Europe. Great chains of mountains ranging from Spain to India have appeared. The Pyrenees, Apennines, Alps and Himalayas have come to give earth a framework.

All over the Earth this Tertiary Period is characterized by the advance of the trees. These are no longer pines and firs, remains of the first, evergreen vegetation, but trees that bud and lose their leaves with the seasons, that bear flowers and fruit.

The first that set off en route for the Equator were palms and ferns, then figs, laurels, camphor-trees and cinnamon; the last to descend were the oaks, acacias and maples, which went to the plains and the grasslands.

Up to the middle of the Tertiary Era nothing hampered the advance of the trees, and they inhabited the entire globe. At the extremities of the poles the temperature was still high; Ireland enjoyed a climate like that of the South of France today, and even at Spitzbergen the climate was as mild as that of the South of England now.

In the latitudes farthest from the Equator, in the coal-bearing strata, there are traces of this great passage of the trees — the same that, today, have withdrawn to the temperate South of Europe: tulip-trees, plane-trees, walnuts, cypresses, poplars, hazel-nut trees and vines. The presence of this tropical and semi-tropical vegetation can also be explained by a violent shifting of the poles.

Now we see grassy valleys, forests alternating on the mountain-sides with rich pastures, and there we see the Earth's new inhabitants. The race of great lizards inhabiting the swamps and rivers has degenerated. The saurians have shrunk in stature to the size of our alligators and caymans.

The pilgrims of the rain have changed shape. Their enormous heads now carry the long trunk that allows them to pluck leaves and pull up grass as they walk along. They are now 16 or 20 feet high. They go in herds, like giant elephants. Some of them, the brontops and mastodons, are armed with heavy tusks. Others, like the dinotherium, are as unshapely as the creatures of the previous period. Nature amuses herself by elongating them, stretching them. She models them as if wanting to make kangaroos and tapirs out of this massive family of elephants.

The herbivores, eaters of grass, and carnivores, eaters of flesh, have teats to suckle their young: bears, rabbits, wolves, hyenas and also the manatee, a sort of aquatic elephant out of which legend will make the mermaid, the siren which sings at the bottom of the sea.

Away in the distance, across the savanna, bound troops of graceful, light animals: giraffes, antelopes and gazelles.

For centuries Nature has been green and dumb, but now she becomes gay with bird-song and colour.

Big pelicans and marabou storks perched on one leg fish in the vast swamps, and above them ibis and flamingos fly about the sky in trails of blue and pink. A cloud of white egrets alights on a mass of mangrove, the red roots of which twine and twist above the mire.

THE ADVENT
OF·THE GLACIERS...

EARTH is now in the fourth period of its life. It has cooled considerably. The onward march of the glaciers is about to upset the geography of our planet.

Four times, the glaciers from their base at the ice-caps of the pole, attack the world. You can still follow the track of their four invasions across the mountainous districts of Scotland and Scandinavia, in the Alps, and on the northern plains of Germany, North America and Siberia.

The ice took with it masses of striated stones, the moraines. These stones were rolled along, worn down and made smooth by the slow progress of the glaciers, and now lie scattered all along the course the glaciers took. We know, too, where the invasion of the glaciers was halted. The streams born of the melting ice carried down masses of broken stone that have accumulated along the sides of the valleys.

The queer blue night that envelops the lands of ice will see the end of the last of the fantastic creatures. The cold of the Great North will destroy all those that do not flee before the glaciers. A troop of mammoths roams the frozen desert of Siberia; their thick brown fleece is matted with snow. They are so weak that they can no longer hold up their huge heads, and they walk along with their curved tusks resting on the ice, like sledge-runners.

Here are bears and the giant hyena of the caves, herds of elk and reindeer, driven down by the cold to the plains of Central Europe in search of food and grazing. Later, when the steppes have thrown off their covering of ice, they will move up north again.

In the south, the rhinoceros, hippopotamus and elephant have also retreated to the lands of the sun and henceforth the bush and the tropical forest will be their domain.

Our film will end with this fourth age, the Quaternary Era, of the world. The last few shots will show us this jungle and a lion emerging from his cave to go hunting with his lioness. The huge elephants will continue all their lives plodding along in the wake of the rains. The Beast is sovereign in its kingdom. Earth belongs to it.

But not for long.

...AND OF MAN

Soon Nature will reveal a great secret. One day, the elephants will halt suddenly as they snuff the wind with their trunks, worried by the sour smell of an unknown animal. The lion will tell his lioness that a horde is camping in their hunting grounds and, without yet showing itself, is attacking their herds of zebra and antelope.

And one day the great monkeys, hiding behind trees, will be astonished to see creatures pass, walking erect on two feet and swinging their arms like they, and talking as they go.

The first troop of people, the first clan of naked people making their way across the savanna!

two witnesses

COAL
PETROLEUM

COAL

I is six o'clock in the morning and the engineer is going to go down the mine with the head overman. The latter, an old foreman who has spent his life 'below', is ready equipped and waiting by the winding-shaft. He wears an old suit of overalls with nothing underneath, large leather hat well down on his head, and has a safety-lamp ready, hooked to his belt.

The old man grumbles. He tells the engineer that he is not a surface man, but belongs down below. That he will consider himself finished if he has to stop going down. He does not feel so old that he has to be put onto overseeing people picking up stones at the mine-head, the sorters, or to giving orders by whistle to the trains of trucks taking debris and slate to be tipped on the spoil-heap.

The old man is haunted by the threat of being retired to the surface, as inevitably he will. For thirty years he has been overman down below, in the galleries and at the working face. Today, however, he has something else on his mind.

'We're not going to be able to go on working the seam at face 7 as we are doing,' he grumbles. 'The wall's sounding . . .'

The wall is that of the gallery.

The engineer knows that he can trust his old overman, and he is in a hurry to see what conditions are like at face 7. The two men get into the iron cage and down they go at a speed that takes your breath away when you go down for the first time.

In less than a minute the cage has reached the bottom, nearly 2,000 feet underground. A descent at that speed scarcely leaves you time to glimpse the flashing, fleeting glow that marks the entrance to each working at the various levels, from mine-head to the bottom where the galleries are.. When level with the last of the lower workings, the sweating of the wall is such that it is a flowing lining to the shaft. This is disquieting, for a pit is easily flooded, even though there are pumps working day and night to draw off the water that oozes from the galleries and flows into the sump. The engineer makes a mental note that he must report this water to the specialists, who will come down and block the fault with an injection of cement.

At the bottom, the two men step out into an atmosphere like that of a furnace. There they are subjected to the heavy pressure of great depth which feels like a crushing weight on your chest. The large, central gallery seems to vanish into the distance. The short

36

beams of their torches serve only to light up the two gleaming lines of the rails.

At a bend in the gallery a halo of light appears, and the two men flatten themselves against the wall, pressing against the huge pipe that carries compressed air for ventilation and to work the motors, and those others that take water from the galleries. Then, with a deafening clatter, a train of some thirty tubs laden with coal rushes past down the slope. Soon they will come back empty, pulled up the slope by a winch and a steel cable.

All along the galleries are openings leading to faces that are being worked. The black dust is so thick there that you can scarcely make out the yellow splodges of the lamps and the reflection of their light on the miners' shoulders and bare torsoes, glistening with sweat. Kneeling or lying, the men attack the seam of coal with their picks. Pieces crumble and fall even on to their bodies. They work away to the accompaniment of the staccato hammering of the compressed air drills, like those with which streets are dug up, and of the shrill squeal of the electric saws and undercutters that cut, stope and clear, and of an infernal scraping of shovels. This noise is punctuated by the crash of blocks of coal being flung on to the iron conveyor belt that shifts tons of coal and, at the mouth of the gallery, pours it directly into the tubs.

'These props must be shored up! And have this coffered quick!'

The overman sees everything. The safety of the mine depends on the timbering team. They work behind the hewers who cut and dig out the face, erecting stout props, uprights and carriers all along the wall, building a whole lining of props and planks that prevents the sides from caving in.

Here the gallery widens out. The men have built a huge scaffolding, an enormous column of tree-trunks to support the 'roof', that is to say the ceiling where the roofing timbers that prevent the gallery from collapsing intersect.

The overman halts and waits till there is a gap of silence in the din of the drills, and listens. It takes the practised ear of an old-timer to hear the timbers 'speak', to distinguish that all but imperceptible groan of props and stays in danger of giving beneath the weight of the gallery.

'Quick, double those props,' the overman orders. 'Come on, men, drop your picks, everyone help shore up. Everyone, I said. Understand?'

'Right, boss.'

The overman moves on to complete his inspection, while the engineer stays at face 7 with the ten men who now are also alive to the danger. In feverish haste they set up auxiliary props along the walls, driving them home under the cross beams with great sledgehammer blows.

Suddenly, while they are hard at it, they are flung to the ground. The roof caves in, sending down a shower of stones. The next moment the entrance to the gallery is blocked. Someone, scarcely on his own feet, seizes the engineer by the shoulders and, thrusting with all his strength, sends him rolling to the face, to which the others have already rushed. There, huddled together in the dark, they wait for the fall. All their lamps have gone out, been blown out. Shouts ring through the darkness, but are immediately drowned in the roar of an

Almost 300 million years ago large parts of the Earth were covered with immense forests. These have been engulfed, just as the prehistoric animals have disappeared. This vegetation buried in the ground has produced coal.

lay bare the seams of coal, and dredgers that scoop it up in their bucket-chains and pour it on to aerial conveyor belts, miles long, that will discharge 135,000 cubic feet an hour directly into the factory.

Will there come a time when we shall have used up all the coal there is in the bowels of the earth? Undoubtedly. But we shall have to wait thousands of years for that.

World production is large, almost 1½ thousand million tons a year. If all the coal mined in a year in the five continents were loaded into waggons and made into a single train, that train would reach five times round the earth.

The world's reserves of coal are considerable and will last a long time: there are 5 billion tons in North

The same phenomenon took place all over the surface of the globe and it is certain that under the sea, fringing the continents, there are considerable deposits of coal and lignite.

avalanche of huge blocks of coal. The whole fault has collapsed.

Now the only sound is the moaning of the wounded, for two of the men were caught by the fall. Groping, the others manage to free them. And then hours and hours pass. The ten men wonder if they are going to die of asphyxiation. Can help reach them? They are already growing sluggish from lack of oxygen when they hear the first blows of a pick above their heads. The moment the breach is made, down come ropes and up they are pulled, one after the other, the wounded first.

The breach is no larger than a man-hole, but it is enough. From there they have to crawl on their stomachs 500 yards down a sort of mole's tunnel, pulling the wounded by ropes fastened round their shoulders. Thus they are saved.

It was the old overman who had thought of breaching the roof there and remembered that old abandoned shaft.

●

Being a miner is a fine, manly job. Because the work is so hard and dangerous, there is a wonderful team spirit among the men — the engineer, the overman, the miner, timberer, and the shotfirer, the one who digs the sap in the seams of coal too hard for the pick and fires the shots that blast it out.

They get every least bit out of the seam. The black diamond, coal, is precious and none must be wasted, when you have to go down many thousands of feet to get it. In the world there are certainly more than a million men working in the bowels of the earth, or in the open as in the lignite areas of America and Germany. But there, it is machines that do most of the work: excavators that strip off the covering of dead ground to

America alone; 2 billion tons in Asia; 800,000 million tons in Europe; 150,000 million in Australasia and 100,000 million in Africa.

The history of each piece of coal goes back to the birth of the world, to the Primary Era when the great forests were engulfed with their swarms of giant dragonflies, the wings of which have left the impress of their filaments on the shining leaves on anthracite, the oldest form of coal. Later, other forests were buried in their turn, giving seams of brown coal, or lignite, which is sometimes found lying open. Peat is immature coal, and the bogs with their black mud and decomposing plants and dead trees are making coal for the future. On such bogs, of an evening, you will see little flames dancing here and there, chased by the wind — what people call will-o'-the-wisps. These are caused by a tiny puff, a bubble of gas suddenly igniting as it escapes from the bog into the air.

People have always had a superstitious fear of these will-o'-the-wisps, but it is not much more than a hundred years ago that man realised that coal could give off gas and be used for other things than just heating. At the end of the 18th century scientists were working on the idea of extracting combustible gas from coal by distillation, and this was first successfully done by William Murdock who, in 1779, introduced the first system of gas lighting. Before that people had used candles made of resin, tallow and beeswax.

And do not forget whale oil! For fifty years the whale was hunted in all the seas of the world, and the only thing that saved these graceful monsters of the deep from extermination was the invention of gas lighting. The progress made since then, however, is astounding. Today, gas works are veritable chemical factories.

The coal, distilled in immense retorts, gives off gas which is drawn off with a blower. Air is kept from the coal during the process of distillation, so that the coal is not consumed. Raised to a white heat, it melts and gives off volatile products that constitute the crude gas. This is then filtered and stored in metal bells, giant steel cylinders in which it is kept under great pressure. In some countries, such as France and America, the gas works cannot stock enough gas for the great cities. In

Coal conjures up ideas of combustion, heating and comfort, of travelling by train or boat, of machines providing the power to manufacture a great number of everyday objects. But did you know –

France there is a gas pipe-line from the coke-works of Lorraine to Alfortville 230 miles away which delivers about 25 million cubic feet of gas a day. The French are also planning to use the American method of storing gas by compressing it in beds of porous sand 1,200 feet or so underground which would thus act as natural reservoirs.

Coal gas, the main use of which, before the invention of the electric bulb, was for lighting, is today mainly used as a fuel. It is often used to heat the radiators and bath-water in our houses and for cooking. It has a variety of uses in industry. It provides a source of heat that can be regulated easily and for that reason is used in glazing china and silvering mirrors. It is used for vulcanizing and retreading tyres, and for melting the metal with which the printer casts the complete lines of type that

come from his Linotype machine. It is also used for sterilizing surgical instruments.

It takes about 2 million tons of coal to provide the gas consumed by a large city in a year. This is enough to make a train of 100,000 trucks, and the gas itself would inflate a ballon 4,000 feet in diameter.

In the country, where there is no gas laid on, people use butane gas for domestic purposes. This, like methane propane and pentane, is one of the many constituents of carbon and a by-product of the distillation of petrol. It is an excellent fuel and easily liquifiable, which makes it convenient to transport in the small metal containers with which most of us are familiar.

But to return to coal. The chief residue of its distillation is coke. Part of this, still glowing, can be used straight away to heat the furnaces. The rest is extinguished and later used in blast furnaces and in the boilers of central-heating systems and domestic stoves.

There seems no end to all the things that can be extracted from coal — all the by-products we get from the black diamonds that have brought man such wealth . . .

First, there are the hot, violent derivatives: the two fuels, gas and coke; and benzol which is used in the manufacture of explosives and, purified, as a fuel for motor car and aeroplane engines.

Then there are the cold, placid by-products: ammonia, which enriches fertilizers; sulphur and tar. From tar we get phenol, which is a medicine and disinfectant, naphtaline and aniline which yields lovely mineral dyes, heavy oils for motors, and, lastly, asphalt for surfacing roads.

Coal is one of the oldest relics of prehistoric times when cataclysms engulfed the forests and the flying saurians and monsters of the Primary Era, and buried them all deep in the earth where man now digs his mines, the mines in which, for all his care and precautions, a gallery occasionally caves in and imprisons some of those who obtain this wealth for us.

– that coal is used to make motor-car tyres, telephones, combs, gramophone records, fertilizers, paints?... And lots of other things to which we shall come later.

PETROLEUM

THE other witness of the beginnings of the world is OIL. The people of the Orient called this oil from the earth naphtha. The Romans called it 'Oil that comes from stones', and the Persians *radinake*. These latter obtained it from wells, using buckets and ropes made of goat-skin.

The oil-fields were formed very much in the same way as the coal-beds. They do not come from giant forests being buried in the bowels of the earth, but from the sea burying tiny little creatures in its depths, enormous beds of sticky creatures, molluscs, a swarming mass of microscopic marine organisms that were as much vegetable as animal.

This is the plankton that whales eat. Masses of these live particles of the seas eventually sank down and down to the bottom of the ocean, piling up in layers one upon the other, until billions and billions of tons of these dead molluscs covered the floors of the oceans with a thick, sticky silt. Millions of years passed. Currents transported this silt and filled the deep ocean trenches with it. Slowly the waters of the seas receded and the dry land expanded. The sea-bed creased and puckered like the land, and as a result the masses of plankton were squashed and imprisoned. Above these pockets beneath the waters, the centuries amassed deposits of salt. Compressed by the vast pressure of the deep, protected from the air and its oxygen, the mass of animal matter did not decompose but turned into petroleum.

It is the presence of this salt which guides the prospectors in their search for oil-fields. These pockets lie underground in those parts from which the sea receded millions of years ago. Some fields are only just below the surface.

Two thousand years ago, under the Ts'in dynasty, the Chinese discovered petroleum in searching for — guess what? — salt! The layer of salt covered an oil-field.

The oldest known oil-field is that on a peninsula of the Caspian Sea. Several centuries B. C. hundreds of fountains of flames used to shoot up from the ground there. Sailors saw these great flaming torches by night. For two thousand years there was a religion in Persia – it has not totally vanished – which was a sort of fire-worship. Their god was called Ormuzd.

The Chinese were the first people in the world to sink drill-holes. They sank more than 600 wells using cranes, levers and drills — the same implements, in rudimentary form, as are used today. Teams of oxen turned the huge wheel that forced the drill into the ground like a gimlet.

Let me tell you, too, about the extraordinary adventure that happened to a Russian general called Tsitsianov, who was an emissary of the Tsar of all the Russias. He had come to Hassan Koali Khan, who at that time ruled over the land of petroleum, to demand that he recognize the Tsar's sovereignty over the oil-wells of Baku. In his audience room, Prince Hassan, the last of the Khans, severed the poor general's head from his body with one blow of his yatagan. He then had the head salted and sent it to his sovereign, the Emperor of Persia, by one of the camel caravans that every month used to take 2,000 bourdiouks, which were great copper jars filled with naphtha, and distribute them through the empire.

It was Colonel Drake who, in 1859, bored the first modern oil-well at the foot of the Allegheny Mountains. He only had primitive drills and lived in a tent throughout one terrible winter, when he and his men were half dead with cold and hunger. People thought him crazy, because he wanted to look for oil at depths of thousands of feet. It was this same Drake who erected the first boring-derrick at Titusville.

●

The oil-fever began even before the day of the powerful drills that we now have. The adventurers of the world set out to look for petroleum. It was the Gold Rush all over again.

Since then man has sought the precious oil in the deepest strata of the earth and under the sea. Nowadays we drill wells on the seashore, in the sea itself and in lakes. Oil-fields that lie under water are being exploited in California, Texas and in the lagoons of Lake Maracaibo in Venezuela. Maracaibo is the best-lit town in the world. It has grown up in the course of a few years on one of the richest oil-fields that there are, which extends along the lake and under its waters.

Petroleum was first used as an engine of war in Syria some fifty years B. C. A small town halted a Roman fleet under Lucullus at the battle of Samosate. A crowd of men, women and children ran to the harbour and emptied vessels full of petroleum into the sea. The petroleum spread in a film across the water, and when they set fire to it most of the attacking fleet were enveloped in a sea of flames. The few survivors had to row for their lives to get away. The Romans had to abandon the fight when the flaming petroleum rained down on them from above, penetrating their cuirasses.

41

In that area they have dug 7,000 wells — 7,000 pumping derricks stand there, on the shore and in the water, so close as almost to be touching. At night the 7,000 derricks are lit up, and their pumps work without stopping, sucking up the black oil and driving it along the conveyor pipes, 200,000 tons of it every 24 hours.

Which is the deepest well in the world? One in the U.S.A., at Wyoming, where the drill went below 20,000 feet.

There is, too, a lake of asphalt; yes, a complete lake of bitumen. This is on the island of Trinidad, the humming-birds' paradise in the Antilles. The lake is only about 500 square yards in area, but it is inexhaustible. The layer of bitumen in this great pond scarcely gives

at all beneath the weight of the light railway track and of the little trucks that take the asphalt away. They dig the asphalt out with picks, and it only takes a night for it to fill up the holes and make the level the same as before. In the days of the corsairs, the filibusters used to put in at Trinidad, to the little port of La Bréa. There they repaired what damage their ships had suffered, and, instead of pitch and resin, used the bitumen of the lake to caulk and plug their hulls.

How does one drill an oil-well?
Powerful motors turn the drills which have special bits at the end. They dig down a dozen yards or so and

then the whole column of steel is withdrawn for the drill head to be changed. Once below 12,000 feet, this great drill weighs some 100 tons. It is hung in steel wires passing through blocks to a winch. The actual boring-bit is like an enormous dentist's drill, and it wears down very quickly when piercing rock.

Eventually the drill penetrates into the oil-bearing stratum. What it encounters there is not a liquid surface like the water at the bottom of a well: the oil-bearing pocket is more like a vast sponge of sand and limestone impregnated with naphtha, which it stores in its pores. At the top of this dome-shaped pocket, gas accumulates under great pressure, and if the drill pipe reaches the gas first, this is liable to escape and catch fire. Then it is necessary to drill a second hole to reach the oil, which will have to be sucked up by pumping engines, the flow being controlled by a system of valves.

●

The largest producer of oil in the world is the U.S.A.; then come Venezuela, the Middle East, the U.S.S.R. and Mexico.

How many wells are in production throughout the world?

More than 900,000! World production exceeds 22,000 million cubic feet. Such figures mean little to us, but if the people of London used oil instead of water, it would be eight months before that quantity had flowed through their taps. That will give you some idea of the size of the giant pipes used to convey this mineral oil from the wells to the refineries or loading ports.

These pipe-lines are made of steel tubes welded together, and the tubes can be anything up to 32 inches in diameter. They are either buried in trenches or lie in the open. Pumping stations along the pipe-line ensure that the oil flows steadily.

At Maracaibo there is more than 170 miles of pipe-line, and in Iraq and the Lebanon nearly 1,400 miles. In the U.S.A. itself the total length of pipe-lines would encircle the globe six times. The oil passes through these pipe-lines roughly at the speed of a person walking. At the ports it is stored in tanks and then pumped into tankers which take it to the refineries.

As with coal, distillation allows by-products to be obtained at various stages as the temperature increases. The most volatile bodies, that is those that evaporate most easily, such as benzine, are the first to be given off.

Petrol is given off at 250° C., gas-oil at 300°, fuel oil at 500°, asphalt at 800°.

In simple distillation, the vapours of successive by-products are drawn off the raw material into separate vessels, leaving the heavier material behind. In 1913, a new process called 'cracking' was perfected in order to get still more value from the raw material by using higher temperatures and decomposing even the heavier portions of the crude oil. 'Cracking' causes a chemical change — unlike distillation, which merely separates the different parts of the oil — and its introduction was soon followed by many new refining processes. Today it is possible to make dozens of special oils in whatever particular quality industry may demand.

Heavy oils for lubricating machinery, greases for protecting razor-blades and other such things and for making cosmetics and even printer's ink are all derivatives of petroleum. With gold and coal this mineral oil is one of the three most precious substances in the world. Unfortunately, it will become exhausted quicker than coal.

The world's known reserves of oil are in the region of 10,000 million tons, while those of coal are about 8 billion tons. It may be that in twenty years there will be no petrol left to drive a car or an aeroplane.

However, there is little doubt that other oil-fields will be discovered, thanks to the intensive prospecting that is being carried out. They even use aerial photography in impassable country. Also the fields under the sea will be being exploited before those beneath the land are exhausted. There are still unexplored parts of the world, especially the virgin forests of South America, where adventure and perhaps a fortune await the pioneer.

ONCE the city of Ys was enclosed, like a fortress, behind a high wall against which beat the waves of the Bay of Biscay. It stood not far from the present village of Plomarch in Douarnenez Bay. A great dike protected it from the fury of the ocean, and in this dike was a secret door whose only key was kept by King Gradlon.

THE FORMATION

What relics are there of the fabulous days which shaping of the Earth has been accompanied by towns and even continents of which we now know tell you the legend of the King of Ys

From this door the waves retreated one day to allow the lords and their men-at-arms to embark in the ships that were to take them to a distant war. At the head of those who embarked into the first ship was Perceval, the betrothed of Dahut the Fair, his cousin and daughter of King Gradlon. He was as handsome as she was lovely, the proudest knight among the gallant warriors of that little kingdom.

A year passed and the city of Ys remained without news of the gallant adventurer who had set out dreaming of conquering unknown lands to lay at the feet of his king and his lady.

Then, one day — a day of both rejoicing and mourning — the waves withdrew from the door in the dike to allow the returning conquerors to disembark from their ships. The city of Ys celebrated and all its bells rang. In the streets people sang and shouted. But in the palace Dahut was crying heartbrokenly, for her betrothed had perished in a distant land.

That night, in the midst of the festivities, the princess stole away from the banquet given by King Gradlon to his warriors to celebrate their return and ran to the secret door, the door to the sea that spoke and called to her with the voice of Perceval, her knight. The waves and the wind brought his dearly loved voice to her from the other end of the world, and so, wishing to join the one whom she had loved above all others and whose voice she thought she could hear in the sound of the waves, Dahut opened the sea door with the key which she had stolen from her father and the roaring waves rushed in through this breach.

Meanwhile in the palace, warned by Guénolé, abbot of Landévennec, King Gradlon and his knights mounted their steeds and galloped to save the princess. The king succeeded in snatching her from a foaming wave, and with his daughter behind him sought safety in frantic flight.

The king escaped, but alone. Dahut the Fair let herself slip from his horse as it dashed through the bellowing, panic-stricken crowd, and soon the waves had caught her up and engulfed her.

By the morning the city of Ys had vanished, swallowed

At a depth of 150–200 fathoms under the sea a piece of the earth's crust of several cubic miles subsides. This sudden commotion causes a submarine earthquake. The water, drawn into the great hole, flows back in gigantic oscillations, devastating the coasts for miles inland, before it finds its level again.

OF THE EARTH

our most distant ancestors witnessed? The slow
local cataclysms and upheavals that have engulfed
nothing beyond what legend has to tell. Let me
and of his daughter Dahut the Fair.

In other parts of the world such subsidences or quakes
have forced the lava up into the chimneys of volcanoes
and made them erupt. All observatories in the world have
an instrument called a seismograph which registers any
tremors that shake the earth's crust, which are thus
called earth tremors.

up by the sea.

Now, when fishermen returning from their grounds
come within sight of Douarnenez, they sometimes hear
the sound of the bells of the engulfed city ringing in the
water beneath their boats. This, very muffled, is the
alarm that all the bells of Ys rang on that terrible night.
It is probable that this legend was inspired by actual
events. There is no doubt that the city of Ys existed,
and it was probably submerged by a tidal wave.

Nowadays, millions of years after the geological
upheavals of the early ages, earthquakes and other
cataclysms, volcanic eruptions and horrible tremors still
occur in certain parts of the globe. And we still get tidal
waves after an earth tremor or submarine eruption that
have nothing to do with the tides.

When the waters of the sea are suddenly drawn to
where the earth's crust has fallen in, enormous waves are
set up before the water can find its own level again.
These waves have caused ocean-going ships to be swept
several miles inland and left there high and dry. In 1775,
at the time of the Lisbon earthquake, a 40-foot wave
swept the quays and wharfs of the city and carried off
the 30,000 people who had taken refuge there.

The people of antiquity were frightened when they
saw the earth quaking and thought that Vulcan was
hammering on the anvil in his smithy at the bottom
of the crater of Mount Etna, forging weapons for the
gods and heroes of legend. It is from Vulcan, the name
of the smith to the gods of Olympus, that the word
volcano comes.

In the other direction, lava, being subjected to sudden pressure,
is thrust into the chimneys of volcanoes, rises rapidly and reaches
the top, expelling through the crater rocks 'swept' from its long
chimney. This sudden emission of fire is often as catastrophic in
its effects as the violent onslaught of the waters on land.

Legend apart, people often have an entirely wrong idea of volcanoes and how they come into being. A volcano, no matter how old, is never a mountain in which a crater has been made. A volcano forms itself by spewing out and piling up its own lava, cinders and scoria.

Here is the story of the birth of one of the youngest volcanoes of the century, Paricutin, which came into being in 1943 near a little Mexican village and then grew like a mushroom.

In the night of 20 February 1943, after a series of violent tremors, tall flames could be seen rising from a field some mile or more from the village. In the morning, the men who went to the spot saw a crevasse and a mound of lava that seemed to be swelling and growing, but which was then no taller than an ant-heap. Two days later the volcano, which they could see growing, was already 200 feet high. On 26 February there was an outflow of lava from a crater that had opened at the top of the mound, which had by then attained a height of some 600 feet. A torrent of molten lava poured down towards the village, and the inhabitants had only just time to get out of their houses.

On 14 June this mountain of lava produced a baby volcano Zapicho, the fiery mouth of which opened in the

side of the parent mountain. Within a few days the baby was itself 250 feet high.

Both volcanoes have since continued to grow side by side. In 1946 Paricutin had already reached the 1,500-ft. mark and its debris covered an area as large as central London. The lava from the outflow of three years constituted the enormous mass of 14,000 million cubic feet — that is, a cube with sides more than seven times the height of Big Ben's Tower. The ash thrown out has been carried by the winds as far as Mexico City, more than 200 miles away.

Are there still active volcanoes?

Yes, indeed, and lots of them. In the different parts of the world there are more than four hundred volcanoes that are still active. Three are in full eruption in the Galapagos Islands in the Pacific, and another, Erebus, which is more than 13,000 feet high, spews its flame and black lava in the cold white desert of the Antarctic continent. There are more than a thousand volcanoes

The volcano Paricutin was 3 feet high in 1943. Ten years later, after growing at such a rate you could watch it, it was 7,000 feet high. It has been quiescent for some time; but has it said its last word?

46

There are thirty-five volcanoes in Japan. The most famous is Fujiyama, a perfect cone over 12,000 feet high.

that are extinct or dormant, marking faults that have opened in the crust of the earth throughout the ages.

This crust has been subjected to upheavals that have left it wrinkled into mountains or it has fallen in and caused crevices and faults.

The Pacific is ringed by a 'belt of fire'. The Atlantic has a chain of mountains running across it and these perhaps mark the remains of a vanished continent. The Mediterranean basin is still the scene of volcanic manifestations. In Japan 1,800 tremors have been registered in thirteen years. The Japanese no longer pay any more attention to them than we do to thunderstorms. Their legends have it that the islands of Japan rest on the back of a giant dragon which, being irritated by its burden, is continually shifting.

There have been so many great cataclysms that have appalled the world during the centuries that it will be enough to quote the most dreadful.

The eruption of Vesuvius in the year 79 is described in the letters of Pliny the Younger. The town of Pompeii was buried beneath a thick layer of cinders, and these were not cleared away until quite recently, when the town was rediscovered. It had been completely mummified at the time of the eruption which had brought all life there to a sudden stop.

Then, in 1883, Krakatau, a little island of only some 15 square miles in the sound between Java and Sumatra, was completely destroyed. First there was a terrifying eruption of the island's volcano, Perbuatan, which threw up into the air almost all the rock on which the island

An aerial view of the crater of Vesuvius.

rested, and then there came a tidal wave that swept over it and in a few moments killed 40,000 people. The smoke and the ash were carried by the wind as far as Europe, where for two years they caused such fantastically magnificent and spectacular sunsets as had never been seen before.

In 1923 the city of Yokohama, in Japan, was utterly destroyed: 450,000 buildings were razed to the ground and 250,000 people killed or wounded.

In 1902, Mount Pelée destroyed the town of St. Pierre in the island of Martinique and killed its 30,000 inhabitants. Less than a minute after the eruption, a hurricane of flames enveloped the town. This cloud of fire sucked up the sea like a large geyser, or rather like an enormous waterspout, for a geyser is a fountain of hot water spurting upwards. You can see several of them in Iceland, and there is one in America called 'Old Faithful' which sends a jet of water more than 60 feet up every 65 minutes. At St. Pierre, all the ships were sunk by the waterspouts, while a rain of ashes blotted out the daylight.

Mount Pelée only threw up clouds of fire, but most volcanoes in eruption spew up, as well as lava and ashes, a surprising amount of debris including volcanic 'bombs' and pumice stone. This latter is a whitish stone made very light by being inflated with thousands of tiny bubbles of air. Pumice stone will float in water, and its lightness has caused it to be used in building. The dome of St. Sophia in Istanbul is made of it.

'Old Faithful', one of the eighty-four geysers in the Yellowstone National Park (U. S. A.). These are real steam engines that Nature has made.

queer evidence of such things as the leaning tower of Pisa.

The sea has not always encroached upon the land. There are places from which it has retreated, even several miles, as it has at Rye in Sussex and at Aigues-Mortes in France, which also was once a port, that from which St. Louis set sail on the seventh and eighth crusades; yet now both towns are well inland.

•

Throughout the centuries the erosion of the sea has altered the shape of the continents. The periods when water and fire were supreme first set the globe in upheaval, then modelled it. The fires are still lurking there inside. Following the cracks in the earth's crust they continue to find outlets through the volcanoes, which are nothing but great pimples on the skin of our planet. Every day the face of Earth grows older, becomes furrowed with wrinkles and eroded by water, glaciers, winds, beasts and man.

As well as such violent upheavals, there are other slower processes that have gradually changed the face of the Earth. Along many of our coasts you can see how the sea has encroached and conquered the land. Mont Saint Michel, off St. Malo in France, was isolated by a huge subsidence. It used to stand in the middle of a vast forest, and even now after a violent storm the trunks of trees that used to grow in that forest are sometimes found in the mud. All along the west coast of France are islands that can still be reached on foot at low tide, when for a few hours the water leaves a practicable ford. Elsewhere there are the remains of Roman roads leading out into the sea and lines of menhirs or standing stones.

The largest subsidences have been those that destroyed not a town, like the city of Ys, but a whole continent, as was the case with Atlantis, the mysterious country of which the Ancients spoke as extending beyond the pillars of Hercules. The Azores, the Canary Islands and Madeira are the only traces left of this fabulous continent, if it ever really existed.

Part of Holland has been recovered from the sea, and people now inhabit what used to be the Zuyder Zee and the polder of Haarlem. Endless dikes protect the land there which lies lower than the sea level. Then there is the famous Dogger Bank, a favourite fishing ground in the North Sea, where people have dredged and brought up the bones of mammoths and prehistoric tools.

Long, long ago, England was joined to the Continent. The Channel was then a great valley in which the waters of the two rivers Thames and Seine met and flowed on elsewhere.

In other parts the subsidences have been tiny, no more than a slight flexure of the beds of clay, and Nature has left us no trace of them: in fact, we would not know that they had occurred were it not for the

To reclaim land from the sea, the Dutch made dams to enclose large areas of water, and then enclosed further sections or 'polders' within these non-tidal lakes. Water was pumped from the polders into the lakes and then into the sea, until gradually the whole area was drained.

For centuries, at each high tide, the waves have beaten against the foot of the cliff. They have eaten away the rock, which is more or less friable, digging out a cavern and causing cracks in the cliff, into which sea-water and rain-water filter. Then the part undermined collapses, the waves rake over the fallen rocks, dragging them away little by little at each ebb. Then the destructive play of the waves begins again and at the end of several more centuries the sea nibbles a few more inches of cliff.

The rains and the winds have long had their own invisible routes along which they come and go each season.

Without ever losing their way?

Why not?

You should see with what impatience the African negroes await the arrival of the first tornado. It sometimes happens that the rains are late. In the villages the negroes have already sown their millet and pea-nuts, yet the rains do not come. Can they have mistaken the way and got lost? When such doubts arise, the people of Bandiagara, for example, will try to summon the laggard rain by beating their tomtoms night after night at the foot of their cliffs. Their witch doctors talk to the wind, and a great prayer is addressed to the waters of heaven, sung by the women and danced by the men. The dancers, leaping and bounding, cover their faces with masks, the rain-masks made of wood, with horns and a huge bird's beak painted red.

But, you say, we have got a long way from erosion. Not so far, really. The rains *have* changed their routes in the course of the centuries; the Sahara is now a desert, yet the scorched mountains of Tibesti are still scored with the furrows made in them by the torrents that used to foam down their sides thousands of years ago. There, on those desolate plateaux, in the pools that lie in the hollows, you find tiny crocodiles, no longer than your hand, which are the degenerate descendants of the great saurians.

In these ponds you can also find a drop of water as old as the world itself that has flowed in streams and rivers, been in seas and clouds, and which, as it fell, along with all the others in some downpour, carried away a tiny particle of clay from the column of one of those rocks that the rain has carved like the gargoyles of a cathedral, which you see on the sides of mountains. Some of these are most elegant, gracefully shaped columns with a sort of hat balanced on the top, a mushroom of harder stone that has worn less than the column which it now protects like an umbrella.

These drops of water may have covered the world before they find themselves gathered at the fountainhead of some little stream, which then swells and finally throws itself into a river and so ends up in the sea.

•

Rivers are not all of the same age. There are those that are wild and swift, which rush down steep slopes, take leaps and tumble over rocks. These are young.

The mirror of water in which these 13th-Century ramparts are reflected is a brackish pond. The place is called Aigues-Mortes, which means 'dead waters'. It is the port from which the seventh and eighth Crusades started, but the silt of the Rhône delta has gradually overtaken it and it is now five miles inland.

For thousands of years this pyramid, which the geologists call a 'fairy' or 'hatted column' has been slowly denuded by the rain. The stone surmounting it acts as a little roof and slows down the action of the waters. It will take several more thousands of years before the stubborn, corrosive rain has destroyed this queer phenomenon.

THE NIAGARA FALLS. An avalanche of water that day and night pours down tons of water to irrigate flourishing valleys and contribute to the well-being of man.

Still impetuous, they sometimes dig potholes in their stony beds in which the water seethes as though in some giant's cauldron.

Other rivers are wise and sedate and just saunter through their valleys. Others, the very aged, no longer have the strength to deepen their beds. They are slow and meander along, twisting and twining across their plains.

One and all, however, continue to model their beds. They dislodge and carry away soft rock, cut out the curve of a loop, wear down the shelf of rock over which they leap like the famous Niagara Falls between Lakes Erie and Ontario. At this latter the river digs out its gorge by about a yard every year, and in fifty years has moved the 160-ft. terrace from which it makes its thundering leap a distance of from 10 to 100 yards.

Niagara is an Indian name meaning 'thunder of the waters' and is not the name of the river, which is the St. Lawrence.

Many rivers have a delta, but not many have two. One of these is the Rhône in France. It has one delta in the Lake of Geneva and another in the sea. The one in the lake is a stretch of more than 12 miles of silt and has advanced only just over a mile since the days of the Roman occupation; while the other, the marine delta of the Camargue, has encroached 7 miles on the sea in the same period. The silt deposited there in one year amounts to some 15—20 million cubic yards of soil, which is roughly the amount that had to be excavated to build the underground railway in Paris.

Deltas form in sheltered seas or where the tide is weak. The Ebro, Po, Nile and Tiber, which flow into the Mediterranean, all have deltas; so has the Danube, which flows into the Black Sea, and the Volga that mouths into the Caspian. The huge delta of the Mississippi has taken shape in the natural shelter of the Gulf of Mexico.

One aspect of the SAHARA, a vast expanse of desert that the white man can only cross with difficulty, going from one water point to the other. The Targui (plural – Tuareg) knows how to protect himself against the wind that picks up the sand.

For a delta to form, the river must itself bring down a huge quantity of silt, and this must strike a submarine bar. The line of the bar then swells and grows, and gradually becomes a triangular island shaped like the Greek letter △, which is called delta. The river then divides into arms and these form fresh little islands of the same triangular shape. Thus, slowly, the delta advances, moving out into the sea.

Another who helped to shape the earth was Aeolus, King of the Winds, who used to keep the tempests shut up in caves in the Lipari Islands and loose them to range the seas in packs. It is they which have polished the long tables of stone, the bare plateaux of the Sahara, until they are as smooth as glass.

It is, too, the wings of the wind that have smoothed the face and the huge paws of the Sphinx in Egypt.

The desert wind is always laden with sand that penetrates everywhere, especially into people's mouths, noses and ears, and that is why the men of the nomadic tribes, the Tuareg, whom we call the 'men of the veil', cover their faces except for a slit for their eyes.

The sand carried by the wind has eroded the *hamada* and chiselled out 'mushrooms' in the limestone rock. It is the sand, too, that has made the deep grooves in the pyramids.

Wind is a mysterious thing, like all the forces of Nature. It is the cause of the slow march of the dunes in the desert, driving the sand, grain by grain, from one slope to the other. Thus the dunes are always on the move, travelling slowly in the direction of the wind.

A sandy desert like the Grand Erg, where the dunes creep along in slow progression, is a land of which one dreams. It is the haunt of *djinnee*, jinns or spirits of the sand, which the wind sends twirling in mad dance across the desert, giving animal shape to the whirling clouds of dust.

There are some lovely legends about these lands of thirst, these vast expanses scorched by the sun, where the Blue Men pitch their tents. These Blue Men, it seems, still tell of their ancestors, the Psylles, famous horsemen of the wind, the wind that was their enemy. Every year, it is said, they used to set off on their camels and horses to meet the wind, to challenge it and fight it with their lances. When they encountered it they charged and drove it to the very confines of the desert.

Today, the war chiefs of the Tuareg tribes still put thin metal rings round the heads of their lances, in which the wind whistles as they ride along, just as it did in the old days when the Psylles charged the wind in the midst of the turmoil of a sandstorm.

Such is the legend of the land where the sand dunes march like armies. Sand is, indeed, all but invincible. On the French coast of the Bay of Biscay, the sand has made two ports, Mimizan and Cap-Breton, quite unserviceable, and so it has that of Zuydcoote, near Dunkirk. Though you cannot, perhaps, conquer it, you can sometimes fix it, as has been done in France in the district of which we were just speaking. There they have planted a million acres of sea-pines, creating a rich and lovely forest, which can be accounted one

51

Rain is not the only thing that carves rocks. The eddies of the wind round these rocks ten feet high have given them the shape of mushrooms.

of man's great feats of transformation, worthy to be mentioned along with the canals he has dug through the isthmuses of Panama and Suez, and with the dams he has built, the rivers he has turned aside, and the mines he has dug. Everywhere man makes himself felt. Sometimes Nature favours him and at other times is against what he wants to do.

•

The world is changing every day, being changed by even the smallest of its plants and animals.

The soil is the realm of innumerable burrowing animals: ants, termites, larvae, moles, rabbits, etc. Metal and stone are the only things that can resist the attack of the termites, and one can almost say that tropical Africa belongs to them rather than to men.

Plants attack rock and turn it into loam.

In tropical seas are the reefs of atolls. These are colonies of live coral growing a fraction of an inch every year and topping submarine craters or submerged islands.

At the two poles, bits are continually breaking off the ice, which at the South Pole is 6—10,000 feet thick, and drifting away. These are icebergs. Sometimes they have a bear or some penguins as passengers. These icebergs are not pieces of pack ice. An iceberg is an enormous piece of glacier, that is of frozen fresh water, while the pack ice is the surface water of the sea that has turned to ice, ice which always remains slightly salt.

•

The drift of the icebergs makes one think of the comparable movement of great masses of rock. These movements are infinitely slower and the effects are only discernible after millions of years, though they have probably helped to model the shape of our continents.

This hunter seated in his kayak is an inuk, which in the language of the Far North means 'man', and not an Eskimo, which is an offensive term that we use out of ignorance. The man has stopped paddling and is watching the water on the surface of which he expects to see the head of a narwhal come up to breathe. If his harpoon goes home, it will make his fortune. Its 6-ft. ivory tusk will serve as money in one of the white man's trading posts. The skin, when chewed, will provide the vitamins he needs for health. The blubber will be salted in barrels and kept in reserve for the winter. The meat will be eaten straight away, and his hungry dogs will have their share.

WEGENER'S THEORY

1. The continents have not always been shaped as we know them. 2. At the beginning of the Quaternary Era, that is to say long ago, when the first men appeared, the continents were closer together. An immense ice-cap covered a vast expanse from the North Pole downwards. It stretched as far as the middle of the U. S. A. and over a large part of Europe. 3. At the beginning of the Tertiary Era – that is to say more than 70 million years ago – the Old and New Worlds were joined at several places: in the South, Africa was joined to South America, and Cape San Roque, at the end of what was to become Brazil, seems as though it would fit into the gulf of Guinea; in the North, America is almost touching Europe, which is largely covered by shallow seas called 'epicontinental'. 4. Finally, in the Primary Era, the Later Carboniferous – that is, 280 million years ago – the continents formed a compact block covered by a thin skin of extensive epicontinental seas. The South of Africa was then occupied by a cap of ice, for at this time the earth's axis of rotation had not the same inclination as it has to-day, and the Antarctic polar zone was round what we call the Cape of Good Hope.

The sphere of Earth consists of concentric zones. It is rather like a fruit: first there is the envelope, a crust as thin as the skin of an apple; then the flesh, a viscous mass 700 miles thick, and in the middle the kernel, 7,000 miles in diameter. Scientists call these three layers: sial, sima, and nife . . .

SIAL because the crust of the earth is particularly rich in SIlica and ALuminium; SIMA because the intermediary layer consists mainly of SIlica and MAgnesium; and NIFE because the central kernel is held to be formed of the same matter as the meteorites, those pieces of the stars that sometimes fall on the Earth, and will thus be composed of NIckel and FErrous iron.

There is still a lot of argument about the earth's kernel: is it liquid, solid or gaseous? Or is it a combination of all three states? The estimates of its temperature range from 6,000° C to 10,000° C.

No one really knows how the Earth's continents gradually acquired what is their present shape. It is reasonable to suppose that the Earth, starting as solar nebula, gradually cooled and that on its surface a crust formed like a raft floating on the viscous mass of sima. That crust is the ancestor of our present continents.

Cracks appeared in this first crust, and the continents, which originally had been all of a piece, became separated. Imagine a break-away of great pieces of sial, like a compact group of icebergs, sliding across the more elastic sima at an extremely slow speed for millions of years.

If you cut America out of a globe, it is possible to fit it in places into the European-African bloc. Not only the coasts, but even the mountains fit together: the mountains of Norway and Scotland correspond to those of Canada; the plateaux of Africa prolong those of Brazil.

There is an ingenious suggestion — which is worth no more than any other — which would explain the mountain crinkles bordering the west coast of the Americas. This is that, as it drifted along this land acted like the prow of a ship deep in the, water and raised a sort of bow wave that piled up sima on it.

What is there in the wake of the land? Pieces that were broken off, a scattering of rocks strewn in its path, chaplets of islands: the Antilles, the Sunda Islands, Japan.

Yes, the world is a marvellous place, perhaps all the more marvellous because we know so little about it. That is why I like to subscribe to this theory which is by no means accepted by everyone.

There is no end to the wonders of the astounding secrets of the world and of Nature. How I envy the scientists, often poets in their way, who busy themselves with such questions.

One can never grow tired of hearing about the sea in whose abyss mountains form, whose waters are salt because the rivers carry into them the salt taken from the earth by erosion — of our blood which is also salt; and of the manatee of the coast of Gaboon, nice big beasts which have followed in the wake of the Americas across the seas and thus are also to be found on the coasts of Brazil.

Can one prevent oneself dreaming when one sees this drawing of the shoulder of Africa like the thick-lipped face of a chimpanzee gazing across the ocean — its eyes probing the distance towards the Gulf of Mexico and the line of the Antilles, a coast which, perhaps, once long ago bore the impress of this same grimacing face?

54

THE DISCOVERY
OF THE EARTH

THE first clan of naked men we saw crossing the savanna beneath the astonished gaze of the great apes set out to conquer the world. Traversing seas, crossing mountains and deserts, in the course of centuries they spread over the surface of the globe. Not infrequently what astonished the explorers as much as anything was the fact that, wherever they went, they were met by other human beings like themselves.

The first discovery of the Earth made by our distant ancestors had to be made over again, sometimes several times, so soon did it become impossible to distinguish truth from lies in the extraordinary stories told by travellers.

There is no more absorbing adventure story than the tale of the early voyages of those who discovered unknown lands and islands. The distant past has become covered with a sort of scrub of legend, and this has to be cleared away to enable one to get at what may perhaps be the truth; as the early explorers of America had to do in actual fact when, in making their way through what they thought was virgin forest, they came across ruined temples and columns and giant statues, like those of Easter Island, relics of vanished civilizations.

It was the attraction of the unknown that impelled these early explorers to go off into the blue—that and, one must admit, the lure of riches, the hope of finding rare stones and precious materials: amber, incense, spices, ivory and, above all — gold! Throughout Antiquity and the Middle Ages the discoveries were made in a rather haphazard way, exploration being directed by the needs of commerce.

Seventeen hundred years before our era began the Egyptians, searching for the Incense Road with a fleet manned by Phoenicians, who were brave and daring seamen, discovered a marvellous country that they called Pouânit. This was probably the coast of Somaliland, and from it they brought back aromatic spices for embalming their dead, incense, ebony, electrum, ivory and — monkeys.

A thousand years later, HANNO, one of the chief men of Carthage in those days, left that city with a fleet of sixty vessels each rowed by fifty oars, on a most grandiose expedition in which thirty thousand people took part. This Hanno was the first of those who groped their way along the continents, the first to have passed his hands over part at least of the gorilla-like profile of the African continent. Hanno passed through the straits of Gibraltar, founded a base at Agadir, sighted the Cape Verde Islands and sailed far enough south to see flames of an eruption of Mount Cameroon. It was no doubt in that area that he had what he thought were very hairy men killed and skinned. In reality they were gorillas. The skins he took back to Carthage.

With the foundation of the city of Marseilles in the seventh century B.C. the Greeks' gods of Olympus set foot in Gaul, landing from a Phoenician galley come from the coasts of Asia.

In those days sailors did not dare go far from the coast, but rather they hugged it, as Pytheas, the man from Marseilles, did when in his one ship he followed the Atlantic coast of Europe northwards in search of tin. He landed in Britain and seems to have sailed right round it, for he describes it as a triangular island. He even went right up to the 'lung of the sea', the wonderfully imaginative name that the Norwegians give to the Arctic Ocean, where the thick mist caused by the cold air meeting the warmer water is like the smoky breath of the exhalation of some gigantic creature. Pytheas was heading for Thule, the legendary city supposed to be at the 'edge' of the world.

In those days people thought that the world was flat like a plate, and that at its edges the sea tumbled over into a bottomless chasm.

Then, about 400 B.C., great explorations were made by land or in a great train of boats that crept along the shore. ALEXANDER THE GREAT set out to conquer the world. He made a great triumphal march across Egypt and founded numerous Greek colonies, thus enabling science and commerce to make considerable progress.

It was the Romans who first realized Alexander's dream and made themselves masters of the world, a world that was then tending to expand beyond the Mediterranean. During the reign of Nero, Roman legions discovered the sources of the Nile, and in 552 the Emperor Justinian sent emissaries from Persia to China. These opened up the SILK ROAD, bringing back the first cocoons in a piece of hollow bamboo. As a result, it was thought outside China that silk was a floss from the buds of the bamboo.

The VIKINGS were undoubtedly the most intrepid navigators of the Middle Ages. Not only did they sail up the rivers of France, round Spain and into the Mediterranean, but they went as far as Iceland, Greenland and Canada — which they called Vineland because they discovered some wild grapes there. Some of these Viking chiefs may even have ventured into the interior of America. In Dakota there are Indians, called Mandans, who are very tall and have fair hair and blue eyes.

When these Redskins want to make rain come, they dance as the natives of Bandiagara in Africa do, wearing their horned masks; but the Indians also loose their arrows at the sky, in the same way as the old Nordic warriors, who are perhaps their distant ancestors, used to pepper the sky with their arrows to help their gods when they were warring in the clouds.

One cannot properly call the Crusades voyages of discovery, any more than the journeys of GENGHIS KHAN who swept over Russia in 1224; but nonetheless these expeditions were responsible for enriching Europe with the knowledge of the Oriental civilizations which were finer and more luxurious than our own. In addition they knew how to use the compass and how to measure time and the height of the stars with wonderful instruments.

In 1271, a young Venetian called MARCO POLO, who was then only seventeen, set out with his father and uncle, Nicolo and Maffeo Polo, on a journey to China. He got back, but not till sixteen years later, and then he wrote an account of his extraordinary adventures in the countries of the Great Khan, in what he called his Book of Marvels. He even described the mysterious island of Cipangu, which was Japan, though he never went there, and how the courtyard of the prince's palace there was paved with gold and the throne itself of solid gold. It was always gold that preoccupied them.

The first person to discover a sea link between Europe and India was VASCO DA GAMA. On 8 July 1497 he sailed from Lisbon with a little squadron of four ships. He doubled the Cape of Good Hope, sailed up the coasts of Mozambique, crossed the Indian Ocean and so reached India.

The one who had seen most of Africa in those days was undoubtedly a man of Toulouse called Anselm Ysalguier, who was a companion of Jean de Béthencourt, the Norman who sailed the African coast and founded a kingdom in the Canaries. On one occasion, having gone ashore on the coast of Rio de Oro, 'River of Gold', Ysalguier was captured by the Moors, with whom there was already some trade by barter. The method of trading used was this. On arrival, the ship showed itself in the roads to which it was guided by fires the Moors lit on top of the cliffs. At night, a boat

EUROPE

ASIA

AFRICA

VASCO DA GAMA
1497 - 1499

MARCO POLO
1271 - 1295

VAN-LOUP

Vasco da Gama's route.
Marco Polo's route.

pulled away from the ship and rowed hard for the coast. The sailors then climbed the cliffs and laid the sacks with their goods there on top. These goods were glass beads, knives and cloth. That done, the sailors returned to the ship. The Moors then came to view the presents and in exchange left bags of gold-dust. Then they too withdrew.

The men from the ship returned. They left a few more trumpery trifles for good measure; for, if the natives did not think they were getting value for their gold, they took nothing, but left the goods lying. And so it went on. After several trips to and fro, from ship to land and back again, agreement would be reached without the Moors and the sailors having ever met. They made fire signals to tell each other when the cliff top was vacant.

Ysalguier was probably captured one night when the Moors were not playing quite fair. At any rate he became the first European to cross the African desert

from West to East. He was taken by nomads to Goa and there sold. In Goa he married a black woman. He lived in the north of the Sudan for nearly ten years, and he may even have visited the secret city of Timbuctu. In the end he became homesick, and with his wife, daughter and three black slaves, travelling with caravans, he crossed the entire Sahara and reached the Mediterranean and so was able to return to Toulouse.

•

Methodical exploration of the globe did not start until the end of the Middle Ages. Then, in less than fifty years, a number of sensational discoveries were made and the first circumnavigation of the globe accomplished, thus at long last giving man an exact idea of the world in which he lived.

It is true to say that the voyages made before those of the Spaniards and Portuguese in the 15th century left little trace but their wake, which was quickly smoothed out by the sea. After Columbus, da Gama, Amerigo Vespucci and Magellan, the true discoverers of the world were those who, thanks to the recent invention of printing, were able with the help of books to spread the knowledge they had acquired of the Earth as a whole, for it is really of no importance now whether or not the Vikings reached the New World five hundred years before Columbus or whether Timbuctu was visited by a European four hundred years before Caillé.

Though the lure of gain was often the principal cause of voyages of discovery being undertaken, and it was the glint of gold that made Cortez and Pizarro conquer Mexico and Peru, it was religious dissent and the watchword of liberty that sent the French and Spaniards into the heart of the New World. Religious faith has sent innumerable missionaries to preach the gospel to primitive peoples; and now, in the twentieth century, it is almost a competitive sporting spirit that is behind our efforts to remove the last 'blanks' from the atlas.

Since the world is round . . .

THIS period of the Renaissance is studded with the dates of famous discoveries which made Ptolemy's prophecy, that 'the girdle of the globe would expand and reveal to man an earth that was vast and unknown', come true.

'Since the World is round . . .' thought Columbus as he sailed west; and yet, though Grand Admiral of the seas, he never realized he had found a new world.

He set out on 3 August 1492 from the port of Palos in Spain, armed with letters to the Great Khan and convinced that 'since the world was round' he would reach China by steering his caravels, *Santa Maria*, *Pinta* and *Niña*, ever westward.

'Another three days and I will give you a world,' Columbus shouted in the midst of a storm to pacify his crew which was on the verge of mutiny. At last, on 12 October, more than two months after leaving Spain, the caravels reached an island which the natives called Guanahani and which Columbus re-named San Salvador. This was one of the islands of the archipelago of the Bahamas.

Columbus's second expedition took him to the Caribbean, to Dominica and Marie-Galante, which he called after his own ship's original name, and to Cuba. But in Spain they were still expecting a golden harvest, looking for the caravels to return with their holds stuffed with gold, paving stones of gold and cloth of gold from the palaces of Cipangu.

On his third voyage, the winds took Columbus to Trinidad—'the earthly Paradise that sends four rivers flowing into the world.'

No, Columbus did not realize that he had discovered America. He had the bad luck on his first two voyages to run his prow into a sprinkling of islands and when, on his third and fourth voyages, he did reach the mainland, he thought that he had just discovered larger islands lying in the seas off Asia. He never suspected the existence of a new continent, of America.

Cabot touched the mainland in 1498, but the new world is actually named after Amerigo Vespucci who, in the following year, reached South America and there realised that he had touched not merely a group of islands but a new continent.

In 1513, Balboa, a Spaniard, landed in the Gulf of Panama. In 1519, Cortez landed in Mexico at the psychological moment. The Aztec kings there ruled their vast empire by terror, and the Indians were expecting liberators to fall from heaven, this having been prophesied by their sorcerers; they took Cortez and his Spaniards to be they. Thus one reign of terror was substituted for another.

In 1523 Francisco Pizarro set out with a mere handful of men (50 horse and 200 arquebusiers) and conquered the fabulous realm of the Incas, giving Spain Peru.

Until then the discoverers of the world, those who had sailed round Africa or who had sought India by sailing westwards—da Gama, Columbus, Amerigo Vespucci—had only brushed the coasts of unknown lands, as they gropingly sought haphazard for a passage westward. With Cortez and Pizarro, however, begins an era of conquest, the age of the *conquistadores*, daring soldiers of fortune, pirate knights as it were. And, as always, it was the lure of gold that drew them.

Throughout Peru the Spaniards plundered the towns, tearing down the golden plaques that decorated the walls of the temples and palaces of the Incas. Gold was sent back to the coast in convoys, and the waiting ships filled their holds with it.

The Spaniards did not get all the gold. The priests are said to have gathered together all that they could rescue from the Spaniards and to have thrown part of it into Lake Titicaca; then they themselves fled into the mountains. The Spaniards who pursued them never found any trace either of the treasure or of those who had carried it. Despite recent searches, the lake has not given up its secret and it is probable that the treasure of the Incas will never be found, any more than fabulous Eldorado.

At the time of the conquest, Francisco Orellana, who was a sort of visionary, said that during an adventurous journey he had been received in the city of Manoa, which was the capital of the 'Man of Gold'. The king was powdered all over with gold dust so that his body glistened and gleamed and made him look as if he had been carved out of a block of the yellow metal.

The city itself was built on piles in the middle of a lake, and the piles were of solid gold and supported golden palaces and avenues paved with gold.

NORTH AMERICA

EUROPE

AFRICA

SOUTH AMERICA

VIKINGS

CABOT
1498

CORTEREAL
1500

CARTIER
1534

VERRAZZANO
1524

PONCE DE LEON
1512

CHRISTOPHER
COLUMBUS

1492

1493

1502

1498

CORTEZ
1519 - 1521

VESPUCCI
1499

VESPUCCI
1501

PINZON
1500

PIZARRO
1532 - 1535

MAGELLAN
1519

CABRAL
1500

The Discovery of the Americas
between 800 and 1535
Areas then known
Lands discovered but
unexplored

VAN-LOUP

You can imagine how all the adventurers of the world set out to search for this fabulous city. One day it was thought that they had found at least the lake in which the city and all its treasures had been engulfed. This was Lake Guatabita in Colombia. Since it was in the crater of an extinct volcano, they decided to drive a tunnel through the side and empty the lake.

A group of financiers put up the money and the lake was in fact drained, but in its centre was a great hole, so deep that it could not be plumbed. This was the chimney of the old volcano and it remained filled with water. Thus the vast treasure of Manoa has still to be found.

The flood of gold flowing from the New World to Spain made the other nations jealous.

The King of France sent orders to the people of St. Malo that they should go and discover new lands for him, and in 1534 Jacques Cartier from St. Malo reached the mouth of the St. Lawrence and sailed up the river as far as Beaver Dam, which is where Montreal came to be built.

Sixty years later Samuel Champlain founded Quebec.

The penetration of the interior of the continent was slow, however, and it was not till the end of the seventeenth century that Father Marquette and Cavelier de La Salle went down the Mississippi and founded Nouvelle France. The interior of South America, even wilder and more savage, was not explored until the eighteenth century by La Condamine, Alexander von Humboldt and Alcide d'Orbigny.

It should be remembered that the object of all these discoveries of the time of the Renaissance was to try and find a possible route to China. At the very moment when Cortez was landing in Mexico, Magellan, to whom Charles V had given a fleet of five ships, was setting sail from Sanlucar to look for a passage south of the American continent. Magellan was a Portuguese who had taken service with Spain.

The winds kept sending Magellan west on what was to be the first voyage right round the world. Thirteen months after leaving Spain he passed through the strait that now bears his name, and then he sailed up into the Pacific. Famine reigned aboard his ships and the men ate the leather of their boots. After a crossing of 4,000 leagues the ships made landfall at the Marianas. There they feasted on wild pig roasted whole, turtle's eggs and palm wine. Then the flotilla sailed on to the north-west.

Magellan died from the wound of a poisoned arrow that struck him in the thigh while commanding his musketeers on the island of Mactan, the natives of which attacked in force and routed the little troop with which he had landed.

Only one of the ships, the *Victoria*, commanded by Sebastian del Cano, Magellan's second-in-command, returned to Spain after getting the rest of the expedition as far as Borneo and the Moluccas.

The Southern Route was now available, but it was long and the passage of Cape Horn very dangerous. At the end of the sixteenth century Davis, Barents and Hudson made vain attempts to sail round the north of America and reach China via a north-west passage, but they all came up against impassable pack-ice. In England a North-West Passage Company was formed, and while the Basques, English and Dutch quarrelled over the possession of Spitzbergen and the fishing right there, the King of France ordered the Arctic Pole Company to effect a military occupation of the polar straits.

The Lands of the Southern Hemisphere

For a long time sailors had been speaking of a large unknown continent in the Southern Ocean, and various plans had been made for taking possession of it. It was not till 1655, however, that Australia, which had been discovered by Torres in 1606, officially appeared on the map under the name of New Holland.

Since Vasco da Gama's great voyage, the Indian Ocean had been ploughed in every direction. The Spaniards and Portuguese made themselves masters of the Philippines and Moluccas and so barred the way to the Celestial Empire; thus it was that the Dutch turned south to the Sunda Islands which they prospected methodically. At first, the French did not venture so far. They installed themselves in Madagascar and its neighbouring islands in 1642. Then the islands of the south and Pacific attracted other explorers.

Bougainville landed on Tahiti, which Wallis had discovered in 1768, and took possession of it in the name of France.

Captain James Cook explored the South Seas and Pacific until he was killed by natives on the Sandwich Islands.

Then French exploration was given a fresh impetus and La Pérouse discovered Easter Island with its enormous statues, explored Alaska, sailed round Japan and reconnoitred Formosa and Macao, returning by way of Polynesia, Samoa and Australia, after which all trace of his ship was lost. Fifty years later, d'Urville, landing on Vanikoro, found the remains of the French explorer, who had been massacred by the islanders.

D'Urville was the first of those pioneers who have reached and explored the icy world of the sixth continent. After him came the British and Norwegians, Shackleton, Scott, Amundsen; and now many nations are exploring there.

Africa

AFRICA remained a forbidden land long after the Middle Ages and was the subject of the most extraordinary legends. Its savage territories were said to be inhabited not only by fabulous beasts, but also by human monsters. It was said that in the heart of this Dark Continent lived beings who spent their time lying down, one foot in the air. This foot was much larger than the other, and served them as a sunshade or umbrella according to the season! The truth was that, though the impenetrable bush served as refuge for tribes of primitive men, there was at the same time an advanced civilization in the big centres of the Sudan and Nigeria, in particular at Timbuctu, which the Scots explorer Mungo Park made a vain attempt to reach at the end of the eighteenth century.

The Sahara was explored by Barth and Nachtigal. In 1770, Bruce discovered the source of the Blue Nile, and Cailliaud that of the White Nile fifty-two years later, in 1822.

The most extraordinary explorer of them all was undoubtedly Livingstone, who knew how to win over the natives. His chief title to fame is not the fact that he discovered the 'thundering smoke' of the Victoria Falls, but that he fought so valiantly against the slave trade. For some time he was missing and Stanley was sent to find him, which he did in 1871, on the shores of Lake Tanganyika.

At this period exploration had become a sport. In 1880, Stanley, who also dreamed of stopping the traffic in negro slaves and of organising a proper hunt of the 'slavers' which carried this 'black ivory', was commissioned by the King of Belgium to explore the course of the Congo. While doing so, in the heart of Africa he met Lieutenant Brazza, who was doing the same, and the two had what was a virtual race.

What can be the history of the ancient city of Zimbabwe, the ruins of which Adam Renders, one of the most daring explorers, discovered in the heart of the Rhodesian plain in 1868? Renders was hunting elephant in the huge valley of the Limpopo when he came across a ring of giant walls flanked by watch-towers and with a large opening in them that had perhaps been filled by a draw-bridge, the whole buried beneath creepers.

Perhaps we shall never know who built this ghostly city. Perhaps they were people come from India or China. The Bantu, whose imagination is most vivid,

consider these gigantic ruins to be the remains of the
ancient capital of the Saos, the giants of the land of
Live Gold. These Saos are supposed to have been so
tall that they used to cut whole trees to make their
bows. They used to catch hippopotami and crocodiles
in the rivers with their hands. In those distant days,
according to the legend, gold was alive, a sort of winged
creature that used to fly up out of the grass, and which
the Saos caught as it flew along.

Asia

ASIA used to be the best known of the continents.
Commercial relations between the Orient and Occident
were never interrupted and had even increased after
the discovery of the sea route to India round the Cape
of Good Hope. St. Francis Xavier had taken Christianity
to Japan in 1550; other missionaries had been at work
in China, and much had been learned from them.

Certain areas, however, long remained closed to the
foreigner. One of these was Tibet, which Fathers Hue
and Gabet visited in 1846, travelling riding on yaks.
They penetrated into the forbidden city of Lhasa, holy
city of the live Buddha, the Dalai Lama. They visited
the monasteries and saw the monks turning their little
prayer-wheels, and in the merchants' quarter, where the
walls of the houses were made of yak horns joined by
mortar, they saw extraordinary statues made of butter,
which were brought out for the great festivals—pyramids and huge bas-reliefs in rancid butter, carved like
marble. Masterpieces in butter!

For a long time the Himalayas remained inviolate.
In 1921 Colonel Howard-Bury led an expedition that
attacked the peaks of Everest, which was finally climbed
by Edmund Hillary and the Sherpa Tensing in 1953.
Annapurna, the first of the giant peaks (26,000 feet)
to be climbed, was conquered in 1950. It is here, in the
highest mountain range in the world, that the yeti, an
unknown and unidentified animal often referred to as
'the abominable snowman', is said to live. It may,
however, not exist at all.

63

The poles

It is only comparatively recently that the POLES have tempted explorers, but it is largely to their expeditions that we owe our knowledge of the extreme North and South. The Eskimos of the Far North, in winter huddling round a lamp of seal-oil in their igloos, which are huts built of snow, are in some ways as superstitious as savages. Their sorcerers, called *angakoks*, tell them that the paradise to which their dead go is on the moon. The Eskimos have never seen a tree, for none grow in their deserts of ice. The only wood they have is driftwood, or wood from ships wrecked in the ice—fallen, as they think, from the forests of the moon.

Thus, when Ross and Parry's expedition reached Prince Regent Bay and the Eskimos saw white men for the first time, the little yellow people thought that they had come from the moon, for nowhere else could they have found enough wood to build their big ships.

In those days the British Parliament had offered a prize of £20,000 for the first person to discover a polar sea route to China, but it was the North-East Passage that

There is still plenty of unexplored country in the world. Much is in the South Polar continent which is only now being explored properly. The depths of the great forests of Africa have not yet been penetrated, nor have the jungles of such islands as Sumatra and Borneo, which may well conceal lost tribes such as those which were discovered in New Guinea in 1954.

And then there are the forests of the Amazon.

Explorers have told us of the vegetable inferno of the Sierra Parima, land of the Mariquitare and fierce Guaharibo Indians. It appears on the first maps of America made by the Spaniards and Portuguese in the sixteenth century. It was there, in the heart of the Amazon

was first made. This was in 1878 and the man who did it was the Swedish explorer Nordenskjöld. Then, in 1893, Nansen had the idea of letting himself be imprisoned in the ice and so drift across the icy cupola of the world. This he did in his ship *Fram*. He was away three years, and though he himself failed to reach the Pole, *Fram* came through successfully.

On 6 April 1909, Robert Peary, an American, reached the North Pole.

In 1926, Amundsen, a Norwegian as Nansen was, who had already achieved the North-West Passage in 1903, flew across the North Pole in an Italian dirigible, *Norge*. Amundsen was killed in 1928 while searching for General Nobile, an Italian, who was attempting to repeat this feat in another dirigible, *Italia*.

In 1908, Charcot opened the route to the South by way of the Sea of Whales and Adelaide Land. Three years later Amundsen, and an Englishman, Scott, both took expeditions to try and reach the South Pole. Scott chose a more difficult route, and when he reached the spot where the invisible axis of the poles pierces the world, it was to see the Norwegian flag fluttering from two skis that Amundsen had planted in the ice on 14 December 1911, only a few weeks before.

jungles, that the enchanted city in Lake Eldorado was supposed to lie, capital of the 'Man of Gold'.

Centuries ago the Indians were themselves great discoverers. They traversed the vast lands of the south from west to east, from the Amazon to the sea. They established themselves in the Antilles, then in Florida and Louisiana, crossing the sea that bears their name, the Caribbean, in canoes which were made of tree-trunks hollowed out.

One can still dream of making discoveries. To the south of the Orinoco, between Venezuela and Brazil, there are vast expanses where the forest is still inviolate and has never yielded its secrets to anyone.

THE explorers of the most distant times had no maps by which to draw up their routes. The marine charts of the earliest navigators were sung. Yes, they were songs, in the chorus of which the names of the towns, capes, ports and islands to be met when following the coast were repeated in their right order. In that way they were remembered.

The soldiers of the Roman legions used to write their stages on their shields, which is probably the origin of the saying 'All roads lead to Rome', for to Caesar's soldiers Rome must certainly have been in the middle of their long shields.

In the day of the Roman, Pliny the Elder, they knew of only three continents and divided the surface of the world between them in this proportion: Europe, one third; Africa, one quarter; Asia, one fifth; the rest being water. Even with only three continents instead of six, the Ancients thought that there was twice as much land as there really is.

The Ancients imagined the most extraordinary shapes for the world. To the Greeks, Delphi, where the famous temple of Apollo stood, was naturally the centre of the universe.

About the year 1000 Macoudi drew the world as a bird spreading its wings in flight, Africa being the tail and Mecca the head.

The Arabs had already divided the grand circle of the globe into degrees. Each degree was equivalent to 25 parasangs. Each parasang represented 12,000 cubits, a cubit 24 digits, the digit 6 grains of barley, a grain of barley 6 mule's hairs.

In the Middle Ages they began drawing the lands and seas on pieces of parchment. Some clever craftsmen even made an extraordinary planisphere of solid silver that weighed 450 Roman pounds and was engraved with an engraver's burin. This carried the names of the towns,

the contours of the lands and even seven bands corresponding to the seven climatic zones from South to North. This was made in Sicily in 1154.

Now we know that the surface of the globe consists of one-third land and two-thirds water. The Pacific Ocean is fifteen times the size of Europe. The Atlantic is a sort of funnel lying between the Old and the New Worlds, and is prolonged by the Arctic Ocean. In the Southern Hemisphere there is the Indian Ocean. The Southern Ocean is the only one that links with all three great oceans, which it does because of the shape of the continent it surrounds. Yet, even so, the surface of the oceans do not constitute a level plane surface, but there have been found to exist changes in level caused, it is

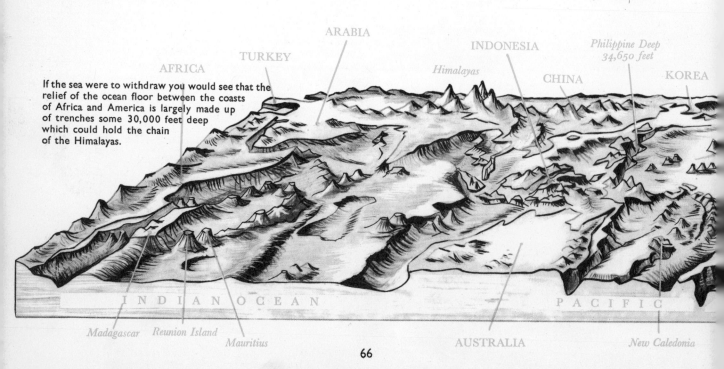

If the sea were to withdraw you would see that the relief of the ocean floor between the coasts of Africa and America is largely made up of trenches some 30,000 feet deep which could hold the chain of the Himalayas.

AFRICA TURKEY ARABIA INDONESIA Himalayas CHINA Philippine Deep 34,650 feet KOREA

INDIAN OCEAN PACIFIC

Madagascar Reunion Island Mauritius AUSTRALIA New Caledonia

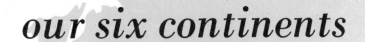

our six continents

Europe	3,900,000 sq. miles
Asia	16,500,000 sq. miles
Africa	11,500,000 sq. miles
The Americas	16,100,000 sq. miles
Australasia	3,500,000 sq. miles
Antarctica	11,500,000 sq. miles

When you look at the map of the world you see that the continents are unequally spread about the surface of the globe. The greater part of the land is in the Northern Hemisphere. The Southern Hemisphere is almost entirely covered by sea.

It is usual for maps to show the North Pole at the top and the South Pole at the bottom. It would be amusing to draw a planisphere that reversed the pattern. One would then have a picture of the world inside out.

It is also amusing to look for strange portraits in the outlines of the continents. Europe is a very complicated shape with its peninsulas and isthmuses; the Scandinavian peninsula resembles the dragon's head that the old Vikings used to have on the prows of their ships, and everyone knows that Italy is like a high boot.

Asia is like a dragon asleep, or like a stretching octopus.

Australia is like a rabbit wrinkling its nose to sniff at a carrot, Tasmania.

The most imaginative picture, perhaps, is that of North America as a huge lasso opened out; in which case South America would be the holster of the gaucho's revolver.

The shape of the different continents, however picturesque it may be, does not matter much to those who

thought, by the attraction of the continental masses or else by differences in salinity.

The Bering Sea, Sea of Okhotsk, China Sea, Yellow Sea, Caribbean Sea and North Sea are surrounded by archipelagoes. They are not so deep as the oceans. There are, too, enclosed seas like huge lakes, such as the Aral Sea, the surface of which is 160 feet above those of the open seas, while the Caspian Sea and the Dead Sea are respectively 84 and 1,200 feet below ordinary sea level. There are other seas like the Mediterranean and the Red Sea that only communicate with the oceans by straits, and this gives them some of the qualities of closed seas: weak tides and greater salinity.

The area of the continents is now known:

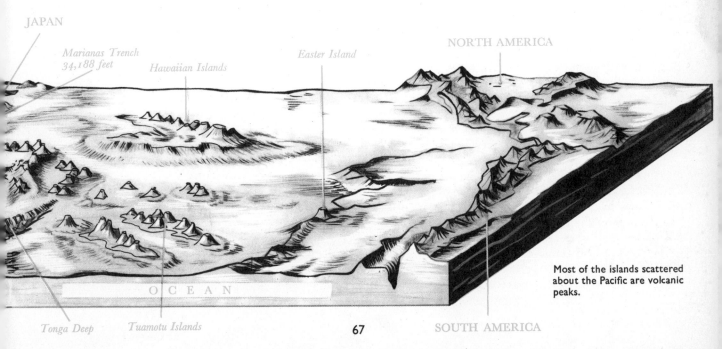

JAPAN

Marianas Trench
34,188 feet

Hawaiian Islands

Easter Island

NORTH AMERICA

Most of the islands scattered about the Pacific are volcanic peaks.

O C E A N

Tonga Deep   Tuamotu Islands

SOUTH AMERICA

MARINE CURRENT
WINDS

live in them. Though a country's position can sometimes influence the activities of its inhabitants, as is the case with Great Britain, which has bred a nation of sailors, more important in this connection are the factors that determine climate.

The chief of these factors is, perhaps, relief, and that means mountains, which can be more or less rugged, depending on their age.

How does one tell the age of mountains?

The first mountains go back to the Primary Era, and they have been worn by the rain and wind for millions of years, with the result that they are now very low. They provide the isolated massifs: the Scottish Highlands, the Armorican highlands, the Ardennes, the central massif of France, the nose of the Australian rabbit and the Brazilian plateau of South America.

The young mountains are those which came into being during the Tertiary Era in the day of the mastodon when Nature was amusing herself by stretching antelopes to make the giraffe, and when the trees came down off the mountains and marched out over the plains.

These young mountains have pointed peaks and sharp needle tops. They are not spread about the world in solid lumps, but stretched out in long chains. They follow two main directions: one runs from east to west, comprising the Himalayas, Caucasus, Carpathians, Alps, Apennines and, after the gap of the Mediterranean, the Pyrenees and the Atlas mountains of Morocco; the other line, running from north to south along the Pacific, is made up of the Andes and the Rockies.

And following the young mountains there is a chain of volcanoes, lying along the line of faults in the earth's crust: Perbuatan in the island of Krakatau in Oceania, Fujiyama in Japan, Popocatepetl in America, Etna and Vesuvius in Europe.

Starting from the Equator are the latitudes rising and descending to the north and south. Altitudes are piled up from the base to the top of a mountain. By reason of its height a mountain is a summary of the two hemispheres of the planet. As you climb it, you find all the varieties of vegetation that you would find if you travelled from the foot of the mountain to polar latitudes.

Thus, in Africa, though the foot of Kilimanjaro is set in the green sea of the tropical jungle, at its top you will find snow, lichens and frozen tundra.

Other factors that vary and so influence climate and the way people live are temperature, winds, rain and marine currents.

In the Northern Hemisphere, the atmosphere is divided into two great regions: that of warm air in the equatorial zone, and that of cold air at the poles.

In the temperate zone, which is where the two masses of air collide under the impetus of the winds, there is bad weather.

The winds are antagonistic and, in the Northern Hemisphere, seem hemmed in by two walls: a polar wall and a tropical wall. The line of the trade winds and the cyclones extends round the Earth, following the two walls.

The rains follow the winds, at least those which water coastal areas and the mountains. Then there are the tornadoes of Oceania, the Amazon basin of South

America and central Africa; these are downpours of moisture that has evaporated during the day and become condensed again in the evening—water that thus does nothing but go up and down.

In the Southern Hemisphere, below the zone of the trade winds, there are only constant westerly winds. Finally, in winter time, the poles are themselves swept by fierce cyclones that often reach as far as the temperate zones.

Marine currents have a great influence on the climate of the continents whose coasts they wash. There are five great submarine rivers in the oceans: two in the Pacific, two in the Atlantic, and one in the Indian Ocean. One of the Pacific currents is a warm one, the Kuroshio, and warm too is the Gulf Stream, an astounding river nearly fifty miles wide that starts in the Caribbean Sea and the Gulf of Mexico and flows at a speed three times that of the River Thames. Its water has a temperature of 29° C. and its deep blue colour stands out against the green of the ocean. It takes three years to make the crossing to Europe, where it helps to make the climate so mild that in some places, such as Campbeltown, it is possible to grow palms.

Can you guess how it is possible to calculate the time taken by a marine current, the Gulf Stream for example, to complete its journey? You do it by throwing in bottles which contain a piece of paper on which is written the date and the place where the bottle was launched.

Then there are the two cold currents of the polar seas: Oyashio in the Pacific and the Labrador current in the Atlantic. This latter passes close to New York and is the reason why in December there is snow there, while in Naples, which lies on the same latitude, the temperature is 10° or 12° C. and people can sit and warm themselves in the sun. Spring in Naples is leisurely, but in New York it only lasts two weeks, and then summer bursts upon the city with a dry heat.

The action of the winds and consequently the rains, together with temperature, which depends chiefly on latitude and altitude, give a country its climate. Climate has been split up into four principal zones: equatorial, tropical, temperate and glacial. These divisions are characteristic on the whole, but there are some curious

ARCTIC ZONE

CLIMATES

TEMPERATE ZONE

TORRID ZONE

TEMPERATE ZONE

ANTARCTIC ZONE

exceptions resulting from modifications due to mountains or winds.

Polynesia enjoys perpetual spring with fresh, balmy breezes, warm rain and moderate heat. You can bathe all the year round, have pineapples and garlands of flowers; life is idyllic in that earthly paradise which is not far from the Equator and on the same latitude as the terrible sandy desert of Australia and of Iquique on the coast of Chile, a place where it never rains — a place of absolute drought.

Why is Polynesia so favoured?

This privilege is due to these islands being situated in the midst of an immense ocean as vast as the Atlantic and the Indian Ocean together. Hot and cold currents circulate there, chasing each other incessantly like bicyclists on two huge tracks on either side of the equator.

Why do Canada and the U. S. A. have winters that are mainly severe and summers that are fearfully hot, while certain shores of the Great Lakes enjoy a milder climate? Why are Lakes Superior, Erie and Ontario open for shipping, while Lakes Huron and Michigan and the St. Lawrence freeze?

This is because of the influence of that huge inland sea which is known as the 'Fresh-water Mediterranean' and which in winter releases the calories it has stored up during the summer.

Why will fruit trees (almonds, apricots, oranges) grow in California on the same latitude as the 'Living Desert' in the middle of the mountains where Walt Disney made his famous film?

Because of the ocean which gives humidity and tepid heat to the orchards, while the desert and famous Death Valley, where the thermometer rises to 60° C, lie on the other side of the mountains, on the other slopes of which the clouds have already discharged all their rain.

Perhaps, too, the warm Kuroshio current has some effect.

Why is it less cold at the North Pole than in Siberia and the North of Canada? Why do seals frolic in the ice-free sounds, and why have astonished explorers seen a blaze of flowers blossoming on little islands near the Pole?

This may be because there are warm currents flowing

under the ice and because of the sunshine of the short summer when there is no night.

The South Pole is said to be much colder and so it is; yet in 1947 an American Expedition discovered the presence there of huge lakes that were quite free of ice. Their seaplanes landed on these lakes and the pilots were even able to bathe as they gathered moss, lichens and algae.

How is one to explain that anomaly on the fringe of the vast dead continent? (Though it has not always been dead, as we know, for coal and fossil plants have been found there.) The almost tepid temperature of these lakes may be due to volcanic phenomena or to geomagnetic causes. They are still a mystery.

Rather similar phenomena are to be seen in mountains where there are what the geologist calls 'glacier gardens', that is colonies of plants growing in certain sheltered parts of the glacier area at a height greater than that at which the plants are normally found. For example, there are two such 'gardens' in the massif of Mont Blanc at Talègre and Argentières, both well known to alpinists.

The influences of the sea are not always strong enough.

New Orleans, which is on the latitude of Cairo and on the Gulf of Mexico, has severe winters when the thermometer can go as low as minus 9° C. This is because the north wind which blows down from the Pole and across Canada continues down the basin of the Mississippi and has enough strength to reach the mouth and freeze everything there with its icy blast.

There is another sort of anomaly due to country being mountainous. In the mountains on the Equator the people who live above 6,500 feet enjoy a mild and pleasant climate. Quito, capital of Ecuador, which is on the Equator, and Bogota, capital of Colombia, which is only five degrees north, are the best examples of this influence of mountains. The mountains induce the formation of coastal clouds and force the air to rise; then the clouds, having cooled and reached a rarefied atmosphere, break in rain on the slopes.

This is the way in which the water vapour given off by the Indian Ocean and driven over India by the summer monsoon turns into clouds which empty themselves on the southern slopes of the Himalayas. (The record rainfall of the world is that of 468 inches at Cherrapunji, there.)

Thus India, which ought to be a desert because it lies in the tropical zone, receives as much water in half the year, during the period of the summer monsoon, as the Equator does during the whole year.

India, however, also provides the exception to the exception in the desert of Thar, one of the most awful places in the world.

Beyond the 'windward' Himalayas, that are watered, lie the arid plateaux of Tibet. Having crossed the peaks of 20—25,000 feet, the air drops, becomes compressed and absorbs the little water vapour there is on the other side. It dries everything. On that 'leeward' side of the Himalayas the sky is a deep blue, while on the other side it is laden with clouds.

AMERICA

Area : 16¾ million sq. miles

Population : 320 million

EUROPE

AREA: 2,085,000 sq. miles
POPULATION: 560 million

Aberdeen
Dundee
EDINBURGH
Glasgow
Newcastle
Londonderry
BELFAST
York
Hull
Manchester
Liverpool
DUBLIN
Norwich
Birmingham
LONDON
Cork
CARDIFF
Thames
Southampton
Plymouth

DUBLIN
NORTH SEA
Thames LONDON
AMSTERDAM
Elbe
ENGLISH CHANNEL
BRUSSELS
PARIS
Scheldt
Rhine
BERNE
Po
Venice
ATLANTIC OCEAN
LISBON
MADRID
Ebro
Barcelona
Tiber
ROME
Pillars of Hercules
MEDITERRANEAN SEA
AFRICA

COMPARATIVE LENGTHS OF THE RIVERS OF EUROPE

River	Length	
THAMES	(210 m.)	
SCHELDT	(250 m.)	
GARONNE	(405 m.)	
PO	(415 m.)	
SEINE	(480 m.)	
RHONE	(505 m.)	
NIEMEN	(515 m.)	
ODER	(540 m.)	
EBRO	(560 m.)	
LOIRE	(635 m.)	
VISTULA	(665 m.)	
ELBE	(685 m.)	
RHINE	(820 m.)	
DNIEPER	(1210 m.)	
DON	(1305 m.)	
DANUBE	(1775 m.)	
VOLGA	(2295 m.)	

ARCTIC OCEAN

ASIA

Murmansk

STOCKHOLM

HELSINKI

Leningrad

TALLIN

RIGA

Niemen   Vilno

Vistula

WARSAW

Volga

MOSCOW

Dnieper

Kiev

Don

Stalingrad

Odessa

ENNA

APEST

Danube

BELGRADE   BUCHAREST

SOFIA

CASPIAN SEA

TIRANA

ISTANBUL

Baku

BLACK SEA

ASIA MINOR

ATHENS

Mt. ARARAT 16,950 ft.

MATTERHORN   Mt. ROSA   Mt. KAZBEK
14,713 ft.   15,226 ft.   16,540 ft.

Mt. BLANC 15,782

PIC d'ANETO 11,163 ft.   MULHACIN 11,417 ft.

ETNA 10,741 ft.   OLYMPUS 9,463 ft.

CRÊT de LA NEIGE 15,599 ft.

BALLON d'ALSACE 4,100 ft.

EIFFEL TOWER 985 ft.

Sea Level

The same thing occurs in the temperate zone on a smaller scale. The western slopes of the Vosges Mountains receive three times as much rain as the eastern slopes. Farther north you find the same thing again: the mountains of Norway are glistening with rain from the sea, while Sweden, lying behind them, is relatively dry.

France and Poland are both in the so-called temperate zone; yet the winters in France are relatively mild, while in Poland for months the thermometer registers minus 25° C. and the rivers are frozen.

Great Britain is especially favoured in respect of climate. In so many other countries the seasons are crazy and abrupt, icy and torrid in turn, but our four are well-disciplined. Spring brings the flowers and prepares us for the heat of summer. Autumn ripens the fruits and the winds scatter the leaves to give us warning of the advent of winter. We have a wonderful variety of animals, birds and plants, but no monsters or horrible creatures, no poisonous spiders, or 30-ft. snakes, no big beasts of prey or carnivorous fish in our rivers like the terrible piranhas of the Amazon. We have no wolves, no wild boars or dangerous beasts, we can walk anywhere and bathe in safety. Ours is a gentle and very pleasant land.

Not everybody has thought this, of course. Tacitus, a great Roman, said of England: 'The climate is objectionable, with frequent rains and mist.' However, he added: 'But there is no extreme cold.'

In point of fact we have a variety of regional weather conditions which have given the British Isles a wide range of contrasting scenery and contrasting people. Our generally mild climate is due to the influence of the warm North Atlantic, but within this overall mildness there are many variations caused by veering winds which bring air sometimes from the ocean, sometimes from the Continent, sometimes from the tropics and sometimes from the icy north. The familiar radio announcements about cyclones and anticyclones refer to belts of atmospheric pressure: cyclones are low pressure areas which cause unsettled weather; anticyclones have a centre of high pressure, and usually promise a fine spell.

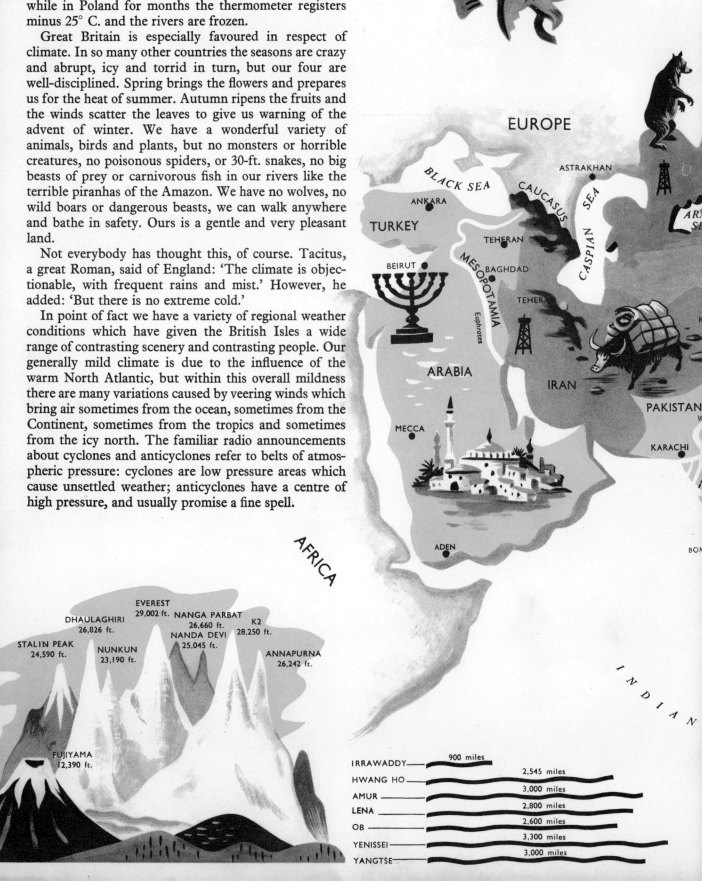

EUROPE

BLACK SEA

ANKARA

TURKEY

CAUCASUS

ASTRAKHAN

CASPIAN SEA

ARAL SEA

BEIRUT

MESOPOTAMIA

BAGHDAD

TEHERAN

Euphrates

TEHERA

ARABIA

IRAN

PAKISTAN

MECCA

KARACHI

AFRICA

ADEN

BOM

INDIAN

STALIN PEAK
24,590 ft.

DHAULAGHIRI
26,826 ft.

NUNKUN
23,190 ft.

EVEREST
29,002 ft.

NANGA PARBAT
26,660 ft.

NANDA DEVI
25,045 ft.

K2
28,250 ft.

ANNAPURNA
26,242 ft.

FUJIYAMA
12,390 ft.

IRRAWADDY — 900 miles

HWANG HO — 2,545 miles

AMUR — 3,000 miles

LENA — 2,800 miles

OB — 2,600 miles

YENISSEI — 3,300 miles

YANGTSE — 3,000 miles

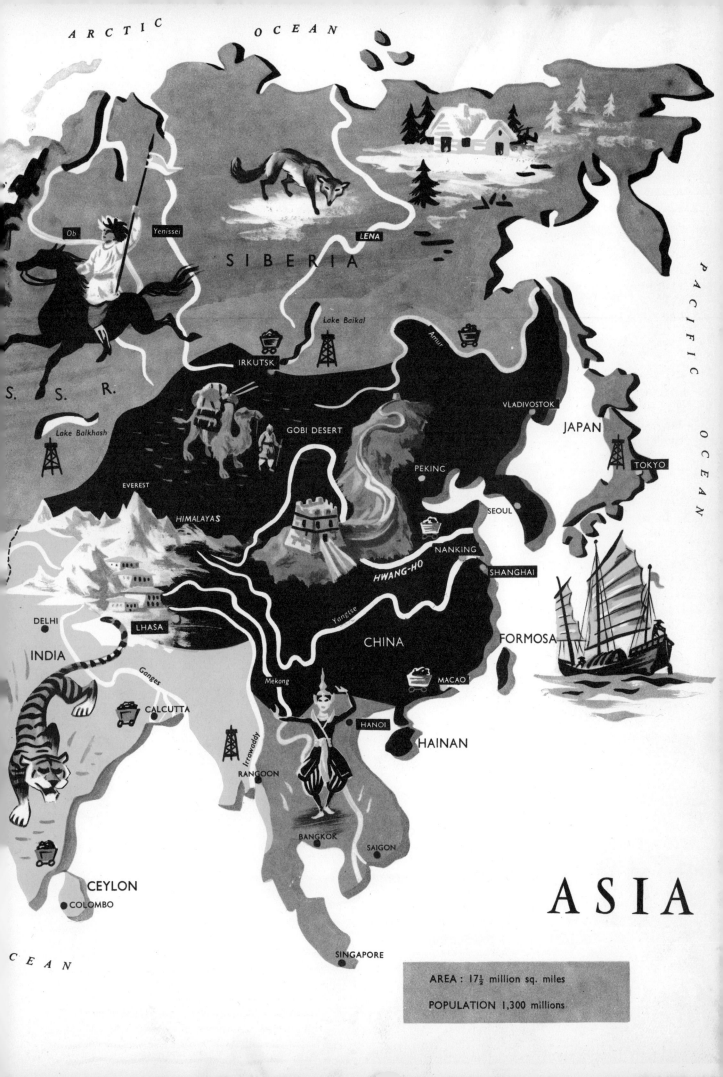

AFRICA

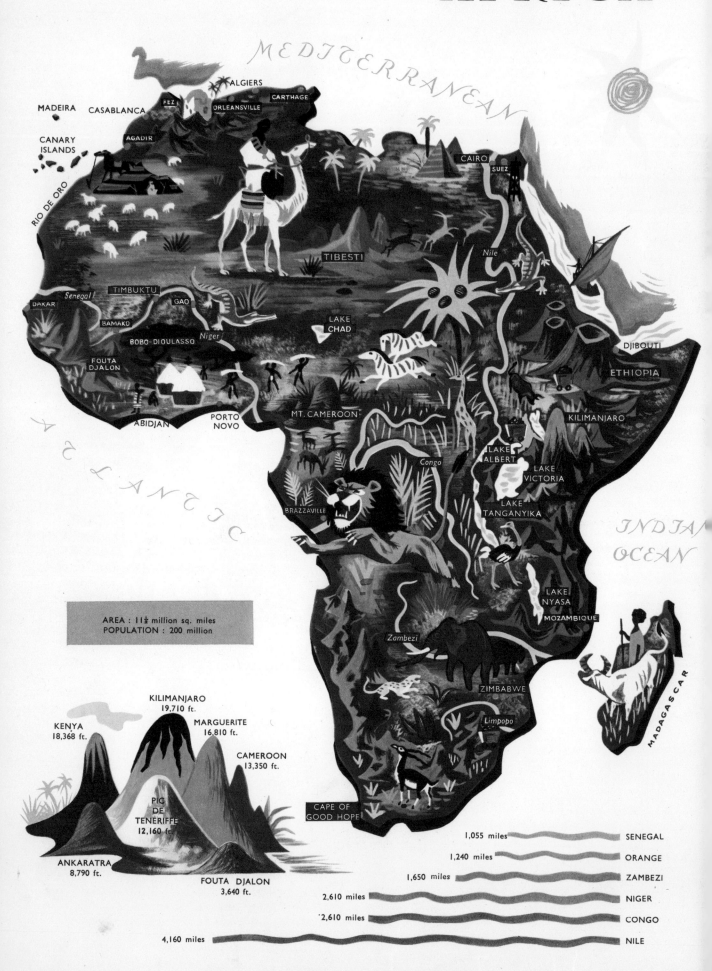

MEDITERRANEAN

MADEIRA · CASABLANCA · FEZ · ALGIERS · ORLEANSVILLE · CARTHAGE
CANARY ISLANDS · AGADIR
RIO DE ORO
CAIRO · SUEZ
TIBESTI
Nile
TIMBUKTU · GAO
DAKAR · Senegal
BAMAKO
BOBO-DIOULASSO · Niger
LAKE CHAD
FOUTA DJALON
DJIBOUTI
ETHIOPIA
ATLANTIC
ABIDJAN · PORTO NOVO
MT. CAMEROON
KILIMANJARO
Congo
LAKE ALBERT
LAKE VICTORIA
LAKE TANGANYIKA
BRAZZAVILLE
INDIAN OCEAN
LAKE NYASA
MOZAMBIQUE
Zambezi
ZIMBABWE
Limpopo
MADAGASCAR
CAPE OF GOOD HOPE

AREA : 11½ million sq. miles
POPULATION : 200 million

KILIMANJARO 19,710 ft.
KENYA 18,368 ft.
MARGUERITE 16,810 ft.
CAMEROON 13,350 ft.
PIC DE TENERIFFE 12,160 ft.
ANKARATRA 8,790 ft.
FOUTA DJALON 3,640 ft.

1,055 miles — SENEGAL
1,240 miles — ORANGE
1,650 miles — ZAMBEZI
2,610 miles — NIGER
2,610 miles — CONGO
4,160 miles — NILE

AUSTRALASIA

AREA: 3,460,000 sq. miles
POPULATION: 13 million

Oceania

When you traverse the lands of the five continents there are considerable differences in degree of ruggedness, climate, seasons and scenery.

One continent, the sixth, which is Antarctica, has neither seasons, climate nor marked ruggedness. It is a dead continent, inert beneath its shroud of ice. It is vast. It is larger than the U. S. A. and Australia put together, and is shaped like a giant wash-basin that shelves down to 8,000 feet, surrounded by a ring of white, blue and pink mountains, like sentries mounting guard. There is no trace of life there: everything is mirage, even the light, even the sun. One almost ought to say 'the suns', for the one sun rises, sets, rises and sets again several times at all points of the horizon.

The continent is covered with a layer of ice 6,000 to 10,000 feet thick; the polar night, which lasts six months, unleashes a fierce wind of 70—100 miles an hour that drives the snow in a dense layer above the head of the explorer. Men and dogs disappear and reappear, all but obliterated in the whiteness. The air is so charged with electricity that a sort of jack-o'-lantern appears at the end of people's noses and fingers, like the St. Elmo's fires that burn so horribly at the mast-tops of ships in a storm.

The subsoil of this continent contains an incredible wealth of minerals. It is not a huge floating iceberg, as the North Pole is. It could be made into a granary, a refrigerator for Europe and the rest of the world. Iron does not rust there and wood does not rot.

Thirty-five years after Captain Scott's last expedition, Admiral Cruzen landed his helicopter near the huts of Scott's base camp. The planks of which the huts were made were like new. Not a nail had rusted. The tins of food were still intact and the food edible. A dead sledge dog was standing frozen on its feet beside an open magazine that might have been bought the day before, and seemed to be waiting for its food.

The civilization of Ancient Egypt has similarly been preserved for thousands of years in the tombs of its kings, handed down and finally revealed to us.

Farming and life in general in different parts of the country are affected by the prevailing conditions: the winds that sweep the Orkneys and Shetlands enforce a routine of existence far removed from that of, say, the orchards of Kent.

Man, however, is the hardiest of all the animals and can live anywhere, in any climate, in any latitude whatever. He can stand a heat of 50° C. in the inferno of the Australian desert, as well as 60 degrees of cold in the frozen wastes of the Eskimo.

Man will eat anything. He adapts himself to the food that matches the climate, eating seal blubber in the lands of the Eskimos, who even give tiny pieces of it to babies which are still being fed by their mothers, and elsewhere juicy beef, spaghetti, rice, locusts, guava, bananas and coconuts.

The various climates have coloured, tanned and chiselled the face of man; but whatever his race, he is always man and like other men.

That is not so with the animals, large or small. They have escaped to the zones of climate that suit their way of life. They never make a mistake about the seasons, latitudes, winds, rains and cold.

Why, then, do we not talk about the climate of the elephant and the rhinoceros, the climate of the zebu, the climate of the camel, of the reindeer, of the llama, of the horse, of the polar bear or of the walrus?

DE KERGUELEN

KERGUELEN
ISLANDS

AMUNDSEN

DUMONT D URVILLE

SCOTT

BISCOE
14,000 ft.

MT. EREBUS
13,100 ft.

ADELIE
LAND

SOUTH VICTORIA
LAND

SOUTH POLE

ROSS
SEA

RO

FALKLAND
ISLAND
DEPENDENCIES

LARSEN

ADELAIDE
LAND

BYRD

COOK

CHARCOT

ANTARCTICA

The Antarctic continent could be an inviolable open-air tomb. Scott's dog, embalmed, as it were, by the cold, could have stood there indefinitely and been preserved for longer than the magnificent Pharaohs in their wrappings and basalt sarcophagi.

But, you say, can it be possible that at the South Pole there is not even the smallest living creature?

The pack ice and some of the islands off it are inhabited by fauna comparable to that of the Arctic; but the heart of this white continent has only one visitor, a strange bird, the Arctic Tern. This is a little live bundle of feathers weighing next to nothing, and yet it has the wing span of a large gull. It cannot bear to live long in night, so every year it flies 27,000 miles from one pole to the other to take advantage of the six months' day that is to be had now in the extreme north, then at the southern end of the world, going as far as the aurora, borealis or australis, hums its song — for it really does make a noise.

The Arctic Tern makes the journey down the meridians twice a year, flying from one pole to the other where the sun is multiplied and the searchlights of the aurora intersect. It is the bird of eternal day.

SECOND PART

OUR
HISTORY
THROUGH
THE AGES

THE LIFE
OF PREHISTORIC MAN

IT was thousands of years ago that our most distant ancestors, industrious even then, but in no way advanced, began to spread outwards from the hot areas of Asia towards Europe.

In the Quaternary Period, man, who had had to contend with the invasion of the glaciers, was already able to protect himself against cold. He knew fire, and he had manufactured his first weapons to help him in his struggle against the beasts.

Clad in badly scraped hides, his body hairy and his head hair like a mane, he was just beginning to develop his powers.

He was on the march.

He lay in wait near a pool or a stream where animals went to drink as dusk began to fall, and he killed because he was hungry. There he camped and spent the night round the embers of his fire. In search of a refuge, a cave in which to shelter, he followed the bank of a subterranean river, leaving prints of his bare feet in the mud.

Now, after thousands of years, a passionate desire for knowledge has sent other men to hunt for traces of prehistoric man, so many of whose tracks have been obliterated, for we want to know what sort of life was led by our ancestors in the day of the aurochs and reindeer.

To-day, some explorers are able to boast that they have met prehistoric man in the flesh. And that is true, for in certain remote parts of the world, in Asia, Ceylon, South Africa and America, in the jungle and elsewhere, islands of primitive peoples have been found living the same sort of life as did the naked men of the Stone Age or Bronze Age.

The first men did not think of using pieces of chipped flint straight away. Chipped! The first flints were splinters and, having discovered that they could cut, men used them as they were, to improve their normal weapons, which were probably just clubs and spears made of wood.

But, you ask, how could they fashion and point their spears?

With the help of fire, the first and strongest of the wild beings that man has tamed. It was probably the women who on the tribe's marches carried the wooden receptacle in which the fire, covered with ash, lay smouldering on a bed of clay. They tended it, fed it with dry twigs, blowing up the embers.

How did man get hold of fire?

Certain tribes that lived among the rocks on the slopes of volcanoes would have been able to obtain burning scoria. And we must not forget the lightning, which must have caused forest fires, when all man had to do was to pick up a burning brand.

It is probable that man learned quite early how to make fire by the friction of a hard pointed stick being twirled round and round between the palms of a person's hands in a hole made in a piece of softer wood, a method that is still used by plenty of primitive peoples, in particular the Guarani Indians of Venezuela. It was not till much later, in the Iron Age, that man invented the tinder-box with its flint and steel.

Apart from the club and spear, one of man's earliest weapons was the sling: two thongs of skin or bark, or pieces of creeper, which were swung to launch a stone. They must also have known how to use the *bolas*, but perhaps you do not know what that is? The bolas is made of two or three balls of soft stone, the size of large beads, that are pierced and threaded on thongs or cords knotted to keep them in place. When thrown at an animal's legs the bolas wraps itself round them, hobbling the animal and sometimes even breaking a leg. Certain Indian tribes still use them to capture wild horses or the vicuña, which is a sort of llama, and remains of bolas, or a similar weapon, have been found in prehistoric caves.

Let us make a rapid tour of the world and enumerate these last survivors of the primitive peoples of long ago.

In Australia you can still meet people whose way of life gives us an idea of that led by our ancestors in the Stone Age. They belong to tribes who were for a long time cannibals; they still fight with clubs, and those who lived in Tasmania when it was first discovered did not even know fire. For a hunting knife they use a splinter of stone crudely set in a ball

of resin to act as a handle. The only tool they have for sawing through a branch is a snake's jaw. Instead of the bolas they have another weapon that they throw.

You have guessed? Yes, the boomerang, that curved piece of wood that, if it misses the animal or target it is meant to hit, rebounds and returns to the person who threw it.

We mentioned the people of Tasmania. Tasmania is an island lying to the south of Australia. In 1800 it had about 3,000—4,000 native inhabitants. Seventy years later there was not one of their kind alive. The race was extinct. They were peaceable savages, with rough black skins and good hearts.

Perhaps it is what he eats that makes man cruel. These Tasmanians were gentle, like their food. They lived on fish that they caught with bone harpoons, wild fruits and the eggs of the big birds that nested among their rocks. The only animals they could have hunted were the timid phalanger and the kangaroo, both of which carry their young in a ventral pouch, as black women carry their babies on their hip wrapped in a length of cloth.

The Tasmanians have disappeared off the face of the earth, but there are still the Veddas of Ceylon. They are true savages; they roam about and are unable even to build a hut of branches, so they shelter in trees or under rocks, like chimpanzees. They are great elephant hunters and collect the honey of wild bees. They do not have a single musical instrument, and when they dance they accompany themselves by slapping their bellies and thighs with their hands.

And then there are the Papuans. They are of bigger stature than the Pygmies but still underdeveloped. They build huts in the trees and paint and tattoo themselves by clans, as the first men did when they began to wage war. The marks and patterns on their skins enabled the members of the tribe to recognize each other. The custom of painting faces and tattoing undoubtedly originated in this need to be able to identify one's friends and enemies.

The prehistoric people of the Stone Age lived in a cold, humid climate. The fossils of animals that have been found in their caves and the crude drawings they left on the walls show that the fauna of those days consisted of the large animals which now inhabit our hot countries: elephants, hippopotamus, rhinoceros, monkeys, etc., all of which were then accustomed to cold.

They must have led the same sort of life as do the Pygmies of the Congo or the Ubangi today, and our ancestors must have caught the beasts in their forests in the same way as I have seen the Pygmies catch antelopes — in nets.

The Pygmies of today use proper nets, but primitive man of the past probably did not yet know how to make nets and instead used a web of tangled creepers into which hunters drove the animals. The frightened creatures, being surrounded, would plunge into the tangle of creepers and then the hunters only had to finish them off with their clubs.

No doubt they also used fire, the barbarous method of hunting that was practised in Africa not so very long ago and which is now forbidden. I was once all but caught in the ring of one of these 'packs of red hounds' and I shall never forget the sight of that inferno of flame. In the centre of it was a clearing in which some lords of the rains, great elephants, were being consumed alive. Every now and again one of the surrounding trees would suddenly burst into flame from crest to foot and blaze like a torch, and meanwhile lions and panthers made fantastic leaps in their attempts to escape the ring of fire.

It is possible that our ancestors also used fire for hunting, for presumably they knew all the tricks and ruses of the Pygmy. We have found bone whistles with which perhaps they signalled to each other in the forest when closing in on their game and unable to see each other. No doubt, too, they took council of their witch-doctors, as do the little people of the Ubangi. Their sorcerers presumably also organized tom-toms and magic dances round the fires before they went off into the forest to hunt.

It is probable that they could communicate with each other across the bush as the negroes do, using their tom-toms to give warning of danger or news of some great event. They employed a rudimentary form of Morse, consisting of drum-beats. They also blew hunting horns made from a hollowed tree trunk; perhaps too they received visits from the Elephants' Dwarfs.

But you do not know the legend of the Elephants' Dwarfs to which the Congo Pygmies' superstition has given rise. Let me tell it to you.

These dwarfs are invisible to the eye of man. They follow the elephants on their unceasing march. When the great beasts halt in the hunting grounds of the Pygmies, the dwarfs go to where the little men have camped and listen to their talk as they sit round their fires. The Pygmies sense their presence, and for that reason they never speak the word 'elephant' aloud, but always refer to them as the 'Big Ones'. Thus when the dwarfs return to the elephants in the jungle, climb up their legs to their shoulders and then slide right into their huge ears, there to tell them what they have seen and heard, they are able to say that the savage naked hunters have no idea that the herd is in their territory, for they did not mention them in their talk round their fires. They never spoke their name.

Yet the next morning the little naked men will try their luck.

The tribe of Pygmies has halted in the heart of the forest.

The elephants are in the vicinity. The chief of the Pygmies has had his men see to their weapons, assagais, arrows with iron heads, and spears.

The primitive Pygmy can neither smelt nor forge iron, but he gets it by barter, and the possession of it is a great step forward. His ancestors were unable to have it and had to be content with pikes with points hardened in fire. Today, when the Pygmy is in need of iron, the young men go by night to the huts of the big negroes who are smiths, and there under a tree at the entrance to the village they place

83

some bunches of bananas and elephant tusks.
When they return the following night they
will find that the negro smiths have removed
the presents and in their place put crude iron
weapons and salt. It is exactly the same procedure as the early adventurers of the sea
employed with the Moors on the cliffs of the
Rio de Oro.

That evening, using branches and large
leaves, the tribe build low huts which they
will occupy for only that one night. They are
little more than lairs, like those of their cousins
in the forest. Ouoro, the chimpanzee, lives one
storey up in a fork of the branches; but
Ebobo, the gorilla, is content to occupy the
ground floor, flattening the low bushes with
his enormous weight. The Pygmies sleep on
the ground, on beds of grass.

The trackers are on their way before dawn,
using the aerial route, jumping from branch to
branch high up in the trees. Having located
the elephants, they return and find everyone
afoot — men, women and children. The whole
tribe goes to meet the elephants.

Now they march along under the trees.
Before they approach their great prey, the
hunters gather round their chief. They have
rubbed themselves with mud and elephant's
droppings, so as to be able to get close
without the salt smell of human sweat betray-
ing their presence to the great animals.

When within arrow-shot the hunters halt.
The chief squats, removes the amulet hanging
round his neck, plants it in the ground and
mutters an incantation, a prayer to the lords
of the bush: 'Father Elephant, we are small.
Our stomachs are flat and we are hungry...'

So the chief of that tribe of men humbly requests
the leader of the herd of animals for permission to
kill a fat member of his herd and make it their food.

Now the rites are all performed. The men crawl
forward behind their chief, who is to have the honour of striking the first blow. They approach to
within a few paces of the elephant they have marked
down. The Pygmy chief crawls on all fours until he
is right under the animal. Shouting a cry of victory,
he cuts the tendon of one of its forelegs with his knife.

Startled, the elephant dashes forward, but the first
step on its wounded leg tumbles it over, and it is
not given the time to get up again. The little men
swarm all over it and, in spite of its terrific struggles,
finally succeed in killing it.

No sooner is the elephant dead than the feast begins. The huge carcase provides a gargantuan repast for its tiny slayers. That evening, gorged with meat, their stomachs stuffed to bursting point, they will build their huts of branches near the remains of the beast which 'Father Elephant' gave them to feast on.

Pieces of crude pottery covered with magical signs have been brought back from Africa by many travellers. Sorcerers made those signs in the clay with their thumbs, but we do not know what they mean. Apparently those who drink from such magical earthenware pots find at the bottom strength, courage and sometimes death. But friendship may also be the reward. There is, in a remote place, a tribe where 'brothers of the hunt', two boys the same age going on their first hunt together, used to drink from such a magic cup a beverage in which they had mingled some of their blood.

Nowadays quite a little industry has grown up manufacturing masks and imitations of the fetish pots of the primitive tribes which are sold as curios to travellers.

Excavations made in search of cavemen have brought to light a wealth of prehistoric relics, many of them imitations which fortunately will not bear serious scrutiny. Even so, certain paleontologists with too much imagination have let themselves be duped by unscrupulous forgers.

The study of rock drawings, stone weapons and bones capable of giving us a glimpse of the living conditions of prehistoric man is a real science. It has been necessary to identify the fauna of the period and the climate there was then.

The Cro-Magnon man lived long after our first troglodytes, and his tools are proof of considerable ingenuity. His fossils have been found in several places in France among heaps of horses' bones beneath coals and cinders.

The Cro-Magnon man was essentially a hunter. He invented the notch in the arrow-head that made it stick in the wound, the first step towards the harpoon. He perfected the industry that gave him his stone weapons. He had a wooden hammer with which he split his flints without breaking them. He began to chip with artistry. With him appeared the first bone implements: scrapers and various forms of awl that the Eskimos still use, a spoon-shaped spatula and, what represented a tremendous advance, the needle, which he used to sew himself clothes.

There are still representatives of a more developed form of this civilization living the same sort of existence at the southern extremity of South America. These are the Indians of Tierra del Fuego and the Magellan Straits. They are called Fuegians. Their

arrows have flint heads; they fish with hooks made of bone, as do the Lapps, and they paddle bark canoes. Their simple huts are built of tree-runks.

The Cro-Magnon man, already considerably taller than his ancestors, had to stand a climate that was almost glacial. The frozen tundra that today lies just below the pack-ice of the poles then extended as far as the south of France. The animals there then were those that you find in Canada today: musk-oxen, blue foxes, caribou, walrus and seals, and of course bears.

As a result primitive man had to change his way of life completely. He took refuge in caves and dressed himself in the skins of animals.

Rudimentary art appeared. Man learned to carve bone, and strange and most artistically ornamented 'commander's batons' have been found.

What use did they serve?

If you look and see if you can find the same sort of thing surviving among the primitive peoples in Africa or America, you will discover that the Indians of the Mackenzie River still use these batons. The chiefs there possess a number of them, carved with

their own device, if one may call it that. These batons are easily recognizable even by the most distant or loosely associated member of the tribe. When the king wishes to send someone an order, he has the messenger who is to take it learn the text by heart, which he repeats when he reaches his destination. To prove that he comes from the king and by his command, he shows one of these batons, which thus acts as a royal seal.

People have found thousands of carved caribou bones as well as drawings cut in the walls of caves. Many rock-faces are decorated with pictures, painted in black and red. The artists who did these drawings thousands of years ago depicted every kind of animal that the hunters brought back from the chase: aurochs, wild goat, bear, hyena, bison, caribou, either fighting or being caught by lasso.

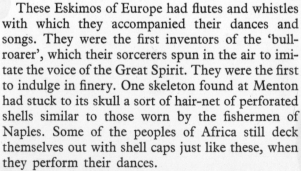

These Eskimos of Europe had flutes and whistles with which they accompanied their dances and songs. They were the first inventors of the 'bull-roarer', which their sorcerers spun in the air to imitate the voice of the Great Spirit. They were the first to indulge in finery. One skeleton found at Menton had stuck to its skull a sort of hair-net of perforated shells similar to those worn by the fishermen of Naples. Some of the peoples of Africa still deck themselves out with shell caps just like these, when they perform their dances.

Man now became less bestial and more sensitive. He began to ponder great problems, and he took to honouring his dead, burying them, probably in his cave, and thus the idea of family was born.

Slowly the glaciers withdrew. The mammoth retreated to the steppes of Siberia; the bear, caribou, musk-ox and blue fox sought refuge in the Far North. The ibex, mouflon and chamois had taken to the last of the snow-peaks.

In Europe, primitive man now enjoyed a milder climate. He was still a hunter, but now his weapons were finer. Having chipped the stones for his axes and arrow-heads, he polished them by rubbing them on hard stone with fine, wet sand.

He began modelling clay. The women used a basket of woven branches to hold the wild fruits they gathered: beechnuts, acorns and chestnuts; and the first pot was probably made when someone hit upon the idea of lining one of these baskets with clay and using it to carry water.

Then man began to sow and cultivate. Man or his first slaves, the women? Undoubtedly the latter. To save themselves going into the forest to gather fruits, they sowed seed round the huts, having once noticed that seed dropped by accident germinated and grew. Thus the first fields came into being, plots with palisades like those of the black peoples today.

The women looked after the herds and flocks, milked the cows and made the cheeses. They span and wove cloth. They were kept hard at it by their lords and masters, the men.

The men hunted. But first and foremost they protected the clan. As tribes became organized, it became possible for hunting grounds to be invaded by an enemy, and when that happened they had to be defended.

As a protection against attack, our ancestors built what we call lake-dwellings — whole towns of houses built on piles in the water of lakes. Remains of these have been found in Switzerland, Italy, France and Poland. A temporary lowering of the level of the Lake of Geneva revealed more than ten thousand tree trunks set as piles in the mud.

Some primitive peoples and fishermen still build huts on piles in marshes or on the sea-shore. The people of Dahomey do so in the lagoon of Porto-Novo and so do various tribes of South America, the Malay peninsula and New Guinea.

The ornaments of the people of this age of polished stone consisted of necklaces, pendants and bracelets. The shells which have been found in great numbers and sometimes far from the coast were perhaps even then the coins with which they bought things, like the cowries of black Africa which the famous dancers of Man wear threaded on cords round their wrists and ankles, where they stand out strikingly against their black skins.

Pearls and turquoises have been found in the dolmens of Brittany. These dolmens, and the menhirs, belong to the Neolithic period of polished stone. These 'megalithic' monuments — that means formed of large stones — are the most remarkable of the tombs of the Neolithic period. Vast subterranean halls have been discovered, like the tombs of the Hova of Madagascar. The Hova are a noble caste and even today their funeral rites are most curious. On the occasion of the ceremony of *mamadika*, a joyous festival, each family goes with drums beating and violins playing to the cave-tomb of

its ancestors. There they turn the dead over on to the other side, so that they can lie in a different position.

Megalithic monuments have been found all over Europe, especially in Spain and even in North Africa. It is even possible to imagine that once there was a road of dolmens that began away in Egypt.

Though the road the ancient civilizations took is still marked out, the tracks of prehistoric man's first adventurous wanderings have been blotted out. Man was already then an adventurer, worthy ancestor of those who were to become explorers and discover the earth. He ventured out into the world and brought back seeds of barley or flax, the pips of an apple or a pear.

Agriculture is said to have started in Mesopotamia and Egypt ten thousand years ago. It came to Europe by way of Libya, North Africa and Spain. This road along which travelled barley, flax, the apple and pear, is also that of the corn-mill, the awl and the round stone. It is also that of the dolmens and menhirs which so strangely resemble the Egyptian obelisks of the Nile Valley.

Legend is even more wonderful than reality. Popular imagination has attributed a fairy origin to these standing and recumbent stones. Others are said to have been carried to their sites by miraculous means, like that of Poitiers which St. Radegonde is supposed to have carried in her apron.

The fairy to whom most stones are attributed is undoubtedly Melusina, whose emblem, that originates perhaps in the lost continent of Atlantis, can also be found graven on the stones of the temples of the Incas.

Today we live in the age of uranium. What a long way we have travelled down the centuries from the chipped flints of the cave men to our feverish age of discovery!

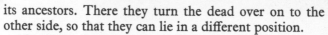

Before the age of bronze, alloy of copper and tin, man smelted and worked copper. The great South American civilization of the Incas, which did not know the wheel, had halted at the copper stage.

The appearance of bronze tools in western Europe is proof of the current having reached there from the Near East, where civilization was so much in advance of its time.

Bronze was fused and moulded. It was only used for weapons, axes and swords, and for ornaments, bracelets, pendants, hairpins.

Tribes were now beginning to group in villages of several families. In each tribe there must have arisen a caste of metal-founders. The lake-dwellings and fortified villages, the beginnings of life in societies, gave the first impetus to the formation of a class of artisans. Each clan now had its families of potters and tanners, for man had learnt how to cure and soften skins. The women spun flax and wool, and the weaver set up the forked stakes of his loom in the open, as is still done in Sudan and Dahomey. A big stone served to keep his skein of fibres taut. His shuttle, made of bone or wood, was pointed at either end. The canoes they made out of tree-trunks hollowed with axe or fire, we would consider tiny.

Men early took to grouping themselves in castes according to their trades. In the rust-coloured hills they smelted iron. Their tall clay furnaces were built up against a cliff, as at Tingrela, in the Sudan, and in the mountains of Mandara in the Cameroons. While this magic was being worked — for anything concerned with the smelting of metals was considered magic — a musician sang invocations to the god of fire, accompanying his song on a primitive guitar.

Stones from the sea-shore or river-bed did duty as hammer and anvil, and with them the smith fashioned his axes, arrow-heads and the first hoe for those who worked in the fields.

There was a cobbler to cut sandals from the skins of the buffalo, the first shoes man ever wore, which were fastened to his heel and big toe.

There was a jeweller who fashioned pendants and bracelets, and who also made the little objects that all hunters in all jungles carry in a leather case hung round their necks on a thong: the iron needle and pincers with which they extract the thorns that have stuck into them while travelling in the bush.

Even so early as this sorcerers were making amulets to protect the wearer against misfortune, a panther's tooth or piece of antelope horn sewn up in a small coloured bag of sheepskin.

The tombs of these primitive peoples demonstrate the slow stages of the onward progress of civilization.

The dead became more and more demanding, as did the living who honoured them. The former now required that in the funeral chambers arranged for them under the tumuli they should have their arms; and often, as in the crypts of Egypt, be supplied with provisions placed in earthenware jars for their use on the great voyage to the next world.

Then the custom of burning the dead became general all over Europe. After burning, the ashes were enclosed in pointed urns which would only stand upright on the earthen plate made for them.

Those who lived in Europe at the end of the Ice Age had to contend with a terrible climate. They were backward in their evolution compared with the peoples of the temperate countries. Without the migrations which followed the march of the sun across the heavens, Europe would probably have remained inhabited by backward peoples. The hunter was still all but naked, as are those of the Congo, and attacked his prey and his enemies with wretched weapons.

However, the roaming tribes from the temperate zones heard the secret promise of the soil. Here and there a tribe halted in some valley where millet and maize grew wild, and there they followed the example of the plants and took root. Thenceforward man hunted round his first cultivated fields, and took his herd of tamed buffalo out to graze on the plains and at night brought them back into an enclosure of dried thorns that protected them from lions.

Had it not been for travellers coming from the Levant we would have remained on the barbarous level of the undeveloped peoples, at the same stage of civilization as those groups which have been relegated to the peninsulas or imprisoned in the depths of the jungle without contact with the other inhabitants of the earth. We would never have advanced.

We have only to look at the herdsmen of the Sudan, the fiery warriors of the Kirghiz steppe and the fisher-peoples of Oceania or Africa in their pile-dwellings, to be able to imagine how our ancestors lived before the Roman invasion, which made them so much more civilized.

Rome . . . Greece . . . and beyond, though still in the Levant, light and sunshine . . . !

The Levant is not merely a symbol. It was there, in the East, in Mesopotamia and Egypt, that we of the West had to look to see the bright dawn of our world.

THE
PRIMITIVE
CIVILIZATIONS

IT is possible that some of the most savage and
backward countries, such as New Guinea and
the lands of the Papuans and other primitive
peoples, may have been brushed by the radiance of
the great ancient civilizations, and that the naked
peoples who now inhabit those areas have relapsed
into the primitive state.

In the age-old customs of these peoples you can
find fascinating relics of a past of which we know all
but nothing, as also in their legends which are as
bright and colourful as butterflies.

When one tries to pierce the mystery surrounding
the fabulous empires of the Sun, all of which have
vanished, one is still dazzled by the last gleam of
their reflection, the last fires of a golden sun on the
mottled wings of the butterfly legend.

North-west of Australia, in the archipelago of the
'black islands' which comprises the New Hebrides,
the Solomon Islands, New Guinea, etc., live tribes
whose customs show that though the people have
long forgotten their Golden Age, some of their
customs are survivals from that age of the gods and
giant kings who could carve huge stone menhirs and
enormous temple figures.

To-day, the natives in their jungle cannot even
work stone at all. Nonetheless, though unable to
erect huge carved stones, they still set up great
wooden pillars that end in a head, a sort of roughly
hewn mask. At the great festivals, their sorcerers
beat their wands on these heads as on gongs, thus
producing the voice of their ancestors.

On a high plateau in the Andes, near famous Lake
Titicaca, lies a town that used to be the capital of
a long-vanished kingdom. There lived one of the
first peoples to call themselves children of the Sun,
as did the Incas who came thousands of years later
to those same highlands where the monumental
ruins of Tiahuanaco now conjure up a fabulous past
and one of the most ancient civilizations of the world.

Three hundred thousand years ago, the sea must
have lapped this plateau in the Andes that now lies
13,000 feet above sea-level. The erosion of the rocks
caused by waves and the sea-shells left lying there
forms a distinct line 100 feet above the present level
of Lake Titicaca, the waters of which have remained
salt.

91

Several miles away beyond the lake are the ruins of the capital, Tiahuanaco, enclosed within a ring of Cyclopean walls. A massive gateway opens into this citadel, the famous *Puerta del Sol* or Sun Gate. Among a welter of hieroglyphic signs and carved emblems you can distinguish the god Viracocha, who has the head of a puma, sacred animal of the Indians.

At the great religious festivals they used to set out golden images in the centre of this vast square, effigies of their divinities, of the creator Sun, of the Thunder, of the Lightning. On thrones of solid gold sat their dead sovereigns, brought out embalmed from their tombs for the occasion, and in front of them they made impressive sacrifices of llamas. As in ancient Egypt, these Indians knew the secrets of embalming which have now been lost.

The desert that this plateau in Peru now is has witnessed the death of two great civilizations: that of the first Indians who were the children of the Sun and who, like the Pharaohs of the Valley of the Kings, built mountains of dressed stone for their temples and tombs; then that of the Incas, the last descendants of the Sun. What is there left, apart from ruins, in this stony desert where once great empires flourished?

There remains a salt lake 120 miles long and 33 miles wide, in the middle of which lies the ancient island of the Sun. In the low, swampy ground are huge reed-covered islands inhabited by tribes of wretched Indians, who live there like animals, keeping to the thick, tall grass and having no contact with other Indian tribes. They have no weapons. They chew the pith of the big reeds and swallow its bitter juice; and they fish in the lake from tiny canoes made of reeds tied together in bundles.

In fact, these people are in the Reed Age. They are true primitive beings from the beginning of the world. For them the sun went out for ever after the eclipse of the old religions of the Sun-King.

Or of the Moon. For although Indian legend tells of giants coming down from the Sun to rule over the little red men, in Africa it was children of the gods — like the great Aziza of Dahomey — who came to live in the forests in order to teach the animals and man to talk and sing. (There was a time when animals talked!) These messengers from Heaven came to Earth down a long liana fastened to the horn of the crescent moon.

We live in the age of speed. With our perfect, swift means of transport western civilization will penetrate to the remotest corners of the world.

It was not thus thousands of years ago. And yet, since his very origins man has developed because of his contacts and exchanges. Where did this evolution begin?

Where was its cradle?

Was there one cradle or several?

That is a great question. Five thousand years ago man, who for thousands of years had roamed about the globe without leaving traces of his passage, suddenly took to writing and left durable records. Man, from having been a roaming barbarian, scarcely organized in clans and tribes, became civilized and sedentary. Nations came into being owing allegiance to a single chief, a king.

Why, one wonders, have some peoples evolved and others not? How is it that in the world today, where the races are strictly all of an age, some seem young, others old?

Indeed, the primitive peoples of America, Africa and the big 'black islands' seem very far removed from us.

Suppose there were twins, one of whom stopped growing and developing at the age of, say, three. When they were both eighteen, people would be astounded when told that they were of the same age.

All people are our twins, but between the most highly evolved peoples and the least developed there is a difference not of fifteen years, as with those twins, but of five thousand years. But what is even five thousand years compared with the many thousands that separate Neanderthal man from both a Jivaro of the Amazon basin and a Londoner of today?

The Jivaro and we are both as old as humanity, going back for as long as there have been people on earth. The only difference between Mr. Smith of London, who has a gun in a Berkshire Syndicate and shoots on alternate Saturdays, and Kobo the Jivaro hunter, with his bow and arrows, is — can you guess?

It is that during these five thousand years time has not passed in the same way for them. For 195 thousand years Kobo and Mr. Smith experienced the same slow evolution, but during the next five thousand years Mr. Smith progressed more and more rapidly, while poor Kobo just went on hunting, as naked as he was born, in his virgin forests.

There is another difference. If Mr. Smith wants to know whether or not to take his mackintosh, he has to consult the weather forecast in his newspaper. Our meteorologists, however, are not as good at predicting as the sorcerers of Kobo's clan. These sorcerers can even summon the rain and make it

come. At least, Kobo believes that they can. What is certain is that the primitive peoples have always been ahead of us in the occult sciences of sorcery and magic. And it is probably the influence of their sorcerers that has caused the backward peoples to remain in their primitive state, bowed by fear. They have been the victims of their own magic.

But let us not exaggerate. Above all they have been the victims of their isolation. They were lost in the heart of their jungles, in the impenetrable bush. They were content with what grudging Nature gave them: the flesh of wild animals and the fruits of the trees in the forest. They had the misfortune to live in a land without oases.

An oasis is a real centre; it favours groupings and has seen the birth of the world's first civilizations. The most brilliant of these — the Egyptian, Chaldean, Indian and Chinese — which suddenly came into being some thousands of years B.C. developed in these oases, these privileged countries. Their soil was very rich. They were fertile enclaves, real oases scattered about the earth. All these civilizations flourished in the generous light and fertile heat of King Sun, in climates that were good. That is why all these peoples who then experienced their Golden Age were ardent worshippers of a Sun God.

This was especially so in Egypt which, along with Mesopotamia and Chaldea, was the cradle of our western civilization. The empire of the Pharaohs and the kingdom of Babylon . . .

The Babylonians claimed to have occupied the rich valleys of the Tigris and Euphrates since the dawn of humanity. As for the Egyptians, come from no-one knows where to the narrow corridor of the Nile, in three thousand years they built one of the proudest civilizations of the world. And remember that this river flows through desert for over 3,000 miles of its length and that the fertile strip over which it deposits its silt is nowhere, except in the delta in lower Egypt, more than 35 miles wide. The empire of the Pharaohs was thus ridiculously small, no larger than Sicily.

Let us look at a map of Ancient Egypt. Run your finger down the twisty course of this great river, the only one to have managed to cross the desert. The White Nile, which takes its waters from the great equatorial lakes, does not have enough strength left when it reaches the first cataract to continue on its way. There, however, it is reinforced by the Blue Nile, which comes down like a torrent from the highlands of Ethiopia. The White Nile falls asleep, while the impetuosity of the Blue Nile gives the river the vigour it needs to break through the rocky barriers of the five cataracts.

At the same time its waters have been picking up the thick mud that will fertilize the royal valley; this is the 'black earth' from which Egypt takes its native name, 'Khemi'.

The fertility of the soil and the generosity of the sun would not in themselves have been enough to make people settle there, if this uninterrupted stretch of 700 miles, this great oasis that extends from the mountains of Ethiopia to the sea, had not been protected on all sides. In every direction is desert: to the east is the desert of Arabia; to the west the Sahara and the sands of Libya, the land of the dead where the sun sets and the Pharaohs had their tombs built in the Valley of Kings.

These deserts protected the country by closing its frontiers. They compelled the people to stay there, preventing both immigration and emigration. Thus the race was kept pure; there were no half-breeds in Ancient Egypt.

The consequence? The consequence was a swift transformation of the clans into kingdoms grouping together peoples of the same race, and then, finally, their unification in a single empire of the two kingdoms of Upper and Lower Egypt.

What made it possible for the eastern civilizations to extend their influence so extraordinarily from the 'ribbon oasis' of the Nile and the 'fertile crescent' of Mesopotamia is that these privileged areas were situated at one of the crossroads of the Ancient World, at the intersection of caravan routes and sea routes, the places where people had most opportunity to make contacts and exchange goods and ideas.

Commerce, the exchange of goods, was the origin of the evolution of social life. It made it necessary to invent some way of accounting, money, writing and the calendar. Round the open spaces of the first markets people built shops, depots and then, to house the merchants come from elsewhere, vast caravanserais with enclosures for camels and pack-oxen.

Towns were built and soon the permanent association of citizens and strangers passing through required an administration, an organization to ensure food supplies and medicine. These great centres soon saw industries develop; they favoured the division of labour and specialization in crafts: smiths, masons, carpenters, etc.

Finally, as craftsmanship progressed, as new needs arose and people made fortunes and wanted to live better and embellish their homes, art was born.

Egypt and Mesopotamia proved well in advance of all other peoples in this respect. Their inventions spread very slowly and gradually till they reached Gaul, where the bronze plough replaced the flint hoe. It took three thousand years for the menhirs, the standing stones that are crude imitations of the Egyptian obelisks, to line the roads through the corn-fields as far as the peninsula of Brittany.

THE MEDITERRANEAN CIVILIZATIONS

CORN originally came to us from the Valley of the Nile. Recently it has done so once again, but this time the corn of the Pharaohs came by aeroplane.

Beside some sarcophagi in the Valley of Kings earthenware bowls containing a few handfuls of a very fine kind of wheat were found. They had been put there as provisions for the dead person on his great journey into the Beyond. The germ of the wheat was dormant, having lain asleep in the heart of the grain ever since it was buried. This wheat was now sown and so, five thousand years after being harvested in the black earth of the Nile Valley, it sprouted and yielded a harvest in its turn.

I should prefer to say nothing of the improvements the ancient Egyptians made to the manufacture of their weapons and arms. It is deplorable, but each time that civilization has progressed, man has done his best to manufacture engines capable of making war more and more murderous.

The real criterion of development, however, is the development of the arts. A great event now took place in Egypt that was to transform the mutual relations of people in their social life: this was the invention of writing.

The hieroglyphics found on the walls of the funerary chambers would seem to point to this form of writing having originated in tombs. The purpose of these drawings was to preserve memories from being forgotten. In the chamber containing the mummy of the Pharaoh various things were placed beside the sarcophagus: a handful of wheat, the weapons and jewels, sometimes even a mummified dog that the king had loved. But how could a powerful monarch, one who had ruled an empire, take with him all that he had loved, all his possessions? To make this possible, artists drew on the walls of the burial chamber representations of the horses, servants, soldiers and musicians of the king, in a word: his memories. The Egyptians believed that in the darkness of the tomb these drawings would come to life, detach themselves and come down from the walls.

Soon this hieroglyphic writing, that at first had only been used to honour the dead, found another use in the world of the living, being used to transmit orders on papyrus, to make notes of purchases and to register sales.

That was a great advance on the days when messengers learned their messages by heart and identified themselves by showing a 'commander's baton' which proved that they came from the king. That was all right as long as the messenger had a good memory.

Messages in those days often took a different form, the recipient having to decipher not a hieroglyph, which was a drawing of an object, but the actual object itself, which was often most puzzling.

Let me tell you the story of the messenger sent by the Scythians, whose provinces had just been invaded by Darius, King of the Persians.

The message that this messenger brought and which he laid at the feet of Darius consisted of a bird, a rat, a frog and five arrows. In their attempts to decipher this remarkable missive the Persians arrived at two solutions, one the opposite of the other.

The fact that the animals lived in three different elements made some people think that the Scythians

were fastened in a bundle like a horse's tail. There were mixed threads, some in twos or threes, and with knots in them that were counted. It was like an alphabet of colours. One missionary has recorded that he once met an aged old Indian woman who had one of these skeins of cord at her belt, and that she could read it like a book. It contained the story of her life. It was all there in detail: her youth, her travels, the things that had happened to her family, the ages of her children and grandchildren.

In reckoning the Indians counted by tens, as did the Egyptians. This choice of the decimal system is easily explained. Man began counting with the fingers of his two hands, thus in lots of ten. It is probable that in all the ancient civilizations man could count before he knew how to write.

It took thousands of years to arrive at the simplification of the alphabet. At first hieroglyphics represented actual objects: gradually they came to represent *sounds*.

were abandoning to the victor their provinces, land, water and air, and that the arrows meant that they were laying down their arms. Others interpreted the message the opposite way: 'If you cannot tunnel underground like a rat, fly through the air like a bird or dive like a frog, you will never see Persia again and you will all perish from our arrows.'

Did the South American Indians use hieroglyphs? Carved images have been found on the walls of Aztec temples that are a sort of embryo writing; but the Incas were not able to write. They used knotted cords to help them remember things that had happened. The cords were of all colours and were called *quipus*. They

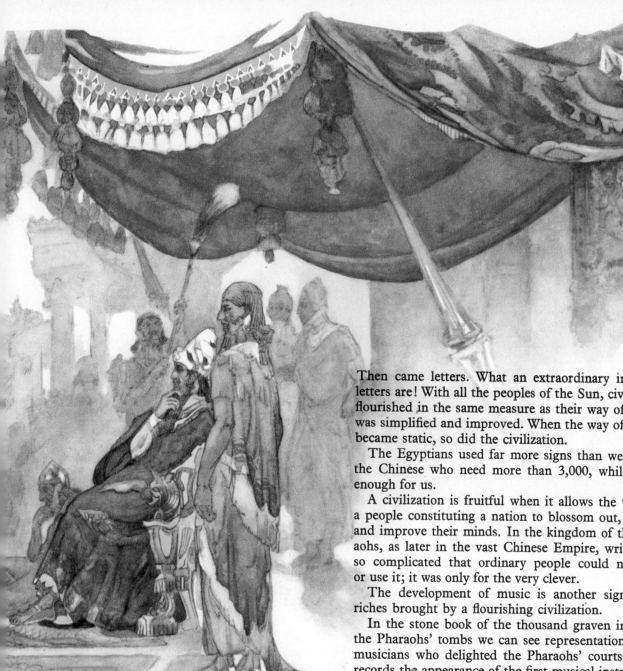

Then came letters. What an extraordinary invention letters are! With all the peoples of the Sun, civilization flourished in the same measure as their way of writing was simplified and improved. When the way of writing became static, so did the civilization.

The Egyptians used far more signs than we do, like the Chinese who need more than 3,000, while 26 are enough for us.

A civilization is fruitful when it allows the whole of a people constituting a nation to blossom out, to learn and improve their minds. In the kingdom of the Pharaohs, as later in the vast Chinese Empire, writing was so complicated that ordinary people could not learn or use it; it was only for the very clever.

The development of music is another sign of the riches brought by a flourishing civilization.

In the stone book of the thousand graven images of the Pharaohs' tombs we can see representations of the musicians who delighted the Pharaohs' courts. It also records the appearance of the first musical instruments.

At first people accompanied their songs by banging together flat pieces of wood or castanets, as primitive peoples still do today. The dancers tied bangles of bells to their wrists and ankles, as the Negroes still do. The Egyptian musicians played a flute, *nai*, and the first oboe, *mait*, and they invented the harp. They did not write down their music. Songs and tunes were handed down like legends. Musicians and singers learned them and repeated them like the entertainers of the Middle Ages.

For example, the name Woodbridge could be represented by the picture of a person of that name — that is, a drawing — or one could divide the word into its parts, as it is pronounced — Wood-bridge — and depict it with two symbols that conjure up the sounds 'wood' and 'bridge'.

That is how the Egyptians divided their words into syllables. The first Pharaoh whose name has been found written in two syllables on a piece of stone is Narmer. The sound *nar* means a fish; the sound *mer*, a tool. Thus Narmer was written with two images, a fish and a tool; while the name of his predecessor was represented merely by the one image of a scorpion.

In time writing became simplified. In Mesopotamia, the brilliant civilization of Babylon, just as original as that of Egypt, elaborated cuneiform writing. This consists of graphic signs like bunches of horseshoe nails.

The dawn that rose over Mesopotamia and Egypt was to spread its light throughout all the countries of the west.

Agriculture prospered. They selected the grain most suited to man.

Then a Pharaoh held a census of his subjects and their names were inscribed on the tax lists.

Scriveners, men of the law, registered the deeds of

97

Medes and obtained supremacy over all Asia Minor, founding an immense empire. These conquerors, 'barbarians' as the Greeks called them, were certainly less polished and artistic than the latter; but they knew how to make and use enamel with which they decorated their brick palaces, which they built on terraces, Assyrian fashion. Their religion, taught by their sages since Zarathustra, invited man to take part throughout his life in the struggle between fire and darkness. For the Persians, the world was divided by the war being waged by Ormuzd — fire, god of good — against the god of evil, Ahriman. As a rule the good man gave himself to serve Ormuzd by being upright, loyal and frank.

sale and purchase of properties. A social order was set up and a civil discipline established. The individual was no longer more than a unit of society.

At this crossroads of the Ancient World fairs and markets were held on fixed dates. Payment was made there in bars of gold and silver. We know the dates when these fairs took place thanks to the calendar, which had now been invented.

The Egyptians, who had studied the heavens, drew up their calendar in accordance with the visible movements of the sun, which does not rise at the same point of the horizon every day. Before it rises at exactly the same spot again 365 $\frac{1}{4}$ days pass, that is to say a year. This year began on July 19, which was the day when the inhabitants of Memphis and Heliopolis saw the sun and Sothis-Isis, our Sirius, rise in the same dawn. On that same day the first wave of foaming new water appeared in the all but dry bed of the Nile. The Egyptian seasons were thus those of the great river.

Technical progress gave a considerable impetus to the arts and to industry.

At the moment of her greatest prosperity, when Egyptian civilization was at its height, 2,500 years before our era began, the first social revolution took place. The peasants left their fields and pillaged the towns and the tombs of the kings.

It was the magical symbols reserved for the caste of their masters that they pillaged and destroyed; they made away with all that was *written* — the tablets of the laws, the parchments, and papyrus. In this extraordinary revolution all that the people wanted was to get hold of the fetishes.

Then the Pharaohs regained power. Order was restored, the same old order with the same servitude for the lowly, the same oppressive inequality among people.

While the civilization of the Near East was enlightening the western world, half-starved hordes of nomads wandering round the fringes of these rich countries were tempted to make raids into them. Often the victor was able to assimilate the civilization of the conquered and even to modify it out of his own genius and so take it a stage or so further.

Sometimes it was the conquered who benefited. The invasion of the Hyksos taught the Egyptians to use horses and chariots.

The Persians simplified cuneiform writing. In a hundred years this small nation from Iran conquered the

The Phoenicians, who traded with the entire Mediterranean world, brought it the alphabet. This nation of sailors, which had a genius for business and commerce, were the successors of the Cretans who had had a brilliant civilization 2,000 years before Christ and been masters of the Mediterranean.

But the Phoenicians, who were crude and without originality either in their art or religion — in fact they were still making human sacrifices — are known merely because they brought the first echo of the oriental civilizations to barbarian Europe.

During three thousand years Egypt was the great initiator, the mother of all civilizations. When her race was run, the torch was taken up first by Greece, of the poets, and then by Rome, home of the jurists. In just a few centuries they built the foundations of our civilization.

We know of the early beginnings of the Greeks, ten centuries before Christ, from the immortal epics of the poet Homer, the *Iliad* and the *Odyssey*.

In the midst of a number of little states, comprising a sort of Europe in miniature in the Mediterranean basin, one city, Athens, grew great and at the end of the 5th century had acquired the status of intellectual capital of the western civilizations of its day. Already the concept of fatherland had linked together the small communities and these now grouped round two great cities,

Athens and Sparta, in order to repulse an invader who was attacking with considerable force.

The attacker was Darius, proud emperor of the Persians, who had put himself at the head of a powerful army. The Greeks ought to have been crushed by numbers, but they were already a nation. And they were free men. They were fighting to defend their liberties, their families, their country. They inflicted two heavy defeats on the Persians: one on land at Marathon, where a desperate charge by Miltiades hurled back the great Persian army that had just landed in Attica; and another at sea, off Salamis, where Greece was saved by an Athenian fleet built in haste on the initiative of Themistocles.

Once again the people of Greece showed that they were capable of the national discipline that assured them of victory. The poorest citizens, those unable to scrape up money enough to buy arms, were enrolled as rowers and laboured on the benches of the galleys, which were normally occupied by slaves or mercenaries.

The Persians succeeded in setting fire to Athens, but Xerxes' fleet, caught between the coast and the island of Salamis, suffered a great disaster and was forced to fly towards Asia.

After this a group of these small states organized the first democracy, the form of government where each

citizen is admitted to the popular assemblies and the people elects its own chiefs and votes to decide matters affecting the prosperity and defence of the country.

Under Pericles, famous strategist who has lent his name to the most splendid century of Greek history, a whole people practised the cult of beauty. Greece experienced a flowering of the arts and letters with writers of genius like Aeschylus, Sophocles and Euripides, Herodotus and Thucydides the historians, and philosophers like Socrates. The chisel of Phidias brought life to the marble and stone of the statues of the Acropolis that dominates the Parthenon, that marvellous temple of the goddess Athene. There, in the gardens of the sacred hill, the gods descended from Olympus were

depicted in supreme examples of the classical expression of human beauty.

To the Egyptians, the peoples of the Far East and the Indians of the fabulous ages of Peru, the gods were mysterious beings who ruled by fear, were greedy for sacrifices and usually as cruel as the beasts whose form they took.

The Greek divinities, while remaining invisible and immortal, could take on the semblance of people. They loved, hated, married and fought like people, these gods whose head was Zeus, sovereign of the world. Olympus resounded with the sound of the attack of the Titans.

Most famous are the feasts given in honour of Zeus. Seven hundred years B.C., crowds came to Olympus from all over Greece, where they worshipped the same gods, to fill the seats of the Stadium in which the Olympic games were held. The winners, who included singers and poets as well as athletes, were given their palms and laurel crown in front of the temples of Hera and Zeus.

The games went on, despite the wars that exhausted both city rivals of Sparta and Athens, and their rich neighbour, Thebes, and despite the domination of the Macedonians and the conquests of Alexander the Great, whose armies opened the road to India beyond the vast empire of the Persians, thus introducing the organization and civilization of the Greeks even into the East.

The stage that Athens and Greece represent along the path of civilization from its origins in the lands of the sun is that of the intellect. What the Greek intellect achieved has since enriched all humanity.

After the conquest of Greece by the soldier-peasants, Rome in her turn adopted the Hellenic civilization.

The poets and artists of Rome went to the Greeks to learn, so that the spiritual influence of Athens gave a certain amount of soul to the city of Romulus and Remus, the twins who had been suckled by a she-wolf. However, Rome was fated to be ever forging the shield and the sword, to advance its 'robot warriors' who alone were able to check the Carthaginian, Hannibal, before being crushed in their turn.

Rome, the merchant, attracted to it all the riches of the world. In the religion Rome set up, the proud and greedy gods whom she worshipped had the same appetites as human beings and liked to haggle over the sacrifices to be paid for their favours.

However, one must not forget the influence of Rome as home of the jurist and the administrator. Rome was much more than just the powerful, helmeted warrior and ruler.

In the first century of our era peace at last allowed Rome to enjoy its Golden Age. This was the age of Tacitus and Seneca.

When Caesar conquered Gaul, the people of Gaul had already reached a stage of civilization that was relatively advanced for the ancient world. Their methods of smelting iron ore and working iron had enabled them vastly to improve their agricultural instruments. The craftsmen of Gaul — jewellers, potters, coopers, tanners, cobblers and especially those who made the harness for their horses — were already distinguished.

The soil of Gaul was rich. Around each village, itself a group of huts with roofs of thatch, was a ring of well-worked fields. At first the Gauls resisted the Roman invaders. Their young chief Vercingetorix put up a heroic resistance, his faith and courage uniting his divided people to a first display of patriotism, but nevertheless he and his country were conquered. Then it was the turn of Britain.

For a long time Gaul and Britain were administered as Roman provinces. They enjoyed peace internally and great prosperity. New methods of tilling were introduced. The Romans built a network of metalled strategic roads which linked the different parts of the country and made a rapid expansion of commerce possible. As a result, big towns and cities grew up.

The Roman civilization was quickly absorbed by a people whose mental powers had previously been little exercised.

Gradually the Latin tongue was adopted. People acquired learning and refinement. Schools were opened in the towns, and an élite grew up that soon began to help in the administration of the country.

THE CIVILIZATIONS OF AMERICA AND ASIA

THE Mediterranean civilizations are of especial importance to us, because we are their direct heirs; but other civilizations, also enlightened by the ancient religion of the Sun, have flourished in numerous other parts of the Earth.

When Cortez and Pizarro landed in America they were amazed by the civilization of the Maya and Inca peoples. India and China both had their Golden Age long after Egypt. Like Tibet, these two powerful centres of the Orient must have profited by the great currents of civilization that reached them from Mesopotamia.

Under these princes who called themselves children of the Sun, civilization took immense strides forward. That cannot be denied. Yet the empires of these princes resembled each other. There were the same magics, the same superstitions, the same grandiose imaginings which found expression in the cult of huge stones and statuary, cyclopean monuments, and the stone calendars of the Sun.

The same worship of the Moon ... In India and Egypt, the cow, whose horns have the shape of a crescent moon, is a sacred animal.

More recent and better known to us are the Inca civilization and the extraordinary administrative organization of the four great provinces of that empire. The Supreme Head of the State, the Inca, Child of the Sun, ruled over the great dignitaries of that aristocracy of power, the two privileged castes of the warriors and the priests, and below them the mass of the people. The latter, kept in passive submission, had no liberties. They were looked after entirely by the State, which distributed their food to them, allotted them dwellings, fixed and supervised everyone's work, and provided popular festivals and games.

This powerful organization, extending to all sections of the hierarchy, from the central power to the smallest district, made it possible to obtain fine harvests of maize and potatoes from the reluctant soil of that mountainous country. The land was worked in terraces, ranged one above the other on the mountain sides and irrigated by a network of channels which brought water from the glaciers right to the arid sands of the coast. Large numbers of llamas were bred, and these provided a plentiful supply of meat and wool, which latter the women wove into fine materials.

The empire of the Inca was criss-crossed by well-built roads that linked the provinces, crossing rivers on bridges, climbing mountains or piercing them in tunnels cut out of the rock.

Yet neither the people of the Inca, nor yet the Mayas and their great ancestors of Tiahuanaco, knew the windlass or crane. They used levers and rollers to move the enormous blocks of stone with which they built their palaces and temples and the impressive ring walls of their fortresses. We know from the accounts of the Spanish conquistadores what riches had been amassed in the temples, how their walls were covered with carved plaques of gold and silver, and with mosaics of precious stones, and how in the fabulous crypt of the Temple of the Sun in Cuzco, the capital, was a row of embalmed sovereigns seated on thrones of solid gold. On temple porticos and the sacred stones on which the children of the Sun, the Mayas and Incas, had carved the emblems of their religion, you will find rosettes and solar wheels.

With several centuries in between, two great Maya empires developed one of the most ancient civilizations in the world in the heart of the tropical jungles of Central America and Mexico. The forest has since returned and engulfed the last vestiges of it, and these the archeologists are today endeavouring to disinter — the cities of massive stones, with paved streets, temples with monumental façades ornamented with strange sculptures of violent, barbarian inspiration. Like the Egyptians, the Mayas built pyramids, tombs and altars made of giant blocks, the piles of which have defied time. Did the ancestors of the Mayas come from Egypt

by way of Asia, as some scientists suppose? It is possible. Although it is difficult to determine to what remote epoch the ancient civilization of these people goes back, the jewels, materials and artistic potteries which have been found, and above all the inscriptions in stone, the designs and stylized emblems which prove that the Mayas used pictographic writing, enable us to judge to how great a degree their civilization had advanced.

In the days, long before the Incas laid the foundations of their vast empire, when the sea ground at the slopes of the Andes at the high altitude of Tiahuanaco, the mountains sheltered a people who, like the Mayas, have left us proof of a past that is lost in the mists of time, monumental ruins of stone citadels. These first inhabitants of the cordilleras mummified their dead and, in order to honour their gods, threw into the lakes, from which some have been recovered after all these centuries, statues, delicately chased jewellery and a quantity of ceramics which prove that these ancient people possessed a marvellous artistic sense.

During the two thousand years preceding the Christian era, two civilizations whose roots went deep into the mysterious prehistory of Asia developed in India and China. This took place when the kingdoms of the Nile and Mesopotamia were already at their height, yet they were caught up and out-distanced both in brilliance and in durability. India and China have

prospered and persisted until the present in lands as vast and populous as Europe itself.

One cannot speak of an Indian race, but there is a spirit of tropical India, and when invaders of a white race conquered the country, far from trying to alter this, they adopted it and gave it fresh vitality; though at the same time, by introducing the caste system they condemned Indian civilization to progressive paralysis.

How to explain the caste system? One could compare India to an enormous pit into which water has repeatedly flooded without the water of each flooding being able to mix with that below. At the bottom, the first occupants have become slaves, pariahs, untouchables; above them are the peasants and artisans, who have themselves been dominated by new masters who form the warrior caste. On the surface of all this is the Brahmin caste of priests and the learned.

In India the influence of climate caused this system, that other conquerors also imposed on ancient Europe, to be pushed to the verge of inhumanity. Just as nature has done in the tropics where, in her exuberance, she suffocates the plants that are unable to rise to the light.

The vegetation that grows so fast in the warm rains of the monsoon that you can almost see it growing has even influenced art. The statues of gods and goddesses have sinuous bodies and supple limbs that twist like lianas. The façades of the temples and palaces are covered with a riot of sculptured vegetation. Nature and art enfold each other. Banyan-trees clasp abandoned temples in their aerial roots and seem to be lifting them off the ground. In this oppressive climate where life is short the life of the individual has never counted for more than that of a mayfly that dances for a few hours above a river's bank. It is no more than a fleeting manifestation of manifold life, life that is ever falling back into the unity of death.

If India was slightly reminiscent of ancient Europe, China was too far away to be influenced by the white races. Characteristic of the spirit of the Chinese race is its respect for man and the entirety of Nature, of which he is a part. Man can live free in a free nature, even if he is poor.

It is not surprising that the Chinese were intelligent observers of Nature, which revealed several of her secrets to them long before she gave other peoples the benefit of them: silk, glass, explosives, the magnet; discoveries which the Chinese only used for the religious ceremonies celebrating the return of the spring.

With the Chinese, love of Nature was mixed with awe: they feared certain evil spirits of the sky, earth and waters. Respect was the basis of their character, and that is why the poor never felt jealous of the educated

people who governed them. These had passed difficult examinations after twenty years of study, for it took that length of time to learn to read and write only part of the signs that composed Chinese script.

Thus a literary education allowed a minority of high imperial functionaries to let their nails grow in order to demonstrate that they were not obliged to do manual work.

Writing facilitated the unification of China, while India remained divided into little kingdoms and, after the Middle Ages, even split into two hostile blocs: Moslem Pakistan and the Brahmanist rest of the country. The Chinese script was a system of simplified drawings of objects. Each sign had a pictorial value and did not depend on the sound of the words. Northern China and Southern China spoke two very different dialects, yet they could read the same characters though pronouncing them differently. The unification of the Celestial Empire was achieved in the third century B.C. This script was used as well by neighbouring peoples: Japanese, Koreans, Manchurians and Annamites, whose languages were very different. It served as a vehicle for Chinese civilization in the Far East, where China has played the same role as Ancient Greece did in Europe. Long before the Roman conquest, the Gauls used Greek letters to write Celtic. The Latin alphabet was itself merely a variant of the Greek. But twenty-five characters were enough to transcribe the entire oral language, while the Chinese needed thousands of signs to represent objects and conjure up ideas and sentiments by means of images. Thus Chinese writing, after being an instrument of progress for two thousand years, ended by killing the spirit of invention in the Chinese people. The Mandarins did not wish the people to have the opportunity to study and, having no rivals to fear, they lived in a rut. The Great Wall, built by the Emperor Ts'in, was ridiculously ineffective as a means of keeping out the Mongol horsemen; whereas the columns of characters of a Chinese book were an invisible but most effective wall that kept out all Western influence.

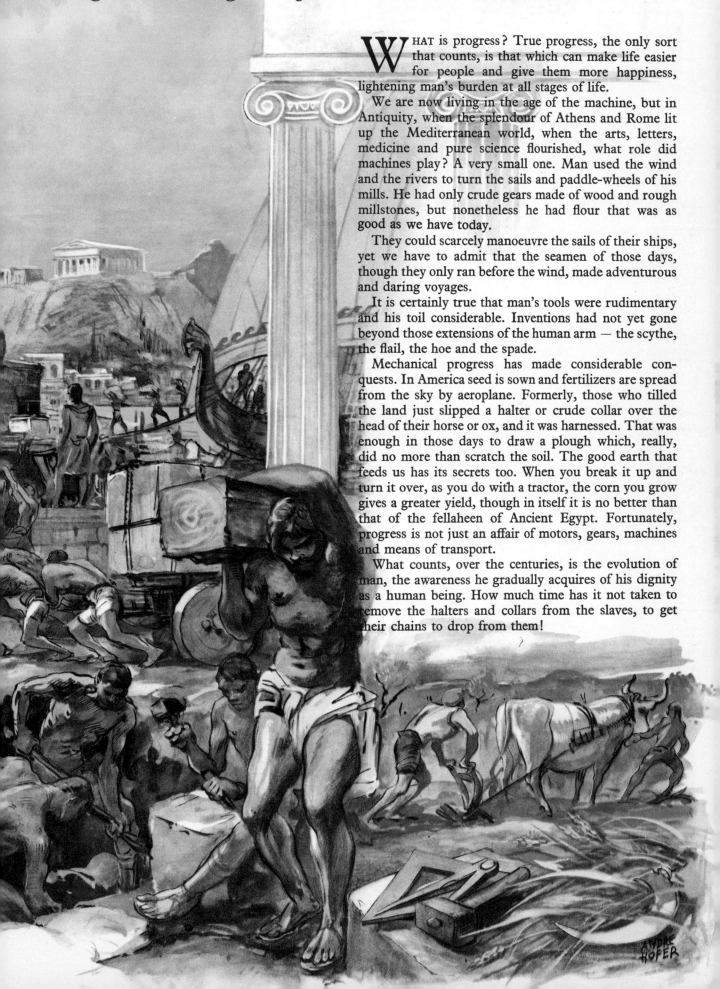

The great stages of WESTERN CIVILIZATION

WHAT is progress? True progress, the only sort that counts, is that which can make life easier for people and give them more happiness, lightening man's burden at all stages of life.

We are now living in the age of the machine, but in Antiquity, when the splendour of Athens and Rome lit up the Mediterranean world, when the arts, letters, medicine and pure science flourished, what role did machines play? A very small one. Man used the wind and the rivers to turn the sails and paddle-wheels of his mills. He had only crude gears made of wood and rough millstones, but nonetheless he had flour that was as good as we have today.

They could scarcely manoeuvre the sails of their ships, yet we have to admit that the seamen of those days, though they only ran before the wind, made adventurous and daring voyages.

It is certainly true that man's tools were rudimentary and his toil considerable. Inventions had not yet gone beyond those extensions of the human arm — the scythe, the flail, the hoe and the spade.

Mechanical progress has made considerable conquests. In America seed is sown and fertilizers are spread from the sky by aeroplane. Formerly, those who tilled the land just slipped a halter or crude collar over the head of their horse or ox, and it was harnessed. That was enough in those days to draw a plough which, really, did no more than scratch the soil. The good earth that feeds us has its secrets too. When you break it up and turn it over, as you do with a tractor, the corn you grow gives a greater yield, though in itself it is no better than that of the fellaheen of Ancient Egypt. Fortunately, progress is not just an affair of motors, gears, machines and means of transport.

What counts, over the centuries, is the evolution of man, the awareness he gradually acquires of his dignity as a human being. How much time has it not taken to remove the halters and collars from the slaves, to get their chains to drop from them!

The Greeks, highly civilized though they were, never imagined any other family or state except one in which there were inferior members, mere instruments equipped with physical strength, beings who were born and died as slaves. In Athens, people did not beat their slaves any more than one did a horse that served one well.

In front of the rich villas of Rome it was not unusual to see a slave-porter chained by the door like a dog, an iron ring round his waist. The condition of slaves in Rome was dreadful. They were mostly prisoners-of-war who had been sold at the fairs and markets. They had lost their status of free men and were put to all the base tasks: turning mills, digging mines, etc. They rowed Rome's galleys chained to the bench on which they sat. They were made to work like animals. They were human machines, intelligent mechanisms that were easily replaceable when they wore out.

True progress is far from being a question of perfecting material or machines. It is less than two hundred years since black slaves captured on the coasts of Africa were kept chained in the holds of the ships that took them to the West Indies and America, where white men who called themselves civilized sold and bought these cargoes of 'black ivory'. These were men like they, capable of loving and suffering like they, only their skins were black.

THE MESSAGE OF CHRISTIANITY

Yet it was then almost two thousand years since the voice was heard that had astounded man. It had been heard, modest but very fervent, in the fishing villages of Lake Tiberias, then in Judea and even in Jerusalem. It was the voice of the son of a humble carpenter. His name was Jesus. He said that all men were brothers and that he had come to redeem by the love of his Father who was in Heaven the poor and the rich alike, the slave and the merchant.

The Jews, who were expecting a Messiah wearing a king's crown, let this prophet whose kingdom was not of this world perish on the Cross, where he stretched out his arms to all, so that we might set our hands in His and, starting with Him, might form a chain of fraternal hands reaching across the derisory frontiers that separate the peoples.

The religions of Greece and Rome had no ideals and did not serve as a moral brake; their gods were similar to people and all the things that happened to them were human adventures. It was in this world, which had reached the stage where no value whatever was placed on the individual, that this wonderful new Promise rang out.

A religion of love had come into being under the sign of the Cross. It advocated the virtues of the family, love of one's own, and love of others; and suggested to all people, all members of the great human family, that they adopt the fine ideal of self-sacrifice.

The advent of Christianity was the first of the revolutions that from now on were to turn the world topsy-turvy.

In the centuries that have passed since then, right up to the present, you can measure the progress of our civilizations by the stages marked by revolutions and wars. At each of these stages people have sacrificed themselves and died for their faith: their religion, their country, their ideal.

That was what the early Christians did. They were persecuted, chased and tracked down to the depths of the catacombs, the subterranean caves in which they had to hide when they assembled to hold their services. Those who were captured were thrown into prison, where they were tortured to try and make them deny their faith. Those who refused were thrown to the beasts and killed at the games.

RELAPSE INTO BARBARISM

Where was the world going?

With the last steps that the carpenter's son of Nazareth took on earth he carried his cross to Golgotha, where Pilate's Roman soldiers set it up in the rock, never realizing that thereby they were erecting a boundary-post, at which the last of the great Roman roads built throughout the world by the legions of Caesar was to stop.

In devastated Europe Gaul was the first to recover. There the Church supported Clovis, King of the Franks, who had been converted at Rheims along with 3,000 of his warriors.

Before it became what it is today, western civilization — that is to say our way of living, thinking and expressing ourselves — has had to make its way through lots of difficulties, and its evolution has been marked by a number of events, the most important of which we shall mention here.

Where was the world going?

It was now caught up by the great currents of the religions preached by prophets who were the real heads of the wars now to be fought, which were holy to those who waged them. Before we came to the Crusades in which the Christians tried to recover the Holy Land, the Arabs, who had already converted parts of Asia and Africa to Islam, were to penetrate as far as Gaul.

Where was the ancient pagan world going now? Till then Rome had marched at its head. Rome was beginning to fear a threat that her legions massed on the Danube and the Rhine would be unable to halt. The yellow wind blowing from Asia was already bringing with it the sound of hooves as the Huns, the horsemen of Attila, came galloping in savage hordes. The Huns harried the Germans, and they in their turn invaded Gaul.

The invaders made breaches in all the frontiers of the Roman Empire and a flood of barbarians poured through: Franks who settled in the north of Gaul, Burgundians who settled in the east, and Visigoths and Vandals who thrust as far as Spain.

In 406 the Roman Empire collapsed as a result of the invasions of these barbarians. For a whole century the West, abandoned to those nomad hordes, was one great battlefield. There was not a corner that was safe from pillage and sack.

Civilization suffered a tremendous setback. In those days of terror the only help that the citizens of the sacked towns and the peasants of the burned villages could find, and slight at that, was in the Church. During the troublous centuries of the Middle Ages the Church was the only moral force able to assemble the best of the heritage of Rome and develop it.

THE LAST OF THE EMPIRE

Mahomet died in 632. He had made the knights of Allah vow that they would take the scimitar and the Koran to the world. In a few years these knights of Allah conquered Palestine, Egypt and Libya, and had advanced across North Africa to the shores of the Atlantic.

Having moved up through Spain the Arabs crossed the Pyrenees in 711. They dreamed of conquering the world and converting it to Islam, but in 732 Charles Martel stopped them and defeated them at Poitiers. Although defeated in France, they established themselves firmly in Spain.

108

This battle of Poitiers is an important event in the history of Europe.

Charlemagne, champion of Rome and Christianity, fought on three fronts against the Lombards, the Moslems in Spain and the Saxons. Under the rule of this 'Emperor with the flowing beard', as the minstrels described him in their songs — though in reality he did not have a beard at all — a veritable Renaissance took place: commerce revived, intellectual and artistic activ-

ities were resumed, while Europe became Christian. The first schools were opened in the shade of the cathedrals.

Nonetheless the political unity of Europe that Rome had imposed and Charlemagne revived was gone forever. The great empire relapsed into anarchy after its dismemberment by the Treaty of Verdun in 843.

While Charlemagne's successors were busy quarrelling about how to divide up the empire, ships came sailing up the rivers of Europe carrying other barbarians, this time from the north.

These were the long ships of the Vikings, at their prows a dragon's head with gaping jaws. These sea raiders harried the coasts of Europe and penetrated all the major waterways. They would set out in summer and return in due course to their homes laden with plunder; or, in many cases, would settle down in the lands they had terrorized and even establish kingdoms there. They invaded Ireland, Scotland and England, and thrust deep into Germany, Russia and France — becoming, in fact, the direct ancestors of those Northmen (or Normans) who were to invade England under William the Conqueror.

In Ireland the Vikings set up the kingdoms of Dublin and Waterford. In 865 a large force concentrated on

England, overrunning the ancient kingdoms of Northumbria, Mercia and East Anglia. Alfred the Great fought magnificently against the Danes who attacked his kingdom of Wessex, and defeated them: he even persuaded their leader to accept Christian baptism.

For a long time the Viking invaders ruled the northern parts of Britain over what was known as the Danelaw, but gradually they were reconquered, and by 954 England was united under one king, Edred. The Danish attacks still went on, however, and at times it was found necessary to 'buy off' the invaders with money, which was known as Danegeld. The influence of these fearless, pitiless warriors on Europe was to be a lasting one.

THE FEUDAL SYSTEM

Great invasions swept across Gaul, mingling races and abolishing frontiers, and the establishment of the feudal system finally destroyed the patriotic ideal that Vercingetorix had been able to implant in the minds of his people, when he led them against Caesar's legions.

What is fatherland or mother-country, the land that is our home?

In the first place it is the land that has produced those who till it. Not everything will grow everywhere, and in

the last resort people are as much a fruit of the soil as is the corn that grows in our fields. The Greeks who had organized themselves in tiny nations, each in a well-defined little province, and the Roman legionary who, having laid down his arms, went back to his village to dig in his vineyard, both had a very live sense of patriotism, of having a country that was like a vast communal field belonging to a whole people of citizens. This field, enclosed by its frontiers, had become a state, in which life in common imposed duties upon each. Under the feudal system which made slaves of those who tilled the land, these latter had no other ties than those that bound them to their master.

These direct links, man to man, went all up the scale. The petty lord in his turn was vassal of a more powerful prince, his suzerain. Thus it went all the way up from the serf in his hovel to the baron who was vassal of a count, who was vassal of a prince, who was vassal of a king; and the king alone owed allegiance to none.

The same person could be the vassal of several lords from whom he held different fiefs. Instead of the citizen having duties to the state, as was the case in Roman society, the complicated feudal system aroused people's greed and envy and led to endless wars. In order to ensure the loyalty of powerful personages the suzerain gave them lands. Being thus more or less bereft himself,

the suzerain had little more than moral prestige — and that fragile enough — and the question of his successor was frequently the cause of rivalries that brought anything but peace, as we know from the Hundred Years War and the Wars of the Roses.

The feudal system developed rapidly because of the need to protect the various provinces from threatened attack. The feudal lord was first and foremost a soldier. He had no need to be able to read or write; it was enough if he was a master in his profession of arms and a good horseman. Thus the education that the young noble received in his youth was confined to turning him into a man of war, the knight who would spend his life fighting in the service of his suzerain.

The church was the only remaining influence able to impose rules and maintain some order in the feudal world. It instituted the 'Truce of God', which set up four days in every week on which the lords were not allowed to wage war. It extended the radius of influence of its abbeys, where the monks not only acquired knowledge, but also worked in the fields and set the peasants an example by restoring fallow land to cultivation. In the towns the Church had hospitals where the sick were taken in and the misery of the poor comforted.

This was the age when stone cathedrals grew up on

THE CRUSADES

The First Crusade was a Crusade of the people and of pilgrims, who had been carried away by Peter the Hermit. Thousands of men, each of whom had sewn a cross of red cloth on his cloak as an emblem, set off to free the tomb of Christ that had fallen into the hands of the Turks. Starving and ill-armed, they were exterminated by the fanatical Moslems before they even reached the walls of Jerusalem.

Four years later, however, Godefroy de Bouillon took the town at the head of a Crusade of knights, who were responsible for killing half a million people.

In two hundred years there were eight Crusades, but not all who took part were animated by the same idealism and burning faith. The Fourth Crusade, for example, was diverted from its original objective to attack Constantinople, a city of a million inhabitants. This capital of the Byzantine Empire had long been an object of the jealousy of Venice and Genoa. Isolated at the head of its lagoon, the mighty republic of Venice considered itself mistress of the Adriatic. On the day

the site of the old wooden churches that fire had consumed. Massive walls supported the Byzantine cupola, the barrel vaulting and arcades of semi-circular arches of the Norman church. Later appeared buildings in the Gothic style with slender columns supported by flying buttresses well clear of the mass which they seemed to carry at the end of their graceful stone arches, while supporting the nave in a flight of spires pierced with pointed casements. The arches of doorways, columns, capitals and balusters were ornamented with naive imagery in stone; monumental statues stood in niches in the facade, from which gargoyles with monstrous faces spewed the rain-water; ogivals and rose-windows in which the sunlight struck fire from precious stained glass set in lead were similarly framed.

This was the time of the lays composed to glorify gallant knights and champions, like the famous *Song of Roland*. It was the time of tourneys and jousting, of the troubadours and minstrels. Itinerant musicians and tumblers went from manor to manor to entertain with their songs the noble chatelaines whose husbands were away fighting with their lords and who had none but the boring company of their tirewomen. These troubadours also brought accounts of the fighting in the Holy Land to which the knights had all gone on a Crusade.

when he took office its head, the Doge, standing in the prow of his galley, *Bucentaurus*, would throw a ring into the water, thereby wedding the sea; and each year on Ascension Day he repeated the ceremony. When, a hundred years after the First Crusade, the knights of Christ were intending to go off again to try and conquer the Holy Land, Venice lent them her fleet, but on

from the East and cultivated: shallots and buckwheat and elsewhere in Europe rice and apricots.

The Crusades brought about a revival in commerce and industry, especially on the Continent, where the great fairs that were held on fixed dates made an exchange of goods easy and profitable. Thus were imported and exported French wines, cloth from Flanders, silks and velvets from Italy and the East, wool from England and Scotland, glass from Venice.

Those who went on the Crusades saw the luxuries of the East and developed a taste for spices and rich foods.

conditions. That is why the Fourth Crusade culminated in the taking of Constantinople.

These distant expeditions had a considerable beneficial influence on the intellectual and social life in the western countries. The Moslem world had extended its bounds from the Mediterranean to eastern Asia, where the civilizations of India and China were then well in advance of our own. For two hundred years, thousands of people, pilgrims and soldiers, who but for the Crusades would never have left their own country, came into contact with the civilizations of the East. Once again, the lands in which the sun rises brought us civilization and with it a certain taste for luxury: baths, perfumes, precious stuffs, and artistically worked furniture. At the same time the West learned how to make glass, rag paper, gunpowder, cross-bows and the magnet.

The Arabs had already made translations of a great number of Greek works. Their contacts with the intellectual centres of the Ancient World had made them heir — as far as the sciences of mathematics and astronomy went — of the Chaldeans, Egyptians and Greeks. They opened up those fields for us. Our architecture became enriched with the cupola and ornamental arabesque, things that the Crusaders had admired in Constantinople, and these soon appeared in rope-mouldings, volutes and rosettes on the façades of our cathedrals.

Economic life took a great stride forward. Cereals, fruits and trees till then unknown were brought back

They liked having rugs on their floors, tapestries on their walls, and they acquired the habit of wearing underclothes. They brought back damasks, fine armour and weapons and many other things that stimulated the craftsmen in their own countries to imitate and in time even to surpass them in artistry and quality. Then was created a demand for goods that started what we would call a boom; at the same time the lands east of the Rivers Rhine and Elbe were being opened and settled, providing new markets still.

While this economic renaissance was taking place the lot of the peasants was considerably improved by new agreements which were embodied in 'charters'. In these the lords, following the example of the monks, guaranteed a man's freedom to work and reduced the burden of corvées laid on the villagers who cleared their lands and developed their estates.

As well as the episcopal schools in which the priests and monks educated themselves, independent associations of clergy grouped together to form universities to which students came from far and wide, often from abroad, and where instruction was given, always in Latin, in law, philosophy, theology and medicine.

NORMANS AND PLANTAGENETS

In 1066 William of Normandy had invaded and conquered England. His excuse for doing so was the

apparently ruthless way in which Harold, son of the Earl of the West Saxons, had declared himself King of the English within a few hours of the death of King Edward the Confessor. Harold claimed that Edward had chosen him as successor to the crown, and also asserted that he was the only man strong enough to weld the Saxons together and protect the country from its enemies. But Duke William was related to Edward, and many people in England had reason to believe that he was determined to claim the crown — by force if necessary.

The expected attack came. William and his army embarked at the end of September, 1066, and landed at

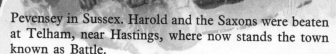

Pevensey in Sussex. Harold and the Saxons were beaten at Telham, near Hastings, where now stands the town known as Battle.

William and his successors relied on a warlike nobility. In 1154 the throne of England was inherited by the Plantagenets, who governed a large part of France and who dreamed of uniting France and England under one crown. This ambition led to long years of feuds and bitterness, often breaking out into open war.

Outright disaster came in the time of King John. He was hated by the people as an oppressor, and regarded by the nobles with contempt because of his cowardice and indecision. In 1214 he rashly embarked on an unsuccessful war with France.

As a result of this and of his attempts to impose heavy taxes and seize money from the Church, the barons threatened to withdraw their allegiance from the king unless he confirmed certain essential liberties in a charter. In its final form this was the famous Magna Carta which, though limited in its scope, became one of the cornerstones of British democracy.

War was to flare up again in the time of Edward III. The death of Charles IV left the inheritance of the French crown in a rather confused state, and it was only after a great deal of political manoeuvring that Philip VI became king. Edward, after apparently recognizing Philip's right, finally declared his own right to the throne. England was now in a mood to claim the return of her old French possessions, and sent armies across to take them.

THE HUNDRED YEARS WAR

The Hundred Years War, whose causes were a mixture of economic conflicts, political disputes and a dynastic rivalry, really started in 1337 when King Edward began operations against the Low Countries to detach them from France. He invaded France itself in 1339, and in 1346 inflicted a crushing defeat on the French at the Battle of Crécy. A year later the English took the town and port of Calais.

The knights of those days were indeed of noble

blood, but they were champions incapable of doing anything but fight, which they did very well indeed. John of Bohemia was actually blind, but that did not prevent him going to war. At Crécy, when the archers of France has been routed, John of Bohemia led the faithful vassals of the King of France in a gallant charge through the scattered ranks of the bowmen.

He wore a suit of gilded armour and he had his horse tied to those of two of his squires, one on either side, who guided him. In the morning after the battle the king and his two squires were found on the battlefield crushed beneath their mounts.

The cannon used for the first time at Crécy were more noisy than dangerous, and they frightened more people than they hurt. In fact they did little more than make a great noise and spew out fire. In time, of course, proper guns were developed, capable of shooting out stones and cannon-balls weighing more than 100 pounds.

It took money as well as brass to found cannon, even those like the famous bombards that thundered at the siege of Orleans, in 1429.

Do you know the story of John of Lorraine and his culverin?

John was a hefty fellow. He shouldered a culverin weighing 200 pounds and went off to where the people of Orleans had blown up one of the arches at the end of the bridge facing Tourelles, where the English had entrenched themselves. There John crouched down by the rampart, like a poacher, and firing through an embrasure he shot the English down like flies.

It was now that Joan of Arc appeared on the scene. A simple country girl, she was convinced that God had chosen her to be the instrument that would free France. Having obtained a following she dressed in man's clothes and rode to battle. Though she herself was taken prisoner and executed, her example gave fresh courage to the people of France.

The Spaniards and Portuguese vied with each other in the search for new sea routes, above all to the Indies. In 1486 Bartholomew Diaz for the first time doubled the Cape of Good Hope at the southern end of the continent of Africa. Then Vasco da Gama, sailing round it in his turn, opened up a new route to India and the East. He reached Calicut on the west coast of India in 1498. Christopher Columbus had discovered the New World, and Magellan accomplished the great feat of circumnavigating the globe.

This was the end of the Middle Ages. Great inventions were in the offing, inventions that were to revolutionize the world.

DISCOVERIES AND INVENTIONS

The brass used in making bombards was also used for other, more peaceful purposes. It was used, among other things, for making the new instruments, the

astrolabe and the compass, which allowed sailors to find their way and make landfall by using the stars, enabling ships to sail across the oceans and, before long, all the way round the world.

A revolution in the method of rigging had given a considerable stimulus to navigation. Ships with a high board could now manoeuvre in all winds, thanks to the complicated setting of the sails. The new navigators set sail to find new routes to the spice lands, the one through the Mediterranean having been closed by the capture of Constantinople and the harrying of the barbarians. Lisbon became a port of such importance that it was to end by ruining the trade of Venice.

It was not only spices that people wanted. Such tales were being told of the riches of China that people wanted to go and see for themselves. In ten years, from 1492 to 1501, the globe which before had been known only from the accounts of the Ancients was criss-crossed in all directions.

Technical progress made great improvements in the method of building ships possible, and new types of vessels appeared on the stocks.

There were now marine charts squared with parallels and meridians. Navigators had the astrolabe with which they could measure the height of the stars in the sky, and the compass which made use of the magnetic needle that the Chinese had known since Antiquity, and which always points to the north. These two new aids allowed ships to hold a given course and make landfall without having to sail by 'dead reckoning' as before.

The art of war was revolutionized by the use of firearms. Castles were no longer impregnable, now that

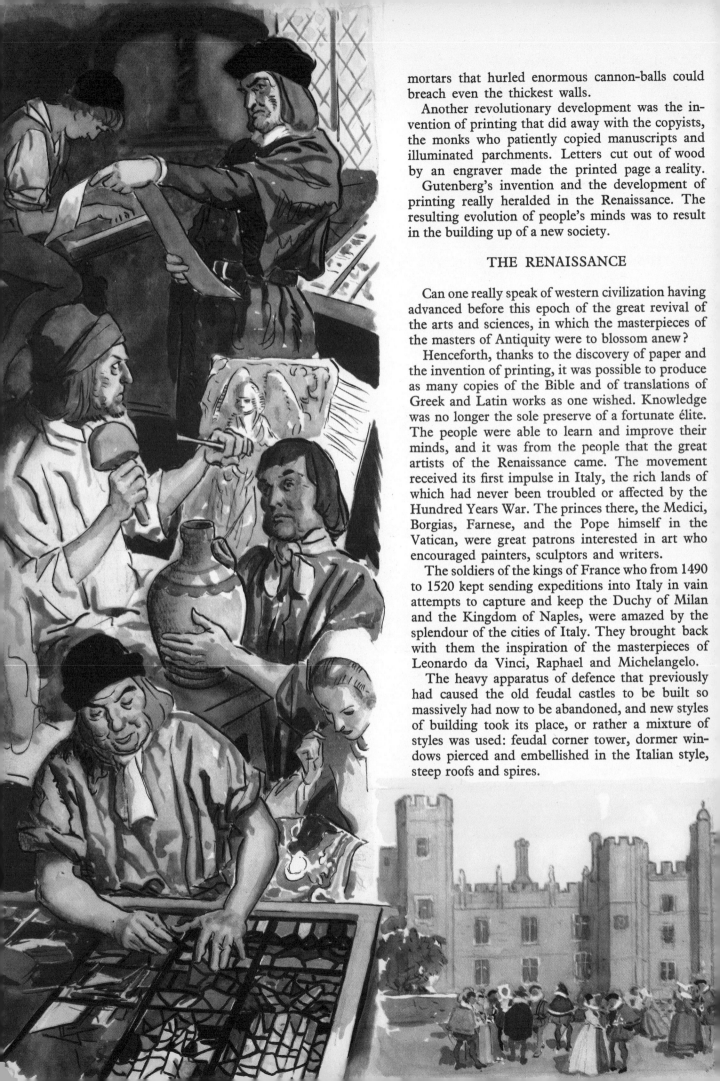

mortars that hurled enormous cannon-balls could breach even the thickest walls.

Another revolutionary development was the invention of printing that did away with the copyists, the monks who patiently copied manuscripts and illuminated parchments. Letters cut out of wood by an engraver made the printed page a reality.

Gutenberg's invention and the development of printing really heralded in the Renaissance. The resulting evolution of people's minds was to result in the building up of a new society.

THE RENAISSANCE

Can one really speak of western civilization having advanced before this epoch of the great revival of the arts and sciences, in which the masterpieces of the masters of Antiquity were to blossom anew?

Henceforth, thanks to the discovery of paper and the invention of printing, it was possible to produce as many copies of the Bible and of translations of Greek and Latin works as one wished. Knowledge was no longer the sole preserve of a fortunate élite. The people were able to learn and improve their minds, and it was from the people that the great artists of the Renaissance came. The movement received its first impulse in Italy, the rich lands of which had never been troubled or affected by the Hundred Years War. The princes there, the Medici, Borgias, Farnese, and the Pope himself in the Vatican, were great patrons interested in art who encouraged painters, sculptors and writers.

The soldiers of the kings of France who from 1490 to 1520 kept sending expeditions into Italy in vain attempts to capture and keep the Duchy of Milan and the Kingdom of Naples, were amazed by the splendour of the cities of Italy. They brought back with them the inspiration of the masterpieces of Leonardo da Vinci, Raphael and Michelangelo.

The heavy apparatus of defence that previously had caused the old feudal castles to be built so massively had now to be abandoned, and new styles of building took its place, or rather a mixture of styles was used: feudal corner tower, dormer windows pierced and embellished in the Italian style, steep roofs and spires.

Lovely châteaux were built in the valley of the Loire in France, many of which we can still admire today. In Paris the monumental façade of the Louvre was built, and the Tuileries. In England Cardinal Wolsey built his palace of Hampton Court.

The King of France published an edict whereby French became the official language in place of Latin. But as well as encouraging interest in the vernacular, he assembled round him men of learning and letters and founded an academy where the ancient languages were taught. In Italy also, the humanists Dante, Petrarch, Boccaccio and Machiavelli brought the study of the ancient Greek and Latin writers back into honour.

Of the writers of those days we still honour the names of Montaigne for his *Essays*, of Rabelais for his witty, truculent tales of the adventures of the two giants Gargantua and Pantagruel, and of Ronsard.

In this 16th century, when England and France had recovered from the ruinous effects of the Hundred Years War, considerable economic progress was made. Commercial and industrial activity increased. The craftsmen of the country towns had their share in the boom. The bourgeoisie — the merchants, heads of guilds, lawyers, doctors and bankers — was growing richer and richer. Little by little it was to dethrone the nobility and acquire a preponderant influence in the country.

Meanwhile England, having lost all her French possessions in the Hundred Years War, was rather isolated in the north-west corner of Europe. By comparison with her neighbour across the channel she was unimportant and rather unfortunate, for she suffered three decades of civil strife. Her population had been reduced and farming had become so unprofitable that some landowners gave up and leased off their land.

The Elizabethan resurgence of England was at hand, but had not yet come, and for the time being it was France that imparted brilliance to Europe, as Europe was to do to the world.

Revolutions were to come and transform the different states, and the origins of these revolutions lay in the spread of knowledge that now began to take place.

THE REFORMATION

The first of these great basic revolutions was the Reformation.

The Renaissance had begun by spreading knowledge of the scriptures and of the Greek and Latin classics by means of books, and this had really allowed a 're-

birth' of the human mind. The humanists, the scholars, studied Greek and Hebrew, the original languages of the Old and New Testaments, to learn there of the acts of love that mark Christ's path in the world. From their studies some scholars arrived at a formal principle, that of the Divine Authority expressed by the Scriptures, and this they set up against the principle of the infallibility and supremacy of the Church.

The Bible had now come within the reach of everyone and even among the masses people became incensed when they compared the recommendations of holy writ with the luxurious and sometimes thoroughly un-Chris-

tian lives led by certain members of the clergy. Their critics did not spare the lower part of the hierarchy, of which the prelates were too often ignorant.

The Reformation was a sincere act of faith. It started in Germany under Martin Luther and ended by destroying for ever the religious unity of the Church that had given Europe some measure of cohesion ever since the collapse of the Roman Empire.

In England Henry VIII drove the monks from the monasteries and seized their lands and wealth, even having many of the monasteries pulled down. He then proclaimed himself temporal head of the church, rejecting Papal authority. Later, under Mary and Elizabeth, there was a wave of religious persecution in England. Mary burned Protestants (those who would not accept the Pope's authority) at the stake, and Elizabeth in her turn harried the Roman Catholics.

The Low Countries and Scandinavia also broke with Rome.

Philip II of Spain wanted to re-establish the Roman Catholic faith in England and to punish that country for letting Francis Drake, Richard Grenville and their fellows plunder his ships in which the treasures of the New World were sent back to Spain, so he prepared to invade England. The invading force was carried in a great fleet, the Armada, which was defeated by Lord Howard of Effingham, Drake, Hawkins and Frobisher, and then scattered by a storm. Thereafter the mastery of the sea passed to England.

England was now great again and a rival of France.

William Shakespeare was writing his immortal plays.

which is said to have given employment to 30,000 workmen throughout his reign. Encouragement was given to sculptors, musicians and painters. Paris itself was beautified with Les Invalides and the colonnade of the Louvre. In her turn France now produced writers of genius, Corneille, Molière, Racine, and La Fontaine. Roads and canals were built to assist commerce, and industries supported.

Richelieu had tried to colonize some of the islands of the Antilles, the mouth of the River Senegal, and Canada, and now this policy was intensified and immigration organized. Twenty thousand Bretons and Normans were sent to Canada. La Salle explored the

The Pilgrim Fathers had sailed to America in *Mayflower* and the first English colonies in the New World had come into being.

Then Charles I quarrelled with his Parliament and in trying to uphold the principle of the Divine Right of Kings brought about a Civil War. Charles I was beheaded in 1649 and for eleven years England was a Commonwealth. After this Charles II ascended the throne and England had definitely embarked on the path of constitutional monarchy.

This was not the case in France, where Henry IV had pacified the country and put an end to religious strife by the Edict of Nantes, by which Protestants in France were allowed the right to worship according to the Calvinistic rite and to have universities of their own. Shortly afterwards Henry IV was assassinated while in his coach, and Louis XIII came to the throne. When he gave powers to Cardinal Richelieu the government of France was in strong and capable hands.

Richelieu brought the nobles to heel. The Protestants, being discontented with the way the Edict of Nantes was being put into practice, took up arms. England helped them and even sent a fleet to La Rochelle, the centre of the Protestant resistance, when it was besieged by Richelieu.

Richelieu died and his place was taken by another great man, Cardinal Mazarin, an Italian. When he died, the government was so powerful in France that Louis XIV was able to reign as absolute monarch, sharing his power with none.

Louis XIV built the wonderful palace of Versailles

course of the Mississippi and brought his country Louisiana, while France acquired Chandernagor and Pondicherry in India, where British influence was rapidly growing.

A grandson of the great Louis XIV ascended the throne of Spain and his grandfather proudly announced that the Pyrenees no longer existed.

This was an age of great absolute monarchs: Louis XIV in France, Frederick II in Prussia, Catherine in Russia.

In 1665 there was a violent outbreak of plague that killed thousands of people in London and was followed the next year by the Great Fire of London, which burned down eighty-four churches and hundreds of wooden houses, destroying many of the filthy, narrow alleyways that had served as breeding places of disease and plague.

At the same time England was engaged in naval war with Holland, but in 1685 James II was deposed and his daughter Mary ascended the throne with her Dutch husband William.

In this same year Louis XIV revoked the Edict of Nantes.

In 1702 in England, Queen Anne, last of the Stuarts, ascended the throne, and English arms triumphed under the great Duke of Marlborough at Blenheim, Ramillies and Malplaquet.

In 1714 George I ascended the throne of England and the following year James Edward, son of deposed James II, made an attempt to recover the throne for the Stuarts. Although he had the help of the Scots his attempt failed, as did that of his son, Bonnie Prince Charlie, thirty years later. Bonnie Prince Charlie, the Young Pretender, got as far south as Derby, but was defeated at Culloden and eventually escaped to France.

As England grew strong, France declined. By the end of the Seven Years War she had lost all her colonies, and the country was faced with bankruptcy. In 1759 Wolfe captured Quebec, and Canada passed from France to become part of the British Empire. Robert Clive was now bringing India under British rule.

REVOLUTION AND CHANGE

In 1789 an astonished world heard that the people of France had risen and triumphed, and that they had issued a Declaration of the Rights of Man which began —

'Men are born and remain free and equal in their rights.'

Those have become deathless words, like the three of the slogan of the Revolution and its armies: Liberty, Equality, Fraternity.

Are not men brothers and really members of one great nation? Are not wars really always civil wars?

Already, in 1783, the English colonies in America, where people had grown tired of paying taxes to the home country, had revolted and declared their Independence. With the help of the French and under the leadership of George Washington they defeated the British troops sent against them and formed a new country, the United States of America.

The Napoleonic era really begins in 1794 when a young officer commanding French forces fighting in Italy realized that he was a military genius.

Before setting out for Italy, a friend had said to him that he was really too young to be in command of such an expedition.

'Don't worry, my friend, I shall be old when I get back,' said Napoleon.

His victories did mature him quickly. For him nothing seemed impossible. He believed in his own luck in a thoroughly superstitious way. One night, in Egypt, a wall by which he was sleeping collapsed, yet not a brick touched him. When day dawned Bonaparte found himself surrounded with debris and felt a small lump in the hollow of his hand. Looking at it, he discovered that he was holding a magnificent cameo from the Augustan age.

'I realized then,' he said when telling the story of the episode, 'that everything that was intended to harm me would always turn out to my advantage.'

When he returned to France from Egypt, he seized power in a coup d'état on 9 November 1799. His first title was that of Consul, but this was merely a step towards the throne and on 2 December 1804 he was consecrated Emperor. When he felt the crown on his head, remembering the modest home in Corsica where he was born, he turned to his brother Joseph who was standing at his side, and murmured:

'If Father could see me now!'

Both the deeds and the very ideas of the revolution were abhorred in Europe, and France had many enemies. Napoleon swept across the Continent from end to end triumphing over the armies of his foes. In 1813, when fighting against Prussia and Russia, Napoleon was at Bautzen with an army. Before attacking, he decided to wait for Marshal Ney, and while waiting thought he might as well sleep. He ordered a cloak to be stretched on the ground and lay down on it.

'Wake me in two hours,' he said, and at once went to sleep, despite the roar of the guns which were keeping up a cannonade. He did not wake till Ney arrived. Then he calmly jumped on to his horse and said:

'Within one hour we shall have conquered.'

Napoleon remade the map of Europe, dethroned kings and created others. Metternich tells of witnessing an incident which, as he said, made him realize Napoleon's power. Metternich had been invited to a gala dinner. Among the guests were Murat, King of Naples, Napoleon's brother-in-law, King Jerome and King Louis, his brothers. The fish was very slow in coming and the Emperor's brow clouded.

'King of Naples,' said Napoleon, turning to Murat, 'go and see what is happening.'

Murat got up and went out. Time passed and he did not return. The Emperor barked out another order:

'King of Westphalia, go and see what the King of Naples is up to.'

Jerome found Murat and came back with him and the fish — just as a third order was about to send the King of Holland from the table.

'How imperious his gestures were! What a curt way to speak to kings! That day I was aware of the *imperator*, the great master.'

Napoleon's military prowess all too often dominates the picture we have of him, so that we forget that other side of him and how he applied his genius to organizing France and Europe. He created many of the institutions that France has to-day, including the Legion of Honour, and he was responsible for the famous Napoleonic Code which has since served as a model for several other countries' laws.

Napoleon was finally defeated by allied armies under Wellington at the battle of Waterloo and sent to St. Helena, where he died six years later.

Meanwhile another revolutionary and epoch-making event had taken place in a very different sphere. In 1807 the slave trade, in which negroes had been forcibly taken from their homes in Africa and sold as slaves in America and the West Indies, was abolished. This was largely due to the efforts of William Wilberforce.

INDUSTRIAL PROGRESS

Gone for ever are the good old days when people did not burn the candle at both ends, but took the time to live, to go for walks and to be idle. Now those days only exist in books.

This is all because of the revolution in transport and communications caused by the invention of the railways.

The first public railway was that between Stockton and Darlington, built by the famous George Stephenson. The engine, named *Locomotion*, pulled the train at the tremendous speed of twelve miles an hour. Four years later Stephenson's *Rocket* achieved a speed of twenty-nine miles an hour at the Rainhill trials. After that it was not many years before trains were travelling almost as fast as they do today.

Steam power and electricity appeared almost simultaneously and began working miracles. It was like a magician waving his wand.

The first steam engine was built by Newcomen in 1712. It made only sixteen revolutions a minute, the vacuum in the cylinder being obtained by injecting cold water. The cold water valve was not worked mechanically, but was opened and shut by hand. This work, which called for no special skill, was entrusted to young apprentices.

In those days people began working at a very early age and children were employed in the mines and factories. This was the case with Humphrey Potter. His job was to stand for ten hours every day beside Newcomen's engine, opening and shutting the cold water valve at each thrust of the piston.

Humphrey was an intelligent child and he noticed that the gesture he was continually making exactly followed the rhythm of the balance-beam of the pump. He then thought out a device, rudimentary enough, for making the machine do the work for him. A system of cords transmitted the movement of the beam to the tap lever and after that all he had to do was to watch the machine and his makeshift invention.

It was not till 1794 that Watt's steam engine, using

WATT

his famous parallelogram, made it possible to make the piston work in both directions, thrusting and pulling.

In 1752 Franklin sent a kite with a long pointed spur into a thunder cloud and thus obtained electricity from the atmosphere. That was the birth of the invention of the lightning conductor, that leads the electric discharges of a storm into the earth.

Did you realize that the first electric battery was a fish: the cramp-fish? John Walsh fixed a lead to the body of one and obtained small electric discharges. Galvani, professor at the University of Bologna, was at the same time experimenting with the feet muscles of a frog and the way they contracted when subjected to an electric discharge.

Volta was interested in Galvani's work. He did not conclude, as did the latter, that electricity could be produced by the nerves of frogs, but thought it could be generated by metal lying in salt water. In 1800, he perfected the application of his sensational discovery and produced the first electric battery.

Volta's battery was like a miner's lamp. It was com-

posed of discs of zinc and copper stacked one on top of the other and separated by circles of fabric impregnated with acidulated water. This produced an electric current in the wire connecting the first copper disc with the last zinc disc.

At the same time as two great new sources of energy, steam and electricity, were thus put at the service of man, the economy of the world was convulsed by a series of mechanical and technical inventions.

Coal, the production of which was increasing, took the place of charcoal, thereby transforming the metal industries.

The genius of Lavoisier gave birth to modern chemistry.

Machines were improved and perfected. Progress even reached agriculture. Ploughs were modernized and farmers began using threshing machines instead of flails. It must be admitted, however, that the real revolution in agriculture consisted not so much in the use of machinery as in the more intensive cultivation of crops like sugar-beet and potatoes, capable of giving a good yield. The proof is that the farmer has remained faithful to his land; his state has not changed; while the craftsman ... Machines now make pots and dishes, weave and forge.

Exploitation of mines and the purchase of machinery called for the investment of considerable capital. Great industrial centres came into being.

The artisan began to disappear and his place to be taken by the worker.

This was revolution, an industrial revolution, and it was not without its dramas.

The invention of the spinning jenny by James Hargreaves (1764), Richard Arkwright's spinning-machine, and Samuel Crompton's mule and Edmund Cartwright's weaving loom initially threw people out of work and there were riots and disorders; some mobs even tried to smash the machines.

In 1802 William Symington built a steam engine to drive a tug-boat. It worked perfectly, but the owners were afraid the wash set up by her paddle-wheels might damage the banks of the canal and so the boat, *Charlotte Dundas*, was never used.

In 1804, an American called Fulton demonstrated a steam-boat that he had built on the River Loire, but he received no encouragement from the Emperor Napoleon. In 1812 Henry Bell built the *Comet*, which was the first steam-boat in regular service. She achieved the great speed of $7\frac{1}{2}$ miles an hour.

The invention of the railway and its rapid expansion, linking all the principal towns and ports, gave a tremendous impetus to the country's economy; yet those who worked in the new factories and mines were often desperately poor and wretched, as were many of the country-people, largely owing to the dying out of the cottage industries of spinning and weaving, tasks which could now be done more cheaply and quickly by machine. Also the old method of strip farming had been abandoned and the land divided into fields surrounded by hedges. Farming methods improved. During the wars with France the price of corn was high and the landowners and farmers were well off.

Lord Townshend had introduced the method of growing turnips for winter fodder instead of letting land lie fallow, and as a result it was now possible to get fresh meat all the year round. A machine for sowing seeds in rows was now in use and the quality of sheep and cattle was being rapidly improved.

The bulk of the people were still poor, however, and writers began drawing attention to this state of affairs and calling for equitable wages and better working conditions. Gradually all this came about.

EXPANSION OF THE WEST

The capture of Algiers in 1830 acted as the signal for the European Powers to occupy Africa and acquire colonies throughout the world.

In 1833 slavery was forbidden in all British dominions and all slaves were freed.

In 1851 The Great Exhibition was held in Hyde Park at which British goods were shown to visitors from all over the world.

In 1854 Britain and France went to war with Russia to prevent her taking Constantinople. This is called the Crimean War. During it, Florence Nightingale became famous for nursing the wounded in hospitals behind the lines.

In 1857 there was the Indian Mutiny, as a result of which the Government took over the administration of India and responsibility for its welfare from the East India Company.

Africa was now being opened up and explored by such men as Speke and Sir Richard Burton, David Livingstone and H. M. Stanley. Cecil Rhodes founded Rhodesia; while in the Congo vast territories were acquired for France and Belgium by de Brazza.

In 1840 England had gained a footing in China and was able to trade there. Japan, too, opened her ports to foreign trade when threatened by the guns of the American Commodore Perry.

Much of this expansion and many of these occupations were essentially humanitarian, and those concerned were anxious to respect the liberties of the natives, at the same time as materially improving their conditions.

In fifty years Europe with its missionaries penetrated two continents, the Black and the Yellow.

THE TWENTIETH CENTURY

In 1914 the First World War began when Germany invaded Belgium and then France. Her armies were halted on the Marne and four long years of trench warfare began. Soldiers lived and fought in appalling conditions. Poison gas was used and tanks were in-

and cutlery came from the kitchen of their own accord and laid themselves on the table.

This sorcerer had an apprentice who was learning the secrets and art of sorcery. One day, when the old sorcerer was out and the young apprentice alone in the house, the latter thought he would test his prowess. Very excited, he muttered the first spells, the only ones he knew, and so set everything in the house working. The pail trundled to its place under the tap which began spouting water, and soon the pail was overflowing. The broom swept the stairs frenziedly; the fire roared and the water splashed: there was a terrible commotion and everything was upside down, the furniture dancing about, and there was nothing the young man could do about it. The sorcerer's apprentice who had started it all had not yet been taught the magic words that would stop the infernal dance of all these objects which were now so very far from inanimate.

Luckily the sorcerer himself returned in the nick of time and pronounced the necessary spell.

The earth, our little sphere in the universe, is today

vented. Aeroplanes were used in battle for the first time and the Royal Air Force came into being.

In 1917 the USA entered the war on the side of the Allies. In 1918 Germany was forced to ask for an armistice, which was signed on 11 November 1918.

For the next twenty years Europe had a breathing space.

Great changes were taking place. New machinery and methods brought prosperity and improved conditions to the agricultural populations. The working classes benefited from shorter hours and the social insurances that were later to become the Welfare State.

Motor cars now became popular and traffic on the country's roads was heavy. In 1922 broadcasting started from Marconi House, and in 1926 Baird gave a demonstration of television. In 1927 the first 'talkie' film from America was shown.

Then in 1939 Germany invaded Poland and the Second World War began. This lasted for six years.

What will the future hold?

Soon, the scientists themselves will be frightened by the disturbing magic of science, like so many sorcerers' apprentices. Do you remember the story?

Once there was a master sorcerer who, thanks to his magic wand and spells, could make all the inanimate objects in his house do what he wanted. One word from him and they all got busy. The pail rolled under the tap which turned itself on, filled the pail and turned itself off again. The draught blew up the fire; the broom swept the room. The furniture arranged itself in the dining-room, and the crockery rather like a house in which a number of sorcerers' apprentices are trying out their spells.

Where is the world going? What promise does the future hold?

Each time that matter or the machine have tried to enslave man's mind and spirit, the intellectuals, the men of learning, the philosophers and artists have risen against the danger that was threatening to degrade man, to reduce him socially and morally. Courageously they have given battle.

Byron died at Missolonghi while helping Greece in her war of independence against Turkey. Fichte, the philosopher, headed a movement in the universities of Germany openly resisting Napoleon.

When he heard that Napoleon had had himself crowned emperor, Beethoven withdrew the dedication of his Third Symphony, which he had made to Napoleon Bonaparte when the latter's star seemed about to shed the light of a peaceful future over all Europe and the world.

The twentieth century has also produced

its generation of artists, despite the dreadful years of its two world wars.

What are we heading for? What will the future bring?

That is a question that has occupied man throughout the centuries.

We must have confidence in mankind, in the people of the future, and look forward with faith and sincerity.

127

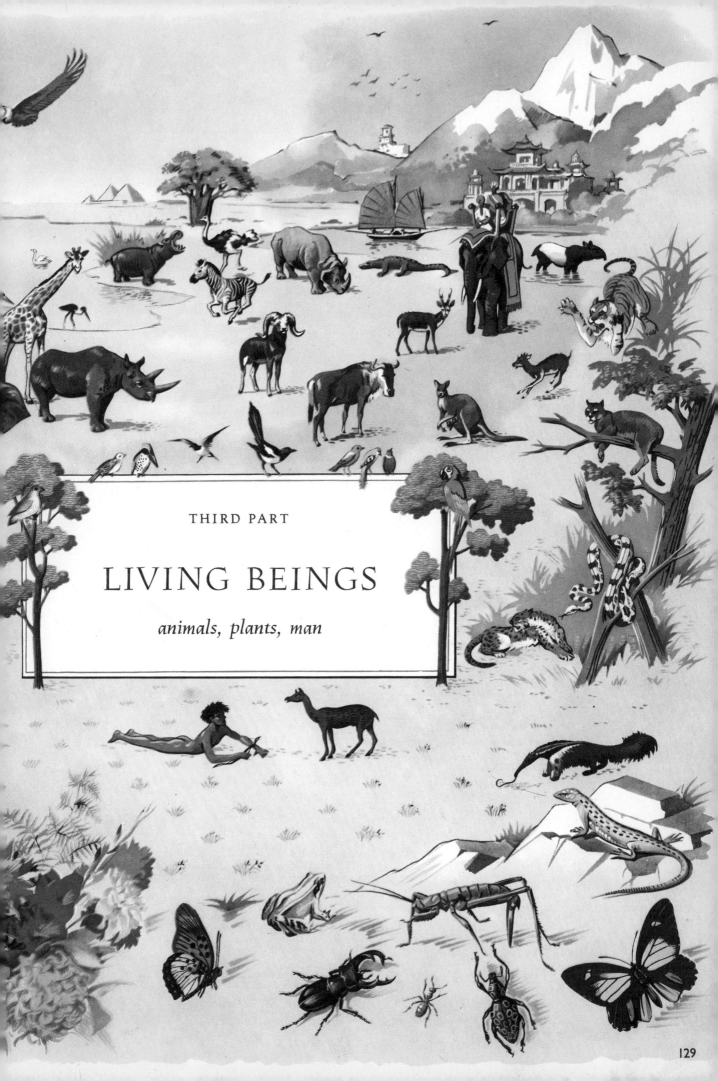

THIRD PART

LIVING BEINGS

animals, plants, man

OUR ANIMAL NEIGHBOURS

NATURE'S freaks are so many mysteries to us. At the time of the reptiles, in the warm, live mud of our Earth, everything was so mixed up — water, slime and air — that there was no great difference between that which flew, that which swam and that which crawled. It is possible that at that time Nature produced a sort of flying tortoise, though to-day we only know the land or marine varieties.

In the course of the centuries, Nature has made a selection of those animals in the making of which she has been successful.

There are many legends of sea monsters, those fabulous beings which, like the one at Loch Ness, have sometimes appeared in horrible guise, rising from the sea in the midst of a storm which had stirred the ocean's depths. Probably the great ocean depths still hide other survivors besides the famous coelacanth, but no fisherman will ever bring them up in his nets.

Why, then, do we call them 'survivors'? Why choose this name for the creatures which are in a way living fossils from prehistoric times? Because, in these days, it is amazing to find proof of the survival of species which, logically, Nature should have completely destroyed.

Logically, because she has always shown herself very intelligent and very ruthless in her methods. Gradually improving each new version, she has suppressed the failures among the animals which she had called into being. But one will never know why to this day she has preserved some ugly creatures whose brains are smaller than a nut and which are hardly more than rough drafts. These are rough sketches, the first crude drafts which Nature has never revised; or, at best, caricatures.

Does the sea-serpent exist? Sailors declare that they have seen them on the surface of all the seas in the world. No-one has captured one, much less photographed one. It is probably a creature of legend.

The dinosaurs consist of a large group linked with the crocodilians by their skull characteristics and the form of their vertebrae, and with birds by the strong development of their hindlimbs and their pelvis. This, say the scientists, would explain the existence of an intermediary type: the crocodile, whose direct ancestor is unknown.

OKAPI
and baby okapi

How are they survivors, these monsters dating back to the world's beginning which have survived up to our day? Because involuntarily one thinks of the continents as having suffered shipwreck, as having been muddy rafts that have ridden the floods of our planet, carrying, like so many Noah's arks, just these our 'survivors'.

The history of the living world of beasts and plants is amazingly like that of mankind. Like the primitive peoples which have never evolved, these 'rejects' of Nature are still met with in South Africa, in the wilds of America, and above all in Australia.

Specimens of some of these freaks are to be seen in the Zoos. This is so with the okapi, the mysterious, elusive animal, long known from the tales of the peoples of the Congo, that at last was captured alive. The okapi resembles both a beautiful antelope and a wild ass. It has striped hind quarters like a zebra. It is also a distant cousin of the giraffe, a sort of giraffe whose neck Nature has not bothered to stretch.

Amongst Nature's 'rejects' one finds everything, ranging from the degenerate descendants of the great monsters, the cayman, the rhinoceros, the gnu, the warthog, the peccary and the giraffe, to tiny animals like the mole and the guinea pig.

The ancients called the giraffe camelopardalis, or 'camel-leopard' because of the markings of its skin. Its actual name comes from the Arabic word zourafa. The giraffe is dumb, but its sight, hearing, sense of smell and intelligence are more developed than in many other animals. When it runs from danger, it moves faster than a galloping horse.

On land, underground and in the sea, where the jellyfish, a survivor, floats like a live umbrella with a funnel ending in a mouth, Nature has preserved to this day creatures whose ancestors can be found in the form of fossils enclosed in the deposits of the Secondary and Tertiary Eras.

The jellyfish that we find stranded on our beaches could fit on to a plate, but there is a giant jellyfish 10 feet in diameter which has fringed streamers 130 feet long.

The hippopotamus (from the Greek hippos, horse, and potamos, river) supports its bulk of 3 or 4 tons on legs 24 inches high. Its skin alone weighs 1,200 lb. Each of its canine teeth provides $7\frac{1}{2}$ lb of ivory as valuable as that of an elephant.

The first warm-blooded animals were quite different from present-day mammals. Some laid eggs, like the fabulous dinosaurs weighing 60 tons, which have been found in veritable graveyards in the Gobi desert. They were still nearly reptiles, but they were no longer cold-blooded.

The world's oldest species at the present are really living fossils which Nature abandoned millions of years ago, having lost interest in them. They have remained half-way between the saurians which lay eggs and the mammals which suckle their young. The two most curious specimens of this sort live in Australia. They are the duck-billed platypus, which has webbed feet and a duck's beak, and the echidna, a sort of hedgehog with a long beak, covered with armour like a porcupine — an animal with no teeth, but which has claws strong enough to break up the old tree trunks in which live the ants on which it feeds; then it only has to sweep the crevices of wood with its tongue which it can stretch out a long way. Exactly the same as an anteater, whose tongue secretes a sort of glue, on which all tiny creatures stick, so that the animal only has to swallow them.

These two prehistoric phenomena, the platypus and the echidna, lay eggs like a snake. They hatch these eggs not in a nest, but by putting them in a pouch under the skin of their bellies. And there the babies live, carried about by their mother, and suckle until they are old enough to jump out of their skin nest and frisk about on their own.

There are no anteaters in Australia. There are some in Africa, such as the aardvark with its donkey's ears, and some in Guiana, such as the great anteater which even the Indians fear. Thanks to its claws, which are as powerful and sharp as daggers, it can defend itself against the attack of a big leopard, whose belly it can slit up.

But, at the beginning of time, Nature amused herself playing with a thousand different creatures, and she was full of imagination. In the Canadian rivers she made beavers and muskrats, animal woodcutters able to fell birch trees and saw up their wood. With this these clever architects build towns for their winter quarters in the running streams. In Europe she made the dormouse, which sleeps all the winter like the marmot and looks like the flying squirrel. In the American continent she made another freak, one with a round face and the snub nose of a monkey, and this lives hanging from the branches of trees.

This is the sloth. So slothful that for all these generations none has bothered to right itself and to see the world any way but upside down. Clinging with its sickle-like claws, it hangs by its long hairy arms; in fact this sleepy animal is its own hammock and rocks itself to sleep.

The sloth is also an easy prey for all the wild animals in the jungle. Jaguars have only to jump up and hook one down to feed to their young; while pythons need only climb up a tree trunk and swallow one as it sleeps, hanging there like a ham or big plump fruit.

You know what one calls the marsupials — those strange creatures which live mostly in Australia and the females of which have a pouch under their belly in which to carry their young. This pouch also contains the teats. When they are born, the young cling to a teat with their mouths and never let go. The baby has not enough strength to be able to suck, so the mother squirts her milk down its throat from her teat. The largest of the marsupials is the giant kangaroo, the one which can be taught to box, with gloves, in a circus.

The opossum, which is an American species, belongs to this family. Stretching out her long, flexible tail to

The sloth sleeps nineteen hours a day. It moves at the rate of just over one mile an hour in a tree. In the same time on the ground it will cover 800 feet.

which the little opossums fasten on with theirs, the mother opossum climbs trees with all her brood on her back. And there are also the 'parachutist' marsupials, the flying phalangers. Then there is the koala which resembles a plush teddy bear. It has tiny teeth with which it rips off the little green flowers among the leaves of eucalyptuses. All these marsupials, with the exception of the opossum, live in Australia, Tasmania and New Guinea.

The armadillo of America, with its armour, is undoubtedly one of the first mammals to have appeared on earth. The Indians there roast it in its shell, which acts as a plate. When empty the shell serves as a basket, or a sounding box for their musical instruments, when it is fitted with a neck and has strings stretched over it like a guitar.

In Africa and Asia, there is another such knight in armour. This is the pangolin. He wears a real coat of mail, made of scales, which fits from the helmet protecting his lizard's nose to the tip of his tail.

And, speaking of lizards, we must remember that Nature has made some pretty horrible little monsters:

The largest of the pangolins, which lives in tropical Africa, reaches a length of 6 feet.

The great anteater – 8 feet long – lives in tropical and central America.

The aardvark looks rather piglike, it has a rabbit's snout, ass's ears and a sticky tongue like an anteater's. None of this prevents it from being a distinct animal.

In Australia the platypus is also known as a 'duck-bill' and 'Australian beaver'.

This terrestrial iron-clad is not a tank but an armadillo. This animal, of the group called 'edentates', can have up to a hundred teeth to chew the insects on which it feeds.

Koalas are the charming Teddy Bears of the Australian forests.

The male kangaroo weighs anything up to 250 lb and can make jumps of 45–50 feet.

The tapir is gentle and timid. The puma cruelly kills it just for the pleasure of killing. Unfortunately both live in the same regions.

the Thorny Devil of Australia that bristles with spines, the Frilled Lizard and the Flying Lizard of Asia.

In Peru lives the tapir. It goes in herds like the African wart-hog and, like it, digs in the mud with its pig-like nose, the end of which is shaped like a trunk. With this it digs up roots, but always one of the herd keeps watch, ready to give the alarm at the first sign of a puma.

With the tapir, Nature has really let herself go. She has begun by stretching its nose, as if she wanted to turn an ugly pig into a miniature elephant. Then she has enlarged its feet, like those of a rhinoceros or hippopotamus, and she has given it four toes on its front feet, and only three on the hind feet. Finally, she has fitted its mouth with a beautiful set of forty teeth — as many as the horse.

This monster is not a dragon but a harmless bearded lizard which lives on ants.

The flying fox wraps its wings round it like a cloak and sleeps suspended by its toes.

When night falls in the elephants' jungle the flying foxes that hang from the trees call to each other with thousands of little cries like the tinkling of bells.

These flying foxes, like the vampires of Africa, which gorge themselves with the blood of sleeping animals, belong to a large family of bats, an astonishing tribe of flying mammals.

In the course of time the bat has been endowed by Nature with radar, which man only discovered some years ago, and which was used during the war for locating aeroplanes that were not visible to the human eye. The bat utters such high-pitched cries that the human ear cannot hear them. These sound waves strike any obstacles, rebound and come back as echoes; these are picked up in return by the animal, allowing the 'flying witch', as it is called in many countries, to detect the presence of the smallest obstacle that may be situated in its line of flight, a branch as easily as a spider's thread.

And its 'wings'! Have you ever noticed the fine skin of the webs on a duck's webbed feet? On each side of it, the flying witch has a similar sort of membrane, between the three long, thin fingers of its hand, its hind foot and tail, rather like the sails of a ship stretched between the yards.

In the Antilles, and especially in Asia, there are giant bats. Some of these grow to the size of a fox-cub, and their heads look strangely like one, which is why they have been called 'flying foxes'.

There are also bats of the sea, for that is what two sorts of fish have been called. One is the squill, an enormous ray which has a spread of 26 feet and weighs 3 tons. It often leaps out of the water and, if there happens to be a boat nearby, it can capsize it. The other is the true 'bat of the sea', an aquatic phenomenon with toad's feet which haunts the waters where the hog-fish and the angler-fish are found.

The angler-fish has a mast on its spine and another at its prow — I should say on its nose. Actually these are fine, flexible fishing rods and they are hung with sort of shreds of flesh which serve as bait. Thus the angler-fish fishes by trawling, putting out its lines in the shoals of hake to attract the small fry. These lines have no hooks, but when its prey comes milling round them, the angler-fish has only to swallow them.

Among the strange creatures which inhabit the waters of the seas and rivers are ones no less extraordinary than those which populate the bush and jungle. In hot countries there lives a very small fish, the periophthalmus, which one might call the lazybones of brackish waters. It is amphibious: it breathes equally well in the air as in the water. To have a rest from swimming, it comes out and climbs up the twisted red roots of the mangroves growing out of the mud. It climbs higher than the oyster beds, for oysters also cling to the tufted growth of these aerial roots. Hanging by its tail and fins, our lazybones takes a sleep, rocked by the river which flows beneath it. In the dry season, this fish digs itself into the cracked mud of the channels and sleeps until the rainy season returns and fills the pools again.

It is not the only one of its species to have in its gills ramifications able to function like lungs and allow it to breathe on the surface. Its distant cousins, the catfish of Africa, called *claria*, also have this advantage. They are called catfish in the Sudan because of their long whiskers.

RAYS

Men equip themselves with frog-feet and glass masks to be able to watch the shoals of small fish as they dart and zigzag in the green light of underwater caves. But imagine their amazement when for the first time they see an immense ray coming towards them flapping its huge, flexible wings like a bird of the deep.

I have seen some of these catfish there. At night they pull themselves out of the soft mud or out of a sort of burrow and go to eat insects on the bank.

But yet it is in our own part of the world, in the lakes of Central Europe, that the biggest catfish weighing up to 450 pounds are to be found. Such large carnivorous fish will sometimes eat small birds.

Among the small fry in the muddy waters of hot countries there is a fish — neither flower of many colours nor bird of paradise — whose fins, or wings or petals, unfold in the water like a gauze dress. This wonder, the fighting fish, also rises to breathe on the surface from time to time. Then it dives, releasing a little ball of air. If it were prevented from getting fresh air to breathe, it would die of suffocation. In other words, here is a fish that can drown!

We have seen how among Nature's survivors there are, on land, egg-laying mammals; in the air, flying mammals; and in the sea . . .

The huge family of cetaceans, which live in the seas, show the different stages at which Nature has sent the experimental types which she had previously accustomed to live on land into the sea, there to live a marine existence. Baleen whales, finbacks, cachalots, porpoises and dolphins all have common ancestors. They are also first cousins of tapirs, horses and giraffes. The seven vertebrae in the giraffe's immense neck can be found, reduced to a length of two inches, in the whale, whose neck is set in its shoulders.

PROTOPTERUS

PARUPENEUS BARBERINUS

TETRODON or GLOBEFISH

GREAT SILURUS, or CATFISH

SEA HORSE

FIGHTING FISH

HAMMERHEAD

GURNARD, or SCORPION-FISH

COFFER-FISH

PTEROIS

thrust. Now! The man drove the long iron harpoon into the giant shoulder with all his strength. Strike! As the whaling song says:

> The whale was struck
> And the line paid out,
> And he gave a
>   flurry with his tail...

The wounded animal dived as it fled, and the rope reeled out at a terrifying speed. A sailor had to damp it as the lengths flew out so that the wood did not catch fire as it rubbed against the edge of the boat. When all the rope had gone out and only the end was left, strained to breaking point but fastened to the bows of the boat, they let themselves be towed along in the wake of the whale. When the monster was finally exhausted they drew close and again attacked with their harpoons. Finally the enormous hulk lay still in the sea, which was dyed red with its blood, and the whalers could tow their fantastic prize back to the ship, where it would be cut up.

These land mammals were not all launched at once. First of all the whales had to take to the sea. Then, much later, seals, walruses and sea-lions — the same acrobats who balance balloons on their noses in the circus — left land for the sea and the ice-floes.

Those animals which live in the polar seas will still take thousands of years to adapt themselves completely to marine surroundings. Once they were quadrupeds on land, and now they have flippers where their hind-legs used to be. But there no longer remains any trace of these hind-limbs on the smooth body of a whale. The whale's fins, which were formerly its arms, no longer help it to swim — they are just stabilizers, out-riggers which steady the monster's course. All the cetaceans, and whales especially, are wonderfully adapted to their element after living thousands of years in the seas. They are as streamlined as submarines. And their powerful tail propels them like a great oar.

Stirring tales have been written about the times before the harpoon-gun was invented, when the whalers sailed their three-masted barques to the ice-packs in the northern seas. The look-out man would shout from his perch in the crow's-nest the call which threw the whole crew into feverish activity, from the captain to the ship's boy: 'Thar she blows!'

Quickly they let the whaling boats down on winches and rowed hard after the whale. The monster dived, then appeared again in the trough of the waves, blowing out the jet of water which had betrayed its presence to the look-out in the crow's-nest.

The small fragile boats rocked about on the waves, but the oarsmen pulled them strongly towards the monster. The harpooner, with his iron spear in his hand, braced himself in the bows beside the rope, 300 yards of which lay coiled in the bottom of the boat. He waited to see the gleam of the whale's little eye before he

The giant of the seas is the finback, the fabulous blue whale, 90 feet long and weighing more than 100 tons — as much as a regiment of 1,500 men! It is the biggest living animal in the world.

The heart inside this gigantic mass is as big as an ox. And the blood circulating in its enormous veins weighs from 8 to 10 tons. This is as much as a family of African elephants would weigh, consisting of both parents and two babies.

Nowadays, whaling has become a real industry. It has floating factories, ships of 25,000 tons, costing a million pounds or more, and these go to the grounds escorted by a dozen whaling boats or 'catchers', equipped with harpoon-guns. In good years the 200 catchers of the whaling fleets that come from ports all over the world from Norway to Japan have harpooned and accounted for 30,000 whales.

●

If one could make a voyage to the bottom of the sea, what unexpected meetings one would have! The porpoise with his humped back rolls through the waves and is regarded as a friend and mascot by sailors all over the world. The graceful dolphin moves like an arrow through the water and has a white belly and blue back. It has given its name to the French province of Dauphiné and also figures in the arms of the French princes. The narwhal has a sword, like the sword-fish. It is rather like a unicorn of the sea and with its sword on its forehead is just as fantastic a creature as the unicorn which is part of the Royal Arms.

No book contains all the secrets of Nature's infinite imagination.

And now, what on earth is this extraordinary creature with a crocodile's tail and a horse's head?

It is the tiny sea horse, which swims upright looking like a strange question mark as though wondering what Nature meant by making it like that.

Perhaps the most extraordinary of all aquatic freaks is the strange 'radar fish' which can be seen in some aquariums.

These fish have been caught in dark caves beneath tropical rivers, and being accustomed to total darkness they have ceased to need any eyes and have become quite blind.

In an aquarium, as in the African caves, the fish makes its way over the small stones at the bottom of its tank by the same means as a bat, by radar.

Still more extraordinary is what happens to this radar fish if its glass cage is brilliantly lit with electric light, so that it is no longer in darkness. Once it has been given light, it simply grows an eye. Just one! An optic nerve develops in the middle of its forehead and an eye takes shape. In a year or two the fish can guide itself with this entirely new eye and without the help of its radar.

This reminds one of the armoured fish of ancient times with an eye in the middle of its head, the famous coelacanth, which was recently caught off the Comoro Islands, and whose ancestors lived millions of years ago at the time of the diplodocus . . . One is also reminded of those other fish which long, long ago grew reptile's feet to enable them to come out of the sea, and lungs and a nose to allow them to breathe on land, and of those extraordinary animals, survivors of a dim and distant past, which are caricatures of the monsters of earth's early ages, and one wonders what could have been the point of the third reptilian eye, traces of which are still to be found behind the forehead in humans.

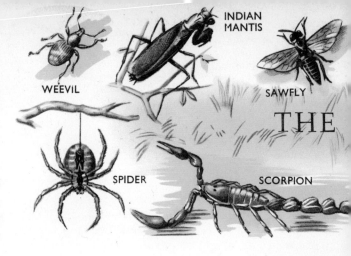

WEEVIL
INDIAN MANTIS
SAWFLY
SPIDER
SCORPION

THE

IT is hard to imagine what the world seems like to a ladybird, or a mayfly which only lives for a day. To an ant, the smallest tuft of grass must seem like a virgin forest. The tunnel hollowed out by a death-watch beetle or a woodworm in the arm of an old chair must seem to them like the dark gallery of a mine deep underground.

And all at once the world, which appears large enough to us, becomes immense by comparison. We sense the presence of this infinite multitude of tiny creatures, the crawling myriads of tiny ants, though we may have observed only one — one which climbed on to our hand, scaling it like a mountain.

How much do we know about insects? Not very much.

There are still many secrets about them known only to the flowers, the swallow, the titmouse and the wood-pecker . . .

Without doubt the insect world is the most secret and mysterious and also the best organized amongst the various families Nature has created. Insects have taken plenty of time to distribute themselves about the earth that they inhabited millions of years ago, long before man. They have founded great empires and provided themselves with laws; they have built cities and learnt to farm as well as to make war. And with their disciplined, united communities they have become dangerous enemies to man.

If one believes the teachings of Mahomet, Nature is so wise that she has worked out the exact number of eggs that a female locust lays and of which it hatches about a thousand during its short life. For the Koran says that if that locust should lay just one more egg, the world would be stripped bare and could no longer support life. The spate of insects would eat down to the roots all the vegetation in the world.

How many species are there in the whole animal kingdom? Millions! There are perhaps five million different species, and four million of them are insects!

They multiply very rapidly. Their lives are brief, but they reproduce themselves with frightening rapidity. In the spring one can sometimes see a huge hatching of mayflies over a river. They rise from the water in a winged cloud, then death comes to them as swiftly as life, and they fall like snow in millions of lifeless flakes.

The leaf and root eaters

ONE cannot turn over a square inch of earth anywhere in the world without seeing some insects crawling. They occupy the entire planet, crawling, burrowing, hollowing and nibbling. Some take flight and, as the Arabs says, are carried by 'the red wind': these are locusts, the most voracious of all leaf-eaters.

It is not the wind that is red, but the countryside on which the flight of migratory locusts alights. They move in a cloud which is like a tornado and obscures the sky. A plain in Morocco or Algeria which may have been a beautiful vivid green is suddenly blotted out. Trees, stripped down to the bark, are left standing, like skeletons. The sticky mass of destructive locusts flows on like a tide of red lava, in which one may sink ankle deep.

So much for the clouds of adult locusts which fly. But these gluttons pass through other stages of life: first as crawling grubs, then creeping flies and finally as the jumping locusts. They move in formation, like ants, and flow on in a veritable torrent, devouring all in their path. Colonies of young locusts have been seen crossing a railway line and holding up a train, the wheels of the engine being unable to get a grip on the rails.

In 1867, an invasion of locusts devastated whole districts in Algeria and brought famine and death to nearly 500,000 people. And the tide of locusts which once swamped Numidia is still spoken of as a disaster after two thousand years.

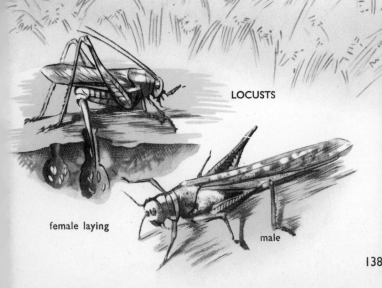

LOCUSTS

female laying

male

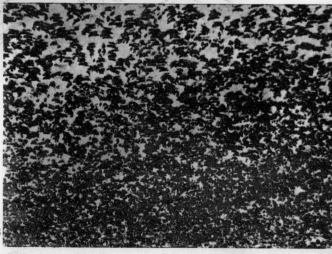

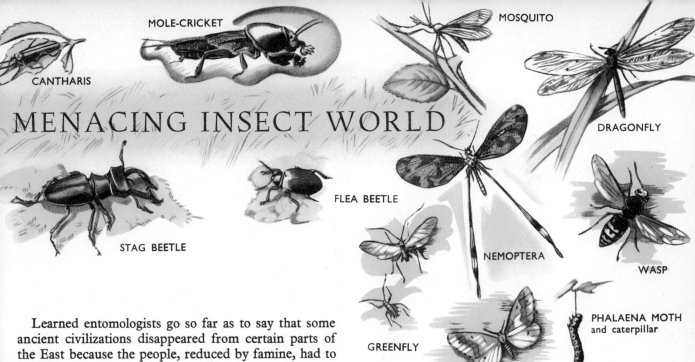

MOLE-CRICKET

CANTHARIS

MOSQUITO

DRAGONFLY

MENACING INSECT WORLD

FLEA BEETLE

STAG BEETLE

NEMOPTERA

WASP

PHALAENA MOTH
and caterpillar

GREENFLY

Learned entomologists go so far as to say that some ancient civilizations disappeared from certain parts of the East because the people, reduced by famine, had to abandon their lands to the locusts, just as immense populations were wiped off the map by the horsemen of Genghis Khan and his Mongol hordes.

In the heart of Africa, locusts assemble all along the margins of streams which flow into the great rivers, and then, obeying a secret word of command, embark in dense clouds on one of their pilgrimages, which at the rate of 100 miles a day will take them in a month 3,000 miles from their point of departure. And nothing can stop them from alighting and destroying.

All over the world war is being waged against these terrible invasions. In the Argentine 20,000 miles of barricades can be erected in a matter of days to stem the devastating flood at the first alarm. In some districts they use flame-throwers. In 1890 they dug 1,250 miles of barricades and trenches in Algeria and the seething

COCKCHAFER
and its larva

mass of locusts piled up in the trenches, where millions of the insects were suffocated.

Cockchafers, or 'Maybugs', as they are quaintly named in country districts, make their flight on fine spring evenings. These insects do not undertake long voyages in the same way as locusts. They are content to feed on the neighbouring farmlands and woods. They live no longer than a month at the most, so they gobble

up their food quickly, as if knowing that their days are numbered.

Before dying, the cockchafer burrows into the soil to make the tunnel where it will lay its small, white eggs, which will hatch the following summer. And there, in the underground darkness, the cockchafer begins its transformation. The grub which hatches out of the egg has no eyes and can only wriggle. While waiting for its legs to grow it burrows and burrows, and during these months it devours every small root within reach. At the beginning of winter it goes deeper into the earth to sleep until the spring re-awakens it. And then the cockchafer's larva comes to the surface to fatten, which it does for two years, increasing in size and weight all the time. Each winter it returns deeper and deeper into the soil to prepare itself for the cold weather. And there the big white grub waits to be turned into the adult insect that has wings and is capable of flight. The chrysalis wraps itself up in its cocoon where these changes occur. Nature is a good fairy to this chrysalis: she gives it golden wings, the colour of the spring sunshine which awakens it one fine evening when it begins to fly and sing, or rather drone its song. It will have a whole month in which to plunder the fields of lucerne.

PHYLLOXERA

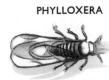

Another plague, this time to the vine-growing countries, was first brought from America. It was imported into France with some plants in 1866 and all the French vineyards were affected. In some districts all the vines had to be pulled up and only those on the slopes of the fine champagne districts of Cognac remained unaffected.

This was the phylloxera.

The Arabs have found a way of getting rid of some of the locusts which alight on their land. They eat them. They cook them in many different ways: boiled, roast, and grilled – when apparently they have a taste like almonds – and also salted, dried and made into a paste. Moses allowed the Hebrews to eat four kinds of locust, described in Leviticus, and we know that John the Baptist in the desert lived on locusts and wild honey.

In ten years this harmful, sap-sucking insect invaded all the South of France. Perhaps it felt out of its element among the French vines, for it has certainly changed and simplified its way of life. Formerly, in America, the phylloxera family had a female for each season — four different types of female! The spring ones ate the vine shoots. The summer ones caused tumours to grow on the roots where they installed themselves, and this killed the vine-stock. Then came the autumn females; these had wings and laid eggs from which hatched others, the winter ones which laid their eggs among the roots, and from these hatched the young females of the next season, the spring.

Whether it is due to the change of climate or to a whim of Nature, the phylloxera has changed its complicated ways of reproduction since coming to Europe. It has not kept the four different types of female in its family, but only one — and that the one most dangerous to the vine, the one which attacks the roots.

To check this plague which was destroying all the vineyards, the French grafted their vines on to American plants, which are resistant to the phylloxera.

COLORADO BEETLE

What we must do next is to discover a plant resistant to the Colorado beetle on to which the potato could be grafted.

The first of these insects arrived in Europe about 1876. They first appeared at Bremen, Liverpool and Rotterdam. Their progress was swift and they travelled about 200 miles a year, soon invading all Germany and England. France was spared until 1922, when the Colorado beetle suddenly appeared in the south-west; by 1935 it had reached the Belgian frontier. The Visigoths had been no swifter in their invasion from the opposite direction!

One would think that mountains would be an obstacle that would stop this invader, but the army of beetles can rise in the air, lifted by ascending warm currents that have carried them over mountains. Some stragglers have been collected at a height of more than 6,000 feet.

The Colorado beetle has already crossed the Alps; it only needs favourable winds for it to cross the Pyrenees.

All these little beasts came from America, which also sent us the 'San José louse' and the Argentine ant. But we presented them with the Hessian fly, a glutton which attacks corn or maize with equal greed, so it is only tit-for-tat.

We must resign ourselves to it, for it is unfortunately part of the exchanges between countries. All these insects are diligently hunted, but no ship's captain can possibly track down all the stowaways that hide themselves at the bottom of his holds. In banana boats tiny snakes and yellow scorpions coil up in the bunches of fruit.

And in Honolulu, where once mosquitoes were unknown, they joke about the ones which arrived to colonize them at the same time as the missionaries.

CATERPILLAR
of the Cabbage
White butterfly

One cannot end without mentioning the thousands of gnawing caterpillars which spin a cocoon in which the chrysalis forms that eventually turns into some marvellous butterfly.

One finds that Nature nearly always begins her transformation play with a ballet of winged flowers, or rather of beautiful butterflies.

In May you sometimes see what look like white petals from apple and cherry blossom drifting across a field or kitchen garden, but it is probably a swarm of cabbage white butterflies. They are graceful and airy, but they plunder and gorge themselves on the juices of flowers. Each female hovers for an instant near a large green leaf on which she sticks her string of eggs. In less than fifteen days these eggs hatch out into minute, greenish caterpillars which start to climb and nibble the leaves which served them as a cradle. In a cabbage field where they have gorged themselves nothing is left but the stumps and veins of the leaves, in the same way as nothing but the skeletons of trees are left standing in countries which are devastated by locusts.

And what a hurry these greedy caterpillars are in! Nature only allows them three weeks to feed before forcing them to retire for the same length of time, when they hang in the folds of their fine silken slings to turn into chrysalises. And at the beginning of the autumn

MORPHO CYPRIS
(Colombia)

CHARAXES DILITUS
(East Africa)

CYMOTHOE SANGARIO
(West Africa)

CALIGO URANUS
(Honduras)

AMBLYPODIA
CURROLPHUS-
ADONIAS (Java)

EUSELASIA UTICA
(Brazil)

HELICONIUS
(Peru)

TIMELOEA MACULATA
(Formosa)

PAPILIO
ULYSSES-OXYARTES
(Aru Islands)

ORNITHOPTERA VANDEPOLLI
(Java)

they will be flitting about as new white butterflies and laying eggs in their turn.

Nature nearly always chooses the hollow silk nest of a cocoon for a chrysalis to grow and turn into a winged insect. Luckily they are not all as deadly as the cabbage white, and some are very useful.

The most unfortunate of all the short-lived butterflies is undoubtedly the silkworm moth, whose eggs produce the caterpillars that we call silkworms. This unshapely moth has no mouth and its wings are so cumbersome that it is unable to fly. When it is time for it to leave the cocoon, the poor thing becomes exhausted with producing saliva to unstick the thread which holds it prisoner and it crawls off laboriously, scarcely better able to walk than to fly.

The wretched mate that this female moth meets is, like herself, already tired of life. And while her mate slowly dies, the female with sudden speed hurries to stick together the 500 eggs which it lays and which make up the 'graines'. This is what the eggs are called in the rearing houses where silkworms are used — and where the short-lived insect lays its eggs in little discs on the mulberry leaves.

A very small handful of this graine, which the breeders hatch out at a gentle temperature, produces 100,000 silkworms which will devour from 10,000 to 13,000 pounds of mulberry leaves before becoming adults. This is equal in weight to the daily ration of grass and leaves of a family of elephants.

This insatiable caterpillar has an amazing capacity. Day and night for a whole month it never stops eating the mulberry leaves the breeders pick for it. But this intake of food certainly suits it, for at the end of 30 days it reaches a length of about 4 inches — a hundred times what it measured at birth. And its weight increases 10,000 times — that is not a misprint, there are no noughts too many — 10,000 times the weight that it was when it hatched from the egg!

An elephant's growth, compared to that of this caterpillar, seems to be no more than that of a humble microbe. If the elephant developed at the same rate as the silkworm, it would be more than twice the height of the Empire State Building at the end of a hundred years!

But let us go back to this worm whose life as a crawling caterpillar is drawing to a close. Suddenly it stops eating and, clinging to a twig, throws its head about to and fro just like a weaver's shuttle. It is spinning the thread for the cocoon which will surround it. In this way it reels out from 1,000 to 1,500 yards of thread in a few days. The thread is almost liquid when it comes out of the salivary glands and is spat out in jets of silk from minute spinnerets in the caterpillar's mouth. This is the silk which is eventually woven into ribbons and expensive materials.

Man has not invented anything new. The mechanical spinners which manufacture artificial silk are no improvement on the silkworm's spinnerets. Like the thread of this insect's cocoon a semi-liquid paste is squirted out from holes in the machine in a fine floss which congeals at once to give skeins of nylon thread.

The spider, which is a distant relative of these insects, also spins by means of spinnerets, which are situated beneath her abdomen.

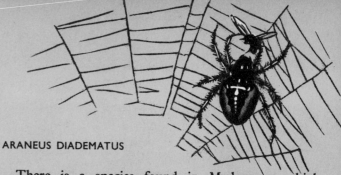

ARANEUS DIADEMATUS

There is a species found in Madagascar which produces a rare and very much sought-after silk. And another enormous spider with a blue belly and hairy legs seems to spin the thread of Destiny for the witch doctors of the Ivory Coast. In the black sorcerer's cabin one can see this little tame monster descend from the thatched roof at the end of its thread. The giant spider knows the sound of its master's voice perfectly well; it comes down at his call and, hanging by its thread, will eat from the man's fingers.

The wood-eaters

IN the forests, where wind and birds sing, there are thousands of little sounds that our ear cannot hear, being muffled by the bark of the trees about which the green woodpecker climbs. The woodpecker, on its daily inspection of its domain, is very familiar with these noises, the scraping sounds of larvae boring through wood. The woodpecker hits the bark with its beak to make the larva come out from the gallery it has been digging into the heart of the trunk. For, before going to sleep for its metamorphosis, the larva has taken its precautions, remembering the insect it is going to become, whether a big capricorn beetle or a fine stag beetle with mandibles sharpened like a lobster's claws. Such an insect, hampered by its carapace, wings and feet, would never be able to reach the end of such a narrow gallery, not being able to move like a worm; so the larva, head turned to the opening, drags itself up to the mouth of its lair before letting itself fall into its miraculous sleep.

Tap, tap! The woodpecker strikes the bark repeatedly, beats a regular tattoo on it, drilling through the bark and the wood with its beak that is as sharp as a bradawl, putting out its tongue that is sticky like that of an anteater and also equipped with hooks that enable it to dislodge the grub it wants to eat.

The wood-gnawers attack both live trees and felled ones, logs, planks and furniture, which they riddle with thousands of 'worm holes'. You can tell old furniture by its shape, its patina and by the numbers of little holes with which the wood is pitted. When he wishes to make imitation old out of new, to make the tiny round galleries that the death-watch beetle or pea-beetle would have taken a hundred years to drill, the 'faker' fires a cartridge of small shot from a shot-gun and riddles the wood that is to restore or make an imitation antique.

But it is in Africa that the wood-eaters really come into their own. That continent is mined like a gigantic termitary, and the bush is studded with little hills of red or grey clay of the queerest architecture varying with the whims of the builder termites. You see them shaped like mushrooms or large umbrellas, like crenellated mountain peaks or palaces out of some fairy-tale; like miniature castles resembling the soukalas of the Lobi or the palaces of Timbuctu.

People have calculated roughly the weight of earth in these cyclopean structures with giant domes that shelter the cities of the termites of the Congo and Central Africa. The surrounding wall of such a subterranean city is twenty inches thick. It is made with the saliva of the insects to cement it and weighs more than twenty tons. It is difficult to imagine the amount of work the insects have put into these gigantic structures, building them one grain of sand at a time.

Compared with these castles of red earth the skyscrapers of New York or the pyramids of Egypt are like mole-hills. For if man were to make the dimensions of his houses proportional to those the termites have used in their termitaries, he would have to build corridors wider than Hyde Park Corner and rooms large enough to hold the Albert Hall, while the whole would be the size of a high mountain.

The termites work secretly. You never suspect that they are at work eating all the woodwork in your house: beams, planks, rafters. They work inside, leaving only an outer layer of wood as thin as a piece of paper. One knock with a broom and you crush it: the wood is quite hollow.

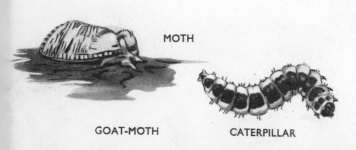

MOTH

GOAT-MOTH   CATERPILLAR

142

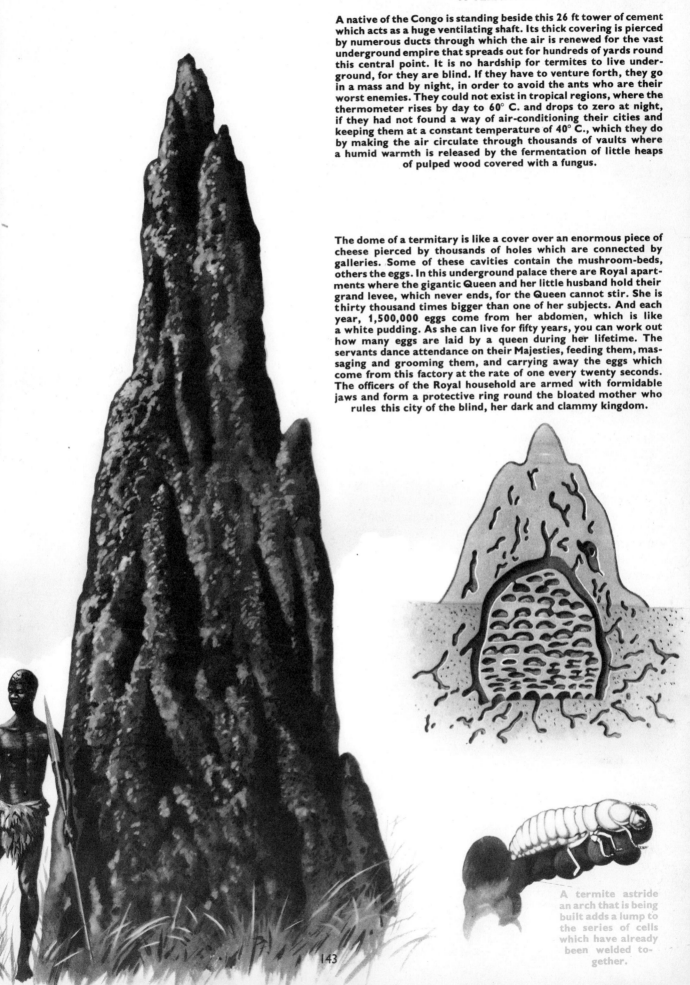

A native of the Congo is standing beside this 26 ft tower of cement which acts as a huge ventilating shaft. Its thick covering is pierced by numerous ducts through which the air is renewed for the vast underground empire that spreads out for hundreds of yards round this central point. It is no hardship for termites to live underground, for they are blind. If they have to venture forth, they go in a mass and by night, in order to avoid the ants who are their worst enemies. They could not exist in tropical regions, where the thermometer rises by day to 60° C. and drops to zero at night, if they had not found a way of air-conditioning their cities and keeping them at a constant temperature of 40° C., which they do by making the air circulate through thousands of vaults where a humid warmth is released by the fermentation of little heaps of pulped wood covered with a fungus.

The dome of a termitary is like a cover over an enormous piece of cheese pierced by thousands of holes which are connected by galleries. Some of these cavities contain the mushroom-beds, others the eggs. In this underground palace there are Royal apartments where the gigantic Queen and her little husband hold their grand levee, which never ends, for the Queen cannot stir. She is thirty thousand times bigger than one of her subjects. And each year, 1,500,000 eggs come from her abdomen, which is like a white pudding. As she can live for fifty years, you can work out how many eggs are laid by a queen during her lifetime. The servants dance attendance on their Majesties, feeding them, massaging and grooming them, and carrying away the eggs which come from this factory at the rate of one every twenty seconds. The officers of the Royal household are armed with formidable jaws and form a protective ring round the bloated mother who rules this city of the blind, her dark and clammy kingdom.

A termite astride an arch that is being built adds a lump to the series of cells which have already been welded together.

143

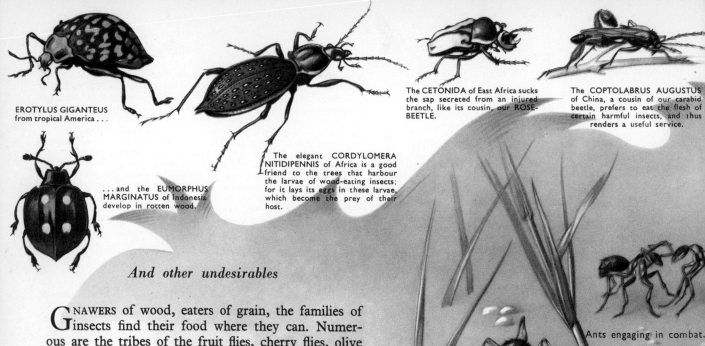

EROTYLUS GIGANTEUS
from tropical America . . .

. . . and the EUMORPHUS
MARGINATUS of Indonesia
develop in rotten wood.

The elegant CORDYLOMERA
NITIDIPENNIS of Africa is a good
friend to the trees that harbour
the larvae of wood-eating insects;
for it lays its eggs in these larvae,
which become the prey of their
host.

The CETONIDA of East Africa sucks
the sap secreted from an injured
branch, like its cousin, our ROSE-
BEETLE.

The COPTOLABRUS AUGUSTUS
of China, a cousin of our carabid
beetle, prefers to eat the flesh of
certain harmful insects, and thus
renders a useful service.

Ants engaging in combat.

Ant with one an-
tenna cut away.

And other undesirables

GNAWERS of wood, eaters of grain, the families of
insects find their food where they can. Numerous are the tribes of the fruit flies, cherry flies, olive
flies, moths like the codling moth, whose egg is laid in
the very heart of the flower.

Then there is the weevil which perforates fresh fruit
as though with a gimlet, piercing acorn, chestnut and
even the hard shell of a hazel-nut.

There is the clothes moth which eats fabrics, furs and
carpets.

And then there are all the cochineals, the cicindelidae,
the plant lice, and all the plant fleas and bugs. These
have cousins, graceful creatures that song and fairy-tale
have presented as rustic poets: firstly, the cicada which
plays in the hot sunshine; and then the ladybird which
has tiny confetti on its wings. Who would ever think
that the innocent ladybird belongs to the fiercest of the
insect tribes? It indulges in horrible massacres of caterpillars and greenfly. In fact, in Australia they breed
ladybirds to loose during the orange and lemon seasons
in flying packs that attack other pests.

The winged insect world is one of plunderers, from
the fly to the wasp, from the wasp to the bee. Half-
opened flowers await the delicate feet that will press on
their corollae and deposit at the bottom of their calyx
pollen taken from another flower. It is life or death they
bring, these travelling swarms, one fertilizing flowers,
another causing havoc among herds as does the anthrax
fly, whose ravages were incalculable until Pasteur discovered the vaccine.

The green shade of the forests of Africa is the realm
of the tsetse fly, the fly that implants the virus of that
terrible disease, sleeping sickness. Many are the species
of insect that hatch in the mire near the stagnant waters
of the African marshes: one of them is the anopheles

As soon as it settles — as the natives of Central and South Africa
well know — the TSETSE FLY
(Glossina) crosses its wings on its
back, which the house fly does not
do. A vigilant eye will spot this,
and one blow can put an end to
its menace.

which transmits malaria; another the yellow-fever
mosquito, one prick from which was enough to infect
a person with the 'black vomit', until the discovery of the
immunizing vaccine.

The insects have set out to conquer the world, and
already certain areas belong to them. The mosquito,
which can acclimatize itself everywhere and stands up to
both heat and cold, is not only ruler of the tropical
jungles, but has extended its domains to the tundras of
the Far North, where it appears with the summer. In
greedy, tormenting hordes it harries the Lapps and their
herds of reindeer.

There are more than fifteen hundred species of lice —
just lice, not counting fleas, bugs and the jiggers that
make their nests in the flesh of people's toes, or the
vermin that eat leather, the skins of animals and the
down of birds, sucking the blood of those victims in
whose fleece they live.

Lice by biting people, can give them such dread
diseases as recurrent fever and typhus. It is only a short
time since a vaccine capable of protecting people from
typhus was first discovered. In the same way as ladybirds are bred, the medical institutes of the East now
keep lice in folds. These folds are little fenced enclosures
set on bare pastures. What pastures? The arms and
thighs of poor Chinese who have had typhus and been
cured and are thus immune. They are paid well and give
their blood to feed the lice, which, after being scientifically treated, are used to prepare the vaccine that now
is saving thousands and thousands of lives.

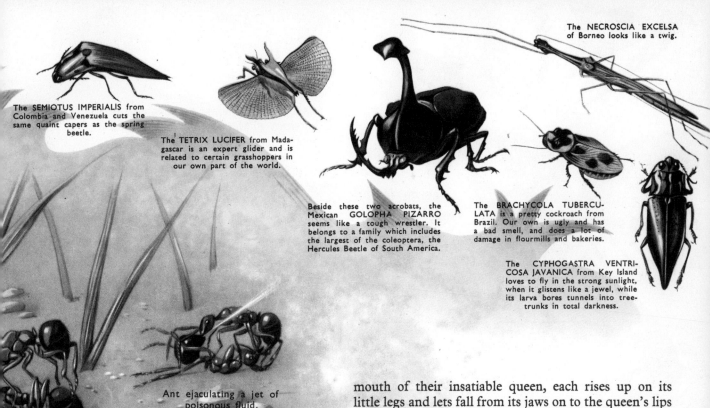

The SEMIOTUS IMPERIALIS from Colombia and Venezuela cuts the same quaint capers as the spring beetle.

The TETRIX LUCIFER from Madagascar is an expert glider and is related to certain grasshoppers in our own part of the world.

The NECROSCIA EXCELSA of Borneo looks like a twig.

Beside these two acrobats, the Mexican GOLOPHA PIZARRO seems like a tough wrestler. It belongs to a family which includes the largest of the coleoptera, the Hercules Beetle of South America.

The BRACHYCOLA TUBERCULATA is a pretty cockroach from Brazil. Our own is ugly and has a bad smell, and does a lot of damage in flourmills and bakeries.

The CYPHOGASTRA VENTRICOSA JAVANICA from Key Island loves to fly in the strong sunlight, when it glistens like a jewel, while its larva bores tunnels into treetrunks in total darkness.

Ant ejaculating a jet of poisonous fluid.

...beheading its adversary.

The dangers of numbers

THE fecundity of insects is staggering. One tiny fly in its short life lays more than 700,000 eggs. The silkworm moth does not lay more than 500 eggs, but the wasp can manage as many as 30,000 and a queen bee up to 2,000,000. Fortunately for us the louse only lays a dozen eggs.

Let us venture a peep into the secret city of the termites where a giant couple, the king and queen, rule the innumerable population of a lilliputian realm.

In the heart of the palace, in the royal apartment, the guard is being changed. The soldiers, in a ring round their queen, standing motionless as statues, now present arms to the relieving guard. Entering, this deploys and dances a ballet of homage, encircling the royal couple.

Now the old guard has gone, while the new has taken its place, the soldiers standing at attention all round that chamber of red earth.

In the middle, enormous belly sprawling on the ground, Her Majesty the Queen lies outstretched, round and seemingly inanimate, like a bright pebble. Close to her lounges her consort, the King, preening himself during the unending march past of their tiny slaves, pouring in through the main entrance in a well-ordered throng.

To minister to their sovereign — who is thirty thousand times larger than they, so that walking round her is like going round a mountain — these servants line up in single file, and as they march past the ever-open mouth of their insatiable queen, each rises up on its little legs and lets fall from its jaws on to the queen's lips a minute drop, the golden colour of honey. This is the royal jelly of the termites.

Circling the giant body of the queen in the opposite direction, so as not to collide with the servants making for the exit, is a second stream, this time of nurse termites. They are even busier than the others, the workers, as they come bustling up to seize and carry away an egg apiece. As each goes through the throng with its precious burden, it licks the egg clean, making it ready to be hatched in its cell among thousands of others, in what is really an enormous incubator.

Between two changes of her guard the queen of the termites will lay as many as 5,000 eggs.

The greenfly only lays one single egg, but this is as large as itself. This little beast belongs to the tiniest caste of insects and can almost be said to weigh nothing; yet, provided the majority of their progeny were not killed, one family of these creatures would in a few years produce a mass of living matter as great as the weight of butcher's meat consumed in England in a year.

The infernal dance of the insects, their incessant procession, is enough to make one see things! Their fecundity is so enormous that it could imperil the rest of the living world. If nothing halted their invasion, the seas would become a mush of plankton and the land would disappear beneath a crawling layer of larvae and caterpillars.

The Australian NEOLAMPRINO ADOLPHINAE, with horns like a bull, is just as harmless as our stag beetle with its antlers.

SWALLOW

MAGPIE

CROW

NIGHTINGALE

ROBIN REDBREAST

GREAT TIT

FIRECREST

FLYCATCHER

MALE BULLFINCH

EASTERN NIGHTINGALE

THRUSH

BLACKBIRD

HOOPOE

CARABID BEETLE

The allies of man

IN her wisdom Nature has created a wonderful balance between all the species and their ability to kill and to defend themselves.

The insects have a considerable number of enemies, particularly birds, the feathered tribe without whom, according to Fabre, famine would kill three-quarters of the people in the world.

All the migrants are great eaters of insects. The wrens, the warblers, the swallows, robins, bullfinches, and orioles consume huge quantities to feed themselves and their young.

You would never think that that slight little bird, the tit, in a year catches in its beak six million insects just to feed itself, and that it thrusts some twenty million other insects down the throats of its babies, as they wait cheeping and with gaping beaks in the nest.

In one day a tit will eat ten times its weight in insects. If a human being were such a huge eater as this seemingly delicate bird, he would eat at his three daily meals 110 stone of beef!

A swallow flies 400 miles a day and eats, as it flies, innumerable winged insects.

And then there are all the birds of our hedgerows and gardens: the blackbird darting from hedge to hedge, the thrush, the garden bunting and the nightingale.

Other great enemies of insects are the birds of sombre plumage.

Nasty things are said of them, perhaps because these crows, magpies and rooks look so dreary, yet they do prefer insects and larvae to the grain we sow in our fields.

Far away, in the tropic lands of sunshine, where the light makes the wings of the migrants glow with all the colours of the rainbow, the eaters of insects include the loveliest of all birds in the world: the little humming-birds, the great family of colibris, the African widow-bird whose tail hangs down like a long train of black lace, and the magnificent birds-of-paradise.

Even though they destroy huge quantities, the birds alone would never have been able to halt the dangerous onslaught of the insects. Nature has found the way to police these invaders by making them to some extent destroy each other.

The carabids, especially the golden carabus, destroy cockchafers and slugs. The calosome, itself as well armoured as a golden scarab and, like the ladybird, spotted with specks of ruby red or emerald green, jewelled like a prince, is content with more humble fare than the common carabid: it feasts on caterpillars.

The chrysope, which has huge green eyes and transparent wing-cases, breeds larvae which come out in froth like that on rose-bushes and feed on greenfly.

To other insects Nature has given a poisoned sting, one prick from which paralyzes its victim. With these

146

poisoned daggers the cerceris stabs the body of a spider, paralyzing it without killing it and using it as a store of live meat for its larvae. It lays its eggs on the actual body of the victim and there they hatch out.

There are other minute insects equipped with tiny drills that make holes in the eggs of other insects and lay theirs in them.

The driver-ants of Africa eat everything, even their own dead. When an army of these formidable black ants comes across a wounded buffalo or antelope in the bush, they devour it without halting, without the flood of these horrible creatures with their fearful mandibles ever coming to a stop. Each of the millions of these voracious little creatures snatches a particle of skin, hair or live flesh as it passes. At the end of some hours, when the river of ants has passed, all that is left is a skeleton of white, cleaned bones.

There are other insects which are content to perform the humble tasks of scavenging. These are the necrophores and the dor-beetles.

Like grave-diggers, the necrophores rush in a body the moment they smell the characteristic smell of corruption from a dead rat or bird. They harness themselves to the corpse of whatever it is, drag it away and bury it. But before covering it completely, they lay their eggs in the body which will feed the larvae when they hatch.

The dor-beetles are collectors of dung, which they fashion into huge balls that they then convey away and bury in little silos to form a reserve of food.

Did Nature foresee that scientists would use the poison of bees and certain wasps, in themselves dangerous, to cure rheumatism?

In creating the mosquito that transmits malaria did Nature think of the scientist and his joy on discovering

BEE
collecting pollen.

an efficacious cure for general paralysis, the dread disease that today can be cured by using another disease, malaria, to increase the heat of the patient's blood?

Nature is a wizard.

For thousands of years she hid from us the secret of the royal jelly, the elixir that bestows long life and with which bees feed their queen. For all these thousands of years in each hive there has always been one of the little Cinderellas born to live, like her sisters the workers, for scarcely twenty days, who by a miracle becomes a queen — queen of the bees. All that was needed to accomplish this miracle was a drop of magic, one mouthful of this royal jelly falling into the cell where the insect was still no more than a particle, a minute seed of a bee.

147

DRIVER ANTS
on the march.

BIRD OF PARADISE

THE MIGRATIONS OF ANIMALS

THE city is asleep. You can scarcely hear its noises now that the first frosts have come; yet, if you listen hard, you will be able to make out one of those cries that the wild-fowler hears so well in the silence of the countryside, when he is lying in wait behind the shelter of a clump of willows on the fringe of some flooded grassland.

The cries come from migrating birds crossing the city. They are not ducks. The great frosts have not yet set in and the weather is not bad enough for the sheldrake to be migrating. The harlequins have not yet left the shores of the Channel. It can only be greylag geese.

High above the city flies a V of wild geese heading south. They are migrating. As every year, they have left the icy marshes of the north and are journeying south. A few couples may make a stop on the shores of the Mediterranean, but the rest will fly on to Africa and the lands of the sun.

At the same time, also fleeing from the winter's cold, though in their case it is the cold of the Canadian steppes, the barnacle geese with white collars and immaculate breasts are making the long journey they undertake twice a year to change their grounds.

It is a strange sight when you see thousands of creatures, generally highly individualistic, assembling and setting off together on the adventure of the long trek that migration is.

The migration of animals and birds is governed by laws that we do not know. What fine promises do the birds hear? Who invites them to leave?

Migrations due to hunger

THE armadillos of North America have embarked on a regular policy of colonization. Just like the old emigrants in their ox-waggons thrusting across the Canadian prairies, clearing the forest and 'making land', as they put it, the armadillos, setting out from Mexico, have moved steadily on until now they have reached Louisiana. The huge obstacle of the Mississippi did not halt their progress, and in 1940 they were penetrating into Florida. These colonists will probably only stop at

the boundary of the polar cold, which they will be unable to withstand.

Like so many others, this migration of the armadillos was due to the need of more hospitable territory that comes to all animals: when it comes, off they go. Many will only undertake long journeys when forced by necessity, by the need to obtain food. It is not too much to say that sometimes their food dictates where they go by going ahead of them.

I am sure that you will have thought of the elephant, the pilgrim of the rain. Brutally the rainy season bursts upon the jungle. The ends of the branches of the trees put out the tender leaves of which the elephants are so fond, and at that signal the bull will assemble his tribe

and they will follow the path of the rains through the corridors of the forest. The Blacks of the jungle know this well. The miracle-working rain has covered their 'lugans', plots round the villages, with green, and at night you will hear the trumpets of the watchers calling to each other from hill to hill. These watchers build huts of branches on the fringe of the millet plots and they sound their trumpets for all they are worth. Warned by this, the elephants turn aside, saving the villages and refraining from trampling the young crops beneath their great round feet.

The antelope of South Africa also migrate with the

It is hunger, not thirst, that drives these nomad creatures across the vast expanses that they share with the men of the blue veils, for both the gazelle and the oryx, with long sword-like horns lying along its back, and the even wilder addax, can go without water for a very long time. In the years of great drought, when, like the Targui with his racing camels, they must search for pastures where the grass has not yet been scorched to the roots, the oryx and addax will grow bolder and venture into lands where normally they are never found.

rains, as do the elephants. In the dry season, the spring-bok with their lyrate horns, white cheeks barred with black like the masks of Kaffir warriors, set off and some-times go as far as the mountains of the south. Then they turn back, returning to their old grazing grounds that the rains have made green again and the drinking pools that they have filled once more. Many of these lovely creatures have been destroyed and their numbers are no longer so huge, but in the old days it used to be a ver-itable tide of reddish-yellow and white that came break-ing into the valleys. Any beast of prey had only to stand up and raise a paw in order to kill.

Almost all grass-eaters roam in order to have fresh pasture. Only the rhinoceros and the giraffe are at all sedentary. Even the heavy hippopotamus leaves his favourite streams at the beginning of the rainy season, and withdraws to mud pools in the depths of the jungle.

The stags and wild boars of the forests of Europe also change their abodes.

In the olden days the bison used to traverse the vast expanse of the prairies of the Sioux when the seasons changed.

And the reindeer . . . The caribou of the Canadian tundra also undertake vast journeys every year. In Lapland the reindeer has been domesticated and now man guides the migration of his herds. The leaders of the herds no longer need to listen for the secret call of Nature.

The true nomads are to be found in the lands of sand, in the deserts, where man himself roams from place to place, like the Moors and the Tuareg.

Periodic migrations

and

the travellers of the seas

THE oceans, too, are traversed by shoals of migra-tory fish following their favourite currents, some of which are warm, others cold. There are winter fish, like the cod and the herring, and summer fish, like the mackerel and the sardine.

The herring never has to take a decision itself. It just flees before the currents of warm water, which is too salt for it. It is, too, a difference in the temperature of the water that sends the cod heading for the banks of New-foundland. These banks are covered with a layer of cold water topped by a warmer zone. The cod, which inhabits the lower layer, rises to the upper layer to seize its prey which lives in the warmer water there, then dives down again.

The sardine and the mackerel do the same as the cold-water fish, but in the reverse direction. The sardine is a blue fish which only undertakes coastal voyages, and none of those of any length.

The most modern methods are now used to find the shoals of migratory fish. In this the marvels of modern science are put to good use; radar and echo-sounding now locate the colonies of fish as they move about at various depths in the ocean.

You know, I expect, that birds are caught and marked with a wire or a ring fastened to their legs so that we can follow their migrations and know their halting places; so that now we know according to the season whence they come and where they are going. And, no doubt, it will occur to you that the same thing cannot be done with fish, because they have no legs. Bigger fish, however, can be marked with a metal disc clamped to their tails, and the Americans have thought of a most original method for making the smaller ones that cannot swim with such a weight on their tails; they make the fry swallow tiny magnetized needles.

That is not a joke! That is what they do, and when the fish are piled on the quayside after the boats return, it is easy to discover any sardines or herrings that have been marked, for an electro-magnet will soon reveal those with a magnetic needle in them.

Just as there are two streams of migratory fish going in opposite directions, one from warm water to cold, and one from cold water to warm, so, too, Nature has made certain species leave the sea in which they live to go and spawn in rivers, and sends certain inhabitants of the rivers to the sea to spawn.

First there is the salmon.

When they ascend the rivers the salmon are magnificent blue fish so strong that they can clear obstacles six or ten feet high in a single leap. They swim against the current until they reach the point where the mountain streams come tumbling in, and there on the sandy bottom they deposit their eggs, which are like little amber-coloured balls. The young salmon are born in fresh water, and after a year, when they are still scarcely four inches long, they go down the river and swim out into the open sea.

It is said that the salmon remember the places where they spawn and return to them each year, just as swallows go back to the same nests.

Salmon have been marked, and so too has the mysterious freshwater eel, with its black back and white belly, which inhabits our rivers. When the eels in our streams and ponds set out on the great adventure of breeding, it is to the Sargasso Sea away across the Atlantic that they go. How, you ask, do those in the ponds reach the sea, when to do that means leaving the water? That does not worry them. They wriggle overland by night when the grass is wet with dew till they reach a stream that takes them to a river, that leads them to the sea.

All eels go to the Sargasso Sea and spawn there. For two years after hatching, the sea rocks the baby eels, which are mere threads and almost transparent; they are no thicker than a hair and about one-sixth of an inch long. They are called elvers.

Borne along by the waters of the Gulf Stream, the young eels finally reach the shores of Europe in a graet mass. There the mass unravels into giant strings, each

of which searches for the mouth of a river. They enter the rivers by night and only move up them by night, and people fish for them from flat-bottomed boats using lanterns.

The elvers go up the rivers in vast shoals known as eel-fares, and so they spread into streams and ponds and there, in fresh water, they grow and become the 'yellow' eels that we know. And after about fifteen years they will start off on the return journey, back to the Sargasso Sea.

The white world of the Far North also sees great assemblies of creatures preparing to migrate.

The caribou know where to find each other when they

Walrus, sea-elephant and seals.

foregather before embarking on their great journeys. The frozen seas of the two poles act as periodic rendezvous for the denizens of the polar regions.

Seals call to each other, barking hoarsely. The sea-elephants, come to give birth to their young on land, are also aware of the change of season. Like stags, which tear off the velvet covering their new-grown antlers by rubbing them against trees, the sea-elephants rub off their old skin by rolling in mud and scraping on the pebbles, baring the new skin underneath. In May, they dive in a herd into the sea and vanish for several months.

Even penguins travel. When tired of walking, which they do on two legs like us, the Emperor penguins dive into the sea, or play at tobogganing, sliding down the slopes of ice on their stomachs. When the courting season comes, the gentlemen penguins lay at the feet of their chosen one a bright pebble which they have selected with great care from among the myriads on the beach. This pebble will be one of those with which their nest will be edged. When the eggs have hatched and the parents have completed the education of their chicks, you will see a whole tribe of them arrive at the water's edge like a troop of shipwrecked mariners. It is not a sail for which they search, but a piece of pack ice that has come adrift. There is one coming. They hold council. They discuss the matter, smacking their white bellies with their flippers, quarrel and finally reach agreement. Shoving the little ones in front of them, they embark on the raft of ice; the marine currents have charge of it and will ground it in the right place.

In some ways the periodic movement of animals from the colder regions of the world to more hospitable climes is reminiscent of the behaviour of our own people, who long for the summer holidays to come round! Human beings leave their homes and become 'temporary residents' of other towns and villages just as animals and birds do. And just as men go away to the seaside for sunshine and a change of food and air, so the animals fall into an inevitable rhythm, year after year, closely allied with the availability of food and warmth — though to them the world 'holiday' has no meaning.

Butterflies in southern Canada and north America mass together in the autumn and fly south to Florida and similar regions. The Painted Lady butterfly, moving in spring in the opposite direction, flies from North Africa into Europe, and has even been seen as far north as Iceland.

There are some so-called 'erratic wanderers' who move about restlessly except during their breeding season, but these are exceptional. The lemmings, those strange creatures from Norway which are suddenly prompted to leave their land and drown in their thousands, are governed by some slower tempo, some undercurrent which we cannot detect; but that the rhythm is there nevertheless, we can hardly doubt.

The longing for food or for warmth; the urge for a change of scene; the command of a mysterious call too strangely pitched for the human ear to detect . . . whatever the reason, there is no denying the regularity of these mass movements. From the Alaskan fur seal which winters in California, to the land crab which moves relentlessly down to the sea at breeding time, or the fish which swim to their breeding areas and later float back on the current to their usual areas, the pattern is a regular one . . .

Nature can be russet like autumn, green like the hills of Africa, or white and veiled in a mantle of snow, but in regulating the procession of the seasons she also gives her children their marching orders and sends them off on their great journeyings.

The long-distance travellers of the air

IN response to the orders of that mysterious thing, instinct, obedient to the laws that govern the seasons, certain great families of creatures assemble in species and undertake vast journeys far from their dwelling-places. This is done by those that swim, creep, run and fly.

In southern Europe, bats, which in this country hibernate, migrate to warmer parts as soon as winter comes. Bats are great eaters of harmful insects and great friends of the farmer, though some silly country people refuse to admit the fact.

Bats have been caught in nets and ringed, using a tiny aluminium ring fixed to their wings, and this has made it possible to trace the routes of their migrations. Bats from the Pyrenees have been shown to go to Morocco, while American bats have flown the six hundred miles or so from their normal habitats to the islands of Bermuda. People have also experimented with bats, taking them considerable distances from where they were caught and releasing them like carrier pigeons, and always they have been able to make their way back, returning to the exact cave from which they were taken.

Swallows do the same. They return each spring to their old nests, repair them with mud mixed with saliva and line them with down. As long as the summer lasts, the air is streaked with the swift flight of these blue arrow-heads, but when autumn comes — autumn with the cold that kills off the insects on which they feed — the swallows assemble, form into companies, and one fine day you find that they have gone. They have flown off to Africa, a flight of many hundreds of miles. They are the first; after them go the swifts.

The storks of Alsace and Holland cover a distance of some seven thousand miles across France, Spain and Morocco to Lake Chad. As though they were an army on the move, they send out an advance guard with scouts to check their position. Having recognized the bald mountains of Tibesti, they know they are on the right course and speed straight for the great African lakes. Yet the return flight will bring them back unerr-

ingly to the same house and nest of branches on its chimney which they left the year before.

All Continental birds of prey flee from the winter, sometimes to this country. Of them, one falcon, perhaps the most common on the Continent, has a great reputation as a traveller. This is the peregrine. When it returns from the south of Africa to which its journeyings mostly take it, it makes its way north without hurrying, in easy stages, halting at each cathedral it passes.

Have you guessed why? It is because it finds an easy prey among the broods of young jackdaws and pigeons in the nests made in hollows among the stones and on the arches or in the bell chamber.

In the old days the falcon was the aristocrat among birds, being used by kings and nobles in hunting. Men on horseback carried the proud falcon on a leather-gauntleted wrist, where it sat, as proud and regal as the sacred bird of Ancient Egypt, its head covered with a leather hood. In the open plain, where the hares were, the moment the game came in sight the falconer removed the hood that blinded his bird, and the falcon, being trained for that very purpose, would set off in pursuit. In Siberia and Ukraine they even trained eagles to hunt wolves across the snow-covered steppes.

The peregrine falcon has also been used by fortune-tellers. Where did it learn the art? Perhaps in the lands of the sun, in the East which is still the realm of magic. In the Middle Ages the fowlers were a powerful brotherhood who enjoyed a great reputation. They sold birds

to the falconers who trained them to hunt, but they also sold others to the mountebanks who at fairs and other places exhibited ones that they had cleverly trained. The mountebank carried the bird chained to his wrist by a little chain, and when its master held out his headgear the bird would bend down and with its beak pull out a playing card or a little square of coloured cloth. The man then foretold the future from the card and interpreted the colour: green was a promise of success, red foretold the dangers of war, and yellow, the colour of gold, promised riches.

On the Continent there are lots of quails which are migrants, and in China they have dwarf quails: the old Chinese used to carry one in their cupped hands to keep their fingers warm during the winter.

Many of the passerines are great travellers. Being birds of passage, one might think that their name came from that, but in reality it comes from *passer*, which is the Latin word for sparrow.

All our song-birds — finches, warblers, wrens, robins and wagtails, normally such individualists and so jealous of their family rights — can join together in flocks

birds, so that now there are no more flocks: it is feared that today the Eskimo curlew is extinct.

Those who have seen a flight of flamingoes coming through the bluey-grey sky of evening to alight on the great river Niger will never forget the lovely sight. First you see them high up; then they spread out and become a riband of blue, the same colour as the vastness of the sky, then down they glide and suddenly alight on the surface of the great river. As they alight the dull waters seem to light up, as though touched by a last ray of the setting sun.

in times of great cold. Some of them migrate, and far away in other parts of the world Nature prepares to receive them.

When the cold of winter first sets in is the time when the wild duck migrate, and when the wildfowler gets into his hide and puts out his painted, papier-mâché decoys. There he waits beside the river, marsh, or stretch of flooded grassland, until some of the duck passing high overhead are tempted to come down to inspect the waters which the decoys make appear to be safe, and so come within gunshot.

One of the most courageous travellers was the Eskimo curlew, which mated and nested in the far north of Canada and then flew right down to Patagonia for the winter. More than two thousand miles of its journey were covered non-stop over the ocean.

In the spring it would head northwards again; but going in this direction it followed the land more, and suffered heavy fire from the guns of hunters. Shooting parties decimated the flocks of

PELICANS

CROWNED
CRANE

When pelicans take off from the waters of their lagoons, they are like great seaplanes. The marabou stork has to fold up its huge stilt-like legs, which it lets down again, like an undercarriage, before it alights. Other such birds are the ibis, the crowned crane with its diadem of gold and rubies, and the pink flamingo.

Migrations whence none returns

MIGRATION is an astonishing thing, but the strangest and most mysterious forms of it are those journeys which are made without hope or possibility of return. This is the case with certain spiders, which take flight hanging from their silken thread, and with many of the butterflies that make mass flights from Central America towards South America. One of these latter is the lemon-yellow callidryas.

Another example is that of the lemmings. It almost seems as though Nature, having allowed one species to prosper, will then lead it to its destruction, for that is what it does with the lemmings of Norway. Lemmings are a kind of vole. For fifteen or twenty years they increase and multiply, until there are lots and lots of them. Then, suddenly, they will all assemble at the foot of a mountain and off they go in close columns, like an army. Some sense or instinct makes them go in a straight line, and from this they never deviate, not even to go round an obstacle they find in their path. All such hindrances they either climb or dig through or under, in long straight tunnels out of which these little rodents emerge on the farther side still in their ranks.

When they come to the coast their numbers will have shrunk, for stoats, martens, gluttons, weasels and foxes have taken toll of them. Bears and wolves will have feasted on them, and the various birds of prey will have accompanied them right to the sea. There the survivors fling themselves into the water and swim off towards the west, driven by some instinct of which we have no knowledge. There the big gulls and petrels attack them, and those who are not killed are drowned.

Another example of migration without return is that of the eel. We have seen how the young eels, the elvers,

leave the Sargasso Sea and, reaching the shores of Europe, ascend the rivers, going far inland and at times even travelling overland, through damp grass, to reach ponds and lakes. After staying in their pond or river, perhaps hundreds of miles from the coast, for ten or fifteen years, by which time the eels will have grown three feet long or more and be most handsomely coloured with a black back and silver belly, they will set off on their mysterious journey back to the Sargasso Sea to breed and never return. Do they die there? Or do they descend into the great depths and there become transformed into monsters of the deep?

●

Like a great travel agency, Nature has carefully organized the routes taken by these colonies of insects, mammals, fish and birds, both those who go and come back, and those for whom there is no return.

But what is the reason for these migrations; why do they go? And what sense guides the swallows in their flight, the lynx of the tundra, and the butterflies? Are they in search of an eternal spring, of lands more kindly and smiling than their own? Or are they answering the call of Adventure?

Another traveller and migrant is the humming-bird, that tiny creature like a gleaming jewel from the mines of King Solomon. These humming-birds do not hesitate to cross the whole of North America to spend the winter in Panama, along the banks of the canal.

HUMMING-BIRD

MUTUAL AID AMONG THE ANIMALS

ONE of the most curious aspects of the strange world of the animals is the fact that not only do animals of the same species help each other, but that there is mutual aid between superiors and inferiors of different species. In fact, animals are often more sociable than people.

Many species of fish, birds and even mammals can live together, sharing the same waters, territories and hunting grounds, without warring against each other. This indifference, or mutual tolerance, is scarcely mutual help, but we do know that between certain clans of animals there are secret associations so strange that one cannot help feeling that here we are dealing with what is tantamount to mutual aid.

Take the hawks. At times they are like feudal lords protecting their vassals. So, too, are vultures. In the heronries, as the towns are called in which the herons group their nests, it is not unusual to find a hawk or, in hot countries, a vulture, living there among the other big birds. It perches in some tree that it uses as look-out tower and from it keeps watch, ready to attack aggressors or any who may come to disturb the peace of the city. It also happens that innocent passerines will seek the protection of hawks. The lordly birds make room for their vassals, allowing them to build their nests among the dead branches and twigs with which they have made their own.

These associations between the strong and the weak are as strange as they are interesting. You will have heard of the little bird that cleans the great mouth of the crocodile, pecking and removing the bits of bad meat lodged between the saw-like teeth of the animal's great jaws. The jungle is full of little birds that live at the court of some such mighty lord. Some act as sentries and veritable bodyguards, like those that accompany the rhinoceros. At the slightest sound these will fly off the rhino's armoured hide, from which they pick vermin, in a flurry of feathers and cries that warns it, even if it is asleep, and allows it to make off and get to safety, or to charge.

Buffaloes also have birds perching on their backs — their protective tufts of white ox-peckers.

These little sentries are only doing their duty in thus mounting guard; it is their way of paying tribute to their lord and master, for we must not forget that these birds feed on the parasites that live on the hides of the

Sometimes a young rabbit, being attacked by a weasel, is saved by a hawk which puts the weasel to flight. It can also happen that if the hawk misses the weasel, it will return for the rabbit.

great buffalo. You will often see starlings and wagtails doing this very thing, perched on the back of a cow or sheep and happily pecking up its vermin.

All these associations are based on an exchange of services, on give and take. In associated clans, some eat what the others leave. That is true of the woodpecker and those kingfishers which inhabit ant-hills, and of the thousands of insects which use the galleries of the mole, or the burrows of the rabbit and marmot.

Where there is true protection, it is that of the stronger protecting the weaker, as with the passerines that go and live in vultures' castles, or of the small birds that hawks receive and which make their nests in the eyries of those birds of prey.

Animals often have need of a creature smaller than themselves. The shark would be helpless without the pilot fish. It appears that not only do shoals of little pilots accompany the sharks on their hunts, but that old sharks carry a tiny pilot fish in the corner of their mouths, by the lip. It is said that black divers on the coasts of Africa can sometimes escape from a dogfish or successfully fight off a shark with a knife if they have been able to tear its pilot fish from its mouth, after which it will swim round helplessly in circles.

Such associations are astonishing enough, but there are others even stranger, especially in the realm of the seas. There is a kind of huge jellyfish that shelters young fish beneath its umbrella, especially the silvery young of the whiting and the cod. These youngsters shelter there, play in that marine playground and grow fat on the remains of the victims caught by their protector, the jellyfish.

There is another enormous kind of jellyfish, the Portuguese man-of-war, which lives in colonies and whose tentacles distil a mortal poison, mortal at least to all fish except the tiny one which it has adopted and which Nature has provided with a protective oil to protect it against the poison that would burn it.

Have you ever heard of an actinia? It is an animal that lives in the sea attached to rocks. It is so close to a plant that it is also called a sea-anemone. It is rather like a big dishevelled dahlia which can open its petals at will, only the petals are really poisoned tentacles. Now there are fish that go and live in the heart of these sea-anemones! Not only do these live, carnivorous 'flowers' share their prey with their lodgers, but they protect the latter against the attacks of other hungry fish.

Altogether, the small fry of the oceans can choose some very peculiar dwellings. There are fish that make themselves comfortable in the stomach of the pearl oyster, and in the belly of a big seaworm or other fish.

Certain crustaceans, like the hermit-crab, use empty shells and sub-let the upper storey, that is the point of the shell at the end of its spiral. There is room there for a large worm, which the hermit-crab thus shelters. This bristle-worm appears to be asleep, but in reality it is wide-awake and listening for the noise made by the crab's mandibles when it starts eating its prey. As soon as it hears this noise, the worm comes down and the crab generously shares with it. In fact the worm even snatches the food out of the crab's mouth.

Often there is even a triple association, such as when a sea-anemone shelters under its live bushy top the shell inhabited by a hermit-crab and its bristle-worm. One fine day the crab decides to change his refuge, so he gives his bristle-worm a signal and the latter makes ready to follow him; then he gives an order to the sea-anemone, which detaches itself from the shell they are abandoning. The crab then makes a bundle of the sea-anemone, shoulders it and plants it on the new shell when he has made his choice. The bristle-worm, of course, follows to the new abode.

Imagine the meeting between an old crab and a young, walking along sideways in its soft shell. The young one does not yet know all the possibilities of the sea, but the old one does and it is carrying in either claw a bouquet of fine sea-anemones which hunt for it and catch its

These young fish circle beneath the jellyfish, but nothing else dare touch it on pain of death.

Animals organized in true clans and obeying their own laws have their own little kingdoms. In these the association between individual members of the one tribe becomes really close. Often they have a chief, a leader of the herd, whom they obey. He it is who gives the orders in matters of defence, searching for food, hunting and building.

•

I remember one strange encounter I had in the jungle while hunting elephant in Africa. A troop of chimpanzees was crossing the jungle path ahead of me and I told my driver to stop. An old male, the leader, his hands on his hips, stood glaring at us from a distance of a few paces. At intervals he intensified his gruntings to hurry up the rest of his troop, cursing the stragglers. I almost felt that he was counting them as they came along.

The last chimpanzee to cross was a terrified female. Suddenly the big male gave a bound towards her, seized her and shook her and grunted at her something we could not interpret. Whatever it was, it forced her to turn back into the bush. She reappeared a moment later, and now, clinging to her back with both hands and feet, was a grimacing little baby chimpanzee, which in her terror she had abandoned.

Then she leaped into the air with her baby in her arms and disappeared among the foliage of the trees. All was now in order, and the old male gave a couple of triumphant grunts, made a gesture as much as to say that the path was now free for me, and disappeared into the jungle, the last of his troop.

prey. The sea-anemones are so fat that they are in two, like a double flower. The old crab feels that it must help its young relative, and so it teaches the other how to hold tame sea-anemones in its claw so that they will hunt for it.

One of the most extraordinary associations is that of the succulent Marennes oyster and a live colour, one of the seven colours of the rainbow. The colour really is alive, for it is imparted to the water of the fattening ponds in which the flesh of the oysters is made to turn green, by millions of microscopic particles, navicules of a deep azure blue.

Nature has made an indestructible bond between the oyster and these particles of live colour. The oyster adores them and makes itself green with them, while the particles themselves can only live in water where oysters are, because of the juices and mucus that the oysters emit.

In this connection there is a nice story concerning the involuntary migration of Portuguese oysters from the mouth of the River Tagus.

The owners of some oyster-beds on the west coast of France were worried because the beds were deteriorating without their being able to discover why, and so they sent to Portugal for some fresh stock. The oysters were dredged off the beds in the River Tagus and loaded into a ship. Bad weather prevented the ship getting farther than the mouth of the River Gironde, and there the oysters had to be tipped overboard, several tons of them. They prospered and multiplied to such an extent that it became a regular invasion, and since 1867, the date of their being jettisoned in the Gironde, they have spread up the coast as far as Vendée, a distance of close on a hundred miles.

How can a bed of oysters travel? The sea sows the oyster's eggs farther and farther afield, and some of the tiny oysters attach themselves in front of the others. Mussels progress by warping, a slow method which consists of putting out a rope with an anchor ahead of a boat and then hauling the boat up to where the anchor is lodged. That is what the mussels do. They detach their filaments from the rock, throw them on ahead, and by them pull themselves an inch or so forward.

In his way that chimpanzee talked. So too does the squirrel when it modulates its cry differently to announce the approach of a man, a bird of prey or a snake. The big cobe of the bush utters a gentle whistle to reassure its startled females or a shrill call if it wants them to take flight.

The oryx of the desert guards the flank of its herd when on the move, doing *chouf* as the Tuareg say, travelling alone, far from the others. Man has copied the animals in putting out sentries and in the outriders that travel along behind the dunes escorting and protecting a caravan or *rezzou* from plunderers.

In hunting, the law of mutual aid becomes a real code of honour for the animals. Often when a stag is all but exhausted and has succeeded in rejoining its herd with the pack hard on its heels, you will see a young stag go and draw the hounds off. The young stag is still fresh and capable of a long run, so off it goes and thereby saves the other. Wild boar will do the same.

You will have heard how a partridge, like some other birds, will trail a wing and pretend to be wounded in order to lure a fox or other animal away from where its chicks are.

I have often been asked whether it is true that ele-

phants will pick up one of their number that is wounded. They do, or very nearly. Wolves and prairie dogs are savages by comparison; they eat their dead or any which are disabled. Among elephants, it is the females which are the brave ones. With legs straddled and foreheads against the shoulder of a wounded male, they will get him on to his feet again, using their tusks as levers. Then, one on either side, they support their lord, shoulder to shoulder, and almost carrying him they get him along without collapsing.

I saw something similar on the Gold Coast. An old patriarch had dropped, mortally wounded by an explosive bullet. Two others, great grey brutes, had helped it up and supported it all the way to the river Volta, across which the wounded animal had swum. For seven

miles we could follow the triple track: the footprints in the centre regular and perfect, the others on either side aslant and dug deeper in the mud, where the elephant's feet had been thrust in to take the strain.

One baby elephant had been unable to keep up with the herd and my trackers had caught it and were tying it up with lianas. Suddenly two elephants appeared, bursting through the greenery, and my men had only just time to scramble up into some big trees. The elephants had come to get the baby.

It is more than an instinct of affection which tells these animals what measures they must take to preserve their race, harden the young and protect them during infancy. Among them solidarity is extended to consid-

erable lengths. It is not unusual to find an orphan adopted by another mother. That frequently happens with certain species of monkey, and is not surprising to anyone who has seen them in their natural surroundings, observing their attitudes, gestures and how they live a social life that is roughly like our own.

Perhaps it is because the big Emperor penguins walk, like us, upright, on two feet, that they are so wonderfully civilized for birds. The first preoccupation of this people of the ice is to preserve their race. Not all the females lay eggs, and each precious, magnificent egg is more the property of the clan than of the privileged one who has laid it. If the mother goes fishing far from her nest of pebbles, another female comes rushing up, instals the egg on her palmate feet to isolate it from the

cold and, covering it well with her plumage, takes a turn at hatching it.

These penguins are quite a well-developed society. They have kindergartens with attendants who teach the babies to play, to dive and to walk in file.

It is, however, among the species that are obliged to act in concert, to discuss things in council and to profit from the experience of the older members, that the social instinct is most striking. These are animals which undertake things requiring a concerted effort on the part of them all.

I am thinking here mainly of the animals which build — for example the elephants, which in times of great drought will build a barrier of tree-trunks, branches and stones to dam the bed of a stream in some valley when the water is getting low. In this way they form an artificial pool deep enough for them to take a proper bath. In Africa you often come across these dams that elephants have made and on which they must have worked as a team.

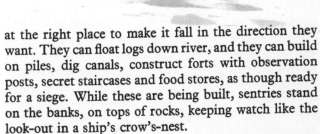

at the right place to make it fall in the direction they want. They can float logs down river, and they can build on piles, dig canals, construct forts with observation posts, secret staircases and food stores, as though ready for a siege. While these are being built, sentries stand on the banks, on tops of rocks, keeping watch like the look-out in a ship's crow's-nest.

The smaller animals are often better organized than the big. In South Africa, the sociable weaver-birds live in colonies and build themselves real aerial towns in the huge trees. Working in teams of three or four hundred, they first build an immense conical roof of straw which shelters their city. Then, underneath, each couple builds its own nest in storeys.

Beavers and muskrats are indefatigable builders. They build locks, which are more than dams. They can fell trees as well as any lumberjack, gnawing the trunk

Marmots also put out sentries when they come out to cut and make their hay. These marmots do really cut and make hay. They use their teeth and work in line just like reapers in the old days. Having cut the grass, they let it dry, keeping an anxious eye on the weather in case it should rain. At the first drop, they hurry to carry their hay back to their burrows.

But we must go back to the world of insects to find true organized communities of members living in cities, where each individual submits to the law of division of labour.

That is the case with the termites which we have already mentioned, and with wasps and bees.

There are innumerable varieties of bees, but the most civilized and industrious is without doubt our own domestic bee, which originally came from Asia. The term industrious, however, does not apply to the males, who are unable even to find their own food among the flowers. They are idlers whom the community feeds, and they do nothing. In the end, however, they are condemned to death and perish, one and all, beneath the stabs of the others' stings. The peoples of the bees include skilled workers: honey-gatherers who go out and plunder the flowers; wax-workers who remove the discs of wax from their bellies; the ventilators which incessantly ply their wings at the entrance to the hive to renew the air inside; sentries, cleaners, and so on. It sometimes happens, despite the vigilant watch of the sentries, that a small creature, an insect or a tiny mouse, makes its way into the hive. It quickly perishes beneath the stabs of thousands of stings, but the scavengers find that they are not strong enough to drag the body out of their city. They then turn themselves into embalmers, enclosing the body in an envelope of wax just where it fell; this prevents it from decomposing.

There are court ladies to wait upon the sovereign, the queen, whose function it is to lay eggs unceasingly throughout her life of three or four years. The queen can lay at will eggs that will hatch into males or ones that will produce females, that is to say drones or workers — or little queens. The latter are entitled to much larger apartments than the modest cell of the others and they are fed by the court nurses with the famous royal jelly.

Of all the thousands of specialist workers who live only a few weeks and kill themselves with work, the most intelligent are the geometricians. They are little mathematical geniuses. If man had wanted another unit for measuring length, another standard instead of the yard he might have taken the length — tiny, it is true, but nonetheless invariable — on which are based all the radial constructions made in wax by all honey-bees throughout the world. Each hexagonal cell always has its six sides exactly equal, and each cell is identical with all other cells in the hive and with all those in all other hives throughout the world.

The most developed, the highest of the insect civilizations, however, is that of the ants. Ants also have castes: large-headed soldiers, slender servants and a whole tribe of slaves debased to the role of navvies, crushers and grinders of grain, scavengers and porters. Among these latter, there are some who need strength out of the ordinary, like the porters of Smithfield or Covent Garden, and there are others who convey the small one on their backs, like nurses with children.

There are innumerable kinds of ants, but one and all are organized in societies that conform to their own genius. There are mason ants which can masticate, powder and mould all soils, and who build their cities with cellars, reinforcing them with a wealth of pillars, buttresses and partitioning walls. In the Americas there are paper ants that build aerial towns with veritable leaves of paper. They manufacture this paper out of wood, pounded up by the worker-ants into a paste, which is kneaded and then spread in sheets.

The industrious bee forages in a flower like a thief after treasure. Her feet are furnished with brushes and combs, and she pushes the golden pollen behind her and makes it into a ball, which she places in cavities like trouser-pockets in her hind legs. At the same time she thrusts her long proboscis to the base of the corolla to suck up the precious nectar which she collects. This undergoes a transformation inside the bee. Under the effect of the bee's saliva and gastric juices, it is turned into honey. There are three hundred males or drones in a hive, and they are real sluggard kings who live at the expense of the rest of the community. But at the end of each summer a revolution in the palace regularly puts an end to this scandal: all the males are exterminated and their corpses thrown out of the hive.

Queen laying an egg in a cell. In this fashion she lays 2,500 times a day.

QUEEN

MALE DRONE

BUMBLE BEE

WASP

Here is the same cell shown like a film-strip: you must look at it from right to left to study the growth of the insect, from the egg to its birth.

Each cell built by the workers is a box with six equal sides. The closed cells protect the sleeping pupa. On the left, the excrescence shaped like an olive serves as a cell for a larva in the process of being transformed into a queen.

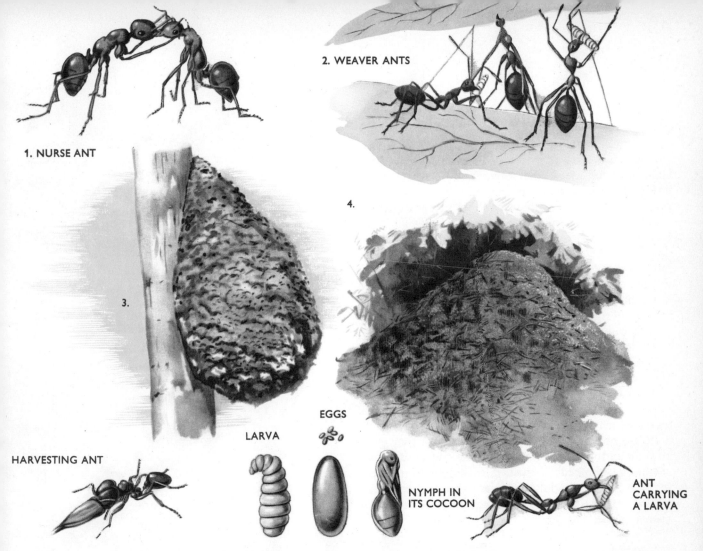

1. NURSE ANT

2. WEAVER ANTS

3.

4.

HARVESTING ANT

LARVA

EGGS

NYMPH IN
ITS COCOON

ANT
CARRYING
A LARVA

1. The ant's stomach contains a reserve of sugary juice set apart from what she swallows for her own nourishment. It is impossible for her to dispose of it for herself, but she can offer it to another ant. 2. In Africa, Asia and Australia weaver ants make their nests in trees by fastening the edges of leaves together with a crisscross binding of sticky threads from their larvae, which act as living shuttles. 3. In Madagascar, tropical America and India, one species of ant builds its nests in the trees; these 'cardboard' nests are eighteen inches high. 4. In our own woods, a dome-shaped heap of pine needles and brushwood 3 ft high and 12 ft round hides a hillock of earth thrown up from the excavations of a huge undeground city, which extends for an area of 50–100 square yards beneath the surface.

In Africa there are tailor ants, red ants, which make nests of green leaves in the trees. They work like real weavers. Hanging one from the other by their feet, the workers form a chain which they set swinging and so pass from one leaf to the other. These leaves they sew together, using one of their larvae which emits a thread that solidifies immediately.

No other creature goes in for mutual aid to the same extent as the ant. Like the rat which lies on its back clutching an egg in its paws and lets the others pull it along by its tail, ten or a dozen ants will join together to transport a large burden like a plum or a nut.

On the journeys they make to replenish their store-rooms, it is always the discoverer of the land of plenty they follow; the one who went out searching and made the find leads the column that goes to bring it in. You ought to see how the ants encourage each other in their work, using their dumb language; for ants express themselves with their feelers, stroking each other's back, belly or feet. It is a language of caresses.

What do ants do when they have to cross a water-course? If any stones protrude, the bridgers get to work. Twig-pontoons are made, and straw-girders used as ground-sills. If the current is strong they launch rafts made of knotted grasses. If there should be any large bushes overhanging the water, they will climb into them, make a chain of bodies and throw a live bridge across. Then the whole colony passes over using the live bridge. If some clumsy one should fall in, another chain will quickly be made, a life-line that can be thrown to it. Brought to the bank, the unfortunate one will be massaged by its companions with their feelers, as it lies on a warm sunlit stretch of sand.

And the activity there is in the city itself, and how perfectly each knows exactly what he has to do! When they attend to their toilet they groom each other, vigorously plying their antennae as brushes; and at meal times the workers, back from the fields, feed those who never emerge from the galleries, putting the food into their mouths. The nurses, for example, never have a moment to spare, so busy are they unravelling the cocoons in which are enveloped the newly-hatched ants that would die if they were not at once exposed to the sun.

'Incidents' are rare in the well-guarded cities of the ants. Sentries are at the gates. You can hear them dragging great stones to block the entrance when the rain pours down. But how has this great caterpillar managed to get there and why have the ants let it in? It is the offspring of the blue butterfly. It has let itself drop from the rosebush in which it has grown up and hurried to take refuge with its friends the ants. There it will feast on larvae, it is true, but otherwise what a help it will be—more use than a thousand scavengers, for it will eat all the refuse.

This caterpillar of the blue butterfly is not the only insect to have a place in the cities of the ants and to live in friendship with them. There are thousands of species of creatures, more or less slaves of the noble ants, which live in the shadow of the ants' nest. The cultivator ants need a large labour force to pound and crush the pile of leaves which they make into a hot-bed; for, just as we cultivate mushrooms in dark cellars where they grow all pink and white, so these ants sow and grow mushrooms on these beds of crushed leaves, obtaining excellent food for the adults, who are able to peel them, while the larvae are content to suck the juice the mushrooms exude.

The mutual aid that can be observed among animals is sometimes rather one-sided. Occasionally an old lion will adopt a motherless cub, or a boar with broken tusks an abandoned young boar. This kindness is not disinterested. These old males know that they are on the decline, and they feel that they have just time to train a page to hunt for them, to pull down a deer for the lion or to root up succulent roots for the old boar whose snout is becoming flabby and soft.

Mutual help among the animals also extends to the people who give the animal shelter and food. You will have seen a blind person being taken about in absolute safety by a guide-dog, and ordinarily we adopt a dog to love us and be a watch-dog, or to put up game and retrieve when we go out shooting. We train and use falcons and carrier pigeons, and we used to send ferrets into burrows to drive the rabbits out. Perhaps in your chair there is a cat lying asleep; stroke her and she may return the caress.

OUR NEIGHBOURS
THE PLANTS

THE world of the plants with its innumerable families, its monsters, species
that have survived from prehistoric times, and its extraordinary vegetable
fauna, is undoubtedly more wonderful than the animal kingdom.

At the various stages of the world's development, during the great epochs
of creation which peopled the continents and the seas, Nature has always achieved
a wonderful harmony between the animal and vegetable kingdoms.

Nature has organized and 'dressed' her two worlds according to the seasons
and climates, with fur for the animals, scales for the fish, and startling plumage for
the birds; and at the same time she has decked the trees and plants with leaves and
flowers.

When man came he domesticated some of the animals, such as the horse and
buffalo, and some wild plants and trees as well. He acquired flocks, fields,
gardens and orchards almost at the same time.

But we are still far from having discovered all the secrets of the plants in
the vegetable kingdom, ranging from giant trees and monstrous algae to microscopic bacteria.

This baobab of the African plains has a circumference of 105 ft at its base.

The ancient city of Palenque in Mexico, abandoned by men, has been reconquered by the exuberant vegetation.

THE GIANTS AND MONSTERS

of the vegetable kingdom

I REMEMBER how in Africa during a tornado I had to shelter myself and my car, for which there was plenty of room, in the belly of an enormous baobab that the rains had hollowed out. Inside, it was like a huge vegetable chimney. High up among the branches was the top opening at a fork, and through it I could see a little patch of blue sky.

I could have spent the night in my car, but I preferred the shelter offered by an abandoned hunter's cabin which had a door, though it did not shut well. To this I took my guns and my box of cooking things. As I was settling down to sleep, I heard the sound of bodies brushing against the dried grass walls and muffled grunts.

I recognized the sound as the dull bark of the dog-headed baboon; and apparently I had a whole pack of these horrid cynocephali round the hut. There was a discussion; they seemed to be planning an attack. I could not tell from where it would come. The walls of the cabin were thick and I had stoutly barricaded the door. But the whole troop jumped on to the roof and it looked as though, if their weight failed to break it in, they would be able to tear off the thatch covering it with their hands. I felt that I must have recourse to a gun. I fired through the roof, twice. There was a stampede. Half an hour later they were back again. The roof looked as though it would collapse beneath their weight. They were most excited, all chattering and yapping at once.

I could not afford the ammunition to keep them away by firing through the roof all night, so I shouted at my undesirable visitors and at once there was silence. They listened, giving vent to *hoohoos* of astonishment, and seeming to be most intrigued by the sound of the human voice. After that I talked and talked, while they, like attentive children, must have squatted in a ring on the roof, huddled one against the other, while the thatch sagged deeper and deeper. I talked to them until the dawn. It was not long before I was bored with my own voice and did not know what to say, so I recited to them all the poetry I could remember, and the music of the poems soothed them and kept them quiet.

At daybreak the baboons withdrew, but I found that the sound of my voice had enchanted another long, green creature, which lay stretched out on the floor of the hut along the reed wall. It was coiled like a snake, head stretched towards me, and its delicate lips were parted like a pink flower. This live liana, this creature that seemed to be stretching out its neck to be caressed, was in fact a plant. Never before had I been made so aware that fundamentally the plants are poor animals vowed to immobility — like sponges and corals.

I went back to my car in its garage in the belly of the great baobab tree, which was a real giant. And yet that monster, which could have sheltered half a dozen elephants in its bark cavern, would have seemed almost a dwarf beside the sequoias that grow in California. 'General Sherman', the most fantastic of the giants there, is more than 300 feet high; a tunnel has been cut through its trunk, and now a road 16 feet wide runs through it.

There is a banyan tree in the zoological garden at Calcutta which could shelter three regiments beneath its branches.

The Mexican cypress is not as tall as the sequoia, but it can attain 130 feet. These are probably the oldest trees in the world—for some kinds of tree do live to great ages. It is wonderful to think that the seed that sprouted and so turned into one of those lovely trees received its first drop of dew at the time when the Pharaohs of Egypt were building their tombs in the Valley of Kings.

Four hundred years ago many of the little squares in front of the churches of France were planted with elms, and some of these aged trees are still to be seen. In Windsor Forest there are aged oaks that must have seen William Rufus ride past when he went hunting. The olives which two thousand years ago heard Christ's prayers in the Garden of Gethsemane still line the road up to the mount that bears their name.

On the Ivory Coast I have seen lumbermen fell mahogany trees 200 feet tall. They had to build scaffolding more than 12 feet up before they reached the round, smooth part of the bole, where they could start to ply their axes. Near the ground the trunk spreads out in buttresses and flying arches like those of a cathedral. It is not unusual to find giant mahoganies whose bases, buried beneath moss, measure 200 feet in circumference.

In this felling of the giant trees there comes a most moving and exciting moment when the tree 'speaks', as the lumbermen call it; speaks and cries out as its last fibres part and the pink blood of its sap pours down the trunk like honey scented with wild strawberries.

As the tree speaks, the black lumbermen fling down their axes and leap madly from the scaffolding. There is an appalling din as the great trunk falls, crushing the other trees in its path and breaking a green clearing, a breach in the vault of the tree-tops in which a strip of blue sky appears. The tree is then cut up; the enormous logs are rolled into the river. Then a train of rafts with little gesticulating naked figures brandishing spikes and poles goes down stream on the current. Eventually they reach the sea, where waiting ships hoist the red timber aboard with their derricks and stow it on deck.

It is the sunshine and the great rains of the tropical countries that give rise to this wealth of vegetable fauna. There the liana strangles and giant mosses suffocate all that does not grow quickly enough to escape asphyxiation.

The effect of Nature's rain and sunshine is magical. They produce violets 60 feet high and turn grass into trees — for all bamboos, which are hollow like straws, are really just giant grasses.

You can achieve astounding results if you start experimenting in the vegetable world. You can never tell what monster may not be created by merely changing a plant's milieu, transplanting it to a different climate.

Which is the oldest tree in the world? Is it the fig-tree of Nerbaddah which may have seen Alexander the Great's army pass by? Or this Californian sequoia, which is said to be about three thousand five hundred years old, the age that Moses would be today?

A root of St. John's wort that was replanted in New Zealand became a tree 50 feet high in the course of 80 years.

In Kenya there is a tree caravanserai, a veritable hotel built in a tree, the flowers of which resemble those of one of our most delicate and tiny hot-house plants. On each of the storeys formed by its branches, to which bamboo ladders lead, there are little dormitories with five or six beds, mosquito nets and an electric bedside lamp. There, in the middle of the bush, you can have breakfast in bed and watch the rhinoceros at their ablutions in the mud of a nearby pool. Before that, the great beasts will have sharpened their horns against the bark of that huge tree, a thing that some might interpret as an act of homage to a sort of Tree-God.

The sea too has its jungle, a luxuriant submarine vegetation out of the midst of which a kind of seaweed, macrocystes, grows branching up to the surface, its thalli measuring hundreds of yards. On the surface they spread out, supported by nodes that act as floats.

In the sea off the coast of Florida you find deep-water algae, the sargasso that has given its name to that part of the ocean, the Sargasso Sea. That is where all eels go to spawn in the warm water, after crossing the Atlantic. The algae there measure more than 30 feet, and intertwine and knot as though in the heart of a submarine virgin forest.

Man often tries to go counter to Nature; he likes to take a giant and model a dwarf. When you see the tiny

little gardens the Japanese make, you wonder how on earth they can ever get a cedar only four inches high to grow in a pot.

It is a job for the surgeon. First they accustom the poor little trees to live on a drop of water in a thimbleful of earth, then they trim them, nip off their buds, suppress some of the roots. They take a baby Andean cactus, which is normally a huge green candle in which hundreds of birds of prey can nest and pumas can take refuge from the onslaught of the peccary, and they turn this into a stunted mushroom on which a ladybird would just have room to perch.

Legend tells of good giants who came down to earth in the days of long ago. They perhaps knew the secret of how to grow enormous plants. Were one to return today he would still find some of the plants he produced in his old garden: the giant arums and geraniums.

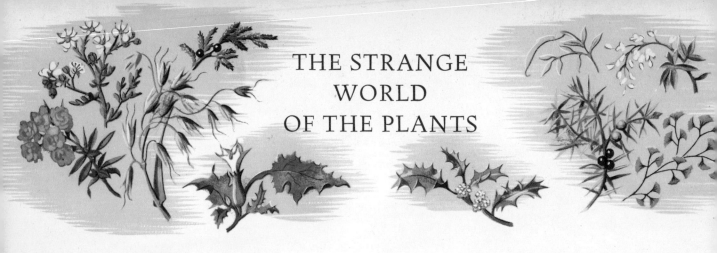

THE STRANGE
WORLD
OF THE PLANTS

Intelligence in plants

Do flowers know the gardener who works among them, as bees do the bee-keeper who looks after them? Have they intelligence and a memory?

There are so many forms of intelligence. The love that animals sometimes so touchingly have for us, especially cats, dogs and horses, is always very secret, but far less secret than that which flowers perhaps may feel for us.

Plants certainly have a secret instinct that governs their behaviour . . . one could almost say their reflexes. It has been observed, for example, that the extent to which cultivated plants will thrive depends more or less on the person who tends them, so that people with 'green fingers' always obtain good results.

Plants are most sensitive perhaps to the effects of the sun. We all know the sunflower which follows the course of the sun throughout the day, and the daisy which closes its corolla to sleep; but have you heard of the 'compass-plant'? The leaves of the dandelion are always so arranged as to receive the minimum of light during the hours of heat and the maximum in the early morning and evening. Thus it is possible to reckon from it the approximate north-south line.

Lianas make unfailingly for the nearest support and twine round it always in the same direction. Try to unroll from the stake it is climbing a liana in the Southern Hemisphere which makes its coils from right to left. Try to make the liana twist in the other direction, as though you were twisting a lock of hair round your finger. The plant will very quickly turn and coil itself round the right way, the way Nature has chosen for it, which is the opposite to that chosen for its sisters in the Northern Hemisphere. These latter climb by coiling from left to right.

Without going so far as to talk of intelligence, many of the reactions of plants leave one wondering.

One plant-lover, a man capable of 'taming' flowers, once turned his attention to a sensitive plant.

Do you know what a 'sensitive' plant is? There are several kinds of them, almost all being members of the large family of leguminous plants, like pears, acacias and mimosas. Those which grow in cold countries are far less sensitive than their sisters in tropical countries, and you have to touch their follicles before they will close up quickly. Do the sensitives that grow on the Equator and become long climbing lianas have, like animals, a whole network of nerve threads, branching out as far as the stalks of their leaves? Whatever the reason may be, the astonishing thing is that if an animal comes anywhere near, its presence will induce a nervous quiver that will be transmitted all along the body of the plant. If something merely brushes the tip of one of the leaves of such a sensitive, that leaf will instantly contract and, at once, all along the coiling body of the plant the leaves will take fright and one by one curl up and close. Not till the danger has passed will the follicles cautiously unfold slightly, as though the plant were venturing a peep. The alarm being over, a signal seems to run down the plant, which opens its leaves once more.

This plant-lover with the green fingers brought up

If placed in the plane of the meridian, the leaves of the wild lettuce expose the minimum of their surface to the sun during the hottest hours of the day. They receive their maximum sun-bath in the mornings and evenings. Thus this 'plant compass' points out the direction of north and south.

168

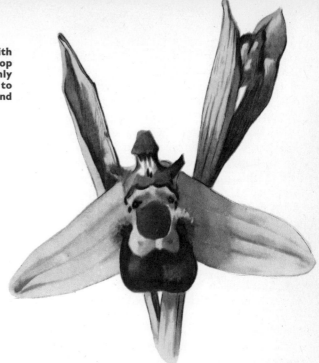

What is this monster with wings spread ready to swoop down on its prey? It is only a simple flower belonging to the large orchid family and is quite harmless.

his sensitive plant as other people might rear a lion cub or other baby wild animal. The plant was itself a wild one, and to begin with the least touch of the man's finger would scare it and make it close.

The man went to the plant every day, spoke to it, caressed and treated it with affection. Before very long, when the man was there, the plant would undulate, and not only did it not close its leaves at his touch, but it stretched out, like a cat, inviting his caresses. How could one say that the plant did not recognize the man who came every day to tend it? Especially as it closed up at once if a stranger entered the hot-house?

Have you heard the legend of the Tree-leader, a good genius who was said to have carried in his tousled hair swarms of bees, the first wasps and the first honey-gathering insects of the world? That was in the days after the withdrawal of the glaciers, when the trees walked abroad searching out the world's ways, the fertile valleys and warmer climes where Nature was about to perform the miracle of creating fruit.

The great horde of wandering trees and bushes got

Did you know that the clover changes its position to sleep?

Two leaves fold up towards each other under the third, which droops to form a little protecting roof. Why? To conserve the dew's freshness longer.

lost in the mud of the African bush. Aziza, who later was to fashion the beasts one by one in order to people the forests, chose one of his sons to act as guide for the horde of wild trees. We do not know what his name was, but he is called the Tree-leader.

The Tree-leader grouped the trees by species, whistling to them like a shepherd to his flocks and blowing a horn to gather them round him, and so he drove them

on without respite, a mad flock gesticulating in the wind and flinging contorted arms towards the heavens as they dragged their roots through the mud. The Tree-leader headed the palms with their metallic-sounding leaves towards the sandy areas: the thorns and the fat baobabs he sent towards the bush, and the giants towards the sea, but they piled up, intertwined their branches and roots and remained motionless for all eternity in the midst of the immense flock that is the forest.

As he went along, the Tree-leader broadcast cochineal insects, bees, butterflies and the innumerable seed of the insects.

One tree alone refused to follow this shepherd whom Aziza had chosen for them. It is called the Defiant Tree and is the only one that does not bend to the wind. It is almost as though, lost in the bush, it stands, trunk curved, spying out its way, avoiding villages and ready to flee at the approach of man.

Plants and animals

As though they were flowers with wings, the insects have had assigned to them an important role in the transport of pollen and the fertilization of plants.

Though most plants are hospitable and gladly let themselves be plundered by wasps, bees and butterflies, there are some which jealously defend the entrance to their corollae and will only admit a select number of customers to their scent shops.

The most capricious of all flowers are undoubtedly the elegant, delicate orchids. Some of them refuse the help of insects and expel all such intruders from their little sugared hearts, but they will gladly open out whenever the tiny little beak of a humming-bird is pointed at their calyx.

Other plants will wither and refuse to flower if the ants which attend to the exchange of their pollen have been sulking or unable to reach them.

169

The most curious case of association between insects and plants is that of one family of small insects that fertilize a very peculiar orchid which has a bean for its fruit, the vanilla. In Mexico, its country of origin, it is a giant liana that climbs right up to the tops of trees more than 60 feet high. When transplanted at a distance from the colony of insects that help to fertilize it, the vanilla stops bearing fruit. If you introduced some families of this insect to the new place where the vanilla is cultivated, they would quickly set about fertilizing the plants there. The insects would multiply, but too quickly, and as they are hard workers they would fertilize every flower without exception. That would quickly exhaust the plants and make them bear none but tiny bean-pods. So, man has broken the association with the insect and taken its place, fertilizing by hand only the finest flowers, which thus yield very choice beans.

Six hundred years B.C. man was already taking lessons from the insects, for that was when Nebuchadnezzar built the hanging gardens of Babylon, near the river Euphrates. Gigantic pillars supported terraces with four storeys. Some of the pillars were hollow to allow water from the river to be drawn up by bucket-conveyors. In more modern times similar gardens, hung between heaven and earth, were built at Granada in Spain and at Isola Bella on Lake Maggiore.

Some of the mason ants of South America build their cities in trees. They bring all the earth in their mouths, powder it and so build their corridors and walls. Then they turn their roofs into hanging gardens, sowing seed that will grow nowhere else, harvesting the grain and storing it.

Like these ants that sow, harvest and thresh the ripe grain in the square of their little aerial cities, the termites grow mushrooms in special beds. These are specially selected mushrooms that the termites acclimatize, and at the same time they go to great lengths to get rid of other kinds of mushroom that try to get in and force themselves upon them.

The *isaria harioti* of Madagascar is a little mushroom that is the parasite of an insect, to which it attaches itself as the mistletoe does to the oak or poplar, growing on its carapace and eventually killing it by degrees.

The fly, attracted by the sweet liquid of the Venus's fly-trap . . .

. . . is caught in the trap which closes round it. The plant opens again as soon as it has digested its victim.

There are other plants that are quite ferocious, carnivorous plants that feed on tiny insects.

We know of a large number of flower-traps. There is a marsh arum that gapes open to make a funnel similar to that which the ant-lion digs in the sand. Any imprudent insect that goes to the bottom finds itself unable to climb back. The flower prevents it, raising along the inner circumference of its calyx a frill of hairs curved inwards and downwards, like the spikes of a grille. At the bottom of this funnel the insect drowns in a liquid distilled by the flower, a sort of mucus that digests it alive. Then there is the sundew which clings on to ants and plant lice by means of shiny, sticky hairs. The pitcher-plant grows a number of red and black jugs rather like pipe-bowls fitted with a lid. Inside the jug is a sticky liquid and hairs which together imprison all incautious insects that venture inside. Then, too, there is the Venus's flytrap, which half opens a pink and fearsome mouth which closes over any flies that are enticed inside by the sugary liquid there.

The astonishing thing is that most of these carnivorous plants are linked with an adoptive family of friendly insects. These are household slaves which come and go about the corridors of the flower, keeping it clean by devouring the remains of the plant-beast's meals.

There are flowers that kill, and flowers which feed a whole hungry tribe, hunting for a little world of their own. There are also flowers that play practical jokes. That is the case with the aristocratic birthwort which jests with bees, powdering any boorish intruder who enters uninvited all over with gold before it sets it free again. When a bee penetrates to the heart of the birthwort, the flower closes round it, and the plant seems

This strange tuft is a mushroom, the isaria harioti, which lives on an insect as a parasite and slowly kills it.

almost to delight in listening to the bee banging its head and beating its wings against the wall of its prison which it fills with frantic buzzing. After much struggling in the cloud of golden pollen, the bee, now gleaming in a coat of gold, sees the withering flower open and restore it to liberty.

There are, too, those astounding plants, the lichens, which must have first ventured ashore in the beginnings of the world, invading the volcanic islands of those days, clinging both to old lava and granite and to the frozen tundra. Long before the march of the trees they came, like explorers, content with little, clearing the way and preparing the ground for less hardy growths, first the mosses, then the grasses.

The lichens adapted themselves to all climates. They inhabit the sea, the dunes, the dry sandy deserts and the icy wastes of the Far North.

To make lichen successfully, Nature created one of the first of the associations between two vegetable organisms, a really intimate one in this case, which is between an alga and a mushroom. That is what the lichen is — a double plant. Man has been able to separate the two. By acclimatizing a lichen to water, one finds that the mushroom will often die and the alga, released, reverts to the independent life of other algae.

Plants and travel

THOUGH plants seem rooted and irrevocably vowed to immobility, that is not altogether the case. Plants become fixed in order to grow, but in their early days, when the seeds are launched on the winds, what intrepid travellers they are!

The seeds of the thistle and aster become detached and take to the air like balloons or tiny balls of down, and the wind carries them along. At the beginning of autumn the catkins of willows and poplars fly off across the fields and many land far away, though not as far as the yellow or white balloons of the cotton plant or the 'Comets' of the milkweed, which are launched in veritable squadrons from hangars superimposed on bouquets in full bloom which then burst their pods. These flying seeds, which have folding wings, antennae that come out at the start of their flight, and the shape of a dragonfly, are rigged to cover enormous distances.

All that man has invented and used in his flying machines — balloons, parachutes, propellers, gliders, helicopters — was invented by Nature before him and used by plants. The fall of the heavy seed of the lime-tree is braked by its wing-apparatus, which acts as a parachute. The propellers of the maple and aspen sweep the air like the blades of a helicopter.

Certain plants prefer to entrust their seeds to running water, and for these Nature has provided the shells and capsules surrounding the fruit with down or floss that makes them float. That is the case with coconuts.

There are other plants which deposit their offspring in the ground itself. The mangrove, for example, its great arms dangling into the very mire of the river bed, deposits its seeds there in front of it, and thus they advance up the bank, warping themselves along, as it were, like a family of mussels.

The ground-nut is another plant that sows its seed around it in a peculiar way. At the first downpour of rain the seed, buried in the ground, sends up a fine tuft of green with spreading leaves that are gracefully carved like those of the clover. Up shoot tigels, and at the end of them a bud forms and bursts into flower. When the flower is a lovely yellow colour and the seed is about to form, the tigel curves downward until it is touching the ground and releases the seed so that it can germinate quickly in the hot sand. The seed then burrows into the ground. In this way the ring formed by the ground-nut can expand almost indefinitely from one season to the other.

The wind, more than water, decides the life or death of the seeds which it carries either to fertile soil or to burning sands.

Then there are the stowaways, which are Nature's favourites. Birds take flight and in their gizzards they carry those seeds, like cherry stones, that are too hard to be digested. These travel with them, as in the hold of a ship, and who can tell where they will be sown?

Do plants warn their seeds about the danger of birds coming and carrying them off, as parent birds instruct their fledglings before they leave the nest?

A seed has only about one chance in a hundred thousand of escaping all the ambushes that are laid for it. One may be pecked by a wood-pigeon, another trampled by the pigeon's companion and thus stuck to the bird's foot by a particle of mud. The pigeon takes

off, withdraws its 'undercarriage' into the warmth of its belly, and there the mud dries and the seed falls — where?

Thousands of seeds can hope to germinate only as the result of some such miraculous chance. A turtle-dove's crop will often be found to contain 15,000 or 20,000 undigested seeds from its last meal.

What Nature does, she does well. Plants are as prolific as insects, their progeny innumerable. If a single head of flax could preserve its 700,000 to 800,000 seeds from the greed of birds and insects and each seed do the same, the whole world would shortly be transformed into a vast field of flax.

PLANTS
AND MAN

THE first people lived on the meat of wild animals and those plants which grew wild around them, such as oat-grass and darnel, stores of both of which have been found in pits in prehistoric caves and in lake-dwellings.

Nature performed the miracle of fruit by herself and without help from man. Man first tamed and domesticated animals, before he began to take an interest in plants. These he did not domesticate till later.

The first people to go in for agriculture were probably the Chinese. Three thousand years B.C., Chen-Nong, Emperor of the Heavenly Kingdom, presided in person at the festival of the Earth. With great pomp and with his own hand he sowed five seeds, one each of the most fertile species that grew in those days: rice, wheat, sorghum, millet and soya.

Most cultivated plants were cradled in the same place, the Asian continent. We owe many to Asia Minor, to Iran and to China; but America, especially the Andes and the Rocky Mountains, has also contributed many.

Just think of the distances these seeds from all corners of the world have travelled before reaching us? You could make a map showing the migrations of our cereals, fruits and vegetables.

Wheat, which is the oldest cultivated crop in the world, was introduced into Europe from Egypt and Mesopotamia, perhaps after having travelled across India and Turkistan, like millet which is nowhere grown more intensively than in China.

Like the sorghum of India and China and the durra of Equatorial Africa, millet still feeds 200 million of the world's inhabitants.

Rice originated in India, whence it was brought back by the cohorts of Alexander the Great, and they again

took it to Syria, from which the Arabs introduced it into Egypt.

Maize has never been found in a wild state. Its cultivation goes back to the earliest ages, when Egyptians and South American Indians, in their respective countries, great though the distance is between them, both used lotus seeds as a delicacy — perhaps a memory of the savoury seeds that flowered on the waters of the lakes of fabulous Atlantis. Now maize is common all over Europe, where it was unknown until the discovery of America.

The kidney bean seems to have originated in the New World: seeds of it have been found in graves in Peru; but the pea and other beans have always lived in Europe. Their seed has been found in lake-dwellings. In the old days they were one of the basic foodstuffs of the Ancient World, as were the cabbage, carrot, beetroot and turnip.

The onion, which grew in the soft sand of Ancient Egypt, was venerated there like a divinity.

Garlic lives in the wild state in the Kirghiz desert, the pumpkin comes from Brazil and the vegetable marrow from Mexico. Pizarro discovered the potato about 1520 A.D. in Peru.

In Africa there is a delicious little tomato which has fruit smaller than a cherry. Did our tomato come, via Spain, from Africa or America? We do not know.

As for fruits, our ancestors used to go into the forest to gather bitter crab apples, wild currants, raspberries and strawberries, but the peach, apricot, plum and cherry all came from China, and the quince and the medlar from Armenia and Iran.

The vine has been grown ever since prehistoric days,

Cutting SISAL in Mexico

Cultivation of RICE in the Far East

CORN Harvest in England

tting SUGAR CANE in Jamaica

OLIVE picking
in Italy

Fields of TULIPS
in Holland

Picking TEA
in China

Timber-felling
in Canada

Collecting RUBBER
in Africa

Growing TOBACCO
in Havana

WINE Harvest
in Alsace

Cutting
CORK
in Spain

and the Egyptians were making wine six thousand years ago.

The banana, orange and lemon, which all live in lands of the sun, originated in Asia.

Our ancestors in their lake-dwellings could not be gourmets. The bees were ahead of them there, having discovered the nectar in flowers and used it to make their honey. This honey and the crushed seeds of the poppy provided the Stone Age man with the sweets of which he was so fond.

HARVESTING COTTON

DRYING COFFEE

BANANAS

COCOA

The sugar-cane was known long ago in India, but it did not appear in Egypt and Spain until the Middle Ages. The sugar-beet, however, is native to the shores of the Channel and the North Sea, though its cultivation as a crop did not begin till about 1810.

Neither tea nor coffee was known in Europe before the days of James II, when tea from China was first imported into England. About the end of the sixteenth century the Venetians began buying coffee from the Arabs, and so its use gradually spread. The Crusaders had lived next door to them without ever suspecting the existence of the precious stuff!

Cacao, the powdered nut of which gives us our chocolate, grows wild in Amazonas. The Spaniards introduced it into the Philippines, and it is now grown on a large scale in Africa, in clearings made in the great equatorial forests.

The Indians used to chew tobacco, and in certain Aztec tombs beautifully worked pipes have been found.

The ground-nut is an immigrant from the New World, now well established in West Africa, for it is about the only plant that will be content with the copious but rare showers of rain which are all you get there.

Rubber originally came from Brazil.

Our ancestors used to spin the wool from their sheep and weave with that, and some, especially the Celts, also used wild flax. The textile plants, cotton, hemp and even the long-fibred flax, came from Asia.

The dyeing industry has been revolutionized by the discovery of chemical dyes, but in Africa and throughout the East those who make carpets and blankets continue to use the old vegetable dyes, which give such remarkable colours as those, for example, in the long-pile carpets of Ouagadougou.

One of the best kinds of paper is a 'rag' paper, but most are made directly from vegetable matter, like the old papyrus. The modern paper and board industry uses millions of tons of soft wood every year.

THE STRANGEST
OF
THE PLANTS

Despite the electronic microscope that magnifies a hundred thousand times — that is, fifty times more than the ordinary microscope — the scientists are far from having discovered all the secrets of the invisible world of microscopic vegetables, though it has enabled us to penetrate into a world even closer to nothing, that of the filtrable viruses, the ultra-microbes, so tiny that they pass through a porcelain filter. You will appreciate that creatures so thin can penetrate almost anywhere. A thimbleful of air or other matter, animate or inanimate, contains myriads of them, as do water, the surface soil, and the flesh of animals and of plants. They are to be found even 7,000 feet below the surface in the great oil-bearing synclinal strata. When examining samples obtained from that depth under the microscope, some scientists were amazed to find live bacteria in the oil. These had only been able to develop after coming in contact with the oxygen in the air. They were the descendants of those which had transformed the dead plankton from the bottom of the oceans of the Secondary Era into petroleum.

What part do these microscopic plants have to play? It is an important one and a dual one, that of destroying and creating.

I T is only thanks to the magic eye of the microscope that we are able to see, enlarged twenty thousand times, the fauna of the invisible plant world, those uni-cellular beings, the microbes. If they are rounded, they are called cocci; if shaped like a rod, they are bacilli or bacteria; and if they resemble corkscrews, they are called spirochetes.

A drop of water squeezed between two thin pieces of glass and seen through the lens of a microscope proves to be a world apart in which rod-bacteria swarm, thread-shaped bacteria twine and coil like snakes, and where tiny corpuscles swim, 'rowing' themselves along by pulling on their vibratile cilia.

A drop of culture is a universe swimming with life. And it is rather frightening.

Some of these microbes, though they creep and crawl, measure less than one ten-thousandth of a millimetre. You would think that they would move slowly, but their speed has been measured, and it is almost astronomical in proportion to their size. One covers about one centimetre a minute, which means that it covers five thousand times its own length in a minute. You can work out the comparative speed of a 30 ft boa. (I get it to be more than 1,330 miles an hour.)

Do microbes die?

As quickly as they are born. They reproduce at lightning speed. Each of them carries its own twin, as it were, and rapidly splits into two. The two twins do the same, and the four thus created follow suit. In fact, the number of microbes doubles every twenty minutes, and in perfect conditions the descendants of a single microbe would cover the earth in a few days.

This is the old puzzle of the grains of wheat and the chessboard. According to the story, a mandarin asked the Emperor, as a reward for his services, to cover a chessboard with wheat, putting one grain in the first square, two in the next and so on, doubling the amount each time. But it proved that all the granaries of the world would have been empty long before they got to the last square.

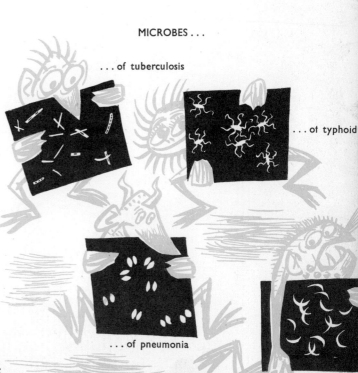

MICROBES . . .

. . . of tuberculosis

. . . of typhoid

. . . of pneumonia

. . of cholera

Certain microbes transform and decompose matter, whatever it is, turning it into something new. All fermentation is due to their secret activity. This is secret in that scientists in their laboratories have not yet been able to cause these astounding transformations except by setting other microbes to work. Without them and their mysterious work man would be unable to make bread, wine, alcohol, butter or cheese.

Microbes can transform soil. No rock can stand up to them; they turn rock into earth.

It is the microbes which, in helping to decompose dead vegetable matter, release the carbon dioxide that is necessary to the plants and the oxygen indispensable for animals if they are to live. It is microbes that enable an elephant to digest two tons of grass a day in its great inside; while if an elephant dies in the bush, other bacteria will digest its flesh and turn it into good earth that will grow tall grass to feed other elephants.

There are other microbes that create instead of destroying. These store the nitrogen of the air in the soil. Nitrogen is necessary to both plants and animals, and these microbes are the only things able to get it from the air. The plants and animals that breathe exhale it without having been able to fix it during respiration; thus the only way of getting the nitrogen to play its part in the life of the earth is through these invisible plants, without which there would be no life on our planet. They develop in the soil, which is aerated by their labours, on the roots of clover, beans, peas and other vegetables. When the roots of these plants rot, the microbes, laden with nitrogen, become mixed with the soil. Other plants sown in that spot obtain this nitrogen through their roots and assimilate it. The herbivores then eat these plants, then carnivores eat the herbivores, and when the carnivores die in their turn, their remains turn into manure under the action of nitrifying bacteria. So the cycle starts afresh: nitrogen from the air, bacteria, plants, animals.

It would be nice to leave the microbes there, making them appear as the great benefactors of mankind; but unfortunately many of these microscopic vegetables cause infectious diseases whose names have the most sinister ring: meningitis, plague, tuberculosis, tetanus, diphtheria, typhoid, yellow fever, cholera, typhus. When they encounter favourable conditions, microbes develop at prodigious speed. They secrete waste, called toxins, and these act as veritable poisons and can cause death. To cure a person infected with these you have to introduce a counter-poison into the bloodstream — that is, the serum taken from immunized animals. This contains anti-toxins that neutralize the effect of the microbe-poisons. It is possible thus to combat certain microbic diseases by introducing into the patient's blood extracts of a mould, penicillin, which is an enemy of microbes, as certain members of a family can be to each other more than to outsiders. This is the same tactic as man had already used against the insect parasites of useful plants, by introducing into devastated areas masses of the natural insect enemy of the parasite, which was then quickly exterminated.

This key opens the door to all the illnesses which are caused by germs. Fresh air and sunshine give strength, happiness and, consequently, good health.

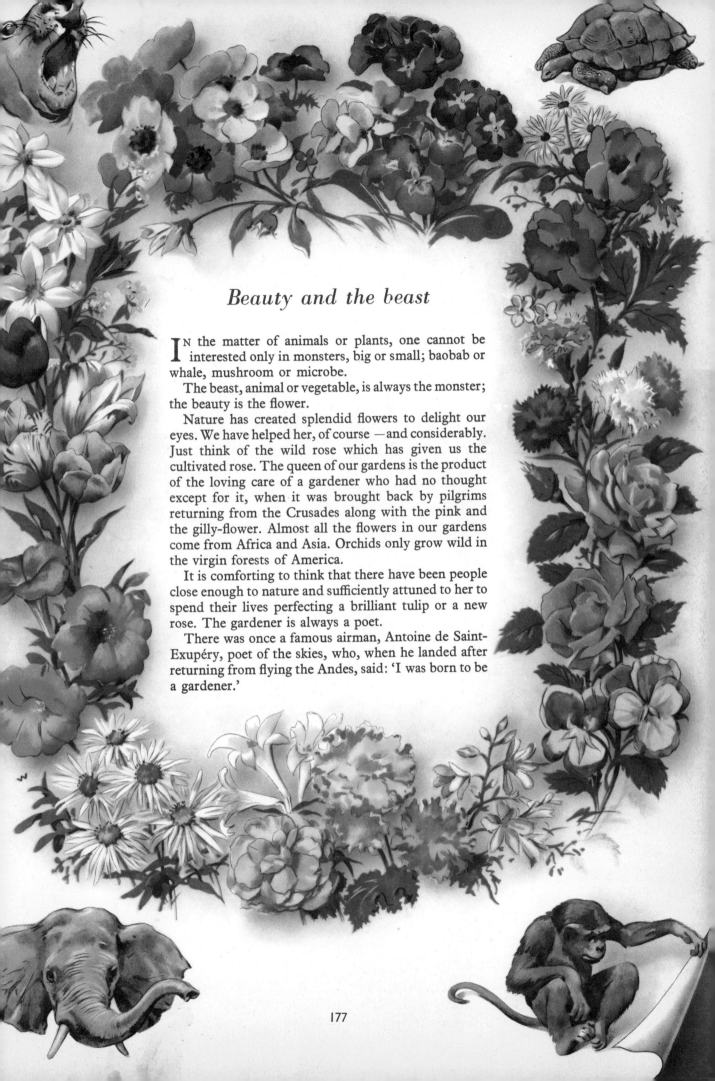

Beauty and the beast

In the matter of animals or plants, one cannot be interested only in monsters, big or small; baobab or whale, mushroom or microbe.

The beast, animal or vegetable, is always the monster; the beauty is the flower.

Nature has created splendid flowers to delight our eyes. We have helped her, of course —and considerably. Just think of the wild rose which has given us the cultivated rose. The queen of our gardens is the product of the loving care of a gardener who had no thought except for it, when it was brought back by pilgrims returning from the Crusades along with the pink and the gilly-flower. Almost all the flowers in our gardens come from Africa and Asia. Orchids only grow wild in the virgin forests of America.

It is comforting to think that there have been people close enough to nature and sufficiently attuned to her to spend their lives perfecting a brilliant tulip or a new rose. The gardener is always a poet.

There was once a famous airman, Antoine de Saint-Exupéry, poet of the skies, who, when he landed after returning from flying the Andes, said: 'I was born to be a gardener.'

MAN

IN the beginning, if legend is to be believed, the beasts were lords of the earth. Later the beasts came to be regarded as a kind of god. The Egyptians, for instance, worshipped them as divine, and the natives of the Congo and of Polynesia erected totems in their honour. Certain natives of the coast of Africa thought that they were descended from sharks. They were not afraid of their great ancestors, and dived right into their midst.

In the Sudan, the lion and the panther are masters of the wilds. The natives have tattooed on their cheeks five marks like scars — the sign of the claw! In this way they show their respect to the masters of the kingdom.

In Egypt the cat did not merely live in the house — he was a member of the family. When he died, people mourned him by shaving off their eyebrows. His body was embalmed. In museums one can see the mummies of other sacred animals — crocodiles, ibises and hawks. In Thebes crocodiles wore necklaces of pearls and gold earrings. In the burial ground at Maabdé, where thousands of their mummies lay piled up on the floors of the crypts, priests were found upright, similarly mummified, mounting guard over each of the entrances to the galleries.

From the wonderful tales of folklore we learn how the elephant, lion and alligator treated with man, who at one time was their vassal. And even though we know that it is only a story, it is fascinating to think of a council of animals adopting a wandering tribe or a group of passing men.

The animals must have been pretty startled when they saw man for the first time. Curious, yet uneasy, for their instinct must surely have told them that this new arrival was of a race very different from theirs, and that the end of their reign was in sight. Just think what naked man could accomplish with his hands!

The beast was only an animal after all. Man had already shown himself to be a thinking machine.

179

THE HUMAN BODY

THE human body is a most marvellous and exact machine. Just imagine how that precise little clock, the heart, in a man of about sixty will have beaten some 2,000 million times without stopping. Here we are, countless generations later, the great-grandchildren of prehistoric man, whom we have seen living in his cave and hunting wild oxen with a stone axe. Like us he breathed, ate and slept — and dreamed. He took his body for granted. And we, who inhabit a similar body, marvel no more than he did to find it so complex, so well organized.

True enough, the tortoise does not bother about its shell, nor, doubtless, has the kangaroo ever asked herself why Nature should have endowed her with that pouch in which she carries her young.

One cannot do better than compare the complexity of the organs and functions of the human body to the workings and installations of a big city.

See how at nightfall the darkness is illuminated by thousands of little dots of light outlining the network of innumerable streets. Like a factory which works unceasingly, the big city continues its nocturnal life till dawn. Lorries filled with food supplies deliver their goods all night. Road sweepers begin their work long before we are awake. And while we sleep, the telephone exchanges, police stations, fire brigades and all the services responsible for our safety keep careful watch.

Tonight, tomorrow, amongst the serried rows of houses children will be born and old people will die.

Our body is a city in miniature; our organs, in fact, are as complex, as well regulated, and some of them work as automatically, as the public services of a great city.

In this living city the inhabitants are all related. Those living in the same neighbourhood are almost twins. They all belong to the family of the nuclei, and all occupy identical dwellings, the cells.

The cells of the body are workshops a thousand times smaller than the cells of a honeycomb, yet furnished with every modern convenience. Besides, the inhabitants do not mind being shut up in their restricted quarters — everything has been provided to assure their well-being. And the same laws apply to them all.

Naturally, here as in any other community, there are certain individuals who prefer to live on the fringe of society. They are evildoers, and they hide, the better to be able to carry out their illegal trade. Their hiding-places are most often cells at the bottom of blind alleys where their sort form unhealthy growths which quickly develop, branch out and bring trouble to the peaceful city, and often death. These clusters of dangerous cells have a frightening Latin name which means crab: Cancer.

BRAIN

SALIVARY GLANDS

TEETH

VEINS . ARTERIES

OESOPHAGUS

DIGESTIVE SYSTEM

PHARMACY

SUGAR MILL

LIVER

HEART

PANCREAS

KIDNEY

STOMACH

KIDNEY

SMALL INTESTINE

LARGE INTESTINE

The food supplies for the city called 'the human body' come from the outside and enter through a large gate: the mouth. They have to pass through a row of factories and chemical works before they can be distributed to the cells.

The first factory is mainly a sort of grinding-mincing machine: the jawbone, which reduces the food to pulp. When the food has been thoroughly chewed and mixed with saliva from the salivary glands it receives a special name: 'Bolus of masticated food'. It is now ready to be swallowed and to start on its journey to the stomach. From now on the work of the other factories will take place mostly during the night.

Jonah was the only being who ever ventured into the second factory, and that was the enormous stomach of a whale. Now suppose that by mischance we swallow some tiny insect which has somehow found its way into the cavern of our mouth; its fate will be like that of a wasp at the heart of a carnivorous plant: it will be taken alive into our digestive tract, and the juices produced by the stomach, liver and pancreas will set to work on it.

Animals like the lion, the tiger or the monkey do not bother about what happens inside their intestines, large or small. They just eat, and what they eat they digest perfectly while they take their siesta, without having to worry their heads about the mysterious chemical processes which transform what they have eaten into a liquid called 'chyle'. This, in passing through the lining of the intestines, will renew the blood and the supply of sugar contained in the liver. But we ought to be more careful, so remember: eat slowly and chew well, and the rest of the process will look after itself!

Our blood circulation is like the traffic of a big town, with millions of red corpuscles travelling along the arteries. They are the delivery vans sent by the heart to all parts of the body in order to distribute the oxygen and other nourishment needed by the cells. For each cell must have its share regularly delivered at the front door.

These corpuscles are minute, about one ten-thousandth of an inch or so, and because of this they can make their way anywhere, leaving the broad highways, the arteries, and travelling along ever-narrowing lanes, till finally they reach the capillaries, which are not even of a hair's breadth.

It takes barely 13 seconds for the average 9 pints of blood contained in our bodies to make a complete circulation. With every six beats the heart pumps one pint, that is 12 pints a minute, or about 2,000 gallons in 24 hours — enough to fill a road tanker. It is this ceaseless process going on within us which maintains the life-giving warmth of our bodies.

In this way each cell is constantly supplied with oxygen, and the nucleus, the cell's occupant, keeps a tiny smokeless fire going, using the oxygen to cook the food brought by the blood. Though the fire is without smoke it gives out plenty of heat — the circulation in fact maintains a regular central heating system in our bodies.

The blood flows always in the same direction, and having left the heart by the arteries eventually returns to it by the veins. On the return journey the red corpuscles purify the parts which they visit, and, in passing, pour the waste down the kidneys and provide the liver with the necessary nourishment, particularly sugar.

The lungs, where the blood is sent by the heart to be

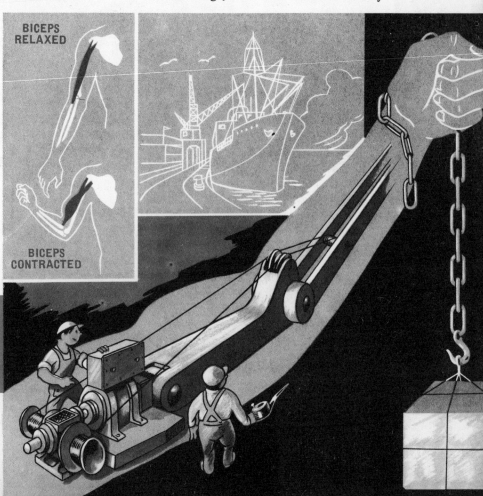

BICEPS RELAXED

BICEPS CONTRACTED

In taking on fresh supplies man is like a ship loading. His arms are the derricks, and he pulls on his tendons and contracts his muscles when lifting a considerable weight, or simply raising a spoon to his mouth.

purified, are also automatic mechanisms. They work day and night of their own accord and without stopping. And the same is true of the two chemical works, the liver and the kidneys.

After it has been supplied with oxygen by the lungs the blood returns to the heart, bright red and as good as new. The red corpuscles now start off again on their 'round trip'. As they go, they may encounter the white corpuscles which act as police. These latter go everywhere, even penetrating into the capillaries and through the walls of the cells, giving pitiless chase to any lurking microbes and pursuing them to the most inaccessible places in order to destroy them.

On one point, however, the human body and a city differ very much from one another. A city stands still, whereas man on his two legs and without the use of machines on wheels or wings covers a distance of thousands of miles in the course of his life.

Directing operations, like the captain on the bridge of his ship, is the brain, which gives its orders to all parts of the machine by means of the motor nerves which branch out to the remotest cells. At a speed of about 100 yards per second the brain sends out an electric current which sets the motor muscles in motion. These motor muscles do not revolve. They become inflated, expand and contract, operating on the levers and bearings of the crane (the arm), the vice (the jaws), the paddle (the tongue), and the mechanical chute (the throat), which acts like the conveyor belt of a coal mine.

The brain is not merely the central electricity control room which assures the supply of power to all parts of the body. It is a transmitter which sends messages and issues orders. But it is also capable of intercepting the waves which reach it from all parts of the city and of recording them.

It does not matter from what neighbourhood the message comes — an arm, the nose, a hand, the back — nor what kind of impression it conveys — a prick, a burn, a blow, cramp or an invasion of microbes . . . however slight the sensation, the brain is alerted at once.

This moving city has its watch towers and its observation posts where the sentinels are always ready to give

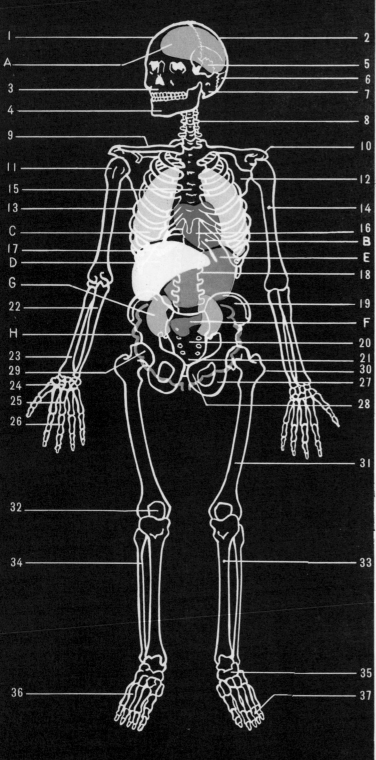

the alarm in the event of any threat of danger from the outside. The eyes keep constant vigil, observing the shape and movement of things. The ears receive sounds and transmit them to the brain. The hands sense by touch, the nose by smell. And the brain records all these sensations faithfully.

In that wonderful log book, the memory, minute and scrupulous records are kept.

'Stop!' commands the brain, or 'Go!' it may say. In order to avoid sudden danger, it is sometimes necessary to brake violently or to put on a spurt of speed. Quick action is required to ward off a threat to safety, and the brain sees to it.

In the Middle Ages, when a city had closed its gates and the curfew had been sounded, the narrow streets were patrolled by the nightwatchman, and throughout the night his cry could be heard: 'It is three of the clock, and all's well!'

Within the city of the body the police are far better organized. The occupants of the cells can sleep peacefully, but, like telephone wires, the nerve fibres — in fact the whole network of the nervous system — remain connected. During the hours of sleep the emergency service can instantly be alerted all along the length of the spinal marrow.

A fly buzzes. It does not wake the sleeper. But the sting in his hand is immediately transmitted to the control room, which instantly sets off a reflex movement. And, without the sleeper's awakening, his hand will brush away the insect and then flop back on to the sheet.

In the morning the city will awaken to a new day. Never for an instant will the sleeper have been aware of the work done by the different organs in his body. It will not have occurred to him that, all night long, his heart and lungs, all the chemical works of his city, have never stopped working. So life goes on!

In spite of the wonderful organization of all the services, the city may be at the mercy of an epidemic. It may happen that the white corpuscles, overwhelmed with work, are no longer able to assure the decontamination of all its parts.

The machinery in one of the factories — liver, kidneys, intestines, spleen, etc. — can go wrong, or the white corpuscles which watch over the general safety may be too weak or unable to cope with an invasion of the city by microbes. And so we fall ill.

Doctors diagnose illnesses and apply remedies which usually succeed in checking or overcoming them.

In the laboratories, notably the Wright-Fleming Institute in London or the Pasteur Institute in Paris, serums and vaccines are developed. Vaccines, such as those against smallpox, bubonic plague or yellow fever are obtained by inoculating animals with the illness to be prevented. The blood and certain organs, removed later from these animals and scientifically treated, are used in the manufacture of vaccines, a small dose of which will render the vaccinated person immune for a longer or shorter period, that is, will stop him from catching the disease in question.

Serums, such as those against tetanus or rabies, are

– 1: FRONTAL – 2: PARIETAL – 3: SUPERIOR MAXILLA –
4: INFERIOR MAXILLA – 5: TEMPORAL – 6: OCCIPITAL –
7: MASTOID – 8: CERVICAL VERTEBRAE – 9: CLAVICLE
– 10: ACROMION – 11: HEAD OF HUMERUS – 12: SCA-
PULA – 13: RIBS – 14: HUMERUS – 15: STERNUM –
16: DORSAL VERTEBRAE – 17: FLOATING RIBS –
18: LUMBAR VERTEBRAE – 19: ILIUM – 20: SACRUM –
21: COCCYX – 22: ULNA – 23: RADIUS – 24: CARPUS
– 25: METACARPUS – 26: PHALANGES OF FINGERS –
27: ISCHIUM – 28: PUBIS – 29: HEAD AND NECK OF
FEMUR – 30: GREAT TROCHANTER – 31: FEMUR –
32: PATELLA – 33: TIBIA – 34: FIBULA – 35: TARSUS –
36: METATARSUS – 37: PHALANGES OF TOES

– A: BRAIN – B: HEART – C: LUNGS – D: LIVER – E: STOM-
ACH – F: PANCREAS – G: KIDNEYS – H: INTESTINES

likewise obtained from animals which have been inoculated with the illness. The serum is administered by injection and is used not to prevent the illness but to check and mitigate its effect if, unluckily, one has already caught it.

Surgery has made astonishing progress over the last fifty years in the repair of the various organs in the human body.

Thanks to the miraculous 'eye bank', surgeons have been able by corneal graft to give sight to people blind from birth, people who have never known light or colour. When a severe injury has destroyed tissue, it is possible to repair the damaged area by grafting on new flesh and skin or healthy muscles. Broken bones can be knitted together. Tainted blood which contaminates the system can be exchanged by transfusion. The removal of a kidney is a common operation. Attempts have even been made to replace the diseased kidney by the transplantation of a healthy kidney from a donor. This operation is far more dangerous.

Soon it will be possible to take to pieces all parts of the delicate mechanism. Already surgeons have operated successfully on the brain and even the heart.

For those who have lost a limb as a result of war injury or serious accident science has been able to devise jointed limbs which are remarkably efficient.

Surgery is even used to improve people's appearance. The plastic surgeon can remodel an ill-favoured face. He can reshape its outlines and make it much better looking than it originally was.

MAN AND THE ANIMALS

THE beehive or antheap are like well-developed cities. Their inhabitants know their place and functions, and social life there is admirably organized.

In the same way Nature, by the arrangement of the cells in plants and animals, has more or less perfected her construction of living things.

Animals belonging to the class of mammals of which man is a member have bodies whose working mechanisms run on much the same lines as our own.

The bodily mechanisms of the lower groups of animals work on very much simpler lines. This is at the same time an advantage and a drawback. The mechanism goes wrong less easily, but if something upsets it, it usually means the end.

Like a good fairy, Nature seems to have endowed each living creature with a gift.

Have you ever been to a steeplechase, or watched the jumping classes at a show and seen horses jump over a rail high enough for them to have passed underneath without more than just bending their heads?

The Swede, NILSSON, clears 6'10".

Since 1935 the American, OWENS, has held the world record for long-jump with 26'5".

ROGER BANNISTER, the first four-minute miler

The record jump for a horse is about 8 feet. After training, police dogs also can jump over obstacles more than 6 feet high.

In athletic contests, records of over 7 feet have been reached — without a pole, of course. So man can jump about as well as a horse or a dog. But not as well as a flea!

With a single leap a flea can reach a height of 300 times its length. If any man were equally agile, he would reach a height of about 1,500 feet. Even our distant cousins, the gorillas, are far from equalling such a performance, though a gorilla can take a river 20 yards wide in its stride. Marvellous feat of strength though that is, it is not the same.

It would be wrong, however, to conclude from this that animals are generally more gifted than ourselves, for this applies only to certain aspects of their physique.

I remember a long trip which I made once in Mauretania as far as the border of the Rio de Oro, crossing the Great Ridge, where the sandstorms are continually obliterating all traces of the tracks, so that they have to be marked out with long stakes to prevent people going astray and getting lost in that huge desert, as could easily have happened to me and the friend who accompanied me on that trip. My friend was a passionate big game hunter and the sight of our first ostriches left him with only one desire: to get an ostrich. Ostriches, however, are 'protected', that is to say that you are not allowed to hunt them without a special permit, and I had quite a job to dissuade my friend from setting off after them. But when, seeming to emerge out of a grey-blue mirage, a herd of great antelopes got up and fled at our approach, I was unable to restrain him. In spite of myself, I took part in the hunt.

I can still see the magnificent pair after which we went, a male and a female, clad in white, bounding along with such supple rhythmic movements that they resembled a pair of aerial ballet dancers, and following them, leap for leap, without ever stumbling, went their fawn . . .

At that point the Great Ridge was smooth and flat, and we were in a fast car. I was driving and my friend sat beside me, his rifle ready on his knees. The young fawn dropped behind, and the mother, realizing that it

was tiring, turned her head to look at it, though without slackening her own speed. I signalled to my blood-thirsty friend to look at the speedometer. The needle pointed to 55 . . . Yes, 55 miles an hour . . . that is the speed of an antelope in the desert!

Then I slowed down. Those magnificent beasts had earned their lives. I saw the two antelopes stop, then lick their fawn which stood bathed in sweat, its slender legs trembling.

A thoroughbred horse will, at the touch of the whip, succeed in maintaining for a few minutes a speed of 45 miles an hour.

The flight of birds can be very fast. A pigeon averages 45 miles an hour, a partridge 50, a swift 105, a golden falcon, when chased by an aeroplane, almost 190 miles an hour. But no bird can rival the dipterous insects in power or even, in some cases, in speed.

It is not so much by their speed, however, that the animals outclass man. It is by their strength. The lion, the bull, the elephant and the gorilla are endowed with tremendous strength.

The dung-beetle can roll before it a ball which it has moulded and which represents three to four times its height. It is as if a man, in the country, were to push a load of hay 4 yards high with his pitchfork.

The mygale spider is a small monster that lives in Brazil, and which attains a height of 4 inches, not count-ing its legs. This spider catches rats and birds. It can successfully take on a rabbit or a hare, and will even pin down a large snake and make it bleed to death.

Nature has been fair in distributing her gifts amongst the creatures of the earth, but she has not always been as generous as one might have thought. She has given strength to some, and speed to others. She has caused certain senses to develop disproportionately: as the sense of smell in dogs and elephants, for instance. The elephant, however, cannot see further than the tip of its

Comparative Speeds

Miles per hour	LIVING CREATURES UNAIDED ● WITH TECHNICAL AID	LIVING CREATURES UNAIDED ● WITH TECHNICAL A...
18000	Husky in artificial satellite (U.S.S.R.)	
3000	Monkey in a stratospheric rocket.	
1000	The 'Trident' SO-900 in a climb. Other jet aircraft in a dive.	
SOUND 760		
393		Sir John Cobb (U.K.)
248		
205		Henri Brachet, driver of the electric train CC–7107 (Fra...
185		Russel Wright (New Zealand on a motor bicycle.
180	Falcon.	
175		Luigi Castelloti (Italy) in a racing car, over a kilometre, flying start.
127	Eagle.	
110	Helicopter.	Cyclist paced by a car.
95	Albatross. Petrel. Vulture.	
75		
70		Cheetah.
65	Wild Duck.	
62		Antelope.
60		
55	Robin. Humming bird. Turkey.	
50		Roedeer. Ostrich. Charging Lion. — Motor scooter.
45	Homing pigeon. Swallow.	
43		Racehorse.
40		Giraffe. Gazelle.
37	Owl.	
33	Magpie.	Zebra.
31	Sea-gull.	Greyhound. Bear.
30	Dragon-fly. Horse-fly.	Kangaroo.
28		Rhinoceros. — Autocycle.
26		
24	Crow.	Elephant. Tiger.
22		Owens (U.S.A.) over 100 metres.
19	Lark.	The fastest snake : the black mamba of Africa.
18		Guido Caroli, on roller skate...
15		Bannister, first four-minute miler.
9	Chicken. Bat.	
6	Bee.	
4	Fly.	
3·97		
0·002		Snail.

Donald Campbell (U.K.) in the speed-boat *Bluebird*

Pravda (Austria) on skis.

...ing Shark.

...rd-fish.

Outboard motor-boat.

Sail skating.

...ny-fish. Dolphin.

The Submarine *Nautilus* (U.S.A.)

...e Shark.

...en Whale.

Ice-skating, over 500 metres.

...ut.

The *Nautilus* diving.

...reland (U.S.A.) swimming
...style over 100 metres.

nose. When it cannot smell the strong odour of the Pygmies on the wind, those intrepid hunters will slip under its belly, and, with one stroke of their assagai, cut the tendon of one of its forelegs.

The dog with his eloquent ears and the goose with her invisible ones have a very well developed sense of hearing. The famous geese of the Capitol gave the alarm when the enemy attacked Rome.

We are certainly short-sighted beings when compared with the vulture or the falcon. The eyes of a bird are often heavier than its brain, and they are finer mechanism than those of the creatures of land and water. In some species of birds the eyes combine the properties of a telescope and a microscope. This gives them a keenness of vision ten or twenty times that of man. In addition birds are gifted with a sense of orientation which man lacks.

Nature has never made a green flower. Those for which she has contrived her most brilliant reds are not even seen by the bees, which cannot distinguish between dark red and green, both of which appear to them equally sombre. Like a bomber, a bee has two large faceted eyes giving it a field of vision from side to side, and three peep-holes enabling it to see danger approaching from below and above.

Each of the big globular eyes of the dragonfly has 15,000 to 20,000 facets.

Variations in intensity of light will cause the pupils of a cat's eye to dilate or contract. The whiskers of the cat, like those of the tiger, act as feelers.

Fish truly possess a sixth sense. It is not so well known as the 'radar' of bats, but is equally astonishing. It has been discovered that fish are aware of the presence of danger without the need of either seeing or hearing it. On each side of its body the fish possesses an array of scales equipped with a line of nerve fibres; this is the 'lateral line' which detects the slightest vibrations transmitted by the water. Thus you can see a school of roach dart away and disappear among the water plants some time before an approaching person has reached the river's bank.

Another of Nature's gifts to some of her animals is the ability to imitate their surroundings, a kind of natural camouflage. Commando troops are camouflaged in yellow and green when being parachuted into enemy territory, so that they will blend with the fields in which they land.

For her beasts, of which each is prey to another, Nature herself has seen to the camouflage which helps to screen them from the eyes of their enemies. The tiger of Asia has a fur striped with black, as if the shadow of the long grass and bamboos in which it hides were painted on it. The giraffe is spotted like the acacia trees on whose leaves it browses.

It can safely be assumed that at one time the sole, like other fish, had one eye on the right and one on the left side of its head. It acquired the habit of lying on its side at the bottom of the sea. Hence the fact that the side resting on the dark bottom is brown and the other is light. Gradually, in the same way, the useless eye, which was always turned towards the mud, has wandered over to join the other eye on the side which faces the light.

The chameleon can change its colour and assume that of the flower or leaf, red, green or yellow, on which it happens to be.

Do you know why? An African legend tells us the reason. A big cloud, like an enormous balloon, descended towards the earth, carrying new beasts, as yet unknown in the bush. Amongst them was the chameleon. When the cloud reached the top of the hills, all the little animals jumped to the ground — all, that is, except the chameleon, which had been so frightened that it shut its eyes. Then the cloud rose again towards the sky, taking the chameleon with it. A tornado suddenly came and tore the cloud apart, and the chameleon, in order to avoid being smashed to the ground, jumped on to a large rainbow. It walked down this, not hurrying, passing from one band of colour to the other as it went — from red to violet, from green to blue. Now, as a result, these are the colours which this little lizard assumes when it is on flowers.

To each creature Nature has given weapons to safeguard and protect its life. An insignificant caterpillar, in order to appear dangerous, can imitate the head of a snake. The 'calico' butterfly frightens and puts to flight the pursuing tomtit by spreading its wings, on which are two brilliant spots which shine like the eyes of an owl.

The cold of the Far North has made its animals dress in white. There bears, foxes and hares wear coats the colour of snow. In those icy seas the graceful dolphin is no longer blue: there it is the beluga, a northern cousin, which is snow-white.

All the animals of creation have their parts to play. The elephant is myopic and the tiger has no sense of smell. If the elephant had the eyesight of the tiger, and the tiger had the elephant's keenness of smell, there would perhaps be nothing on this earth by now except elephants and tigers.

Man alone was put on the world absolutely naked. His life is relatively short. A tortoise lives for 200 years, a falcon 150 years, almost as long as a pike or a carp; an elephant reaches 100 years.

Man has neither tusks nor claws, neither fleece nor feathers. He is truly naked and without weapons. Nevertheless he can adapt himself to all conditions, for, apart from his extraordinary power of resistance, he is gifted with intelligence, memory and willpower.

Of other creatures it is only the spider whose domain is as limitless as that of man.

Man swims and dives like a fish, flies like a bird, and launches himself from the sky with his parachute.

He has reached points of our planet where no other animal can live: the poles and the summits of the Himalayas.

The gift which has enabled man to conquer our planet and to rule there as lord is his spirit of imitation and invention. First, he imitated the beast; he clothed himself in animal skins. Even today, when hunting in the African bush, the black man, who has remained almost naked, crouches, bow in hand, his head covered by a mask grotesquely carved and provided with a long beak resembling that of the hornbill. And pecking the earth with his red wooden beak like a bird, he gradually approaches the wild boar or antelope, until he is within bowshot.

Like the spider which surrounds itself with a bubble of air to dive, man shuts himself into a steel sphere to explore the bottom of the sea.

Man, having begun by imitating nature, has surpassed it by the utilization of his marvellous mechanical inventions.

Man was naked. Man was weak. But he had intelligence. What he has achieved, he has achieved alone and by his own efforts, in the course of the centuries.

And his triumph is the machine.

FOURTH PART

MACHINES
IN THE SERVICE OF MAN

MANY thousands of years ago, man found himself, naked and weaponless, in the kingdom of the beasts, which had already chosen their domains. It was against the strength of the beasts that man had first to measure his own strength. This was not inconsiderable, for our ancestors were strapping great fellows, well built, muscular and powerful.

But after his first encounters with the animals of the forest and jungle, man rapidly became aware that by comparison he was weak. Even if the beast was unable to use its teeth or claws in close fight, it could crush man with the weight of its body. When hunting, the smell of man's salty sweat betrayed his presence to the herd he was after, or he would be spotted far off by its keen-eyed sentries.

Obliged to share the wild fruits of the forest with the beasts, and to hunt wild animals in order to have food to eat, man often risked becoming the quarry himself before ever knowing the triumphs of the hunter.

Man was endowed with intelligence and memory. The beast taught him guile. Very soon our great ancestors learnt to give a name to that which assured the supremacy of the beast: strength. It was this strength which he himself lacked and which he needed to attack or defend himself, to provide himself with nourishment and to build himself a shelter.

In his turn, man promptly set about organizing his domain, for he felt the need to compensate for his weakness. His nimble wit hit upon ways which enabled him to increase and multiply his strength.

The plain, or savanna, where the wild beasts prowled by

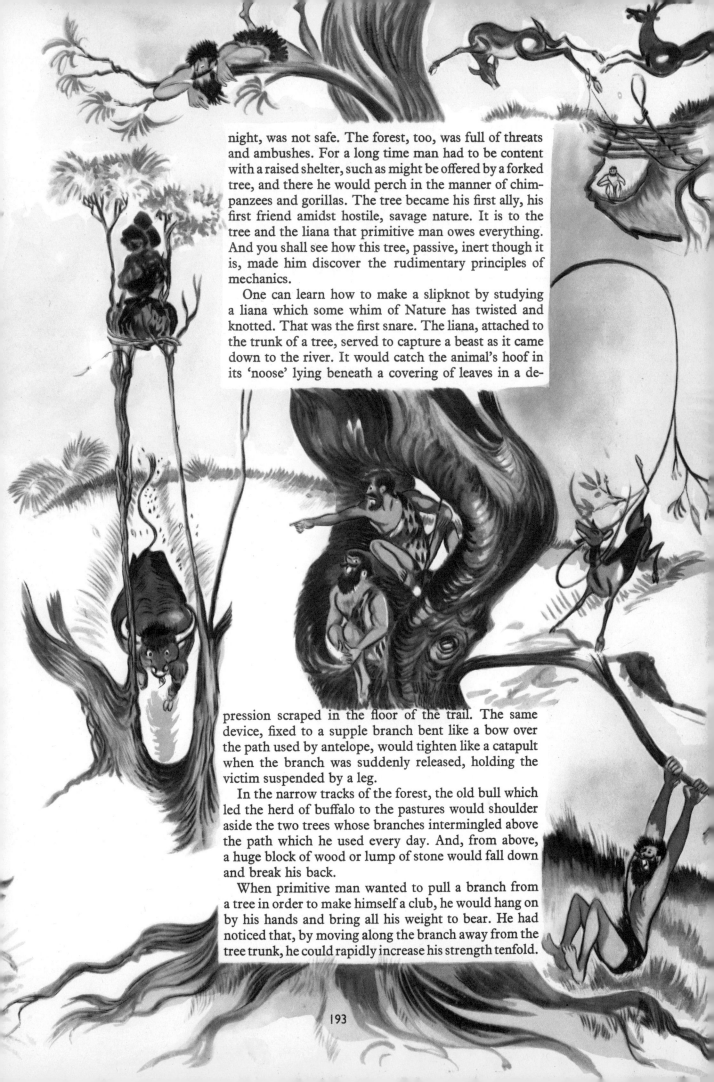

night, was not safe. The forest, too, was full of threats and ambushes. For a long time man had to be content with a raised shelter, such as might be offered by a forked tree, and there he would perch in the manner of chimpanzees and gorillas. The tree became his first ally, his first friend amidst hostile, savage nature. It is to the tree and the liana that primitive man owes everything. And you shall see how this tree, passive, inert though it is, made him discover the rudimentary principles of mechanics.

One can learn how to make a slipknot by studying a liana which some whim of Nature has twisted and knotted. That was the first snare. The liana, attached to the trunk of a tree, served to capture a beast as it came down to the river. It would catch the animal's hoof in its 'noose' lying beneath a covering of leaves in a de-

pression scraped in the floor of the trail. The same device, fixed to a supple branch bent like a bow over the path used by antelope, would tighten like a catapult when the branch was suddenly released, holding the victim suspended by a leg.

In the narrow tracks of the forest, the old bull which led the herd of buffalo to the pastures would shoulder aside the two trees whose branches intermingled above the path which he used every day. And, from above, a huge block of wood or lump of stone would fall down and break his back.

When primitive man wanted to pull a branch from a tree in order to make himself a club, he would hang on by his hands and bring all his weight to bear. He had noticed that, by moving along the branch away from the tree trunk, he could rapidly increase his strength tenfold.

He had, however, no notion that he had just discovered the lever; that lever which served him — always in the form of a piece of branch — to turn a wild ox over on the ground, so as to make it easier to skin, or to roll a lump of rock in front of the cave in which he was sheltering for the night.

Having carved up his game, man looked for a way to keep the quarters out of reach of ants and wild animals. He hit upon the idea of hoisting the chunks of meat to the top of his hut, which he did by sliding them up along two poles resting on the top of the roof. The principle of the inclined plane had been discovered.

The tree which had been cut down, the friendly tree which supplied man with dead branches to feed his fire, one day gave him the idea of using its round, smooth trunk for moving a heavy load by sliding it along on rollers. Man had discovered the wheel. But thousands of years were to pass before he thought of carving out of this long rolling cylinder the two thin wooden discs, joined in the centre by a slender axle, which would lighten the clumsy and terribly heavy primitive roller.

Eventually, the liana, passed over a main branch so that an antelope or wild boar could be hauled up and suspended above ground in the shade of the foliage, provided the first rough prototype of a pulley, where the rope slides over a locked wheel.

If man did not immediately think of these simple machines, we must nevertheless go back to the very beginning of his reign in order to trace their origins in the crude aids which his friend, the tree, gave him to help him multiply his strength. The principle of the lever, the inclined plane and the wheel have thus been known almost since the beginning, and they have been used and applied ever since in man's machines, ranging from the most ancient and primitive to the most complicated and advanced products of modern science.

The inclined plane increases one's strength.

THE ultimate purpose of any machine is to make work easier. All machines put into practice the fundamental principle: a relatively weak force applied over a long distance can replace a powerful force operating over a shorter distance.

In other words: the same effort can be exerted by a weak force as by a much greater one. And thus from variation to variation, always improving, and from combination to combination, becoming ever more perfect, there have finally evolved the marvels of modern machinery.

THE INCLINED PLANE

A ZIGZAG road up a mountain is an inclined plane. It takes longer to get to the top, but it is more comfortable and convenient than the steep path scaling the mountainside in a direct line from base to summit.

Another example of an inclined plane is the ramp used by cars entering a garage several storeys high. A staircase, too, is an inclined plane. This, of course, is

not smooth: stairs have been fixed to prevent the foot from slipping at each step.

Oxen or horses harnessed to a heavily laden cart will not be able to pull it up a slope too steeply inclined. In the same way I should doubtless be unable to lift a trunk weighing 150 pounds, in order to put it in a car whose boot is 1 yard from the ground. If, in order to save my strength, I let the trunk slide over a board 5 yards long, resting on the boot of the car and supported on the ground, the load will have travelled over a distance of 5 yards. In this way, the trunk will have been raised by 1 yard, just as if I had lifted it vertically. I shall certainly have accomplished the same amount of work, but I shall have used less effort; it will not matter to me that I have had to manoeuvre the trunk over a greater distance, if I have been able to achieve my result with less labour.

It is as if the inclined plane multiplied my strength. When the builders of the temple at Ephesus or the Hypostyle Hall at Karnak undertook the construction of their gigantic projects, they had no alternative but gradually to bury the columns in order to build the top. To do this they had to heap up great quantities of earth which formed slopes — again the inclined plane — up which the enormous blocks of stone were rolled by hand. The huge stone slab which formed the crosspiece of a prehistoric cromlech was hauled up in a similar fashion by our ancestors of the Stone Age. The menhirs — the upright stones — were embedded in the ground, crude reminders of the obelisks of Ancient Egypt. These monoliths frequently were of a colossal height, sometimes exceeding 70 feet, and weighing over 600 tons.

The obelisk at Luxor was built about 1500 B.C. of red granite, quarried at Syene in Upper Egypt. This now stands in the Place de la Concorde in Paris, to which it was taken in a boat specially built for the purpose in 1836. Another famous obelisk, known as Cleopatra's Needle, was brought to

195

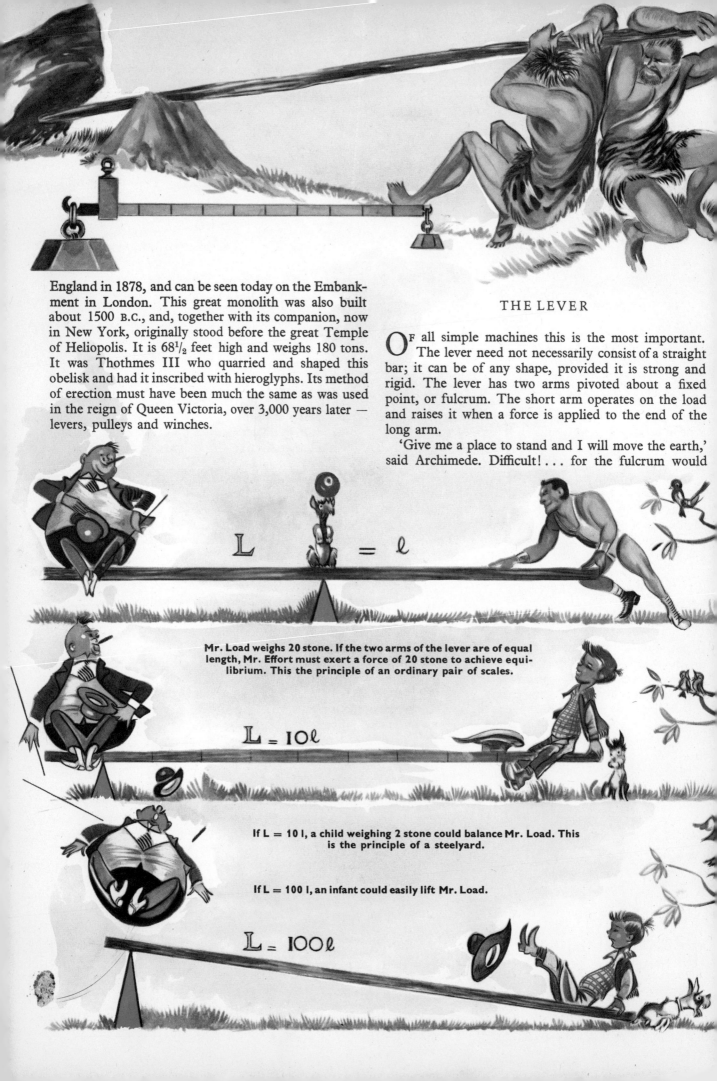

England in 1878, and can be seen today on the Embankment in London. This great monolith was also built about 1500 B.C., and, together with its companion, now in New York, originally stood before the great Temple of Heliopolis. It is 68½ feet high and weighs 180 tons. It was Thothmes III who quarried and shaped this obelisk and had it inscribed with hieroglyphs. Its method of erection must have been much the same as was used in the reign of Queen Victoria, over 3,000 years later — levers, pulleys and winches.

THE LEVER

Of all simple machines this is the most important. The lever need not necessarily consist of a straight bar; it can be of any shape, provided it is strong and rigid. The lever has two arms pivoted about a fixed point, or fulcrum. The short arm operates on the load and raises it when a force is applied to the end of the long arm.

'Give me a place to stand and I will move the earth,' said Archimede. Difficult! . . . for the fulcrum would

$$L = l$$

Mr. Load weighs 20 stone. If the two arms of the lever are of equal length, Mr. Effort must exert a force of 20 stone to achieve equilibrium. This the principle of an ordinary pair of scales.

$$L = 10l$$

If L = 10 l, a child weighing 2 stone could balance Mr. Load. This is the principle of a steelyard.

If L = 100 l, an infant could easily lift Mr. Load.

$$L = 100l$$

have to be placed outside the Earth — on the Moon, for example. However, the learned man wished to convey that even that was feasible, provided the lengths of the short and long arms were carefully calculated in relation to the load to be lifted and the force available. You are probably acquainted with the steelyard,

with a lever 1 yard long in which $1 = 6$ inches and $L = 30$ inches, of the maximum effort which we can exert is 100 pounds.

The formula gives $W \times 6 = 100 \times 30$

$$\text{therefore } W = \frac{100 \text{ pounds} \times 30}{6} = 500 \text{ pounds}$$

To sum up, the two forces Weight and Power (or Load and Effort, as they are technically known) balance each other about the fulcrum, and we arrive at the principle of the steelyard with its arms of unequal length.

In this type of machine the fulcrum is not always placed between the load and the effort. It is in-

which is a particular application of the lever. If the length of the long arm is ten times that of the short arm, a weight of 1 pound will balance a weight of 10 pounds.

From this we can easily deduce the simple mathematical formula of the lever.

Let W be the weight of the load, P the power exerted by the hand, and L and 1 the length of the two arms of the lever. The formula then is $W \times 1 = P \times L$

With the aid of this formula, given any three of the quantities, the fourth can be calculated.

For instance, to calculate P, knowing that $W = 20$ stone, $1 = 1$ foot, $L = 10$ feet, the formula gives

$$20 \times 1 = P \times 10$$

from which it follows easily that $P = \dfrac{20 \text{ stone} \times 1}{10}$

$= 2$ stone.

An effort of 2 stone requires quite a hard push, but if it had been possible to lengthen the long arm to 70 feet the effort required would have been only 4 pounds; that is, a finger could have supported a load of 20 stone.

Let us now calculate the load that could be supported

structive to look around you at the instruments with which you are familiar, to compare the variation in the positioning of the three elements — short arm, long arm, and fulcrum.

In the case of scissors and tongs, the fulcrum is between the load and the effort. In the case of nutcrackers, or of the photographer's guillotine, the fulcrum is at one end, as with a wheelbarrow, which is an example of the lever rather than of the wheel.

And with sugar tongs? — look and see for yourself.

In the human machine the fulcrum is always at the end of the lever. In fact, our joints — as, for example, the elbow, about which the forearm moves — have a fulcrum situated as in the photographer's guillotine. The hand, the fingers of which grip things, is like a pair of sugar tongs.

It was a lever which was used by the fellaheen of Ancient Egypt to draw water from the Nile — a method still used in the *shadoof* of today. This apparatus consists of a terra cotta bucket suspended from one end of a long pole acting as a balance; the other end is furnished with a heavy stone as a counterweight.

THE WHEEL

WE may assume that the wheel came into being accidentally — the round logs cut from a tree trunk no doubt gave someone the idea. In its primitive form the wheel was merely a circle of wood with a hole in the centre. Its main advantage was to do away with the friction caused by pulling a load along the ground. The first cart, the body of which doubtless rested on a wooden axle, was most probably drawn by horses, for it is more than ten thousand years since the horse has been domesticated and used for pulling loads.

The chariots in the royal processions of the Assyrians were sometimes even drawn by lions. Excavations undertaken in Asia Minor, in territories which once were occupied by the Elamites and Sumerians (Medes and Babylonians), have brought to light valuable evidence of civilizations 6,000 years old. Amongst other things figures of terra cotta representing chariots have been found, as well as fragments of bas relief, such as that of Ur where one of those chariots with the great cats is modelled. And one can judge to what perfection the wheel of that epoch had been brought since its first use as a rough circle of wood.

The wheel was now made of crescent-shaped pieces, assembled on a crosspiece turning round a hub, and bound with a copper hoop. Two thousand years later, after the invasion by the Hyksos from the East, the Egyptians perfected the wheel of the chariots of their barbarian conquerors. The rim, fixed on four or six spokes, was also surrounded by a metal band, held in place by nails and clamps and not secured, as it is nowadays, by heating and subsequent contraction of the metal in cooling.

In antiquity, chariots ran on two wheels. They were of all kinds: light and rapid for racing, narrow for battle, and carts drawn by oxen which were heavy and slow.

The invention of a movable front under-carriage, the swivelling action of which facilitated the turning of a four-wheeler, dates only from the sixteenth century.

It is amazing to think that the Incas and Aztecs, at the zenith of one of the most advanced civilizations of ancient times, knew neither the horse nor the wheel before the arrival of the Spaniards.

198

THE SLAVE

how mechanical problems were solved in Antiquity

ALL driving-power at the time of the ancient civilizations derived from the physical strength of man — levers working by the effort of human muscles aided only by other levers made of wood, and by rollers and inclined planes. Horses were rarely used as pack-animals, and the poor harnesses then in use made them unsuitable for pulling loads.

And why, after all, should one make animals work, when the most intelligent and toughest beast of burden, as well as the cheapest, could be bought in the slave market? Why seek to perfect the machine, when manual labour was dirt-cheap? It was the slave, half of whose head was shorn, and whose shoulder was branded with a red-hot iron — as steers are marked on the cattle ranches of North and South America — who was the machinery of antiquity, which was a barbarous time, though it was also so civilized.

If you look at this Assyrian bas-relief, you can see the draught-slaves harnessed to the ropes of a sledge, pulling a gigantic monolith, a winged bull hewn out of an enormous block of stone. You will see the human beast at work, and also the functioning of the rudimentary machines which supplemented the levers of the human arm. The slaves slid rollers under the forepart of the sledge, while, to assist the hauliers bent double over the four great ropes, huge beams were applied as levers to the rear.

Like the galley-slaves, these drudges were driven on with the whip and bludgeon. In front of the sledge, as on the prow of a galley where the gang-leader gave the stroke to the oarsmen with shouts and whistles, a foreman clapped his hands in time to give rhythm to the heaves of the slaves.

199

And it was with these same primitive means — the human muscle, the use of rollers, the lever and the inclined plane, formed by earth heaped up and rising at the same time as the edifice — that the Pyramids were built.

Having lost its smooth outer facing in the course of the centuries — it is this fact which now enables one to climb it rather like a giant staircase — the greatest of the Pyramids, that of Cheops, still measures 451 feet. Apart from a few passages, the pyramid was a solid mass, constructed by the piling up of blocks of stone, the heaviest of which weighed the incredible amount of 55 tons.

If 1,000 fellaheen were insufficient for a task, ten, a hundred, a thousand times more would be employed. Herodotus relates how, in the course of three months, 100,000 men dragged the stones from the quarry to the Nile, then transported them across the river where the building-site of the pyramid of Cheops was situated. But before that, this mass of humanity had laboured for ten years to construct the smooth tracks along which these enormous blocks had to be pulled.

For thousands of years man has continued his research and made progress. But if he has succeeded in improving his material life, it seems that his efforts have been less happy in the realm of mechanics, for he has been unable to find a machine which can, to any

marked degree, make up for his own weakness. Nevertheless, the techniques of the luxury crafts, such as work in mosaics and the art of the goldsmith, were already very advanced in antiquity.

Certain ancient weaving processes are still used in our modern craft as they are by the Sudanese weaver plying his trade in the open market-place of a village. The crossing of the warp and the woof threads, the shuttle's movement to and fro were well known to the inhabitants of the lake dwellings. Our weaving machines work in much the same way as a primitive weaver, only they do the work a thousand times faster.

Much of the decoration and ornamentation of antique

art, whether of gold or enamel engraving or moulding, has never been equalled. But one stands amazed when considering how few tools were used for the construction of edifices, temples and monuments by the Ancients — and yet, how grandly they conceived their projects? The only explanation of these facts lies in the structure of antique society, which was founded upon slavery.

From the fifth century B.C. onwards, a considerable impulse was given to technical developments in those regions of the world then under Hellenic influence. It was the beginning of the scientific era, or at least its first fumblings. It is a remarkable fact that no echo of the ingenuity of the Ancient Greeks, nor of their inventions, crossed the sea and touched the New World, which was to remain in an elementary and even primitive stage for a long time yet.

To the three simple machines of which we have already spoken must now be added the windlass and the pulley, which are no more than variations.

THE WINDLASS

THIS is a rotating lever. It consists of two wheels: one of large radius turned by the effort employed, the other of small radius on to which a cord is wound, thus raising the load. The fulcrum is the axle of the windlass which is common to both wheels. The formula of the windlass is thus the same as that of the lever, but l and L, which in the case of the lever represented the length of the two arms, now represent the radii of the two wheels.

The windlass was used to lift the immense blocks of stone out of the quarries which were used in the construction of the Greek temples. Like the quarrymen's windlass of only fifty years ago, it was driven by man's unaided physical effort. A great wheel, five yards in diameter, was placed above the entrance to the quarry. Round the wheel were fixed the rungs of a sort of circular ladder up which clambered squads of men. In this way the quarrymen turned the great wheel by the weight of their own bodies, thereby rotating the small axle on to which the rope, carrying the huge stone blocks some three tons in weight, was wound.

As with the lever, if L, the radius of the large wheel of the windlass, is 10 times l, the radius of the hub on to which the cord supporting the load winds, a child could raise a weight of 20 stone.

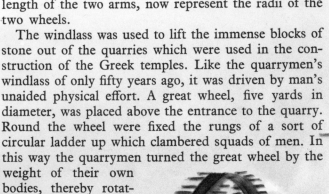

Quarrymen's windlass.

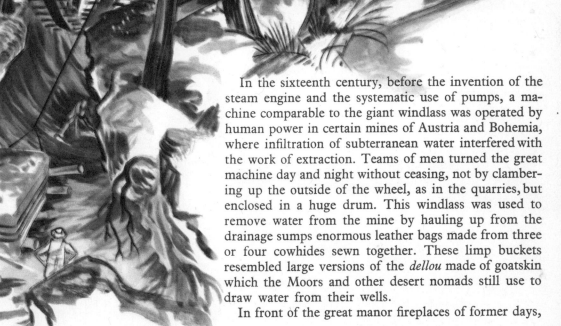

In the sixteenth century, before the invention of the steam engine and the systematic use of pumps, a machine comparable to the giant windlass was operated by human power in certain mines of Austria and Bohemia, where infiltration of subterranean water interfered with the work of extraction. Teams of men turned the great machine day and night without ceasing, not by clambering up the outside of the wheel, as in the quarries, but enclosed in a huge drum. This windlass was used to remove water from the mine by hauling up from the drainage sumps enormous leather bags made from three or four cowhides sewn together. These limp buckets resembled large versions of the *dellou* made of goatskin which the Moors and other desert nomads still use to draw water from their wells.

In front of the great manor fireplaces of former days,

in which whole tree trunks were burnt, were spits on which hares, rabbits and pheasants were roasted. The spit was turned round by an apparatus called a turnspit, which was an ingenious adaptation of the windlass. A little dog, or sometimes a trained squirrel, would run round inside the drum which worked the spit. In the same way, at the beginning of this century, a poodle used to turn the wheel of an itinerant knife-grinder.

In all these examples the same principle of the lever is at work: the application of a small force at the end of the long arm which moves over a relatively great distance, to move a heavy load at the end of its short arm over a small distance.

Another example of the windlass is the steering column of a motor car, where at one end is a large steering-wheel rotating at the other end an axle of quite small diameter which controls the direction of the heavily laden wheels.

There are also many applications of the windlass without any obvious use of the wheel at all. It is, for example, impossible to loosen a tightened nut with the unaided strength of the fingers — we must use a spanner. In this case the small wheel is the nut to be loosened; the big wheel cannot be seen, for it is merely the path traced through the air by the hand holding the end of the spanner. A simple door-handle is another example of the windlass. It multiplies tenfold the strength of your hand, which would never succeed in turning the bolt if you first removed the handle and then tried to turn the spindle directly with your fingers.

THE BLOCK AND TACKLE

THE fixed pulley, fastened by a hook to a beam, is an improvement on the liana sliding over a branch, but only in the sense that it avoids wastage of effort due to friction; in fact, it does not multiply man's strength because the distance travelled by the cord is the same on both sides of the pulley. This can be demonstrated in the following manner: if a sack weighing 2 hundredweight is suspended at each end of the cord, the two sacks will remain in equilibrium. The only advantage of the fixed pulley is to enable the workman to apply his strength in the most convenient direction.

Let us now imagine a combination of two pulleys: one fixed, fastened to the beam, the other mobile, supporting the load to be raised. The cord is fixed at one end to a hook in the beam, passes down to the mobile pulley, then up round the fixed pulley and down again. It is to the free end that a downward effort is applied. Each of the two sections of cord passing upwards from the mobile pulley supports half the load to be raised, for instance the sack weighing 2 hundredweight already referred to. The force applied to the free end of the

cord therefore need only be one half of this load. Thus the strength of the workman is multiplied by the number of pulleys.

Combinations of a number of pulleys are termed block and tackle. The effort required is found by dividing the load by the number of pulleys, or by the number of 'cords' — that is, the sections of cord linking the various pulleys. On the other hand, the cord must be pulled a distance double, quadruple, etc., that over which the load is to be raised.

The development of shipping led to the combination of various elementary forms of mechanisms to form the *crane*. The latter is, in effect, a lever combined with various pulleys and a windlass.

If the block and tackle consists of two sets of three pulleys linked by six cords, the effort which the child must exert will be a sixth of the load to be raised. The seventh cord, the one actually pulled, is omitted from the calculation. To raise the load one yard it is necessary to haul six yards of cord.

THE COGWHEEL AND THE SCREW

Simple pulley. The effort exerted by the two workmen is equal to the load lifted.

To increase the lifting power of this derrick, a first windlass, or capstan, operates on the second.

NEXT came the cogwheel. Before, the circumference of the wheel had been smooth; the ingenuity of this invention was to encircle it with a crown of teeth. The first cogwheels were made of wood, like the gears of which they formed part. Energy was transmitted from one cogwheel to another by a tooth of the first wheel engaging in a depression of the second, moving it round by the distance of one tooth: the principle of reduction-gearing was at hand. In a gear each cogwheel turns round by one tooth in exactly the same time. If the large wheel has 50 teeth and the small one only 10, the large wheel will make one revolution for every five of the small wheel. By means of a system of cogwheels the slowly turning water-wheel of a mill can impart its energy to a succession of small cogwheels, the last of which drives the millstone itself.

Centuries were to pass before the movement of cogwheels came to be transmitted by means of a chain, as on the modern bicycle, which often has a variable gear consisting of several different-sized rear sprockets round which the chain passes. Machines have been developed by man only to save effort. The sprocket on the hub turns round at the same speed as the wheel. When going up a hill the pedals become harder to turn and the jockey sprocket enables the chain to be guided on to another rear sprocket with a greater number of teeth. Thus, we automatically reduce the 'gear' of our bicycle — that is, the diameter in inches of a circle the

circumference of which is the distance travelled by the bicycle with one complete revolution of the pedals.

Let us take a simple example. My chain-wheel has 40 teeth; the rear sprocket in normal gear has 10 teeth. One revolution of the pedals turns the wheel through four revolutions. It is easy to see that, if the diameter of the wheel is 28 inches, the 'gear' is $4 \times 28 = 112$. The actual distance travelled is (taking $\pi = \frac{22}{7}$) 352 inches, or nearly 10 yards.

Climbing a hill, the 40 teeth of my chain-wheel now turn a rear sprocket carrying 20 teeth, so that one revolution of the pedals turns the rear wheel through only two revolutions. The 'gear' is now 56, and the distance travelled 176 inches, or just under 5 yards. To put it another way: going up hill we must turn the pedals twice as often as we do on the level to travel the same distance. You will see that it is always the same principle which applies: my foot presses against the pedal with only half the effort, but travels round with the crank through twice the distance.

At the same time as the cogwheel there appeared the screw, which is merely a revolving inclined plane. The actual inclined plane is the thread of the screw, a ramp spiralling upwards around an axis, like a mountain path.

A jack, used for raising a car to change a wheel, consists of a screw and a windlass.

Larger versions of the jack will enable enormous loads to be lifted by the application of a force of 100 lb. to the end of the operating lever. It is with the aid of powerful jacks and cranes that a railway locomotive is shifted back on to the track after derailment. In the course of constructing the deep tunnels under London for the 'tube' railways, powerful hydraulic jacks were used to shift forward a few inches at a time the 'shields' used to support the roof of the newly excavated tunnel immediately behind the working face.

IN MECHANICS,
the same principle always applies:

a small force moving over a relatively great distance
can displace a heavy load over a short distance.

THE PUMP

THE invention of the pump can be attributed with certainty to Hero of Alexandria, who lived two centuries before Christ.

Before the days of the pump, the machine used in Egypt for irrigation was the *sakieh*. This was a long chain of terra cotta buckets which plunged down into the river and came up again; a sort of wheel fitted with vessels which filled at its lowest point of travel and were then emptied into a cistern. The machine was driven by a buffalo harnessed to a pole fixed to the axle of a horizontal wheel, which in turn rotated the other wheel.

This primitive device is somewhat different from the *noria*, which can be seen even today — for example at Hama on the Orontes in Syria. This machine has high wooden wheels from 12 to 15 yards in diameter fitted with buckets. The force of the current turns the wheel slowly round, lifting the water bucket by bucket.

The Archimedean screw has never met with much success in practice. It consisted of a worm-screw which rotated inside a cylinder. The water followed the moving ramp and was thus gradually raised.

Archimedes will always remain famous on account of his contributions to mechanics: his many inventions are reputed to include the pulley, the block and tackle, the cogwheel and the worm-screw.

In 212 B.C. during the siege of Syracuse, his birthplace, Archimedes held the Roman fleet in check not only by the use of cranes which swung grappling-irons on to the ships, raising them out of the water and causing them to sink, but with the aid also of his famous 'incendiary mirrors'. History relates how, in that country

Archimedean Screw.

of broiling sun, Archimedes is supposed to have succeeded in constructing mirrors for concentrating the sun's rays on to the enemy ships, thereby setting fire to the Roman galleys, which were built of wood.

This scientist of ancient Greece is most renowned for his famous 'Eureka!' (I have found it!), which he shouted on leaping from his bath. Archimedes had been posed a problem by the tyrant of Syracuse, for whom the goldsmiths had made a crown of solid gold. But was it really solid gold? That was the question. The tyrant feared that he had been made a fool of: that the gold of this treasure, instead of being pure, had been alloyed with silver. In his bath, Archimedes felt lighter, as though some of his weight were borne by the water, and he hit upon a practical way of satisfying his master and, what is more important, he discovered the principle which bears his name concerning the density of bodies.

The crown, when immersed in a vessel filled to the brim with water, caused an overflow equal to its own volume. After replacing the water lost, ingots of pure gold were then introduced until exactly the same overflow as before had occurred. If the crown were now placed on one scale of a balance and the ingots on the other, there should be perfect equilibrium, provided both were of pure gold and therefore of the same density.

Through the ages, the wagers of war have profited from the inventions of the scientists. Military art has benefited from the very first steps of technological progress. Hand weapons launched by releasing the levers of the arm were replaced by the first engines of war. The principles of the windlass and of the lever found their military application during time of siege as the ballista and the catapult.

The principle of the cross-bow is well known: the stock of the bow is furnished with a stirrup, enabling the weapon to be held firmly with the foot while the cord is made taut with the aid of two cranks working a small windlass held back by a catch. The ballista is a giant cross-bow which is drawn by means of a windlass operated by a number of men. The catapult consists of a bundle of twisted cords in the middle of which is

206

inserted a beam, which is then pulled right back. The end of the beam is shaped like a spoon; the projectile is placed on it and is catapulted when the beam is released. Balls of stone weighing up to 180 lb. were projected distances of between 500 and 1,000 yards.

The forces of nature — water, wind, heat — gradually came to be used in the service of the more peaceful pursuits of man. Watermills were installed above small cascades quite early, but it was not until the tenth century that the first windmill made its appearance. It was made by the monks of a monastery in France and it was used to raise water from a well.

ROBOTS
the first practical applications of technology

DESPITE the scientific knowledge man already possessed and which could have given a great impetus to practical technique, the ingenuity of inventors was for centuries mostly limited to devising magical machines and animated statues. In those days, when it was considered necessary to hold the imagination of the masses by bemusing them with divine mysteries, it was through the medium of the high priests that the ignorant and superstitious people received the oracles of its gods.

We have already seen how magic, developed to such a degree in some primitive tribes, has kept them cut off from civilization and dominated them by fear of their sorcerers and witch doctors.

The most famous of these machines by which the gods were made to speak are the 'bronze angels', the animated statues of Ancient Egypt. But later on, both Greece and Rome also installed these primitive and ingenious robots in their temples.

With the aid of Hero's automatons, the sanctuary of the temple at Alexandria offered to the faithful a weekly performance of mysterious enchantment. Facing the crowd who had come for the sacrifices, the enormous bronze doors of the temple would open by themselves, as if by magic. The song of birds could be heard — birds cast of the same bronze as the monumental doors. The purification by fire was presided over by priestly

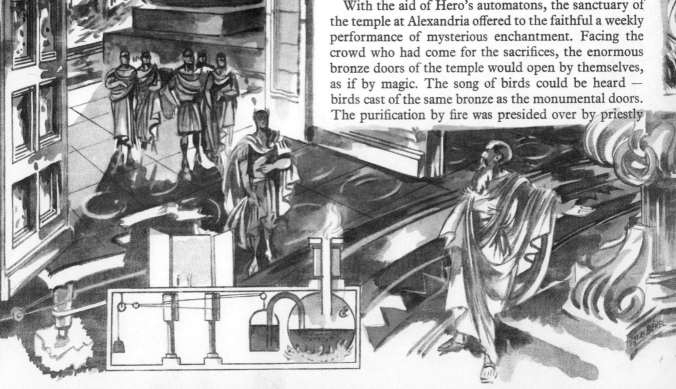

statues of the same metal, which blessed the flames with their brazen hands.

It was the fire lit on the altar which constituted the force capable of animating these mechanical giants. The hinges of the doors were worked by a system of chains, pulleys and counterweights. One of these weights was formed by a huge empty receptacle intended to receive water from a syphon. The whole machinery was hidden beneath the altar. The fire was lit, thus warming the air within a hollow sphere. The expanding air and resulting pressure on the water in the syphon caused it to rise and fill the receptacle which, through its increased weight, came down, putting the system of chains into operation, which, in turn, opened the doors.

The hot air expands in A and forces the water into B, causing it to flow out at C, sprinkling the congregation or extinguishing the fire.

When the fire went out, the air pressure in the hollow sphere diminished and the water would be syphoned back into it. The doors closed.

The bronze priests on the altar, too, were hollow. Inside their arms were tubes, and by means of a similar system of syphoning, in conjunction with a fire and cauldron placed under the platform, water was forced through their arms and flowed from their fingers in a lustral stream with which the faithful were sprinkled.

Temples full of cunning devices, magic fountains, monster-like automatons — those were the things which exercised the ingenuity and genius of the inventors of antiquity.

In certain countries, where the priests conjured up the divine powers by enveloping themselves in mystery, statues in the image of man acted as mediators in the religious ceremonies. Even today, in Sumatra, the

bataks hide a sponge in the hair of a magic doll, and this makes tears roll down the little wooden monster's face through holes in its eyes.

In China, where from times of great antiquity the properties of the magnetic needle have been known, ingenious inventors knew how to put the magic attraction of the Poles to good use. At certain ceremonies, a wooden statue, in the arms of which a magnetic iron bar was concealed, was wheeled about on a carriage, and whatever the direction in which the carriage turned, the statue's arms would always point south.

The East did not show any advance on the peoples of the Mediterranean. The Chinese have continued for centuries to irrigate their rice fields by means of water-mills like the *noria*. They did not even make use of animal power for traction, and their water-wheels were worked by men applying the weight of their bodies by walking backwards and forwards on long planks acting as pedals. These yellow people, who had invented gunpowder, a mixture of charcoal, sulphur and saltpetre, did not use it for a long time for anything but making fireworks — rockets and Bengal lights. But who would complain that the martial thunder of gunpowder was not heard earlier; that it flared only to brighten the great nocturnal festivities of times of peace?

•

The centuries passed. The Roman Empire crumbled; the West recoiled before the flood of barbarian invasion. Darkness spread through the world: all striving for economic progress was abruptly halted, and man, that inexhaustible machine, had to submit to the yoke. In the West, feudal society was maintained and nourished by exploiting the serfs. Centuries were to pass before man could at last hold his head erect and regain his self-respect. Meanwhile, for a long time, human hands were the only tool.

With the Renaissance came an awakening of human understanding. People began to take notice of things

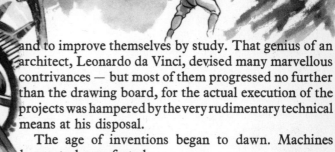

and to improve themselves by study. That genius of an architect, Leonardo da Vinci, devised many marvellous contrivances — but most of them progressed no further than the drawing board, for the actual execution of the projects was hampered by the very rudimentary technical means at his disposal.

The age of inventions began to dawn. Machines began to be perfected.

One of the most impressive mechanical inventions of the seventeenth century was the hydraulic machine at Marly, near Versailles. This was reconstructed a century ago and is still in use today. Huygens and his pupil Denis Papin, who later achieved world-wide fame, had already conceived the idea of a very powerful pump which was to have been driven by the explosion of small charges of gunpowder, but the project did not meet with the approval of the king.

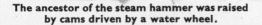

The ancestor of the steam hammer was raised by cams driven by a water wheel.

The machine at Marly was the brain-child of Rennequin, a Belgian engineer from Liege. No less than 221 pumps were employed, spread over the three storeys of the structure. The driving power was provided by fourteen great water-wheels, each 13 feet in diameter; and water could be raised to the height of 530 feet. During the reign of Louis XIV 1,800 men were em-

ployed on its construction over a period of six years.

Up to the end of the eighteenth century the development of machinery continued very much on the lines already initiated by the Ancients, and the effect on industry was very small.

However there was a good understanding of the complicated mechanisms of springs, levers and cogwheels. A good example of this was the calculating machine devised by Pascal, the famous French mathematician. This had a practical application which made it an exception to all the ingenious robots which were the fashion of those times.

Of these robots, the one which enjoyed the longest career was the extraordinary duck made by Vaucanson, a French engineer. This duck was made of little more than old iron. It would peck up corn strewn about on a table; then it would swallow the grain and 'digest' it in its tin stomach, where it was ground up by a series of rollers. This extraordinary duck went on tour in Europe, being exhibited as a curiosity. Eventually it was seen by

Vaucanson's mechanical duck pecked up and 'digested' grain. It toured Europe and was seen by many eminent people.

Did this ancestor of the modern rolling mill ever really work? It was invented by a seventeenth-century scientist and used hot air to turn a turbine which actuated the mill through a system of gears.

the famous poet Goethe, but that day, as the poet tells us, the duck did not seem to have any appetite. Probably the continual tension on the springs and the wear and tear on the wheels had at last caused the little robot to run down.

We have seen how, though the basic principles of mechanics were well known from the days of Antiquity, right up to the eighteenth century their application was limited either to heavy machinery or to cunningly devised playthings — from speaking statues to mechanical puppets.

We owe to the seventeenth century two discoveries which were later to have important applications: the exact measurement of time and the hydraulic press.

The measurement of time

UNTIL the seventeenth century there was never any need for accurate measurement of time or of rapid motion. In this respect the Ancients were concerned more with assessing the passage of time — i. e. its duration — than with determining the exact time of day. The Greeks and Romans used the clepsydra, or water-clock. This 'water which creeps like a thief' — for that is the translation of the Greek word — was already known to the Egyptians and the Chinese, who used it to measure the length of the working day. Charlemagne received a present of a golden clepsydra from the Caliph of Bagdad.

This crude apparatus consisted of two receptacles placed one above the other. The top receptacle had a very small hole in it through which water slowly dripped into the lower one. In Greece the clepsydra was used to measure the length of time accorded to litigants before the tribunals. The speakers were thus prevented from delivering long and rambling addresses, and, to use the expression of the times, took care to 'husband their water'.

Centuries later, when ships had begun to sail faster, the need arose for them to have on board an accurate instrument for measuring time, which, being set to give the time of the port from which the ship had sailed, enabled the sailors to take exact bearings during the voyage. Huygens studied the use of a pendulum for beating out the seconds in the construction of clocks governed by pendulum and balance-wheel. Hooke invented the anchor escapement, and Huygens applied the tension of a spiral spring to precision watches.

The hydraulic press

MODERN mechanical principles, which were to be put to such uses in the eighteenth century, had been formulated mostly in the previous century thanks to the work of Pascal, based on that of Galileo and Torricelli.

It was Pascal who discovered the principle of the hydraulic press.

Two communicating cylinders of different diameter are each equipped with a piston which presses down on the liquid contents. A downward force applied to the piston in the small cylinder will raise the other piston in the large cylinder. If the surface area of the large

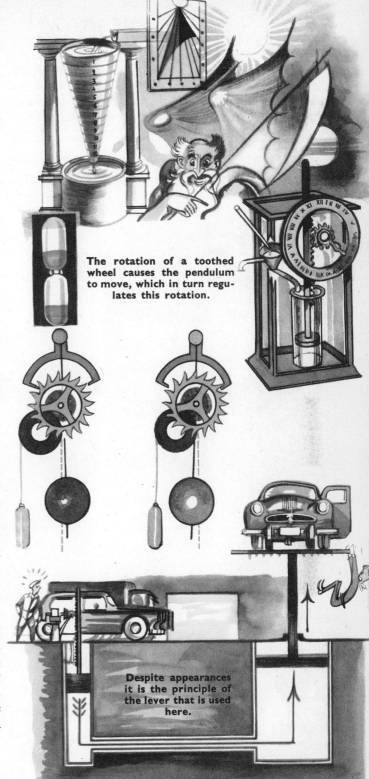

The rotation of a toothed wheel causes the pendulum to move, which in turn regulates this rotation.

Despite appearances it is the principle of the lever that is used here.

cylinder is ten, twenty, fifty, a hundred times that of the small cylinder, a force of 1 pound exerted on the small piston will raise a load on the large piston of 10, 20, 50, or 100 pounds.

The hydraulic press has many applications in modern machinery. It achieves a remarkable multiplication of force. The first lifts were operated on the principle of the 'water lever'. Motor cars are lifted up in the air at service stations by the same means, and many cars have a hydraulic braking system.

THE CONQUEST OF POWER

THE eighteenth century is the century of engineers and of the machine. The evolution of social conditions, the thirst for knowledge, and considerable commercial expansion, encouraged the scientists in their researches and led to an era when inventive genius flourished.

It must be admitted that the advent of the new inventions was received with great apprehension by the workers, who were afraid that the machines would displace much human labour and reduce a large part of the working class to unemployment and misery. The remarkable wooden submarine constructed by Denis Papin, which was propelled by a screw worked from the inside by pedals, was sunk in the river by boatmen. Mechanical looms were burned.

What was needed, before any further substantial progress could be made, was the discovery of a new source of energy more powerful and more easily adaptable than the human muscle or the power of wind and water that had been used hitherto.

The first new source of energy to which men turned their thoughts was steam, for its useful properties had been known for a long time.

THE STEAM ENGINE

PAPIN, a doctor, was a born inventor.
His famous steam 'digester' — or pressure cooker — was not the only invention of his which exploded in the course of experiments. The pipes for the fountains with which he adorned the gardens of the Elector of Magdeburg burst because of excessive pressure. The gunpowder motor with which he intended to drive a horseless carriage also exploded. After each unhappy experiment, Denis Papin was to be seen running into the ruins to recover his powdered wig which had been blown off his head. Before his discovery of the safety valve, an explosion of the steam digester scalded the members of the Royal Society who had been

invited to a demonstration of the device by its inventor.

The principle of the expansion of steam had been well known since Antiquity and the aeolipile of Hero, the great sage of Alexandria. The aeolipile, invented two centuries before Christ to amuse children, was in essentials the ancestor of the modern steam turbine. It was a hollow sphere, free to revolve about a pair of central trunnions, one of them hollow for steam to enter and pierced by two opposed holes, each fitted with a short elbow-shaped tube. When water was boiled in the cauldron, the steam spurting out from the two tubes would exert a pressure on the air and cause the sphere to rotate, in just the same way as the pressure of water squirting from the nozzles of a garden sprinkler causes it to revolve and water an area of lawn evenly.

Papin's cylinder and piston engine was not only the first attempt at a machine driven by the force of expansion of steam, but also demonstrated the considerable power of atmospheric pressure.

Boiling water gave off steam with sufficient pressure to push up a piston supported by a cord passed over pulleys. The steam in the course of cooling condensed back into water, thus producing a partial vacuum in the cylinder. There was just enough time to attach a heavy counterweight to the end of the cord; the atmospheric pressure was then sufficient to press down the piston forcefully enough to allow the heavy counterweight to be lifted. This primitive machine was in fact the father of the steam engine.

Papin died in poverty in London in 1714. He never knew the great success achieved by a development of his brilliant discovery: the 'fire engine', or atmospheric engine, made by Newcomen, which was used to pump water out of many a mine in England.

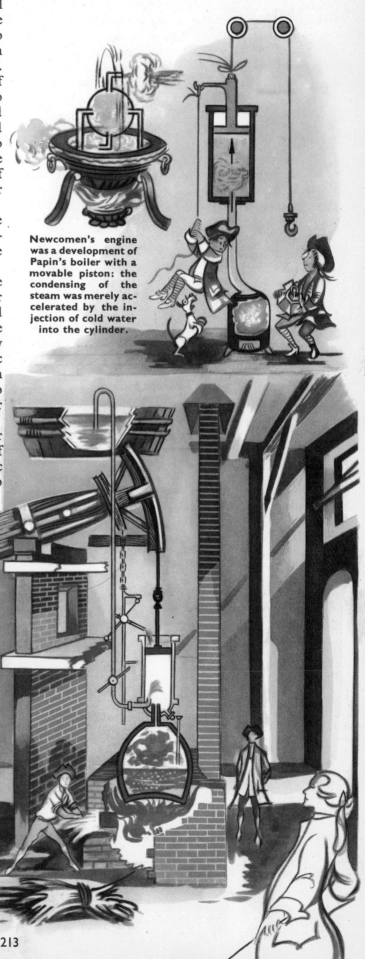

Newcomen's engine was a development of Papin's boiler with a movable piston: the condensing of the steam was merely accelerated by the injection of cold water into the cylinder.

Between Hero's aeolipile and Papin's digester was a distance of eighteen hundred years.

From Papin's digester to Watt's steam engine was a mere ninety years!

James Watt, a Scotsman, was mathematical instrument maker to Glasgow University. Students and professors often gathered in the workshop where he expounded his theories on mechanics. Watt was called in to repair a model of Newcomen's engine and thought of a way in which it could be improved. At first the work was laborious in the extreme. In order to construct the engine which he had devised and at the same time to make sure of keeping the secret, he had to turn himself into both blacksmith and locksmith. His invention of 'parallel motion' helped to increase considerably the output of the pumps used to drain water from the mines. It was Watt who saved the seams of the Cornish mines from flooding; his invention enabled Britain to achieve an early and substantial lead over other nations, and to remain in the vanguard of the industrial revolution which was transforming Europe.

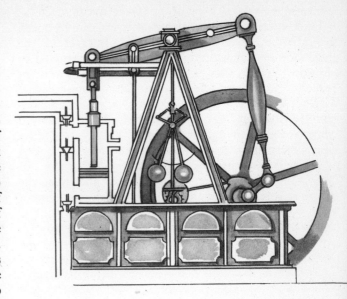

The principle of the steam engine is very simple.

The fire burning beneath a boiler brings the water to boiling point and turns it into steam. In the double-acting steam engine the steam is led by a valve mechanism first to one and then to the other end of a cylinder containing a moving piston. The pressure of the steam is thus exerted alternatingly on each face of the piston, causing it to make a to-and-fro movement.

This action is obtained by means of a slide valve controlled by the machine itself. This device slides within a chamber fed by steam under pressure and, in the course of its to-and-fro movement, alternately opens and shuts the ports at each end of the cylinder through which the steam enters to do its work.

The piston is like an extraordinarily powerful muscle, expanding and contracting as it pushes its piston-rod.

The question now is to transform this movement, which is rectilinear, as is that of the connecting rod fixed to the end of the piston rod and sliding backwards and forwards between its runners. To achieve this, the other end of the connecting rod is jointed to a crank

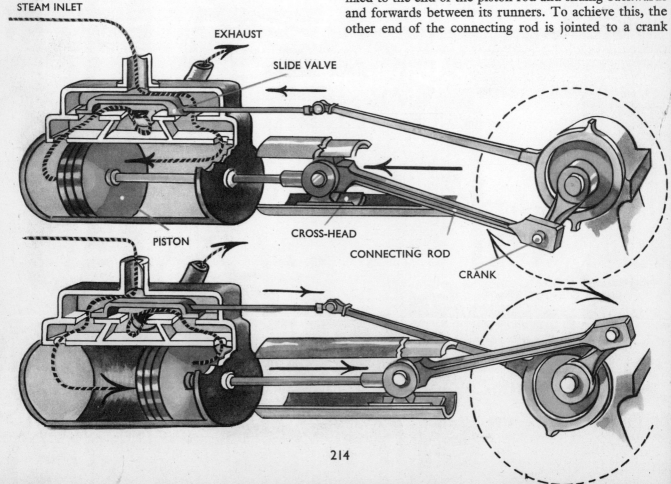

STEAM INLET
EXHAUST
SLIDE VALVE
PISTON
CROSS-HEAD
CONNECTING ROD
CRANK

fixed to the axle of a wheel, turning it and transforming the rectilinear movement into circular movement. If you consider this arrangement, you will encounter once more your old friend, the lever.

One application of the steam engine is the traction engine, the huge flywheel of which carries the driving belt which operates the threshing machine of the countryside; another is the locomotive which, instead of turning its wheels in the air, carries them underneath its frame and moves forward as they turn.

The transition from Watt's steam engine to Stephenson's locomotive (1815) took forty years. But in 1771 Parisians enjoyed the spectacle on the Vincennes road of the steam tumbril constructed by the French engineer Cugnot. This was a horseless cart enveloped by a cloud of smoke and spitting fire.

This engine was intended to serve as a gun-carriage, but its useful career was short — the inexperience of the driver and the hair-raising speed of three miles per hour combined to cause the contraption to come to an untimely end amidst the ruins of a brick wall. The machine is now one of the most venerable exhibits in the Museum of the Conservatoire National des Arts et Métiers in Paris.

The first steam boat, built by Fulton, dates from the turn of the nineteenth century.

The history of mechanical transport and the inauguration of the era of speed began in earnest at the Rainhill trials of 1829, where Stephenson's *Rocket* carried all before it. This famous engine was used to open the Manchester and Liverpool Railway in 1830 and can now be seen in the Science Museum in London. It hauled a truck with twenty people in it at the speed — phenomenal for those times — of over thirty miles per hour.

What progress there has been since that time! On land by rail, on the seas by ships which have grown to the stature of floating cities.

Think of the old three-decker frigates armed with thirty guns which even in those times, thanks to the skilful handling of their sails, could measure their graceful progress against wind and tide. Their passing was less abrupt than that of the stage-coach. The first steam ships were but sailing ships equipped with two

great mill-wheels which threshed the water on either side. The deciding factor which enabled steam to triumph on the seas as it had done on the land was the *regularity* of the Atlantic passage by steam in the East-West direction; the voyage time of the sailing ships was often doubled by adverse winds.

The invention of the screw propeller was the work of the Frenchman Sauvage. It was rejected at first in France itself, but after it had been successfully adopted in Britain, Sauvage's invention was at last taken up in his own country — but not before the inventor had gone mad and died. The man-of-war *Napoléon* was driven by a Sauvage screw, measuring 19 feet across. It attained a speed of 15 knots, which could be matched only by the finest clippers with a sail area of 7,000 square yards — nearly an acre and a half. In 1860 the British launched the *Great Eastern* for the Atlantic run. This great ship was 720 feet long; the hull was flanked by two paddle-wheels as tall as houses, assisted by a screw at the stern. Passengers found this ship rather alarming and shunned

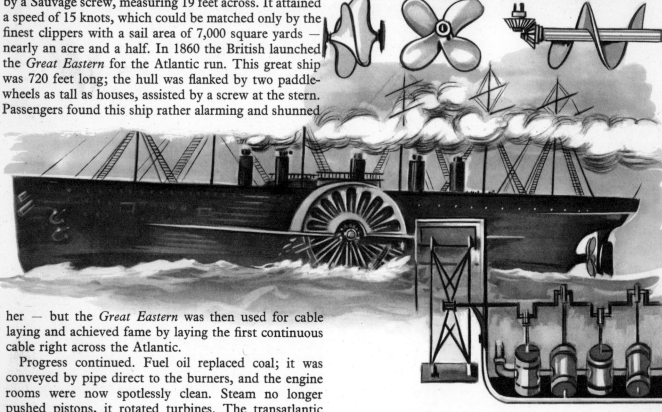

her — but the *Great Eastern* was then used for cable laying and achieved fame by laying the first continuous cable right across the Atlantic.

Progress continued. Fuel oil replaced coal; it was conveyed by pipe direct to the burners, and the engine rooms were now spotlessly clean. Steam no longer pushed pistons, it rotated turbines. The transatlantic shipping companies vied with each other, like teams in some sporting event, for the much sought-after 'blue riband' which trailed in the breeze from the after-mast of the fastest liner. In 1840 the *Britannia* crossed the Atlantic in fourteen days; in 1885 the *Etruria* made the crossing in six days and six hours; in 1908 the *Mauretania* did it in five days.

In attempting to acquire the blue riband on the occasion of her maiden voyage in 1912, the *Titanic* was lost

to the south of Newfoundland after striking an iceberg during the night.

The French liner *Normandie* captured the trophy in 1935. She was 1,027 feet long and displaced 82,000 tons. The following year the *Queen Mary*, another giant of the same size, wrested the prize from her.

Since 1952 the American liner *United States* has held the record with a crossing of three days, ten hours and forty minutes. Though nearly as long as the other giants

(987 feet), she is more slender and is of only 52,000 tons register. She can touch a speed of 40 knots.

Here is a comparison which gives an idea of the progress at sea wrought by steam in the course of a century: it would be necessary to have a train over 40 miles long to carry a load equivalent to the weight of one of these transatlantic liners.

On the railways astounding progress in locomotives was made between 1820 and 1870. A quarter of a century

after Stephenson's *Rocket*, Queen Victoria was entertained by Louis-Philippe in a quilted carriage travelling on the first railway line in France.

This progress is difficult to appreciate without the visual aid of pictures and old prints to stimulate the imagination. For instance, there is the print of the *Catch me who can*, that Richard Trevithick constructed in 1804 for a colliery in South Wales; it ran on wooden rails with the aid of a cogwheel which engaged in a rack-rail.

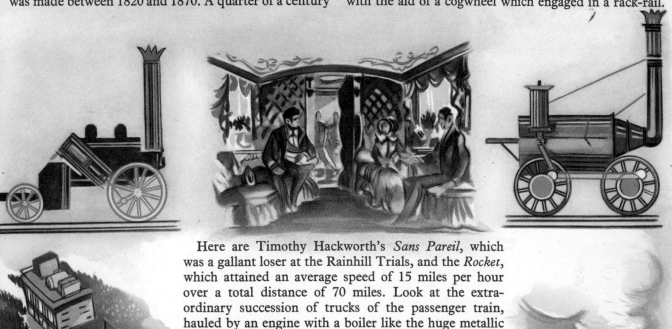

Here are Timothy Hackworth's *Sans Pareil*, which was a gallant loser at the Rainhill Trials, and the *Rocket*, which attained an average speed of 15 miles per hour over a total distance of 70 miles. Look at the extraordinary succession of trucks of the passenger train, hauled by an engine with a boiler like the huge metallic bottle of a still, which inaugurated the South Carolina Railroad in 1830.

The 'Crampton' was an express engine of which three hundred were made in France between 1850 and 1865.

A century later we have the '1442 Baltimore and Ohio' which spreads its own weight of 280 tons over twenty-two wheels, while the French steam locomotive No. 242-A with its sixteen wheels is the most powerful in Europe.

As for speed, the locomotive *Mallard*, one of the A4 Pacific streamlined engines built for the London and North Eastern Railway by Sir Nigel Gresley, attained 126 miles per hour on a trial run in 1938. This still stands as the world record for steam.

However, despite all the improvements which have

been devised, the steam engine yet has two important defects. In the first place, its weight is considerable and it takes up a lot of space; secondly, its efficiency is not very great — that is to say that for a given amount of useful work a large amount of fuel is required. The great power of the steam engine leads to its continued use in heavy industry: for large electricity generating stations, for the turbines of ocean liners, and for railway engines capable of hauling trains weighing 600 tons at a speed of 60 miles per hour.

Almost from the first use of this new form of power, numerous technical improvements have been made with the object of increasing efficiency: one of the most important developments was the turbine. You will recollect that the principle was already known to Hero of Alexandria, who applied it in his aeolipile — or steam reaction turbine.

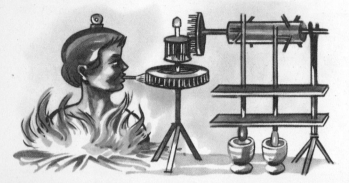

There is only a comparatively minor difference in construction between the modern steam turbine with a conical rotor, to the development of which Sir Charles Parsons contributed so much, and the first laboratory turbine constructed by Branca in the eighteenth century — a wheel turned by the force of a steam jet directed against its vanes.

Two new sources of power, petrol and electricity, were soon to give industry and transport a great new impetus, which could not have been looked for from the use of steam alone.

PETROL AND THE INTERNAL COMBUSTION ENGINE

IN 1858 Drake carried out the first borings for the extraction of petroleum intended for lighting purposes. Twenty-five years later Daimler used the power contained in crude oil to operate the first internal combustion engine.

The principle of the motor is as follows: the energy produced by the explosion of a hydrocarbon fuel (paraffin, petrol, fuel oil, etc.) is transformed into movement by means of a piston moving in a cylinder.

In the steam engine, the fuel — for instance, coal — provides heat energy which is then used to turn water into steam in the tubes of the boiler. It is the pressure of this steam which then thrusts the piston forward.

In the internal combustion engine, the fuel — perhaps petrol in this case — is previously mixed with air and admitted directly into the cylinder where combustion takes place. There the explosive mixture is detonated by an electric spark. The heat produced by the explosion is considerable, the temperature reaching 3,250° F. The gases released suddenly exert an enormous pressure — 450 pounds per square inch, or thirty times the atmospheric pressure — which kicks down the piston with great force.

At a gymnastics lesson the teacher will break up a complicated movement into its constituent parts and will count 'One, two, three, four', which he then repeats over and over again.

In the same way the movement of the piston can be broken up into four strokes, which are repeated indefinitely.

It is important to observe that out of the four strokes only one is the *power* stroke — the third. During the other three strokes the piston is moved by the flywheel, which continues to revolve by virtue of the energy stored up during the *third stroke*.

That is why in most car engines there are four cylinders in which the ignition is staggered. That is to say that, each piston operating one stroke after the previous one, ignition takes places successively in the four cylinders. There is thus always one piston which is delivering power, while the other three are being actuated by the flywheel.

As in the steam engine, the rectilinear movement of the piston is transformed into a circular movement, which is transmitted to the road wheels by the shaft and by a whole system of gears, of which at least those of the gear-box will be familiar to most people.

Man has acquired, in the internal combustion engine, a motor which is both light and powerful, and the possibility of constructing vehicles capable of ever-increasing speeds.

We have already seen, as we follow the course of history, the upheavals brought about by the rapid evolution of means of transport, until we come to our own age — the century of speed. Just think that in the first sporting road event, the memorable race from Paris to Bordeaux in 1903, there were to be seen competing steam carriages which held their own with both open electric tourers and motor-cars run on paraffin. Now in the 'Panamerican', the death race across Mexico which takes place every year, there are super-cars competing which attain a speed of 150 miles per hour.

There are Diesel engines running on heavy oil which are used to propel heavy lorries, river barges, warships, submarines and all sorts of agricultural machinery: ploughs with multiple shares, haymaking machines, mowing and threshing machines. A single machine — a combine harvester — set to work in a cornfield will cut, thresh and winnow the grain, fill it into sacks and bind the straw into sheaves. A single motor will suffice

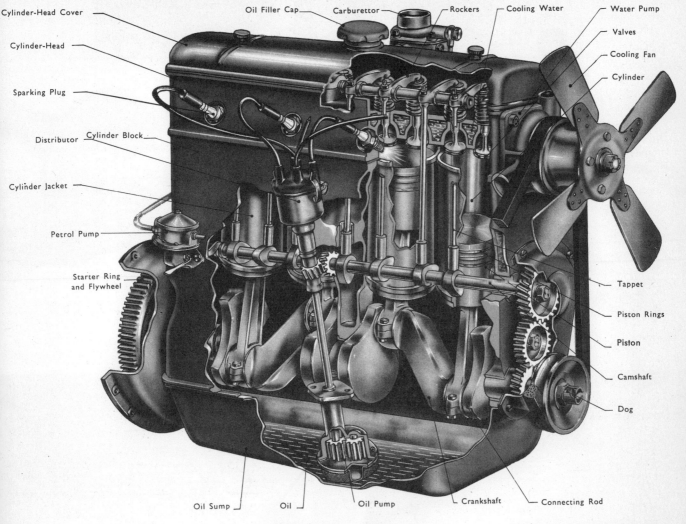

Cylinder-Head Cover — Oil Filler Cap — Carburettor — Rockers — Cooling Water — Water Pump

Cylinder-Head — Valves

Sparking Plug — Cooling Fan

Distributor — Cylinder Block — Cylinder

Cylinder Jacket

Petrol Pump

Starter Ring and Flywheel — Tappet

Piston Rings

Piston

Camshaft

Dog

Oil Sump — Oil — Oil Pump — Crankshaft — Connecting Rod

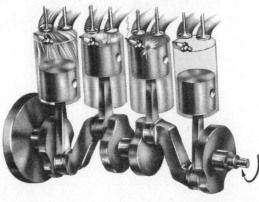

Each cylinder operates one stroke after the previous one; in this way there is always a piston which is delivering power (3rd stroke) while the others are being actuated by the flywheel. For reasons of mechanical equilibrium ignition takes place in a particular order and the second cylinder in order of ignition is not the one actually situated next to the first one. In the diagram the explosion is taking place in the second cylinder.

THE WORKING CYCLE OF A FOUR-STROKE ENGINE
At the start the pistons are actuated by a flywheel.

1st stroke: INDUCTION. The piston descends and sucks a mixture of petrol vapour and air into the cylinder through the inlet valve. At the end of this first stroke the piston is at the furthest point of its travel, at the bottom of the cylinder.

2nd stroke: COMPRESSION, IGNITION. The piston is raised by the flywheel. It compresses the vapour in the combustion chamber which is now hermetically sealed – the two valves both being closed. At the end of the second stroke an electric spark leaps between the points of the sparking plug screwed into the cylinder head forming the ceiling of the combustion chamber.

3rd stroke: EXPLOSION, EXPANSION. Combustion is instantaneous. The two valves both being closed, the hot gases cannot escape and, in expanding, they violently kick the piston, which comes down again and imparts its impetus to the flywheel. The engine starts.

4th stroke: EXHAUST. The flywheel carries the piston back towards the top of the cylinder. The exhaust valve opens and the consumed gases are expelled through it by the rising piston.

20-ton Lorry with Trailer

B. Universal Joint

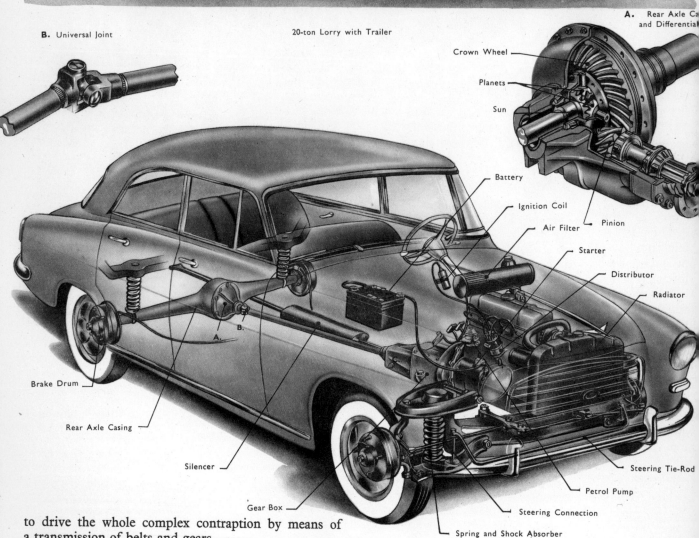

Crown Wheel

Planets

Sun

Battery

Ignition Coil

Air Filter

Pinion

Starter

Distributor

Radiator

A.

B.

Brake Drum

Rear Axle Casing

Silencer

Gear Box

Steering Tie-Rod

Petrol Pump

Steering Connection

Spring and Shock Absorber

to drive the whole complex contraption by means of a transmission of belts and gears.

With its cylinders arranged in a crown around the axle of the propellers, the internal combustion engine drives aeroplanes through the sky and round the world — air-liners, transports, squadrons of bombers, fighters as swift as lightning.

One! Two! Three! Four!... One! Two! Three! Four!... The four-stroke cycle drones on, and a 50-ton seaplane takes off into the air, to land once more in a trough of the waves, like a flight of pelicans on the Niger. The four strokes beat on at a crazy speed for the swarm of stiff-winged insects, buzzing, invisible in the night sky, as they hover above the aircraft carrier. They are waiting for the glowing light signals from the controller, which will summon them, one by one, and guide the steel bees safely on to the deck of the floating beehive.

One! Two! Three! Four!... One! Two! Three! Four!... The four-stroke cycle is about to be superseded. The jet aeroplane, at more than 800 miles per hour, has already broken the sound barrier. And now, in the full flowering of the reign of the internal combustion engine, the era of the rocket is announced!

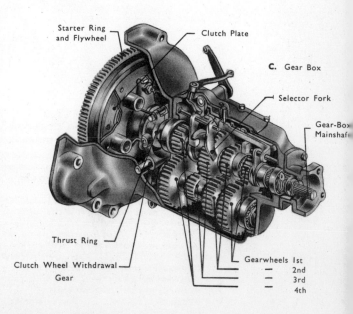

Starter Ring and Flywheel

Clutch Plate

C. Gear Box

Selector Fork

Gear-Box Mainshaf[t]

Thrust Ring

Clutch Wheel Withdrawal Gear

Gearwheels 1st
— 2nd
— 3rd
— 4th

ELECTRICITY

Ever since its first magical manifestations, electricity has been called 'the Fairy' — a fairy who always surrounds herself with the same mystery whenever an application of the invisible force produces some new miracle. She has given us light, and power capable of working the heaviest machinery. This sorceress remains hidden and transforms herself to suit the occasion. We shall describe later some inventions in which she plays her magic part — some of the most remarkable products of man's genius. From Volta's pile (1800), which produced but a feeble current, to the first dynamo (1860) — a true electric motor — sixty years passed.

The two types of engine which we have studied, the steam engine and the internal combustion engine, both turned heat energy into mechanical energy: in other words, by expending heat they produced movement.

The electric motor is *reversible*. That is to say that if one supplies the motor with electric current it will produce power; while if one supplies it with power — by forcing it to revolve — it will produce an electric current.

It is this remarkable property of the electric motor which enables power to be transmitted over a great distance.

One must be careful not to confuse the terms *transmission of motion* and *transmission of power*.

Transmission of motion takes place, in a factory for example, by means of a system of wheels, pulleys, chains, axles, cogwheels, belts, etc.

The transmission of power, on the other hand, is always effected after transforming one form of energy into another. We shall see how a type of power (water, for example) can be transformed and transmitted: we shall examine the route travelled from the waterfall to the power station, to the electric locomotive hauling an express train, or to the more modest domestic appliance — refrigerator or vacuum cleaner.

Michael Faraday, who laid the foundations of modern electro-chemistry, was employed by a bookbinder when young, and eagerly read the books he had to deliver to customers.

The electric motor consists of a fixed frame, the STATOR, a kind of circular cage whose walls carry electro-magnets, and the ROTOR, a large ring of wires which revolves in the centre of the cage.

1. IF WE HAVE AN ELECTRIC CURRENT AVAILABLE we lead the current to the motor by means of wires. The rotor is set in motion and, in turning, its motion can be transmitted, like that of a flywheel, to actuate machines.

2. IF WE HAVE MOTIVE POWER AVAILABLE — for instance, a waterfall or a steam turbine — the power is used to turn the rotor of the dynamo. By rotating between the poles of the electro-magnet an electric current is created in the winding of the rotor, and is then led away by wires.

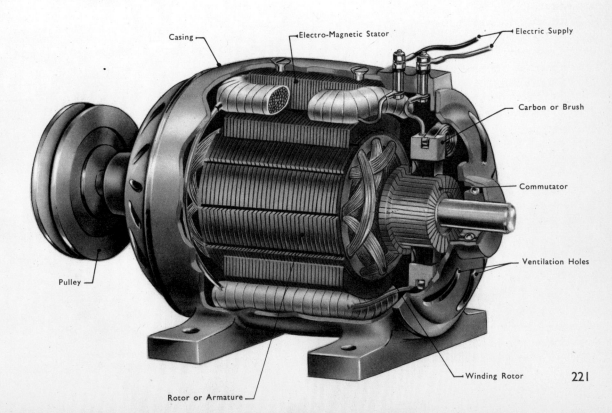

Casing · Electro-Magnetic Stator · Electric Supply · Carbon or Brush · Commutator · Ventilation Holes · Winding Rotor · Rotor or Armature · Pulley

The mass of water in a mountain lake represents energy in a state of repose, but ready to be used. The water is canalized to a dam with sluices that allow the water to be retained or released into huge pipes made of steel of anything up to 3 feet in diameter. The water then plunges through these pipes which run down the all but sheer mountainside.

In the valley is the hydroelectric station. The water follows the elbow of a metal lock-sill that ends in a tuyere. This is a sort of nozzle with a narrow, adjustable orifice, through which the water spurts with tremendous force to strike the 'buckets' of the wheel of the turbine.

The rotation of this turbine wheel drives the moving part of an electric generator, the armature, or rotor, of a powerful dynamo which generates electric current.

The motive power need not necessarily be water, but can equally well be provided by a steam turbine or an internal combustion engine, and this is then called a thermoelectric plant; or the power can come from a wheel with sails that is turned by the wind. Whatever the source, mechanical energy is turned into electrical energy by the dynamo, and the electric current, travelling along wires, makes it possible to translate the original energy to whatever place one wishes.

In a word, when one switches on one's vacuum cleaner and sets its little motor turning, one is really making use of the power of the falling water.

What an advantage this has over the combustion engine, whose power, however much one multiplies the shafting or belting inside the powerhouse, can only be used there, on the spot.

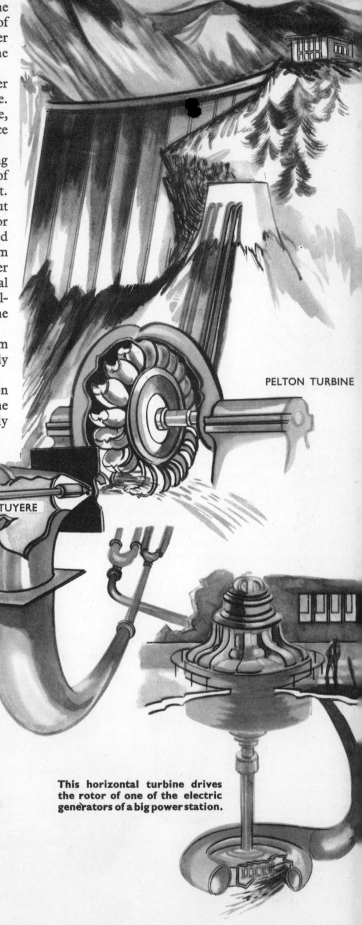

PELTON TURBINE

TUYERE

VARIABLE PITCH
KAPLAN TURBINE

This horizontal turbine drives the rotor of one of the electric generators of a big power station.

From the hydroelectric station in the mountains the current is taken by high tension cables all over the country. You will have seen these wires and the pylons that carry them on shining insulators of porcelain or glass.

Hundreds of miles away this electricity may be used to drive the locomotive of an electric train. One day, perhaps, electricity generated in the Highlands of Scotland will drive the Flying Scotsman on its record run from Edinburgh to London.

Electric motors drive machines of every kind and size. In the home they drive sewing-machines, washing-machines, vacuum cleaners, fans, etc. They provide

most of our power, heat, cold and light. Their use in agriculture has increased the efficiency and yield of the threshing machines, churns, crushers, mills, chaff-cutters, etc. The craftsman uses them for his drills and his saw, and in industry itself there is almost no limit to their use and size.

Thus has man mastered the forces which his ancestors thought could only be utilized by supernatural beings. To-day, by pulling a lever or pressing a button he sets in motion a horde of slaves whose submission to him is absolute. The magic spells of the apprentice sorcerer, his orders, are transmitted instantaneously by the obedient wires to perfect robots, in whose iron bodies are whole nervous systems of coils and magnets.

The same motor that provides the power for this whole metal-works drives a transmission system (belts, pulleys and cams) that works the giant pincers which pick up the red ingot almost as soon as it comes from

223

casting. It sets the power hammer going that flattens the mass of metal in a cloud of sparks like fire-flies. It works the travelling crane that carries the mass to the various machines: the hydraulic press that will start to shape it, the rolling mill that will flatten it between its rollers, the drawing mill that will draw it out.

If a locomotive of 100 tons has to be loaded aboard a ship for export, a crane will pick it up and deposit it on the ship's deck, or in its hold.

If a canal is to be dug, a tunnel made, a jutting piece of rock cut to accommodate a mountain road, it will be done by machines that will raise and remove in one action as much as fifty men could shift in half a day.

All the parts of this motor-car, assembled by conveyor belt on an assembly line, were machined by machines working under man's direction, from the rolling mill to the drill, from the bolt miller to the press that in one movement pressed a sheet of steel into the shape of a car's body. And whether you take the crane, the excavator, the pile driver, the locomotive, power hammer, the press or the rolling mill, you will always find the same elementary mechanical principles employed such as the Ancients knew: the lever, the pulley and the inclined plane.

SOURCES OF ENERGY
OF THE FUTURE

THE twentieth century has witnessed the extraordinary development of the mechanical engine to a state of near perfection. No machine, however, can work without consuming energy. The reserves of the energy now being exploited in the world will not last for ever. However considerable the known deposits of coal and petroleum, we must be prepared for them gradually to become exhausted.

Today, while there is still time, emphasis is being placed on experiments with the natural sources of energy, that is, the wind, the sea and the sun.

Work has been started on an installation for harnessing the tides in the estuary of the River Rance in France, a part of the coast where the tides are very strong. The sea is to be imprisoned. Giant floodgates will open as the tide comes in and close at the flood to store the tidewater behind a great dam. The water will be released later and made to turn turbines as it flows out.

The tremendous energy of the sun is another object of study and research, and it is hoped to exploit it commercially. This is the same idea as that of Archimedes' famous burning mirrors, which set fire to the galleys of the Roman fleet from a distance. In the Sahara, where the radiance of the sun is intense, this source of economical and inexhaustible energy is already being used to work pumps that serve to irrigate vast areas.

Floodgate opened while the tide rises and closed when it reaches its maximum.

Floodgate opened as soon as the level of the ebb tide is below that of the water in the basin; closed as soon as the tide begins to rise.

The principle of these burning mirrors is very simple. First, a huge flat mirror reflects the sun's rays on to a parabolic mirror that concentrates them on to a crucible. Recent experiments have shown that this thermal energy was able in one hour to melt 110 lb. of iron ore by raising the crucible to a temperature of 3,000° C., which is that of an electric furnace and higher than that of blast furnaces.

The speed and volume of transport has increased considerably, but now there is danger of its further progress being retarded in the early future by difficulties in obtaining fuel. A modern locomotive consumes two tons of coal an hour to produce 30,000 lb. of steam, that is to say that in two hours it uses as much fuel as your father will buy to keep your house going all winter. A jet aeroplane uses nine tons of kerosene to cover 500 miles in one hour. Rockets are even greedier. To transport a 2 lb. pay load to the Moon would require 300 tons of liquid hydrogen and oxygen.

2 tons of coal to cover 70 miles.

9 tons of kerosene for 500 miles.

12 lb. of uranium for 238,000 miles.

There is little doubt that in atomic energy man has discovered the long sought-for substitute for coal and petrol, the sources of energy he has used hitherto, but which are threatening to become exhausted. We are now exploiting the atomic pile and already it holds out wonderful promise.

At Calder Hall in Britain, a power station worked by power provided by an atomic pile is already producing electricity. A submarine propelled by atomic power has been launched and can circumnavigate the globe under water without once surfacing.

It calls for the energy supplied by the decomposition of 12 lb. of uranium to feed the nozzles of a rocket travelling from Earth to the Moon.

Those, however, are still no more than alluring prospects of a future that is more or less near.

MAN AND HIS FIVE SENSES

So far, we have merely been concerned with the mechanical aids and inventions which have enabled man to supplement his own physical strength.

It probably did not take our ancestors in their caves long to discover the tool or the weapon which, by adding to the length of their arms, or increasing their muscular strength, enabled them to deal with great weights and to attack animals. It is probable that in prehistoric times people's senses were sharper than ours are today. One must have seen trackers at work in the African bush to appreciate how highly developed certain of man's senses, such as vision, smell and hearing, can still be. These naked hunters, when following the tracks of game, are able, like an animal, to pick up a scent, hear the faintest call and to distinguish the tiny points of gold on the horns of an antelope lying in tall grass.

Of the five senses — touch, taste, hearing, smell and sight — it is sight where faults of perception are most easily diagnosed and which therefore were the first to be remedied.

The emperor Nero, who was short-sighted, had to make use of an emerald, which he held in front of his eye like a lorgnette in order to follow the games in the arena. In the Middle Ages, monks sometimes used this kind of stone, cut in the shape of a thick lens, to decipher unintelligible documents or to embellish parchments with the most delicate illuminations.

It was not until the fourteenth century that scientific attempts were made to correct faulty vision. The first spectacles made their appearance almost at the same time as the bombards which thundered at the battle of Crécy.

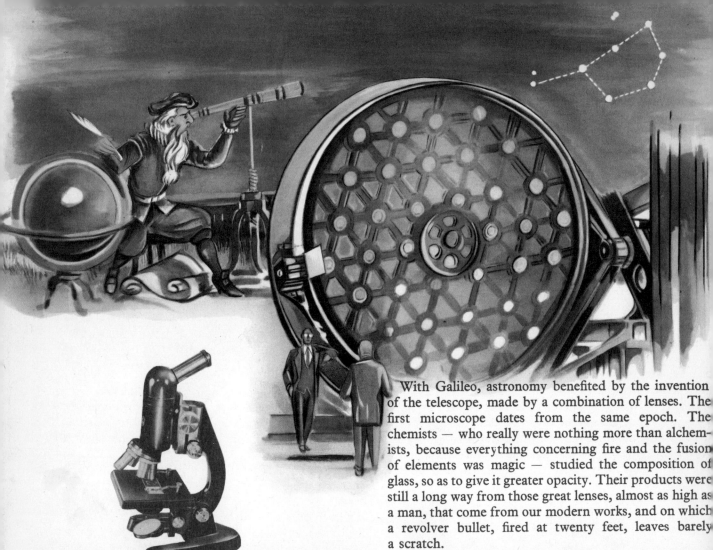

With Galileo, astronomy benefited by the invention of the telescope, made by a combination of lenses. The first microscope dates from the same epoch. The chemists — who really were nothing more than alchemists, because everything concerning fire and the fusion of elements was magic — studied the composition of glass, so as to give it greater opacity. Their products were still a long way from those great lenses, almost as high as a man, that come from our modern works, and on which a revolver bullet, fired at twenty feet, leaves barely a scratch.

At one time, the observation of the small cluster of stars known as the Pleiades constituted a test of keenness of vision. Of this constellation six stars are clearly visible to people with normal vision; those lynx-eyed people gifted with exceptional sight are able to see twelve. The telescope, however, reveals that the Pleiades are really a 'dusting' of stars.

At the observatory of Mount Palomar, the immense field of vision of the telescope, which is 200 inches in diameter and the largest in the world, allows us to explore the frontiers of the visible universe to a distance of 1,000 million light years . . .

In attempting to tackle the transmission of vision over a distance, science has performed other miracles. Images have been caught on photographic film, which makes it possible to reproduce them as prints. Later, these pictures were given movement and colour through cinematic projections, and subsequently a sound track was added. But all this is ancient history by now.

The underlying source of all this magic is always electricity. It is electricity which transmits topical events, gives sight to some blind people, guides ships across the sea and aeroplanes across the sky, allows the deaf to hear . . . For with electricity man is at last able to surpass the animal in the last field in which it remained superior — hearing. Thanks to an apparatus barely th

The microscope enables us to see microbes less than 1/1000 mm. in size, and to look at the marvels and beauties of a world which cannot be seen with the naked eye. Here are cross-sections of a pine root, as fine as a hair; a crystal of sugar-cane; a particle of copper ore; and a tiny fragment of a butterfly wing.

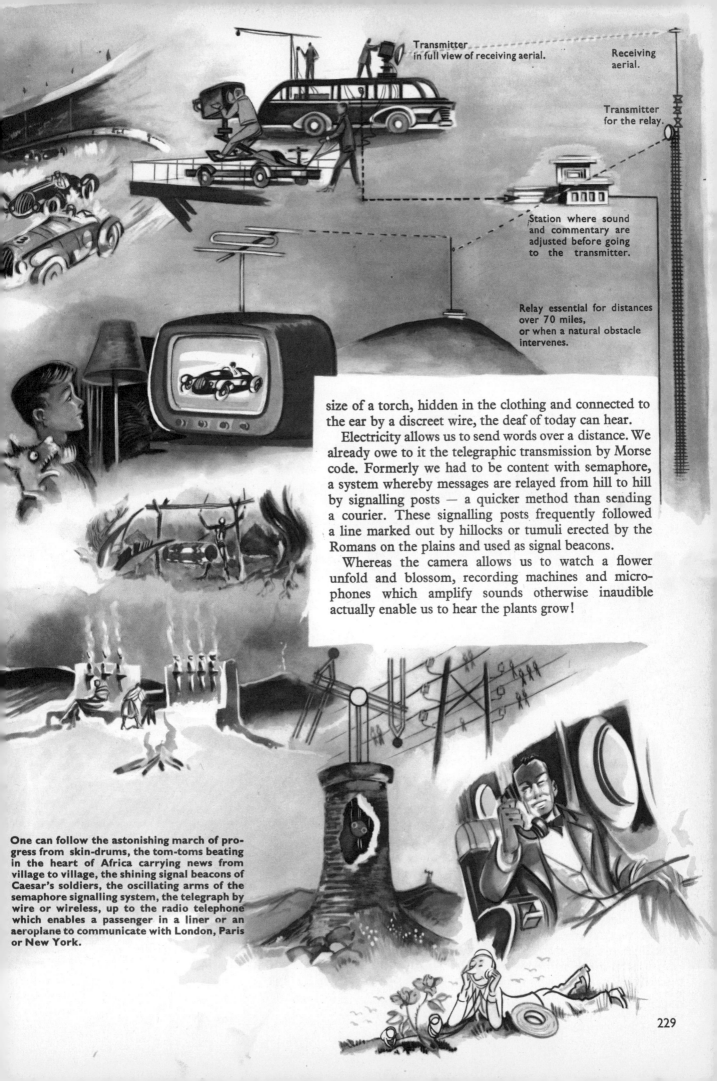

Transmitter in full view of receiving aerial.

Receiving aerial.

Transmitter for the relay.

Station where sound and commentary are adjusted before going to the transmitter.

Relay essential for distances over 70 miles, or when a natural obstacle intervenes.

size of a torch, hidden in the clothing and connected to the ear by a discreet wire, the deaf of today can hear.

Electricity allows us to send words over a distance. We already owe to it the telegraphic transmission by Morse code. Formerly we had to be content with semaphore, a system whereby messages are relayed from hill to hill by signalling posts — a quicker method than sending a courier. These signalling posts frequently followed a line marked out by hillocks or tumuli erected by the Romans on the plains and used as signal beacons.

Whereas the camera allows us to watch a flower unfold and blossom, recording machines and microphones which amplify sounds otherwise inaudible actually enable us to hear the plants grow!

One can follow the astonishing march of progress from skin-drums, the tom-toms beating in the heart of Africa carrying news from village to village, the shining signal beacons of Caesar's soldiers, the oscillating arms of the semaphore signalling system, the telegraph by wire or wireless, up to the radio telephone which enables a passenger in a liner or an aeroplane to communicate with London, Paris or New York.

To increase sensitivity of touch is a far more difficult matter. How can one give a sense of feeling to machines and other inert matter? Here again electricity has come to the rescue, 'animating' machine tools — 'feeling-tools', like the sorting machines used for the grading of beetroots. These machines are capable of making a selection, conserving the best of the plants and throwing out the others.

Now that machines have acquired a sense of touch, it will not be long before they are able to function by themselves. This is especially valuable for the machines that chop, grind and pierce. Until now they had to be fed like babies incapable of feeding themselves, and one had to take the food out of their mouths when one judged them to have chopped, ground and pierced enough. Today all that needs to be done is to set them off and everything goes automatically.

Let us begin with the automatic lawn mower. This is a mowing machine driven by a small petrol engine, pointing its guidestick sideways, in the manner of

to be operated by extremely skilful and accurate workers, who were obliged to remove shavings of metal from the castings, by means of a series of cuts which had to be more and more carefully made as the pieces approached the desired 'tolerance'. Before each fresh 'cut', the workers had to measure the diameter of the piece with sliding callipers or similar instruments. Nowadays many machines perform these operations unaided. To obtain a piece which is absolutely perfect all that is required is to press a button and to follow on a dial the needle which indicates when the required size has been reached.

The hand of the worker guiding and controlling the calibre of the piece has been replaced by a hydraulic, pneumatic or electric 'feeler'. (All three systems exist.) This feeler is the true sense of touch of the machine, a sort of steel finger which exactly follows the template, that is to say the model of the piece to be machined, in the way in which a blind man is guided up a staircase by the handrail.

a blind man feeling his way along a wall. With this guiding rod it feels the 4-inch-high green wall formed by the grass border. It is only necessary to guide the automatic mower along the first line to be cut. After that one can let it go alone on its four wheels, of which the first two swivel and control the direction. Then, by means of its guidestick, it will shift to the uncut part of the lawn, even if this is not shaped regularly in the form of an oval or a circle, but more awkwardly like a bean or potato. It will work by itself, gradually cutting the lawn towards the centre.

In modern steelworks, too, the sense of touch plays a big part. Lathes, planing machines and milling machines operate on the crude steel until it becomes a precision-made article, exact to within a 1,000th or even 10,000th of an inch. Formerly these machines had

The 'Transfert' machine is in itself a chain of manufacturing processes. This chain comprises carriages called 'mounts' on which castings are held in position. A workman at the head of the machine engages the carriage in the appropriate runner and places it in the starting position. Then he sets the machine in motion by pressing a button. The operations take place in the following order: the unbolting and release of the carriages engaged in the machine; shifting of the carriages to their new position of operation; locking of the carriages against the upper runner in their new position; complete cycle of operation of the automatic heads (rapid approach of the tool, operation of the tool and return to neutral position). When a carriage emerges from the last point of operation, the workman placed at that point removes the processed casting, clears the carriage of swarf and connects it to a conveyor, by which it is automatically removed to its despatch point. The complexity of the successive simultaneous movements demands safety arrangements. Thus, a check is kept to see that, before the transfer of the castings, a new casting has been released from its final position, the withdrawal of the tools has been carried out, all carriages have been properly released, all the castings have been correctly put into position after a new transfer, and, finally, that proper lubrication is ensured.

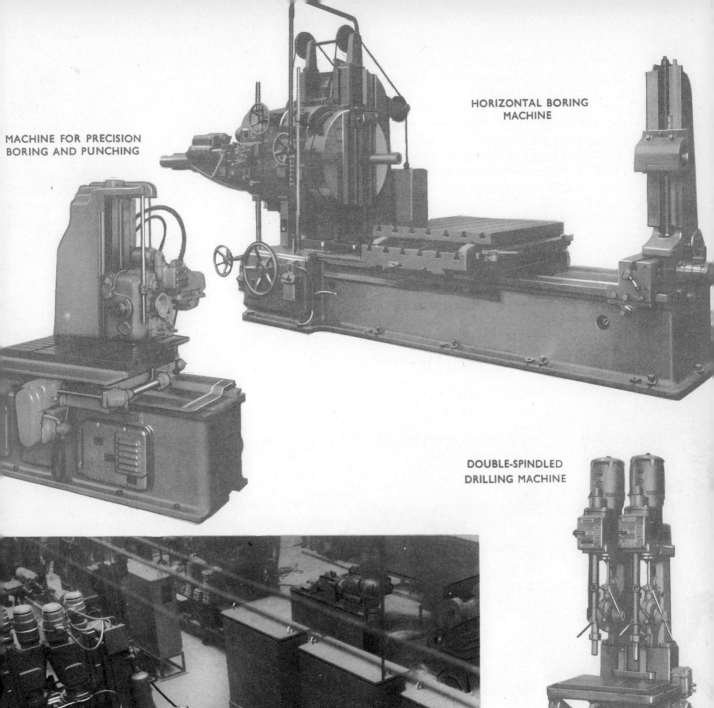

MACHINE FOR PRECISION
BORING AND PUNCHING

HORIZONTAL BORING
MACHINE

DOUBLE-SPINDLED
DRILLING MACHINE

The 'Transfert' machine groups the operations carried out successively by the three drilling and boring machines shown above. The saving of time achieved by this grouping, which was already appreciable at more leisurely manufacturing speeds, reaches considerable proportions at the accelerated tempo of modern conditions.

Man has had to wait a long time before being able to enjoy the help of the machine, but now he is enthusiastically taking advantage of the facilities which it offers him. Machines are in evidence everywhere and are put to every kind of use. Having started modestly by making its power felt in the material world, which is, after all, its proper sphere, it has become presumptuous and now wants to play a part on the intellectual plane.

Some engineers have succeeded, in fact, in endowing certain of their machines with the most mechanical of intellectual faculties: *memory*.

Jacquard, the French inventor of the silk-loom, worked out a principle of recording by means of punched holes, or pegs. The application of this for a long time was limited to the rolls of perforated paper used in mechanical piano-players and the pegged drum of the barrel organ, but it can now be used to run factories without men. A large British motor-car manufacturing company builds its cars on conveyors, fed by parts made in neighbouring factories. The work of assembling and spraying is controlled by punched cards. If it is intended to make during one day twenty black saloons, fifteen red convertibles, and eleven blue tourers, an operative feeds the requisite number of cards, corresponding to the different kinds of car, into the control unit, and in the evening the cars will be delivered ready at the other end of the assembly line.

By rather more complicated processes, using electronics, man is now trying to perfect the mechanical memory of the machine.

Only phenomenal memories are capable of competing with the 'rapid access' storage of certain computing machines. What a long way we have come from the calculating machine of Pascal with its cams, springs and pawls, which solved the problem of 'carrying' in addition and subtraction! In thirty seconds the modern computers can make calculations which it would have taken an expert two days to do. The multiplication of two numbers with ten digits is done in 1/5,000th of a second!

Electronics can now be utilized to maintain a constant control over pressure, speed, current, hardness or length. It sees and hears all. An electronic counter can record the number of objects travelling along a conveyor belt, even if they are passing at the rate of a hundred a second. Suppose it is desired to turn a large number of identical objects on a lathe. It is necessary only to make a single model, which is then examined by electronic 'readers'. The details are recorded by a 'memory' consisting of a length of magnetic tape. From this point onwards the signals recorded on the tape will control the lathe, and the machined objects will emerge automatically, one after the other, with marvellous precision.

Science, it seems, is taking us back to the days of magic and the sorcerer.

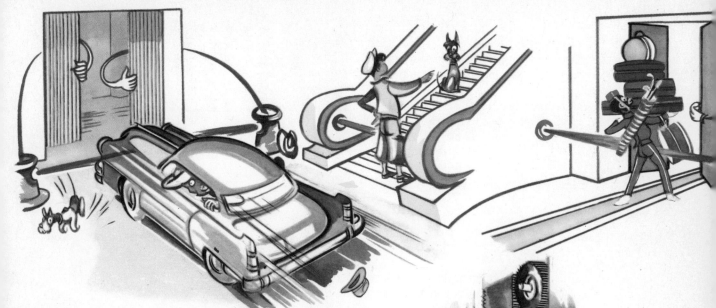

An aeroplane lands, travels along the concrete runway and comes to rest in front of the hangars of the aerodrome. Why does not the pilot get out? There is no one aboard! The aeroplane has been brought down entirely by radar from the control tower. The level crossing gates close, while a warning electric bell rings. A train approaches, drawn by an electric locomotive. You try to make out the shape of the driver behind the glass of the driving-cabin. It is no use peering; there is no one there. The locomotive is controlled from a sub-station thirty miles away. You have been witnessing experiments in remote control in the air and on the railways. In a few years this will perhaps be normal procedure. Already the pilots of airliners only have to navigate their aircraft during the actual flight; a few miles from the landing-ground the pilot's actions are guided by radio-telephony.

Electronics are being used more and more in everyday life. Countless serious accidents are now prevented from happening to those who work blind and dangerous machines like power presses and guillotines; for the hand or arm, which before would have been caught and crushed, now causes the machine to come to a complete and automatic stop by interrupting a light ray acting on a photoelectric cell. This electric eye, which never relaxes its ceaseless vigilance, can also be used as a security precaution. It operates an alarm when a burglar enters a room, or when smoke betrays the presence of a fire.

The doors of a garage swing open when a car, which seems to be about to crash into them, is only a few yards away. At the end of a passage in the Underground there is an escalator; no one is about and the escalator appears to be out of order; but just as you are about to walk up, as if it were an ordinary staircase, the machinery starts up. Who opened the garage doors? Where was the station official who started the escalator?

One's thoughts go back to the bronze doors of the temples of antiquity which, by means of a much cruder device, slowly opened by themselves before the faithful, who had come to hear the brazen voices of their gods.

Man has harnessed the forces of Nature for his own purposes, just as in earlier times he harnessed the beast. Elephants capable of uprooting a tree have been trained by man to carry it on their tusks; they have been trained, too, to crack a nut delicately beneath their huge feet. In the same way, man has trained his machines: elephants of metal, with muscles of steel capable of lifting two tons, but so delicately balanced that they can measure two spoonfuls of oil into a bowl, break in an egg and whisk it into mayonnaise.

Countless other remote-controlled robots are used in atomic power stations to handle radioactive materials, while the human workers direct operations safely sheltered from the dangers of radiation.

Will man of the future know an entirely mechanized world where the robot comes fully into its own? Already in America thought is being given to establishing factories without workers, where human intervention would be reduced to a minimum.

Is that where the future lies? Shall we see specialized operatives going to the factory not to *supervise* the work of the machines, but to give these robot machines their orders for the day? The machines, with the aid of their memory, would then issue intelligent orders to all parts of the factory, thereby controlling all the mechanical operations.

The sorcerer's apprentice has worn many guises and had many names in the course of the centuries. He has been called Hero of Alexandria, Denis Papin, James Watt, Jacquard.

The sorcerer's apprentice, having employed the lever, the wheel, steam and electricity, has now ventured to tame the most stupendous of all magic forces — atomic energy! A few years ago the first revelation of its shattering power burst upon a startled world. The sorcerer's apprentice is at the moment continuing the experiments with some imprudence!

How short the reign of man seems, when we consider that the sun of the ancient fire-worshipping religions still burns for us nearly as youthfully as it did at the beginning of the world! It has shone upon centuries of misery. It has watched man slowly and patiently take possession of the earth and assert his genius.

It is this constant progress throughout the march of time which should encourage us to look forward to a future when science, in the service of humanity, will improve man's station in Life and give him true joy in living.

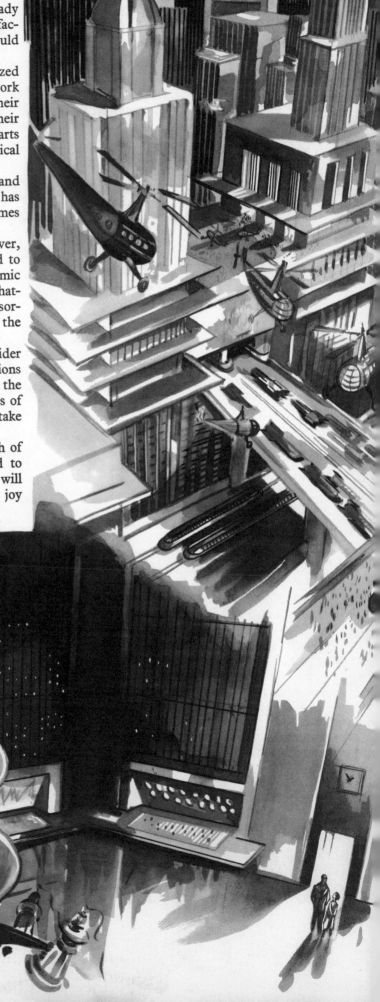

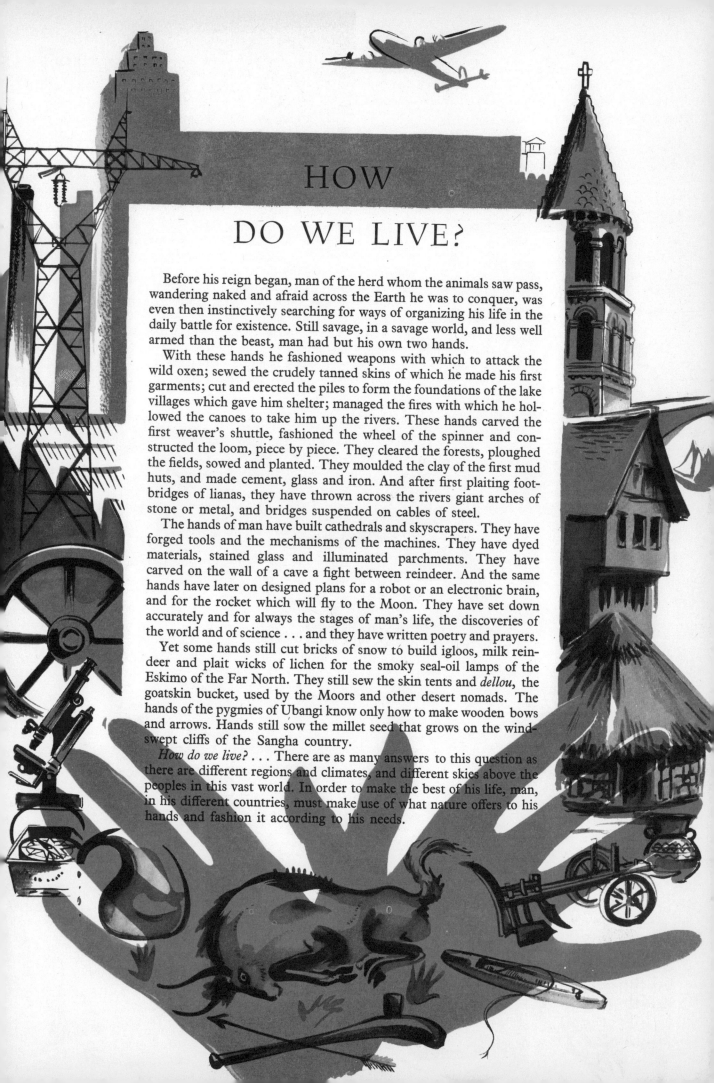

HOW
DO WE LIVE?

Before his reign began, man of the herd whom the animals saw pass, wandering naked and afraid across the Earth he was to conquer, was even then instinctively searching for ways of organizing his life in the daily battle for existence. Still savage, in a savage world, and less well armed than the beast, man had but his own two hands.

With these hands he fashioned weapons with which to attack the wild oxen; sewed the crudely tanned skins of which he made his first garments; cut and erected the piles to form the foundations of the lake villages which gave him shelter; managed the fires with which he hollowed the canoes to take him up the rivers. These hands carved the first weaver's shuttle, fashioned the wheel of the spinner and constructed the loom, piece by piece. They cleared the forests, ploughed the fields, sowed and planted. They moulded the clay of the first mud huts, and made cement, glass and iron. And after first plaiting footbridges of lianas, they have thrown across the rivers giant arches of stone or metal, and bridges suspended on cables of steel.

The hands of man have built cathedrals and skyscrapers. They have forged tools and the mechanisms of the machines. They have dyed materials, stained glass and illuminated parchments. They have carved on the wall of a cave a fight between reindeer. And the same hands have later on designed plans for a robot or an electronic brain, and for the rocket which will fly to the Moon. They have set down accurately and for always the stages of man's life, the discoveries of the world and of science . . . and they have written poetry and prayers.

Yet some hands still cut bricks of snow to build igloos, milk reindeer and plait wicks of lichen for the smoky seal-oil lamps of the Eskimo of the Far North. They still sew the skin tents and *dellou*, the goatskin bucket, used by the Moors and other desert nomads. The hands of the pygmies of Ubangi know only how to make wooden bows and arrows. Hands still sow the millet seed that grows on the windswept cliffs of the Sangha country.

How do we live? . . . There are as many answers to this question as there are different regions and climates, and different skies above the peoples in this vast world. In order to make the best of his life, man, in his different countries, must make use of what nature offers to his hands and fashion it according to his needs.

THE

When a house is being built a great variety of different kinds of workmen are employed in its construction: navvies dig the foundations while masons, carpenters, joiners, tilers, painters, glaziers and others all play their part. At the site itself, however, you see only those who are making use of the wide range of material delivered by lorry — the last ants in this busy community: the builder ants.

One has to imagine the quarry from which the stone was extracted, the brick and tile works where the clay was baked in kilns, the works that supplied the cement and plaster, and those that made the steel girders and the piping. From the lumberman with his axe to the joiner with his plane, making the shutters or some piece of furniture, how many craftsmen have contributed to the building of a house!

Nomads such as Arabs and certain Asiatic tribes used to live in tents which they could take about with them as they roamed; but there are few such wanderers today. Men have tended to settle down and make permanent homes. In all countries of the world, the 'home' is the hearth, the shelter of a family. In Chinese the character 安 (peace) is made up of two signs: 宀 , a house, and 女 , woman.

HOUSE

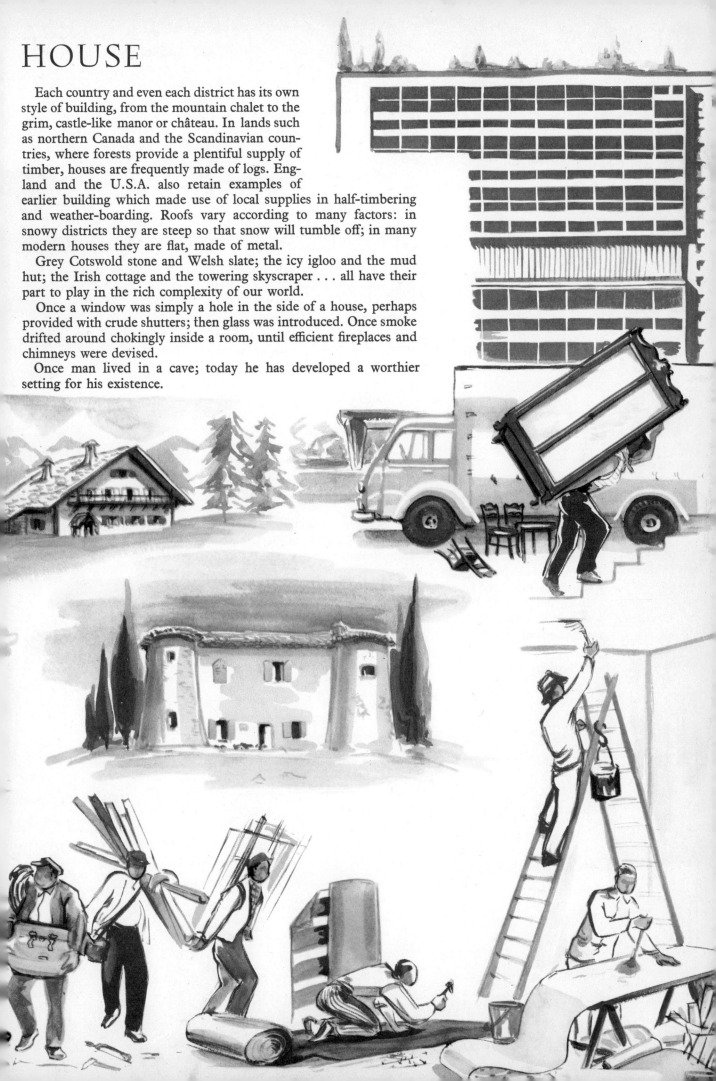

Each country and even each district has its own style of building, from the mountain chalet to the grim, castle-like manor or château. In lands such as northern Canada and the Scandinavian countries, where forests provide a plentiful supply of timber, houses are frequently made of logs. England and the U.S.A. also retain examples of earlier building which made use of local supplies in half-timbering and weather-boarding. Roofs vary according to many factors: in snowy districts they are steep so that snow will tumble off; in many modern houses they are flat, made of metal.

Grey Cotswold stone and Welsh slate; the icy igloo and the mud hut; the Irish cottage and the towering skyscraper . . . all have their part to play in the rich complexity of our world.

Once a window was simply a hole in the side of a house, perhaps provided with crude shutters; then glass was introduced. Once smoke drifted around chokingly inside a room, until efficient fireplaces and chimneys were devised.

Once man lived in a cave; today he has developed a worthier setting for his existence.

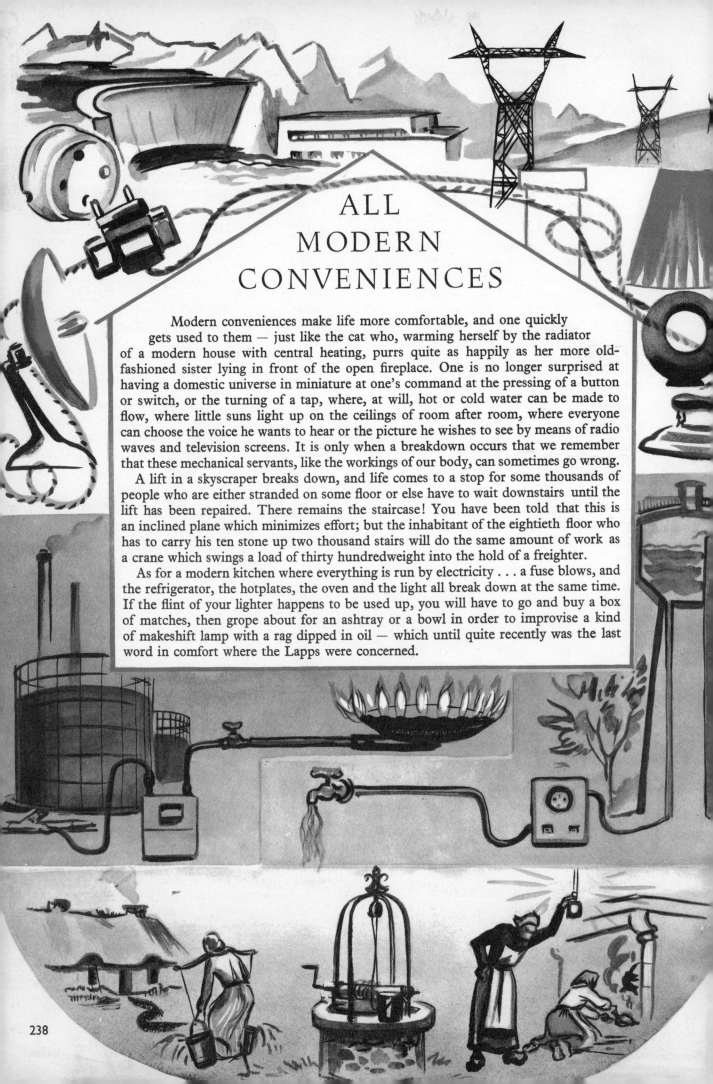

ALL MODERN CONVENIENCES

Modern conveniences make life more comfortable, and one quickly gets used to them — just like the cat who, warming herself by the radiator of a modern house with central heating, purrs quite as happily as her more old-fashioned sister lying in front of the open fireplace. One is no longer surprised at having a domestic universe in miniature at one's command at the pressing of a button or switch, or the turning of a tap, where, at will, hot or cold water can be made to flow, where little suns light up on the ceilings of room after room, where everyone can choose the voice he wants to hear or the picture he wishes to see by means of radio waves and television screens. It is only when a breakdown occurs that we remember that these mechanical servants, like the workings of our body, can sometimes go wrong.

A lift in a skyscraper breaks down, and life comes to a stop for some thousands of people who are either stranded on some floor or else have to wait downstairs until the lift has been repaired. There remains the staircase! You have been told that this is an inclined plane which minimizes effort; but the inhabitant of the eightieth floor who has to carry his ten stone up two thousand stairs will do the same amount of work as a crane which swings a load of thirty hundredweight into the hold of a freighter.

As for a modern kitchen where everything is run by electricity . . . a fuse blows, and the refrigerator, the hotplates, the oven and the light all break down at the same time. If the flint of your lighter happens to be used up, you will have to go and buy a box of matches, then grope about for an ashtray or a bowl in order to improvise a kind of makeshift lamp with a rag dipped in oil — which until quite recently was the last word in comfort where the Lapps were concerned.

...AND ELSEWHERE?

Held captive by the long winters, the people living in the North, in Sweden, Norway or Canada, have provided their log houses with every kind of comfort. With its uprights of bamboo, its sliding panels of oiled paper, the house of the Japanese peasant is as fragile as a bird-cage. On the coast of Africa, the fishers of the lagoons build their lakeside villages on piles as in prehistoric times. The natives of Sumatra raise their leaf roof as high as possible to make it resemble a spire pointing threateningly at the sky, where evil spirits flutter about. Others live at ground level — the Zulu in a hut adorned with boughs, the Bedouin in a low tent, the Mongol in a felt *yurta* that is perpetually filled with smoke.

In the cabins of certain Indians of Colombia, the last word in progress is the incendiary top: a spindle of hard wood placed in a depression hollowed out of a piece of dry bark is made to rotate rapidly between the hands, thereby causing the bark to break into flames.

The nomads, their wanderings determined by the changing seasons, could never have conceived the citadels of the Upper Volta, veritable beehives of red clay, any more than they could have imagined the anthills of the cave dwellers of Medenine in Tunisia.

Luxury for a Tuareg of the Sahara means his *rhala*, the riding saddle of his camel, and the brightly painted wooden chest in which he keeps his treasures: a tinderbox, a box of tea, a kettle and a small copper hammer for breaking his sugar loaf into pieces.

To the Eskimo, comfort signifies his walrus oil lamp, which at the same time lights and heats his smoky igloo. It signifies the narrow opening lit by a slab of freshwater ice taken from the river, the size of two hands and almost transparent, through which the chill light of the glaciers filters to illuminate his hut of snow bricks.

And then one thinks of Le Corbusier's famous block of flats at Marseilles, built of glass and steel, reflecting all the sky in its façade, as in a mirror . . .

239

WHEAT

To make his dough, the baker mixes in his kneading-trough only flour, water and salt. But just think of the journey the salt has made since it left the salt mine; of the miles of subterranean conduits along which that water from a distant river has flowed to reach the baker's. And think of the hands that have helped in the making of a loaf of bread: the hands of the miner, extracting coal, and of the worker at the oil well; the hands of factory-workers manufacturing agricultural machinery, mills, lorries, kneading-troughs . . . just so that a crisp, crusty loaf should emerge from the oven.

RICE

The bowl of rice of the peoples of Asia and the handful of millet which is the basic food of the peoples of Africa are still harvested as they were thousands of years ago, by the black or yellow peasants who themselves sow, thresh and mill their grain.

Rice, of which the chief producers are India and China, forms the nourishment of one-third of the world's population. Its production equals that of wheat: 1,550 million cwt. If one collected together the annual production of either rice or wheat, one would be able to make sixty enormous piles each as big as the Great Pyramid!

WINE

Of the wine-growing countries in the world, France is the most important. There are famous vineyards in the Champagne, in Burgundy, Bordeaux and in the Charente region where the wine is distilled into cognac. The annual output of the French vineyards, not counting the considerable export of wines from Algeria, is 1,100 million gallons. This is enough to fill two long-necked bottles of the shape and dimensions of the Eiffel Tower.

Other wine-growing countries important to British markets are Australia and South Africa. We must remember, too, the port that comes from Portugal and the sherry that comes from Spain.

VEGETABLES · FRUITS
SUGAR

The fruits of the earth are as varied as the countries and climates of the world. Nowadays, thanks to the speed of communications and to deep freeze in ships, people in Europe can enjoy vegetables and fruit ripened under a sun hotter than their own. Fruit and vegetables are perishable foods and do not keep all the year round like the potato, that useful plant which is one of the most important crops in the world.

Although most of our vegetables are homegrown, we do import some from parts where the seasons are in advance of our own — notably tomatoes and new potatoes from the Channel Islands. The majority of the fruit we eat is imported: oranges come from South Africa, Israel or Spain, to name a few; bananas and lemons come mainly from the West Indies. Even a large number of apples are imported from Canada, and we get cherries from Italy.

The greatest fruit-producing country in the world is undoubtedly the United States, thanks to the vast orchards of California and Florida, where selected plants are standardized with a view to intensive output. The fruit consumption in America, however, is so great that only a comparatively small proportion is left for the world market.

Fortunately Nature has put into fresh fruits and vegetables certain mysterious vitamins which are absolutely indispensable for the health of our bodies, although we only need tiny quantities of them.

Sugar, which is used in the preparation of a great many of our foods, in sweets and cakes, is extracted from the sugar beet and sugar cane, which latter is cultivated in the West Indies and Australia.

Sugar is easily assimilated by the body and enables us rapidly to replenish our reserves of heat and energy. The world consumption of sugar is hardly less than that of wheat.

MEAT · MILK · LEATHER

In the Far East, Buddhists and Brahmins do not eat meat. India alone, however, with her 140 million head of cattle, has just under a quarter of the world total. This, like that of sheep, amounts to 650 million head. Pork is really the only meat eaten by the yellow peoples. While the number of pigs fattened each year in the world may well be five times less than the combined amount of sheep and beef raised, nevertheless if all the pigs were put behind each other in single file they would go eight times round the Earth.

In former times meat used to be preserved by salting and drying and smoking it in a chimney as we do with bacon, or it was dried in the sun to make pemmican, in Red Indian fashion. The world trade in meat has been

amazingly extended owing to refrigerated ships and to cold stores large enough to accommodate the carcasses of 5,000 oxen and 10,000 sheep — the weekly consumption of a city like London or Paris.

The production of milk — 25,000 million gallons — equals six times the world production of wine. Selective breeding of dairy cows has led to astonishing yields. The winner of one dairy show in 1955, an eight-year-old cow weighing 1,640 lb, gave an average of $5\frac{1}{2}$ gallons of milk per day. If on one side of an enormous pair of scales one put a bucket large enough to hold all the milk given by this cow in the course of the year, one would have to put thirteen cows of the same weight as she on the other side to balance it.

The Arabs were the first to discover that butter made itself, if goatskin bags containing curdled milk were left to swing in time with the steps of the camels. Modern separators, rotating at 6,000 revolutions a minute, make it

possible to separate all the cream from the milk. The world production of butter now reaches 25 million quintals.

Each country has its own special cheeses: the round Dutch cheese, Swiss Gruyère, Italian Gorgonzola and Danish Blue. From France come a variety of cheeses: Camembert, Brie and Roquefort are among the best known. England, too, produces several kinds, of which Cheddar, Cheshire and Stilton are the most widely consumed, but cheeses like Wensleydale, Gloucestershire, and Caerphilly from Wales deserve to be better known, with their strongly individual flavours and textures.

Stone Age man had already learnt from his friend the tree that the pulp of oak or chestnut bark softened the leather of animal skins. Today we are able to tan the skins of almost all animals: crocodile, seal, snake, iguana . . . The largest amount of leather is, of course, used in the manufacture of shoes.

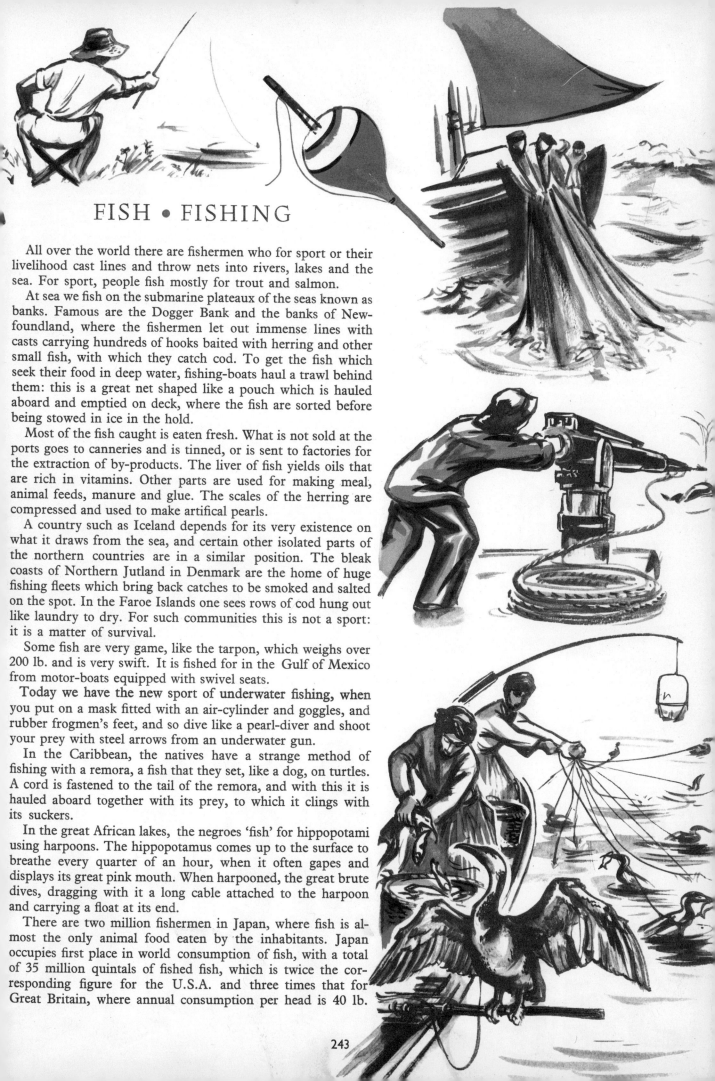

FISH · FISHING

All over the world there are fishermen who for sport or their livelihood cast lines and throw nets into rivers, lakes and the sea. For sport, people fish mostly for trout and salmon.

At sea we fish on the submarine plateaux of the seas known as banks. Famous are the Dogger Bank and the banks of New-foundland, where the fishermen let out immense lines with casts carrying hundreds of hooks baited with herring and other small fish, with which they catch cod. To get the fish which seek their food in deep water, fishing-boats haul a trawl behind them: this is a great net shaped like a pouch which is hauled aboard and emptied on deck, where the fish are sorted before being stowed in ice in the hold.

Most of the fish caught is eaten fresh. What is not sold at the ports goes to canneries and is tinned, or is sent to factories for the extraction of by-products. The liver of fish yields oils that are rich in vitamins. Other parts are used for making meal, animal feeds, manure and glue. The scales of the herring are compressed and used to make artifical pearls.

A country such as Iceland depends for its very existence on what it draws from the sea, and certain other isolated parts of the northern countries are in a similar position. The bleak coasts of Northern Jutland in Denmark are the home of huge fishing fleets which bring back catches to be smoked and salted on the spot. In the Faroe Islands one sees rows of cod hung out like laundry to dry. For such communities this is not a sport: it is a matter of survival.

Some fish are very game, like the tarpon, which weighs over 200 lb. and is very swift. It is fished for in the Gulf of Mexico from motor-boats equipped with swivel seats.

Today we have the new sport of underwater fishing, when you put on a mask fitted with an air-cylinder and goggles, and rubber frogmen's feet, and so dive like a pearl-diver and shoot your prey with steel arrows from an underwater gun.

In the Caribbean, the natives have a strange method of fishing with a remora, a fish that they set, like a dog, on turtles. A cord is fastened to the tail of the remora, and with this it is hauled aboard together with its prey, to which it clings with its suckers.

In the great African lakes, the negroes 'fish' for hippopotami using harpoons. The hippopotamus comes up to the surface to breathe every quarter of an hour, when it often gapes and displays its great pink mouth. When harpooned, the great brute dives, dragging with it a long cable attached to the harpoon and carrying a float at its end.

There are two million fishermen in Japan, where fish is al-most the only animal food eaten by the inhabitants. Japan occupies first place in world consumption of fish, with a total of 35 million quintals of fished fish, which is twice the cor-responding figure for the U.S.A. and three times that for Great Britain, where annual consumption per head is 40 lb.

CLOTHES

To make their clothes, human beings have used the fibres of the bark of lime trees and elm, of flax and hemp and the fluff of cotton, and also the fibres of aloes, jute, raffia, silkworm cocoons, sheep's wool, camel's wool, and goat's and lama's wool.

Three and a half yards of material is enough to make a man's suit; but to weave that amount of material you need seven miles of woollen yarn. The flowing burnous of the Bedouin takes as much. When you think that camel hair is only a few inches long, you find yourself involved in another of those calculations of enormous numbers to which Nature accustoms us and yet which always amaze us. A pinch of silkworm's eggs will hatch into 30,000 silkworms which, in order to weave the envelopes of their cocoons, will disgorge 10,000 miles of raw silk.

Since the invention of rayon in 1880, the manufacture of artificial textiles from coal, cellulose and casein has become a great industry. Now we have cloth woven from the yarn of a fine rain of glass, and there is no limit to the range of colours or to the quality of the materials the dressmaker uses.

Oriental embroidered kimonos, gaudy burnous from Morocco, garish kerchiefs of the West Indies, the overcoat of the northern countries — every country and every age has its costumes and fashions. The women of the land of Bobo in the Sudan have a new skirt of fresh leaves tied to their belt every day. The aboriginal women of Australia use a piece of pointed kangaroo bone to sew the hank of bark fibre ornamented with shells that they tie round their

waists. The Polynesians make themselves flowing skirts of tapa fibre, and the women of Borneo squeeze themselves into corsets made of copper rings threaded one on top of the other, like those that the beauties of the upper Niger put on to give themselves long necks like a giraffe's. Even those men who go about naked feel the need for adornment and use paints and tattooing to decorate their only garment, the one they cannot wear out — their skins!

POTTERY

The first pot made was a basket of woven branches caulked with clay. The potter's wheel is said to be as old as the civilization of Neolithic man; at any rate it was used in Egypt six thousand years ago, and the principle of it has never changed. Moved by the action of the foot, the potter's wheel is really a lathe. The lump of moistened clay turns between the hands of the modeller, becomes round, widens at the mouth, deepens, assumes the shape desired. When the article is dry, it is covered with a glaze or coloured enamel, and so it goes to the kiln.

The use of the kiln goes back to the Ancient Egyptians. It made possible the high temperatures that fuse the glazes of faïence, the first artistic ceramics that the Arabs of the eleventh century used to decorate.

Kaolin, a very pure white clay that becomes translucid after firing, has made Limoges porcelain famous. The products of Wedgwood, Dresden, Sèvres and of the Royal Copenhagen factory are also known all over the world.

GLASS

Modern glass has little in common with the crude stuff that for centuries used to be 'blown' by the force of the glass-blower's lungs at the end of their long tubes. Nowadays unbreakable window-panes are made of 'Plexiglass', a plastic as transparent as crystal, which is even used for spectacles. 'Lucite' can convey light from one end of itself to the other, and has proved of tremendous assistance in surgery, allowing the depths of the gullet or stomach to be lit by means of a flexible cable.

There is no end to what we ask of glass. Drawn out into thin delicate fibres, it is even made into materials that are resistant both to water and to fire.

WOOD

Wood was a good friend of even the earliest man. The trees offered him the shelter of their branches, provided him with his club and his spear, and could be used as fuel for his fire.

In our era of coal and petrol, wood continues to play an honourable part in modern industry. In the first place, it is still indispensable in building and equipping our homes. Even in the U. S. A. sixty per cent of the population live in wooden houses.

The crushed fibres of wood provide the pulp from which paper is made. They also give the cellulose film we use for transparent hygienic packaging, the quick-drying paints that give the bodywork of our cars its glossy sheen, and a whole variety of plastic materials used in the manufacture of steering-wheels for motor cars, handles for levers and knives, and for making celluloid, the cheap substitute for ivory and bone.

The celluloid industry arose out of the efforts made to find a substitute for ivory to use in the manufacture of billiard balls, which used to be made from real elephants' tusks. About 1830, tusk ivory was becoming very scarce, because ruthless hunting had decimated the herds of elephants. Tempted by the offer of a prize of 10,000 dollars, chemists set about looking for a substitute. The fortunate winner was a New Yorker, John Wesley Hyatt. Since then, numbers of patents have been taken out for more resistant plastic materials.

Wood pulp is also the basis of rayon, the artificial silks that have all the colours and sheen of natural silk, with which they successfully compete.

RUBBER

If there are survivors of early primitive man still living in the depths of the forests of Ceylon, Java and Malaya, they perhaps venture sometimes to the fringe of the great trees and wonder at the care with which fair-skinned men from other lands and their teams of natives cherish the hevea trees that they have planted individually. It is from the sap of these heveas that we get rubber.

Like the resin that flows from any injury to the trunk of a pine-tree, 'latex' is gathered in cups attached to the bark of the rubber-tree.

Natural rubber does not come only from these cuts made in the bark of the hevea. In equatorial forests there are big lianas growing wild which can be 'bled' in the same way. In Russia they are now growing intensively a kind of dandelion, *kok-saghyr*, which yields a latex that makes excellent natural rubber.

Then there are other rubbers, manufactured chemically — synthetic resins obtained from coal and petroleum — which are now used to make a variety of moulded objects, from a plate for picnics to a motor-car body.

Despite the wonderful invention of the internal combustion engine we should never have known the tre-

mendous speeds of today without the pneumatic tyre, which absorbs the bumps and allows the wheel to become round again after having taken the shape of inequalities in the ground.

It is difficult to imagine an aeroplane landing or taking off, or a racing car tearing along at 150 m.p.h., on wheels with iron tyres like that of a wheelbarrow!

Will the 'plastics' oust rubber? The annual quantity of plastics used in the world today is more than one and a half million tons. In the U.S.A., where consumption follows its ever-rising production, each inhabitant buys annually nearly ten pounds of things made of plastics. Before long, perhaps, people will be living in houses prefabricated of a plastic material, the colour of which will be varied like the bodywork of a motor-car.

'Let's write book about it!' someone says. What happens next you can see illustrated in the drawings on this page. We'll imagine for the moment that we can trace, right from the very beginning, the way in which most of your books are produced. The studious-looking man in the top left-hand corner is the author; next to him is the editor, who has the job of seeing that all is well with what the author has written. The next man in the chain is called the compositor, and he is sitting at a type-setting machine.

This machine has a keyboard rather like that of a typewriter, and is able to produce metal letters correctly assembled in words and lines. These lines then have to be put together in the right order, and this is being done by the man whom you can see standing just below the compositor.

In the meantime the book will need illustrations, and an artist — the man with the beard and coloured shirt — is hard at work.

When the artist has finished his sketches, they are sent along to an engraver, whose job it is to make 'plates' from which copies of the sketches can be printed.

When all this material is ready, it is put on the printing machine. The man you see in the bottom left-hand corner feeds paper into the machine, and as if by magic out comes a flow of beautifully printed sheets. If photographic illustrations are used, special coatings have to be added to the paper.

Finally the large printed sheets are folded so that the pages come in the right order, and the book is bound. A specially designed book-jacket is fitted on, and at last all is ready for the finished copies to go to your friend and adviser — the bookseller.

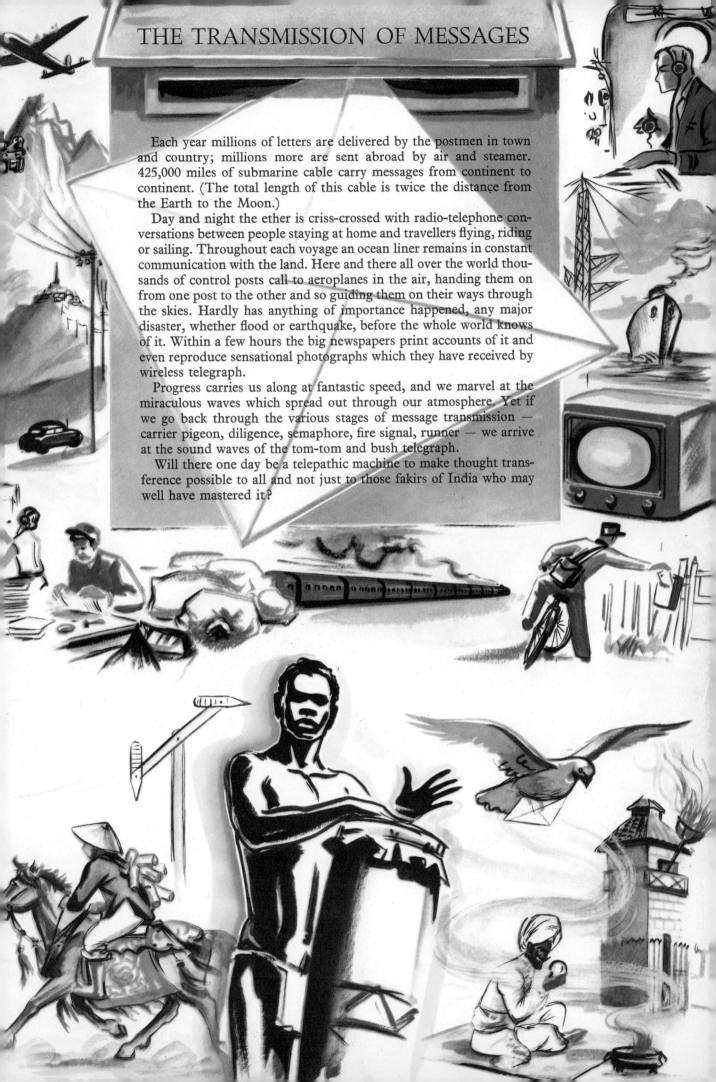

THE TRANSMISSION OF MESSAGES

Each year millions of letters are delivered by the postmen in town and country; millions more are sent abroad by air and steamer. 425,000 miles of submarine cable carry messages from continent to continent. (The total length of this cable is twice the distance from the Earth to the Moon.)

Day and night the ether is criss-crossed with radio-telephone conversations between people staying at home and travellers flying, riding or sailing. Throughout each voyage an ocean liner remains in constant communication with the land. Here and there all over the world thousands of control posts call to aeroplanes in the air, handing them on from one post to the other and so guiding them on their ways through the skies. Hardly has anything of importance happened, any major disaster, whether flood or earthquake, before the whole world knows of it. Within a few hours the big newspapers print accounts of it and even reproduce sensational photographs which they have received by wireless telegraph.

Progress carries us along at fantastic speed, and we marvel at the miraculous waves which spread out through our atmosphere. Yet if we go back through the various stages of message transmission — carrier pigeon, diligence, semaphore, fire signal, runner — we arrive at the sound waves of the tom-tom and bush telegraph.

Will there one day be a telepathic machine to make thought transference possible to all and not just to those fakirs of India who may well have mastered it?

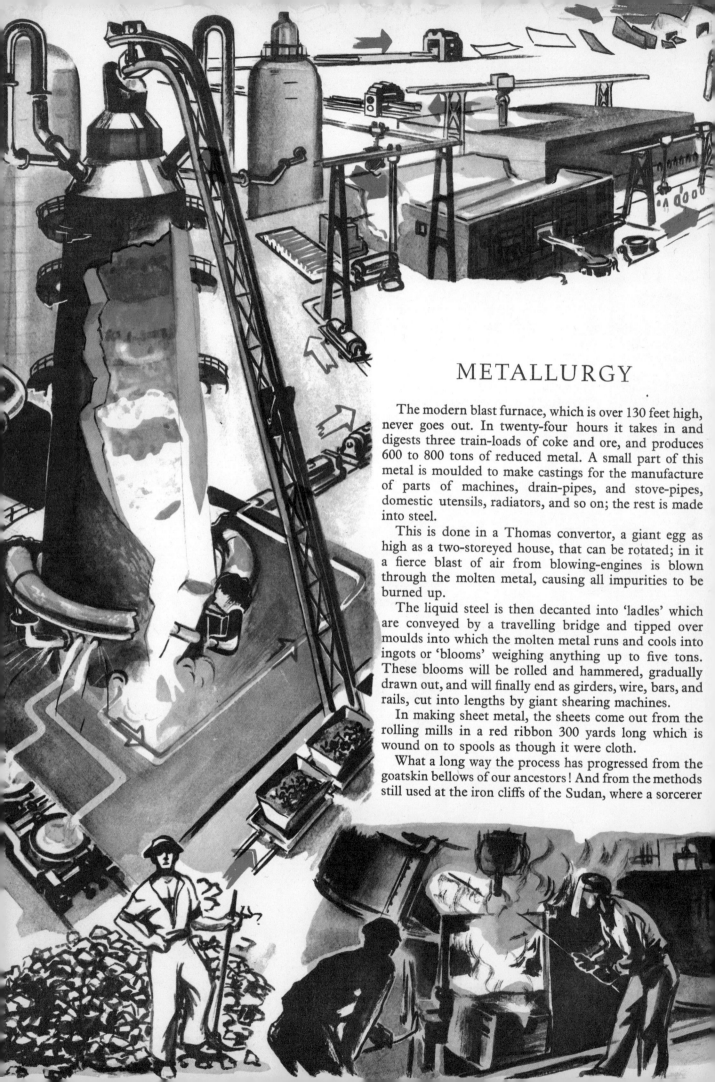

METALLURGY

The modern blast furnace, which is over 130 feet high, never goes out. In twenty-four hours it takes in and digests three train-loads of coke and ore, and produces 600 to 800 tons of reduced metal. A small part of this metal is moulded to make castings for the manufacture of parts of machines, drain-pipes, and stove-pipes, domestic utensils, radiators, and so on; the rest is made into steel.

This is done in a Thomas convertor, a giant egg as high as a two-storeyed house, that can be rotated; in it a fierce blast of air from blowing-engines is blown through the molten metal, causing all impurities to be burned up.

The liquid steel is then decanted into 'ladles' which are conveyed by a travelling bridge and tipped over moulds into which the molten metal runs and cools into ingots or 'blooms' weighing anything up to five tons. These blooms will be rolled and hammered, gradually drawn out, and will finally end as girders, wire, bars, and rails, cut into lengths by giant shearing machines.

In making sheet metal, the sheets come out from the rolling mills in a red ribbon 300 yards long which is wound on to spools as though it were cloth.

What a long way the process has progressed from the goatskin bellows of our ancestors! And from the methods still used at the iron cliffs of the Sudan, where a sorcerer

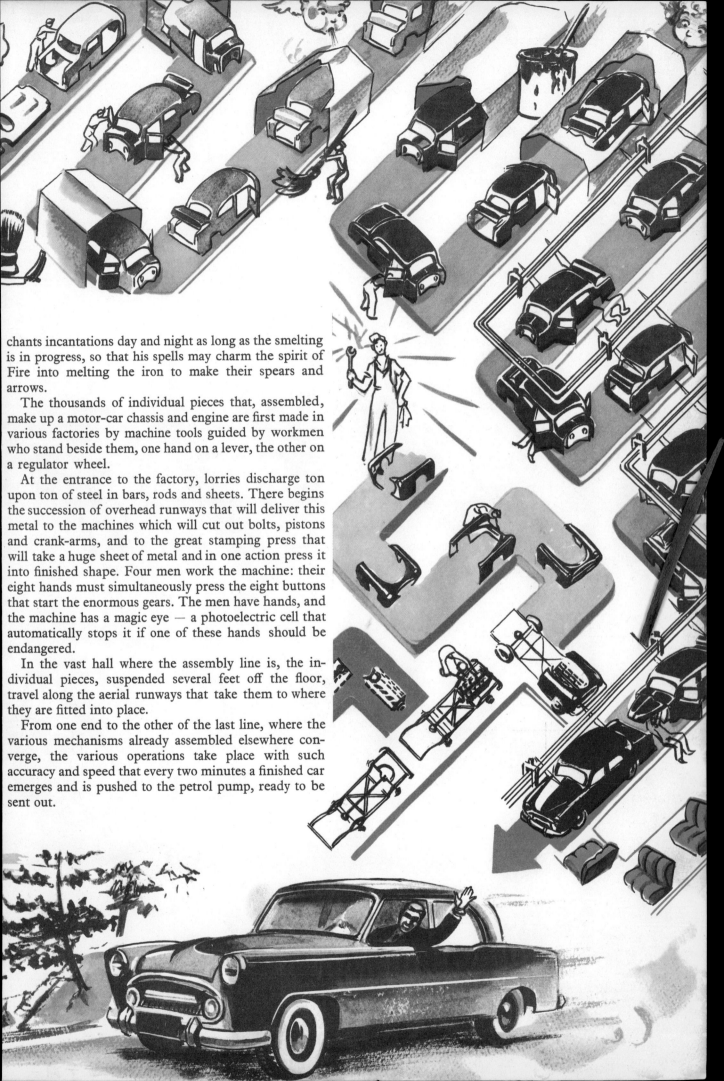

chants incantations day and night as long as the smelting is in progress, so that his spells may charm the spirit of Fire into melting the iron to make their spears and arrows.

The thousands of individual pieces that, assembled, make up a motor-car chassis and engine are first made in various factories by machine tools guided by workmen who stand beside them, one hand on a lever, the other on a regulator wheel.

At the entrance to the factory, lorries discharge ton upon ton of steel in bars, rods and sheets. There begins the succession of overhead runways that will deliver this metal to the machines which will cut out bolts, pistons and crank-arms, and to the great stamping press that will take a huge sheet of metal and in one action press it into finished shape. Four men work the machine: their eight hands must simultaneously press the eight buttons that start the enormous gears. The men have hands, and the machine has a magic eye — a photoelectric cell that automatically stops it if one of these hands should be endangered.

In the vast hall where the assembly line is, the individual pieces, suspended several feet off the floor, travel along the aerial runways that take them to where they are fitted into place.

From one end to the other of the last line, where the various mechanisms already assembled elsewhere converge, the various operations take place with such accuracy and speed that every two minutes a finished car emerges and is pushed to the petrol pump, ready to be sent out.

A port consists of a number of docks lined by miles of quay, fringed with a forest of cranes and great buildings housing Customs sheds and accommodation for passengers and merchandise. A port also has graving docks in which a big ship can lie high and dry to have her hull cleaned or repaired, and also floating docks, which are dry docks that can be moved. The physiognomy of the port is completed by a whole fleet of tugs which bring the big ships in and take them out.

Boats and ships are classed according to their tonnage. A 'ton' is a little less than three cubic yards. A fishing boat is of only a few tons burthen, a banana boat will be of 3,000 tons, a big tanker of 10,000 tons, and a giant like the *Queen Elizabeth* is of 83,700 tons.

252

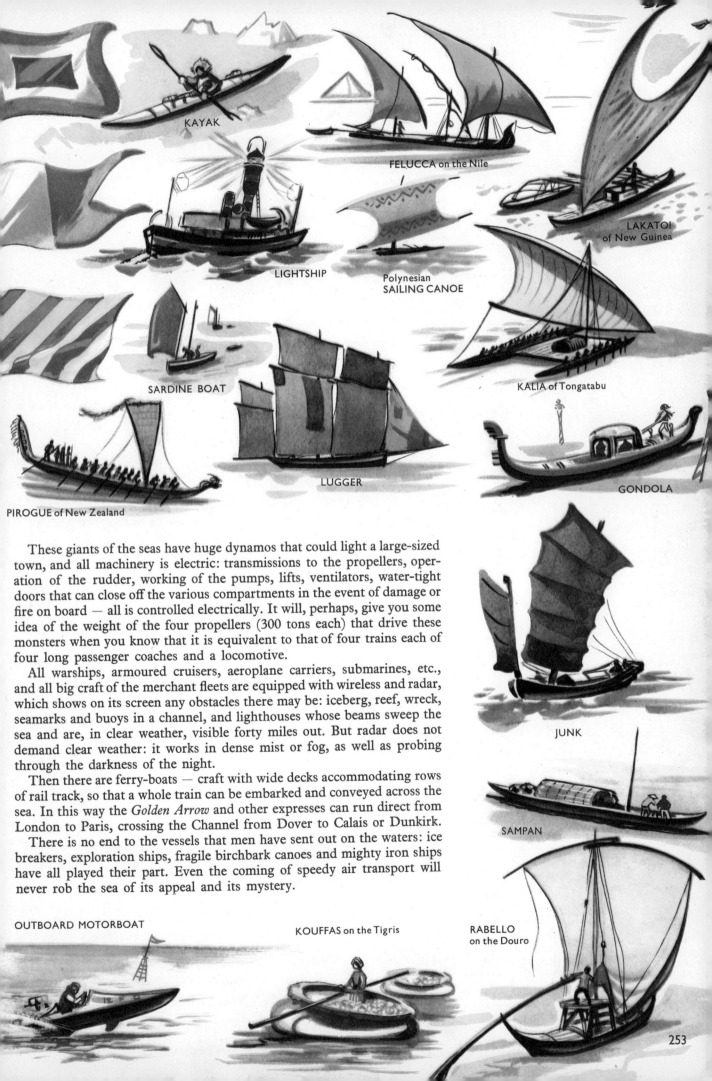

KAYAK

FELUCCA on the Nile

LAKATOI
of New Guinea

LIGHTSHIP

Polynesian
SAILING CANOE

SARDINE BOAT

KALIA of Tongatabu

LUGGER

GONDOLA

PIROGUE of New Zealand

These giants of the seas have huge dynamos that could light a large-sized town, and all machinery is electric: transmissions to the propellers, operation of the rudder, working of the pumps, lifts, ventilators, water-tight doors that can close off the various compartments in the event of damage or fire on board — all is controlled electrically. It will, perhaps, give you some idea of the weight of the four propellers (300 tons each) that drive these monsters when you know that it is equivalent to that of four trains each of four long passenger coaches and a locomotive.

All warships, armoured cruisers, aeroplane carriers, submarines, etc., and all big craft of the merchant fleets are equipped with wireless and radar, which shows on its screen any obstacles there may be: iceberg, reef, wreck, seamarks and buoys in a channel, and lighthouses whose beams sweep the sea and are, in clear weather, visible forty miles out. But radar does not demand clear weather: it works in dense mist or fog, as well as probing through the darkness of the night.

Then there are ferry-boats — craft with wide decks accommodating rows of rail track, so that a whole train can be embarked and conveyed across the sea. In this way the *Golden Arrow* and other expresses can run direct from London to Paris, crossing the Channel from Dover to Calais or Dunkirk.

There is no end to the vessels that men have sent out on the waters: ice breakers, exploration ships, fragile birchbark canoes and mighty iron ships have all played their part. Even the coming of speedy air transport will never rob the sea of its appeal and its mystery.

JUNK

SAMPAN

OUTBOARD MOTORBOAT

KOUFFAS on the Tigris

RABELLO
on the Douro

AVIATION

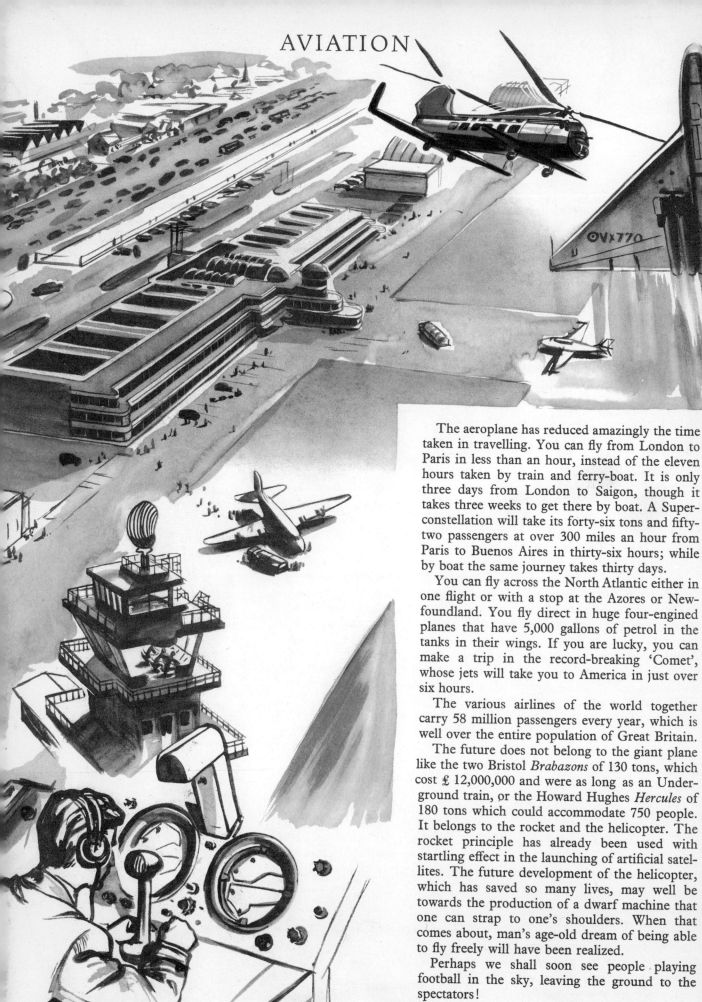

The aeroplane has reduced amazingly the time taken in travelling. You can fly from London to Paris in less than an hour, instead of the eleven hours taken by train and ferry-boat. It is only three days from London to Saigon, though it takes three weeks to get there by boat. A Super-constellation will take its forty-six tons and fifty-two passengers at over 300 miles an hour from Paris to Buenos Aires in thirty-six hours; while by boat the same journey takes thirty days.

You can fly across the North Atlantic either in one flight or with a stop at the Azores or Newfoundland. You fly direct in huge four-engined planes that have 5,000 gallons of petrol in the tanks in their wings. If you are lucky, you can make a trip in the record-breaking 'Comet', whose jets will take you to America in just over six hours.

The various airlines of the world together carry 58 million passengers every year, which is well over the entire population of Great Britain.

The future does not belong to the giant plane like the two Bristol *Brabazons* of 130 tons, which cost £ 12,000,000 and were as long as an Underground train, or the Howard Hughes *Hercules* of 180 tons which could accommodate 750 people. It belongs to the rocket and the helicopter. The rocket principle has already been used with startling effect in the launching of artificial satellites. The future development of the helicopter, which has saved so many lives, may well be towards the production of a dwarf machine that one can strap to one's shoulders. When that comes about, man's age-old dream of being able to fly freely will have been realized.

Perhaps we shall soon see people playing football in the sky, leaving the ground to the spectators!

For landing and taking off, the heavy transport planes which weigh between 80 and 100 tons — the weight of a locomotive — must have a runway built on six feet of foundations. An airport has runways laid out in various directions, so that planes can always land and take off into the wind; then there are ring runways linking the others, a control tower, equipment for blind landings, ground lighting and beacons.

Before taking off, the pilot consults the meteorological map which tells him what weather he will encounter at all altitudes on the flight. While the passengers are boarding the plane, in their cabin with its hundreds of little lights the pilot and co-pilot go through what is known as the 'litany', the responses being given by the mechanics:

Wheel chocks?	— In place.
Servo-drive for wing-flaps?	— Engaged.
Magnetos?	— Circuit open.
Propellers?	— Swung clear.
Navigation lights?	— As necessary.

With the propellers turning, the plane taxies to the end of the runway. The captain speaks by wireless telephone to the control tower and asks permission to take off. The tower confirms the number of the runway he must use, altimeter setting, speed and direction of the wind, and then gives permission to take off. The plane's commander repeats what he has just heard, and the tower confirms that he may take off. Once the plane becomes airborne, the crew go through the litany of the check-list:

Undercarriage? — Retracted. *Flaps?* — Etc.

Fifteen hours later, having crossed the Atlantic, the plane will come under orders of the New York control tower, which will bring it down a level before allowing it to land.

THE RAILWAYS

There is nearly enough railway track in the country to reach round the world, and there are enough sleepers to build a bridge across the Atlantic.

The standard gauge between the double line of rails is $4'8\frac{1}{2}''$, but some countries have wider gauges (including Spain, Portugal and U.S.S.R.) while others have a narrower track (including Japan, Nigeria and Sweden).

Each locomotive has a team of two inseparables, the driver and the fireman. The locomotive is *their* locomotive, and they are proud and jealous of it. Theirs is

a fine but hard job. The fireman has to shovel coal in by the ton on a long journey, though in some countries his labour has now been considerably lightened by mechanical stoking, in which an endless screw conveys the coal direct from the tender to the furnace, where a jet of steam spreads it over the whole surface of the grating.

Electric traction, which is more efficient than steam traction because axles can be driven separately and each pair of driving wheels given maximum loading, has made it possible to increase the speed of trains. France holds the world's speed record of 205 miles an hour, an extra-

signal along all the miles of his route, and must be able to pick each one out even in darkness and fog.

Only rack railways and funiculars can climb the steep gradients one encounters up in the mountains. The record height for a rack railway is that of 11,230 feet, reached by the line to the Jungfraujoch in Switzerland.

Telpher lines, which can also count as railways, really consist of a cabin guided by cables and suspended in the air. A daring application of this system is that built in the Aiguille du Midi in the Mont Blanc massif. It is in two sections, one of 2,810 yards and another of 3,350 yards, without intermediary pylons.

A large modern railway station has huge halls roofed with glass, and perhaps several series of platforms to which passengers go by subway. Such stations, where several main lines converge, have one or more signal-boxes to direct trains on to the track leading to the platform where they are to go in, or to set them on to the correct line as they pull out.

ordinary performance put up by locomotives BB-9004 and CC-7107.

The safety of hundreds of passengers can depend on the driver of a train. In expresses travelling at over 80 miles an hour, the driver must be constantly on the alert for signals: a fully qualified driver must know every

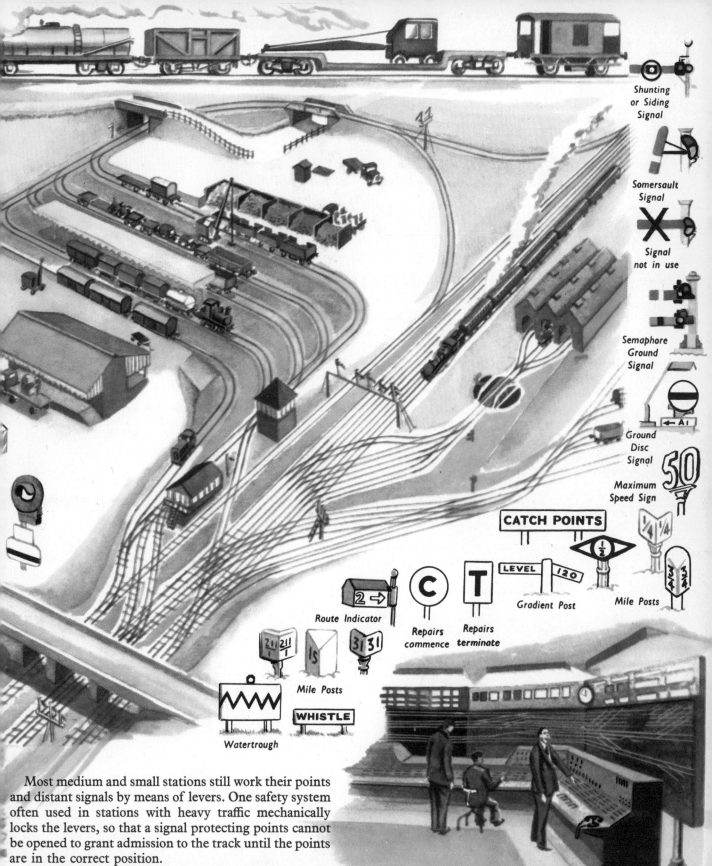

Shunting or Siding Signal

Somersault Signal

Signal not in use

Semaphore Ground Signal

Ground Disc Signal

Maximum Speed Sign

CATCH POINTS

Mile Posts

LEVEL 120

Gradient Post

Route Indicator

Repairs commence

Repairs terminate

Mile Posts

WHISTLE

Watertrough

Most medium and small stations still work their points and distant signals by means of levers. One safety system often used in stations with heavy traffic mechanically locks the levers, so that a signal protecting points cannot be opened to grant admission to the track until the points are in the correct position.

One system, developed in France, uses levers that control not just a set of points or a signal, but open or close a complex of points and signals along the route the train is to follow in entering or leaving a station; this is often quite complicated and can necessitate several changes of track.

Every railway system has its shunting yards, where trains are made up with trucks and waggons brought by other trains from all over the country. Some such yards deal with 4,000 trucks a day, sending them singly or by groups on to the sidings where the new trains are formed. A fascinating modern development is an automatic system which mechanizes the shunting of trucks. As each truck or waggon passes, the person in charge presses the button bearing the number of the track on to which the individual truck is to go. This releases a steel ball which rolls down a tube, along which are the relays of electric circuits which automatically open or close the various points.

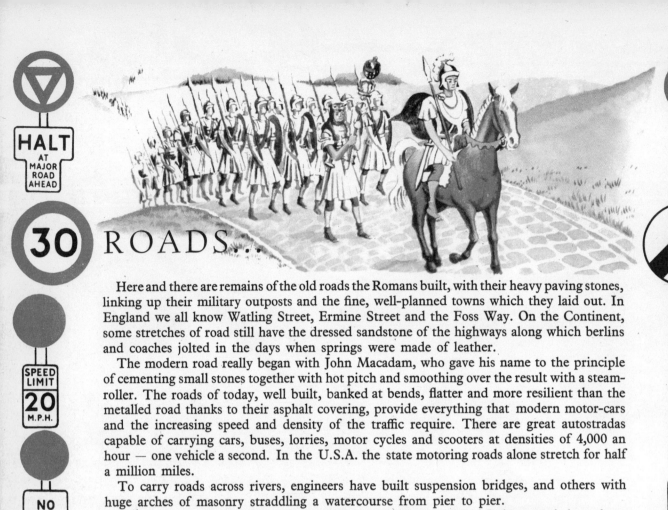

ROADS...

Here and there are remains of the old roads the Romans built, with their heavy paving stones, linking up their military outposts and the fine, well-planned towns which they laid out. In England we all know Watling Street, Ermine Street and the Foss Way. On the Continent, some stretches of road still have the dressed sandstone of the highways along which berlins and coaches jolted in the days when springs were made of leather.

The modern road really began with John Macadam, who gave his name to the principle of cementing small stones together with hot pitch and smoothing over the result with a steam-roller. The roads of today, well built, banked at bends, flatter and more resilient than the metalled road thanks to their asphalt covering, provide everything that modern motor-cars and the increasing speed and density of the traffic require. There are great autostradas capable of carrying cars, buses, lorries, motor cycles and scooters at densities of 4,000 an hour — one vehicle a second. In the U.S.A. the state motoring roads alone stretch for half a million miles.

To carry roads across rivers, engineers have built suspension bridges, and others with huge arches of masonry straddling a watercourse from pier to pier.

Where mountains are in the way, as in France, Switzerland and Italy, tunnels have been driven through them. Soon it will be possible to drive through Mont Blanc along an eight-mile tunnel between Chamonix and Entrèves.

Bulk traffic of heavy goods — iron, coal, timber, grain, oil, cotton, etc. — is preferably carried by water, using lakes, canals and navigable rivers. On the great lakes of Canada and the U.S.A. the lake steamers are giant vessels of more than 12,000 tons.

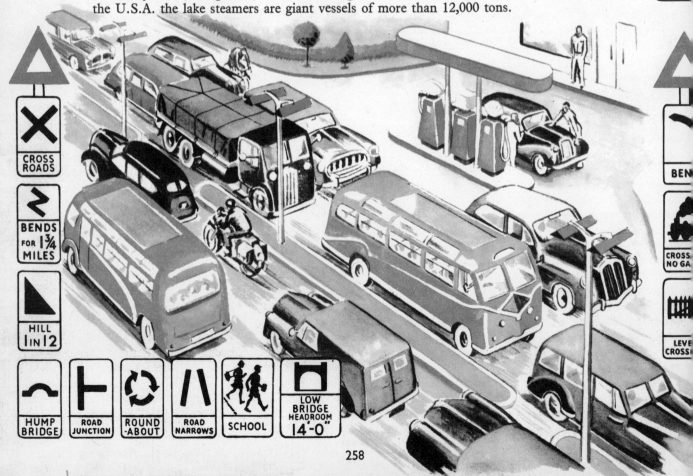

...AND BRIDGES

Though now a somewhat rare sight in England, on the Continent you still see strings of barges, long river craft each of which houses a family of bargees, hauled by tugs, which have now taken the place of the horses that used to plod along the towpath towing the barges. Locks with huge gates that open and shut allow a barge to move up and down a storey when the level of the canal changes.

The network of canals made in old river beds and linking the navigable rivers is so great that you could do a huge tour of Europe without changing your barge. You could start in the Rhône, go into the Saône, pass from it by canal to the Rhine, from the Rhine to the Elbe, the Oder, the Vistula and down the Dnieper to the Black Sea, completing a course of nearly 5,000 miles. You could then return by sea to Marseilles and so complete the circle. The canals may truly be regarded as highways, just as much as the roads are.

The motor car has conquered even the desert where the winds and drifting sands wipe out the tracks of caravans and the Great Salt Road along which, once a year, the 15,000 camels of the Azalai make their way from Timbuctu to the mines of Taodeni.

On the ancient Silk Road, motor coaches piled with passengers scare the buffaloes harnessed to carts with huge wooden wheels. In the narrow streets of Chinese towns, where no bus can pass, one may still see the rickshaw coolie racing along in the shafts of his rickshaw, and the soup vendor pushing his handcart in the coolies' quarter.

On the tracks of Africa, draught oxen and bald little donkeys huddle into the side to make room for huge lorries making for the ferry or the log bridge which the flood may have carried away after the last tornado.

The motor-car is sovereign. It has gone to Tibet by the roads of the lamas. The petty kings of Mossi and the Niger have given up their palanquins and taken to the motor-car, as have the great nobles of Madagascar. Soon the car will be amphibious, and you will be able to drive without stopping across the Congo, under the network of lianas that the negroes have flung from tree to tree to make an aerial bridge across the great river.

MEDICINE

Now that the motor-car has made it possible to get everywhere quickly, the services of the doctor and surgeon are as readily available to those who live in the country as in the town. When a person cannot or should not go to the doctor's consulting-room, the doctor goes to that person's home. In all parts of Great Britain these services are supplemented by the work of district nurses, midwives and health visitors, who do particularly valuable work in country districts.

In every town there is a hospital — several in the larger centres — to which are taken those who have been injured, who need operations, or have an infectious disease. There are surgical clinics, dispensaries, laboratories where analyses are made that guide doctors in their diagnoses, and special institutes for treating and investigating scourges like tuberculosis and cancer.

Surgeons can now operate on every part of the human body. They can even stop a person's heart and operate on it, while the blood is kept circulating in the patient's veins by another person's heart, or by a mechanical heart — for even that has been made.

After the great discoveries of Pasteur it has been possible to prepare vaccines against smallpox, yellow fever, tuberculosis, typhoid, typhus, etc., which, when healthy people are inoculated with them, make those people immune so that they do not catch the disease in question. Serums are also made which can save the lives of those infected by, for example, rabies, diphtheria and tetanus.

Since the discovery by Fleming of antibiotics such as penicillin, which saved the lives of so many wounded during the war, and then streptomycin, aureomycin and others, many of the most serious illnesses have been robbed of their terror.

Every country has its own system, but the medical professions of all countries are united in one thing: the belief that no labour is too arduous, no skill too great, when it comes to fighting pain and disease.

THE POLICE

Modern society, the nation with a past, must safeguard the future of the vast family that it constitutes. Each member who contributes the fruit of his labours is entitled to improve his part of it.

More and more schools have been built, and lavish grants make the highest education available to all. The development of social services, public assistance, free medical services, family allowances, pensions and homes for old people have greatly increased the people's standard of life.

Today children are taught in school what are their rights, their duties and the rules of mutual help among members of society. Society has its representatives who see that the rights of all are respected.

The maintenance of order and the personal safety of the individual members of our great family is the concern of the police. Each police force has its radio cars, and there are call-boxes from which anyone can summon the help of the police. Special detective forces undertake the investigation of skilful crimes — the activities of London's Scotland Yard have provided many a newspaper with front page headlines and many a writer with exciting ideas for stories — and police of other countries often co-operate on an international basis.

People who have committed some offence are taken first to the police station and then, if need be, kept in custody until the time of their trial. Then they are tried either before a magistrate or before a judge and jury at a Court of Assize, according to the gravity of the offence. Everybody can have a counsel to defend him, and if a person is too poor the community will pay for his defence.

Great ports have special police on their docks, and river police are supplied with fast launches, radio, and first-aid and salvage equipment.

The tremendous traffic on our roads has necessitated forces of special traffic police, who use every modern method to control and direct the flow along the major roads of the country, working in conjunction with local town and borough councils.

261

THE FIRE BRIGADE

The alarm sounds at the fire station. It has been given by one of the red fire-alarm boxes in the street, or by an emergency telephone call from a householder.

Above the garage where the big fire-engines stand ready, the men on duty have been lying down fully dressed. The moment the alarm is given they rush and slide down the poles that take them in a few seconds to the ground floor where the motors of the fire-engines are already running.

Speed is everything. Traffic must move aside as the engines roar through the streets. The cause of the alarm may be a fire, or a flood caused by a broken water-main: in either case, swift action is essential.

As fire rages through a building, hoses are rolled out and fixed to the nearest hydrant; ladders are erected — ladders 60, 90, 130 feet high — and up swarm the helmeted firemen.

There are thousands of calls every year. In London alone, there will be about 25,000 calls in one year — of which over 5,000 will be false alarms. But true or false, the men of the fire brigade must answer: they are always ready to risk their lives fighting a fire, saving someone from drowning or from gas asphyxiation, dealing with flooded cellars, rescuing people from a building that has collapsed; no matter what has happened, these men are swift to answer any call for help.

In many factories such as chemical works, where there is a strong fire risk, certain men are specially trained to cope with outbreaks until the regular fire brigade arrives; and every airport of course carries its own fire squad.

WHAT
WAS LIFE LIKE?

And now let us take leave of the present and make a voyage of exploration back into the days gone by. Let us explore past centuries and see the kind of world it was that other children knew. Let us discover how they lived, these children who were born in the days of Queen Victoria or of Cromwell, in the Middle Ages or at the Norman Conquest . . . and long even before that! Back past the houses of stone and brick, back past the thatched cottages until we reach a roughly made shelter in the forest or the jungle, where men learnt to master fire and make weapons from flint, where they hunted wild animals, using their flesh for food and their skins for clothes.

First let us go back to the days when our parents were small. They grew up in those strange years which followed the First World War, when all the world was tired and sad. The War had killed four million men, and with them a world that had been gay of heart. Now the old joys were dead, nothing mattered and nothing seemed worth doing *unless it was something new.*

New dances, new books, new paintings, new plays, new ideas, and new music — the new music called jazz. To our grandparents it was all very shocking, but to our parents it was life and hope.

Then, within a few years, disaster struck again. Not war this time, but poverty and unemployment threatened mankind with endless suffering. Slowly, very slowly indeed, the world recovered. Our parents had learnt many hard lessons, but all would still be well, if only the world could be spared yet another war . . . If only!

Yet for all these disasters and the fear of worse to come, our parents were growing up into a wonderful new world, a world that was changing more rapidly than it had ever done before.

Distances were getting smaller every day — more and more motor-cars were pouring on to the roads; Lindbergh flew the Atlantic, Amy Johnson flew to Australia, two of that small band of pioneers who blazed the trails that are now followed by the great airlines of the world which will carry you wherever you want to go in a matter of hours.

Electricity travelled across the countryside on giant pylons, bringing light and warmth to the remotest homes. Radio, cinema, and, newest of all, television, all had their part to play in changing the face of our world.

Yes, the world of 1939 was very different from that of 1919. One last example: our parents were given a penny or two pocket money, and bought quite a lot with it. It wouldn't go far nowadays, would it?

In the days of our grandparents

Back now a few years to the world of our grandparents. How different it all looks! The women in long dresses and picture hats; the men in drainpipe trousers and colourful waistcoats. And how gay it seems, as though this is a world that is sure of itself and its strength. The streets echo to the singing and whistling of popular songs, robust and rollicking songs from the music hall and the musical comedy. 'Things,' this world seems to be saying to itself, 'are getting better every day,' and it seems to be sure too that they will go on getting better and better for ever and ever.

But let us explore. Take a walk in the evening along a crowded London street. Gone are the fluorescent street lights of the present day. As dusk begins to fall a man appears carrying a long pole. He goes from street lamp to street lamp lighting the gas, for this is the age of gas, gas to cook by and gas to see by, an age which will soon give way to an even stranger marvel, electricity.

If we want to go any distance we can take the underground railway, which began half a century or so ago, or perhaps we should see more by bus. It will probably be a horse-drawn bus of the old familiar kind, but it might perhaps be one of the new motor buses which are just beginning to appear, strange machines with the body of the horse-drawn bus built on to a motor chassis. They are open at the top and have an outside staircase, and as they go puffing hesitantly by we can watch the end of one age and the beginning of another. For many centuries man was able to travel no further and no faster on land than a horse or team of horses could carry him. Then came the railways and now the petrol engine and in a few years the petrol-driven vehicle will give man greater freedom of movement than anyone had ever dreamed possible.

The first motor-cars were already beginning to appear when our grandparents were young, fantastic machines — four wheels, an engine and a seat — which hurtled along the roads at the unbelievable speed of ten or even twelve miles an hour. For the wealthy there was the Daimler or the Rolls Royce, but it was not long before new names appeared — Ford, Morris, Austin, men who designed and produced cheap and reliable cars, the Model T Ford of 1911 and the 'Bullnose' Morris of 1912.

Yes, our grandparents were lucky to be living at a time when the ordinary, everyday things of life were changing. For them it was a thrill and a sign of progress to be able to go for a ride in a motor-car, or to pick up the strange new instrument called the telephone and talk direct to someone many miles away. Then there were the gramophone, the moving pictures which were soon to become the cinema, and the bicycle fitted with the latest of inventions, the free wheel which saved you the labour of pedalling wherever you went, even *downhill*. But most marvellous of all was the aeroplane, a strangely improbable machine which as yet gave only a hint of the air age which was soon to follow.

It was in 1903 that two Americans, Wilbur and Orville Wright, flew a petrol-driven machine at Kittyhawk, North Carolina, and kept it in the air for just under *one minute*. Man had flown before, of course, in balloons and gliders, but if flying was to develop, the petrol engine had first to be harnessed to the flying machine. In 1909 a second milestone was

reached when Louis Blériot flew the Channel, a feat which C. S. Rolls surpassed in the following year by flying both ways in a Wright biplane.

The world was changing in other, less obvious ways. Do you remember how crowded the streets were when you first took a look at our grandparents' world? Nothing much in that, you might think, but there is. Look back a hundred years and you will not find the streets so crowded. It is not just that the population has grown — from 27 millions in 1850 to 41 millions in 1900 — but that there is a whole new order of society, numerically by far the largest, rising up out of obscurity into a position of untold power and influence.

The right of voting in parliamentary elections which had once been the privilege of a few rich men had now been granted to every man over 21. Women too were demanding the right to vote. For a long time past they had been doing work that people had once thought only men could do. Now they were claiming complete equality with men and they caused quite a stir in a peace-loving country by fighting very determinedly for what they believed to be right. Suffragettes, as the women were called who demanded the vote, chained themselves to railings, made inflammatory speeches, and even threw themselves under horses' hooves. All the same, it was not until 1928 that every woman was granted the right to vote.

In Parliament itself the two old parties, the Liberals and the Conservatives, were forced to acknowledge the rise of a third, the Labour Party. In our grandparents' days it was only just beginning and was a long way from its present-day membership of eight millions, though by 1906 it already had twenty-nine M.P.s.

But more important still, everyone or almost everyone was much better off than ever before. This meant that there was now a vast new market consisting of people who wanted to buy and who had the money to buy with, provided the goods were cheap in price. To meet these new demands more and more goods had to be made and industry itself grew bigger and bigger. Small businesses joined together or sold out to more powerful competitors, and so the great combines of the twentieth century were formed. They supplied the goods that people wanted at the prices they could pay, and in their own way helped to raise the general standard of living immeasurably.

One of the things that this great new public clamoured for was news and comment on the news. In the days before radio and television only the newspapers could satisfy this want, and innumerable new halfpenny papers

were started and very soon became famous names in journalism.

There was no doubt about it. The world was growing much richer. But it was still a world of contrasts, as every world is. Beside the new wealth were poverty and destitution, and many evils and problems demanding solution. But people were at last becoming aware that they themselves were responsible for finding the solutions. It had been said for a long time that the government must interfere as little as possible or individual liberty would be endangered. Now it was felt that state must give help where it was needed. Old Age Pensions were one of the first steps in this direction and a corner stone of our own Welfare State.

Yes, our grandparents' world was changing fast. Yet change seemed all to the good. Britain was looking forward to the future with hope.

And before that?

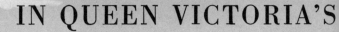

In the early hours of a summer's morning in June 1837 two men of great distinction and importance, the Archbishop of Canterbury and the Lord Chamberlain, drove out to Kensington Palace. They had come to tell the eighteen-year-old Princess Victoria that she was now Queen of England. Nearly sixty-four years later she died at the very beginning of another century, an eighty-one-year-old woman who was not only Queen of England, but Empress of India and symbol of an age.

How her world had changed! From being the Queen of a small island country she had become the head of a great commonwealth of peoples, of a great industrial and trading nation with responsibilities in every corner of the world.

England, of course, was by no means a backwater in 1837. She had a famous past and a great tradition. She had some of the richest farming land in the world and her cargo ships were known in every port. Now she was to prove that she was not content to dwell on past glories, that she had the resources, iron, coal and steel, and the men to take the next step forward into an unknown world where success would bring problems clamouring for solution.

Had you been alive then you would have found poverty and human suffering side by side with wealth and prosperity. In the North Country and the Midlands great new factories were springing up. They were always built close to the coal mines, for in those days it was coal and not electricity which kept the machines going. From these factories poured the iron and the steel, the cotton and the woollen goods which made England rich, and for a time the richest country in the world.

But in the shadow of the factory chimney, in smoke and

GOLDEN DAYS

filth, lived the millions of men and women who worked at the benches, the furnaces and the looms. Their hours were long, as much as sixteen hours a day even for women and children. The conditions were appalling. In other countries there were revolutions and the rich always lived in fear that one day the poor would rise against them.

In spite of this England remained a peaceful country with a long tradition of law and order. There was trouble here and there, of course, but seldom anything that could not be dealt with by the unarmed Peelers, as the men of Sir Robert Peel's new police force were called.

Every year of Queen Victoria's reign saw some new improvement in the way England lived. Both inside and outside Parliament the Government and the factory owners were pressed to make more and more concessions. England was fortunate in having a great many men and women, Shaftesbury, Owen, Chadwick, Elizabeth Fry, Octavia Hill and many others, who were determined to make the world a better place and let nothing stand in their way.

Step by step, hours of work were shortened and conditions improved. Health boards were established and the work of cleaning up the slums which had sprung up everywhere round the new factories began. Pipes were made of a new type of impervious clay, and for the first time it was possible not only to bring fresh water to each house but also to take the sewage away. Medical science, too, was making great progress in the struggle against disease. Smallpox was defeated by vaccination. A great French doctor, Louis Pasteur, discovered that disease was caused by germs, Lister developed antiseptics, and

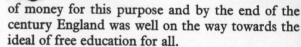

the use of anaesthetics made possible great new advances in surgery. Florence Nightingale devoted her life to the improvement of hospitals not only during the Crimean War but in England for many years after that.

As the years went by more and more men were given the right to vote in Parliamentary elections. Five years before Queen Victoria had come to the throne there had been a great Reform Act, which gave the vote to the middle classes, to the men whom England's industrial expansion had made wealthy and powerful. Two more Reform Acts followed and by the end of the century every man over 21 was entitled to vote.

If a man was to use his vote wisely and well he must be able to read and write and have at least a simple education. England had great schools and universities, but now many more had to be built. Parliament granted large sums of money for this purpose and by the end of the century England was well on the way towards the ideal of free education for all.

It was during the Victorian period, too, that working men first began to speak up for themselves. They knew that if their protests were to have any effect they must act together. But this was just what the Government and the employers, frightened by the terrifying events of the French Revolution, were most afraid of. For a while any kind of combination or union of working men to improve their wages and conditions of work was illegal and liable to be severely punished. In 1834 six farm labourers from the village of Tolpuddle in Dorset were charged with the crime of 'holding combinations of a dangerous and alarming character'. All they had done was to discuss together the idea of asking their employers for an increase of a shilling or perhaps two on their wage of seven shillings a week. Their punishment was seven years in the penal settlement at Botany Bay near Sydney in Australia, where hardened criminals were sent to work in chains and under the lash of the whip.

But all this was gradually changed. Unions of men

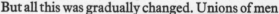

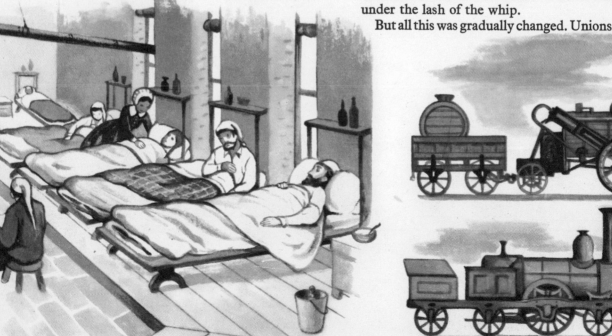

others pointed to the snobbery and arrogance of the middle classes who believed, despite poverty and human suffering, that because they themselves were happy all was right with the world. Underneath this arrogance there lay perhaps a great deal of uncertainty. Two questions were puzzling many people: What was man and what was the meaning of his existence? Archaelogists had proved that the world was much older than the Old Testament seemed to imply. Darwin had said that men were descended from apes. Had science destroyed man's faith in God? What could he believe?

When Queen Victoria died a great deal was still very wrong, but a great principle had been reaffirmed. A wrong could be righted by Parliament. Government must step in whenever its help was needed.

And before that?

working in the same trade not only became legal, but soon began to play a vital part in the life of the country.

What a world of contrasts was this Victorian age! England's wealth and prosperity were summed up in the Great Exhibition held in Hyde Park in 1851. The newest mode of travel was the railway, and as the century went by England became covered with a network of lines serving every part. Rail travel became popular and more and more people took holidays away from home in the country or by the sea where small fishing villages expanded rapidly into large resorts.

Other forms of communication developed too. The year 1840 saw the start of a regular sea service to the United States, and within a few years steamships were making frequent voyages to all parts of the world. In 1858 the United States and Britain were linked for the first time by a telegraphic cable laid on the bed of the Atlantic.

To us looking back one question is inevitable. Was all this change worth while? Most people would have said 'yes', but there were many critics even then. Dickens, Thackeray, Samuel Butler and many

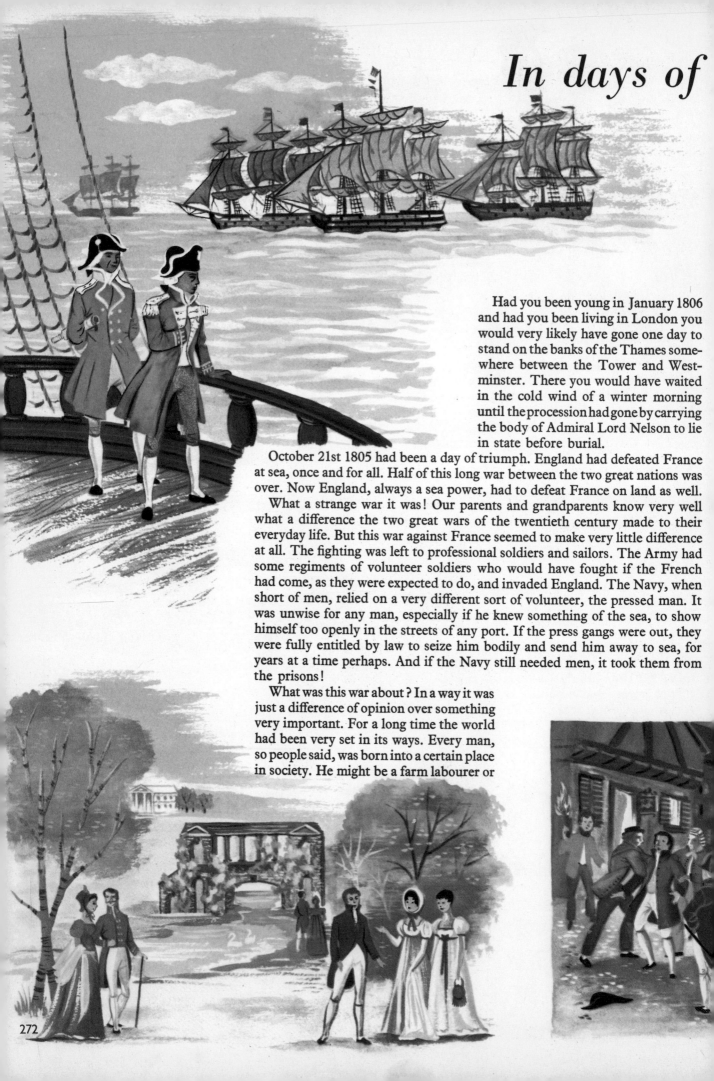

In days of

Had you been young in January 1806 and had you been living in London you would very likely have gone one day to stand on the banks of the Thames somewhere between the Tower and Westminster. There you would have waited in the cold wind of a winter morning until the procession had gone by carrying the body of Admiral Lord Nelson to lie in state before burial.

October 21st 1805 had been a day of triumph. England had defeated France at sea, once and for all. Half of this long war between the two great nations was over. Now England, always a sea power, had to defeat France on land as well.

What a strange war it was! Our parents and grandparents know very well what a difference the two great wars of the twentieth century made to their everyday life. But this war against France seemed to make very little difference at all. The fighting was left to professional soldiers and sailors. The Army had some regiments of volunteer soldiers who would have fought if the French had come, as they were expected to do, and invaded England. The Navy, when short of men, relied on a very different sort of volunteer, the pressed man. It was unwise for any man, especially if he knew something of the sea, to show himself too openly in the streets of any port. If the press gangs were out, they were fully entitled by law to seize him bodily and send him away to sea, for years at a time perhaps. And if the Navy still needed men, it took them from the prisons!

What was this war about? In a way it was just a difference of opinion over something very important. For a long time the world had been very set in its ways. Every man, so people said, was born into a certain place in society. He might be a farm labourer or

Revolution

a shopkeeper, a man of property or a king. But whatever he was, he must remain in the same place all his life. Man was not free and never could be free.

But the world never stays still for long. One man in particular set many people thinking. His name was Jean Jacques Rousseau and in his book *The Social Contract* he roundly stated that man *was* free, and if his freedom was lost he must regain it.

It was ideas like this and hard facts like the failure of the Government to govern properly which started the French Revolution off. Revolutions are dangerous things; so easy to start and so difficult to control.

England, like many other countries, was frightened. The spark of revolution might very easily spread, and her own house might be burned down, for there was a lot of old and rotten wood which would quickly take fire. Parliament did not represent the people, for only a very few Englishmen were entitled to vote at the elections. That there was a great deal of corruption in the Government was very well known. There were many who were rich, the great landowners and the factory owners for example, but there was also much poverty and distress in the farming areas and the new industrial North.

For England was going through a revolution of her own, or rather two revolutions, one industrial and one agricultural. The great English revolution which has long been known as the Industrial Revolution had begun some fifty or so years before. One thing in particular helped to start it off: the invention of the steam engine. There had been a steam engine in use at the very beginning of the eighteenth century, a machine which was used to pump water out of coal mines.

Before that everything had to be done by hand. There was one thing wrong with this early steam engine: it had a vertical up and down action and was no use for turning a wheel for which a rotary action was necessary. It was in about 1760 that James Watt developed a new type of steam engine with the necessary rotary action, and during the next fifty years the use of steam engines became widespread throughout English industry.

The results were astonishing. England was immensely rich in raw materials, coal, iron and wool. Lancashire had an ideal climate for making cotton goods. Altogether England was now in a position to take the lead in producing iron and steel, cotton and woollen goods, and all kinds of machinery, the things in fact which England needed for herself and which every other country wanted to buy from her.

Up went the factories all over the North Country, and to them flocked thousands of people in search of work. Where did they all come from? Many came from the farms, for agriculture was going through a revolution of its own.

For as long as could be remembered much of England's farming land had been common land in which the farm worker had a share. But when there were many owners to one piece of land, it was almost impossible to persuade them to use the new farming techniques which were then being developed. The big land-owners began to introduce bills into Parliament, allowing the enclosure of the common lands. Fences went up round what had once been the property of all; the farm worker lost his share and the large farmer had big new tracts of land on which his sheep could graze, and sheep were very profitable, for the price of wool was high.

So many farm workers were no longer able to make a living and had to leave their homes and seek work in the factories. In a way it was as well that they did, for without enough men to work the machines, the Industrial Revolution might perhaps have failed. But life was very hard and bleak for those who worked in the new factories and lived in the hovels and shacks nearby.

Here was trouble enough to start

a revolution and there has seldom been an English Government as frightened of the people it ruled over as was William Pitt's ministry in the last years of the eighteenth century.

But there were men who were not afraid of new ideas, men of liberal and radical opinions who were ready to challenge those in power. They belonged to the long line of men who century after century have stood out, for good reason or bad, against the Government, and in so doing have accustomed England to government by consent. Men like Charles James Fox and William Wilberforce did not believe that things must stay as they were; they believed that there was a very great deal that needed to be changed and that the sooner a start was made the more likely it was that England would avoid the terror and the bloodshed that France had suffered.

In some ways it was a gracious age, this age of revolution. Men like the Adam brothers were designing houses and furniture in a style which has since become known as Regency. The Prince Regent himself was building a fantastic palace called the Brighton Pavilion. But the future was beckoning.

And before that?

275

In the Eighteenth Century

London was a small place, or at least it would have seemed small to us, but to any man of ambition in the eighteenth century it was a magnet. If you had been born and brought up in the country or in a small town, life might seem to promise very little. But if you made your way to London everything seemed to be possible — adventure, fame, fortune. No matter that very few of those who came to London ever found the success they sought for; there was always the chance and the hope.

London was no stately city where elegance and decorum reigned supreme. London was a teeming mass of men out to make their fortunes and caring very little how they made them. True, fine houses were going up everywhere and the fields and farms of what we now know as the West End of London were being built over with such gracious squares as St. James's in the south and Cavendish in the north. But fine houses filled with magnificent furniture designed by Chippendale and Sheraton, and thronged with men and women dressed in the rich silks and brocades of the time, proved one thing only. They showed that there were fortunes to be made and that the men who made them knew how to spend them well.

Had you been young then, how would you have set out to make your fortune? Most likely you would have tried to attach yourself to someone who was already rich and successful and you would have hoped that he would give you some appointment which would start you on your way. You might have had to go to India, for that was where many of the great fortunes were made, or if Eng-

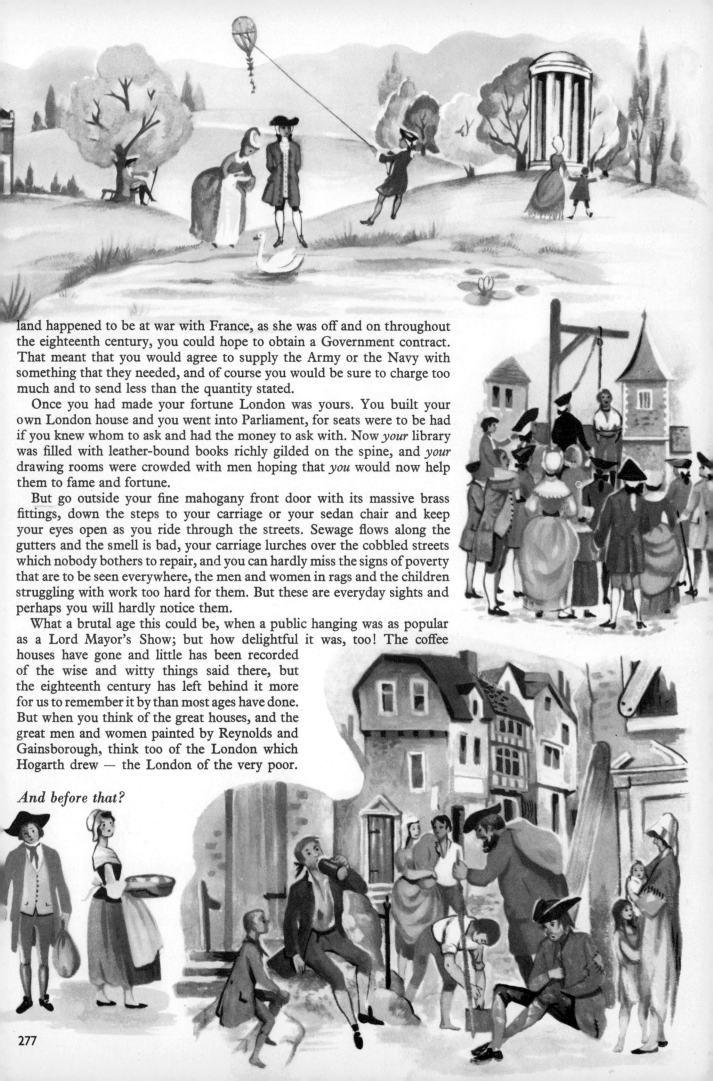

land happened to be at war with France, as she was off and on throughout the eighteenth century, you could hope to obtain a Government contract. That meant that you would agree to supply the Army or the Navy with something that they needed, and of course you would be sure to charge too much and to send less than the quantity stated.

Once you had made your fortune London was yours. You built your own London house and you went into Parliament, for seats were to be had if you knew whom to ask and had the money to ask with. Now *your* library was filled with leather-bound books richly gilded on the spine, and *your* drawing rooms were crowded with men hoping that *you* would now help them to fame and fortune.

But go outside your fine mahogany front door with its massive brass fittings, down the steps to your carriage or your sedan chair and keep your eyes open as you ride through the streets. Sewage flows along the gutters and the smell is bad, your carriage lurches over the cobbled streets which nobody bothers to repair, and you can hardly miss the signs of poverty that are to be seen everywhere, the men and women in rags and the children struggling with work too hard for them. But these are everyday sights and perhaps you will hardly notice them.

What a brutal age this could be, when a public hanging was as popular as a Lord Mayor's Show; but how delightful it was, too! The coffee houses have gone and little has been recorded of the wise and witty things said there, but the eighteenth century has left behind it more for us to remember it by than most ages have done. But when you think of the great houses, and the great men and women painted by Reynolds and Gainsborough, think too of the London which Hogarth drew — the London of the very poor.

And before that?

One day in 1660 King Charles II returned to England after many years of exile. He was a clever, lazy man who had lived abroad long enough to want to spend the rest of his life in England and long enough, too, to be no longer quite sure what the English were really like. He knew they were a touchy, troublesome people who, in a very bad moment, had beheaded his father. But his father had been a very obstinate man who had never learnt that it was sometimes best to give way. Still, governing the English was very difficult because they always seemed to expect so much and want to give so little in return. 'Govern us as we want to be governed,' was what they seemed to ask the king, 'and please do it very cheaply!' So Charles was left with all the work of governing England, and whatever he did someone was sure to speak up in the House of Commons and say that it was a bad thing to have done, and that Parliament should not give the king any more money.

The trouble was that the cost of governing England was going up and up. There was usually a war to be paid for, and what was worse the value of money was always falling, slowly but steadily. This meant, of course, that it was always costing more to do exactly the same things. Everybody found the same; food cost more and so did clothes and all the things that people wanted to buy. Strictly speaking, Parliament should have raised more taxes to help the king balance his budget. But this was something that Englishmen were always very reluctant to face. It was not that they were too poor to pay, for England was a very prosperous country. Agriculture was flourishing, wool and woollen goods fetched a good price, English ships were trading everywhere and there were a great many rich men about. But however rich England might be, it had become a matter of principle for Englishmen to say 'No' whenever they were asked for more money. The reason is quite simple. 'If it is our money that is being spent,' the English

CAME BACK

argued, 'we have the right to say how it should be spent. We won't give money to the Government to spend as they like; they must do what we want.' The problem was to think out the ways and means of governing a country well and yet letting people have a say in what was done. It has taken a very long time to find the answer, and perhaps even now it is not perfect, but we have devised a system of government by crown, parliament, cabinet and party, each with their part to play, that works quite well.

But in Charles II's day people were only just beginning to find out how difficult the art of government was. Fortunately, no one wanted to push things too far at the moment; one civil war in a lifetime was quite enough. In a way the years after Charles came back to England were rather like the 1920's when everyone was trying to enjoy himself. London was a gay place with plenty of amusements. The theatre flourished as it had done in Queen Elizabeth's day; the plays were mostly rowdy, rollicking comedies, but everyone was glad to have the theatre back again after the long and dismal years when the Puritans had frowned on any kind of amusement.

Charles had his serious side too. He was always ready to encourage the men who were exploring a whole new world of knowledge, the world of science. Until now people had been inclined to take the world around them very much for granted. Now they began to ask questions and not to be content until they had found out the facts. Typical of these new scientists were Sir Isaac Newton, who stated the laws of gravity, and Sir Christopher Wren, mathematician, astronomer and one of the greatest of English architects. Wren's great chance came when a large part of the old city of London was burned down in the great fire of 1666. To him we owe the present St Paul's Cathedral and a great many magnificent city churches, built in a style as delightful as any England has produced.

And before that?

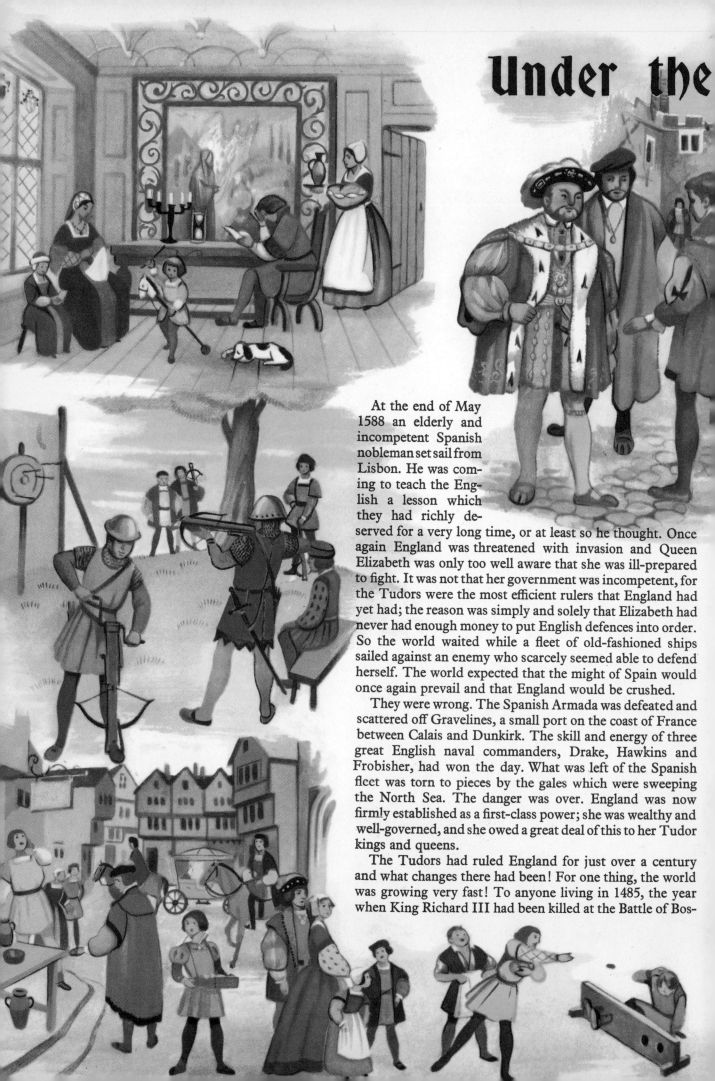

At the end of May 1588 an elderly and incompetent Spanish nobleman set sail from Lisbon. He was coming to teach the English a lesson which they had richly deserved for a very long time, or at least so he thought. Once again England was threatened with invasion and Queen Elizabeth was only too well aware that she was ill-prepared to fight. It was not that her government was incompetent, for the Tudors were the most efficient rulers that England had yet had; the reason was simply and solely that Elizabeth had never had enough money to put English defences into order. So the world waited while a fleet of old-fashioned ships sailed against an enemy who scarcely seemed able to defend herself. The world expected that the might of Spain would once again prevail and that England would be crushed.

They were wrong. The Spanish Armada was defeated and scattered off Gravelines, a small port on the coast of France between Calais and Dunkirk. The skill and energy of three great English naval commanders, Drake, Hawkins and Frobisher, had won the day. What was left of the Spanish fleet was torn to pieces by the gales which were sweeping the North Sea. The danger was over. England was now firmly established as a first-class power; she was wealthy and well-governed, and she owed a great deal of this to her Tudor kings and queens.

The Tudors had ruled England for just over a century and what changes there had been! For one thing, the world was growing very fast! To anyone living in 1485, the year when King Richard III had been killed at the Battle of Bos-

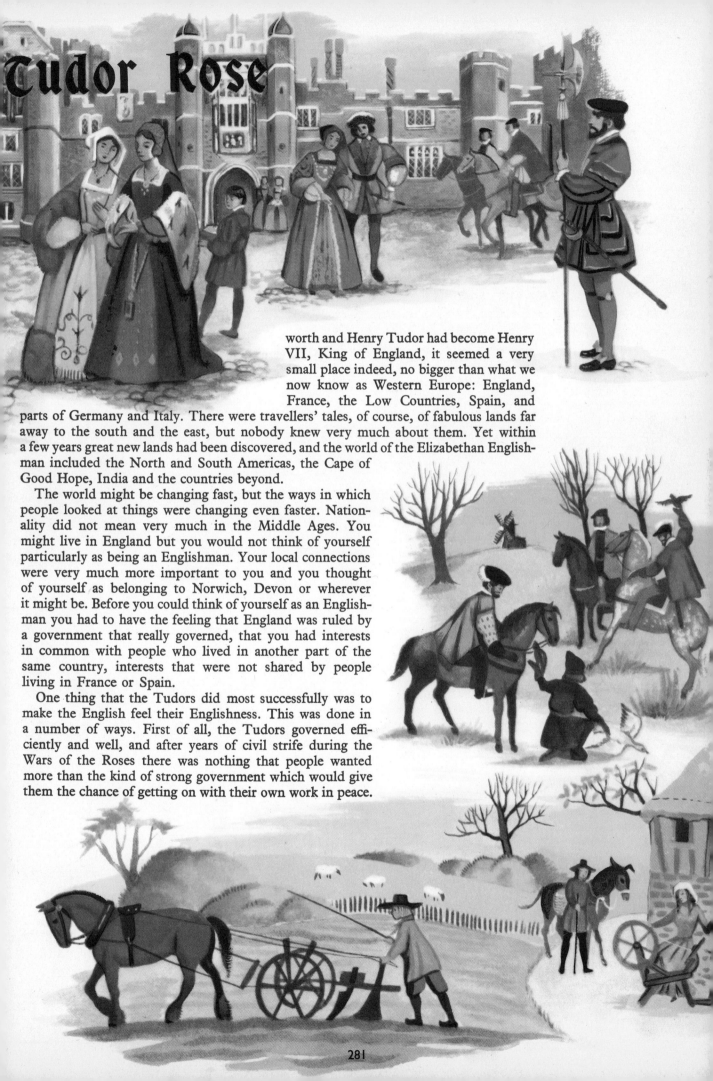

Tudor Rose

worth and Henry Tudor had become Henry VII, King of England, it seemed a very small place indeed, no bigger than what we now know as Western Europe: England, France, the Low Countries, Spain, and parts of Germany and Italy. There were travellers' tales, of course, of fabulous lands far away to the south and the east, but nobody knew very much about them. Yet within a few years great new lands had been discovered, and the world of the Elizabethan Englishman included the North and South Americas, the Cape of Good Hope, India and the countries beyond.

The world might be changing fast, but the ways in which people looked at things were changing even faster. Nationality did not mean very much in the Middle Ages. You might live in England but you would not think of yourself particularly as being an Englishman. Your local connections were very much more important to you and you thought of yourself as belonging to Norwich, Devon or wherever it might be. Before you could think of yourself as an Englishman you had to have the feeling that England was ruled by a government that really governed, that you had interests in common with people who lived in another part of the same country, interests that were not shared by people living in France or Spain.

One thing that the Tudors did most successfully was to make the English feel their Englishness. This was done in a number of ways. First of all, the Tudors governed efficiently and well, and after years of civil strife during the Wars of the Roses there was nothing that people wanted more than the kind of strong government which would give them the chance of getting on with their own work in peace.

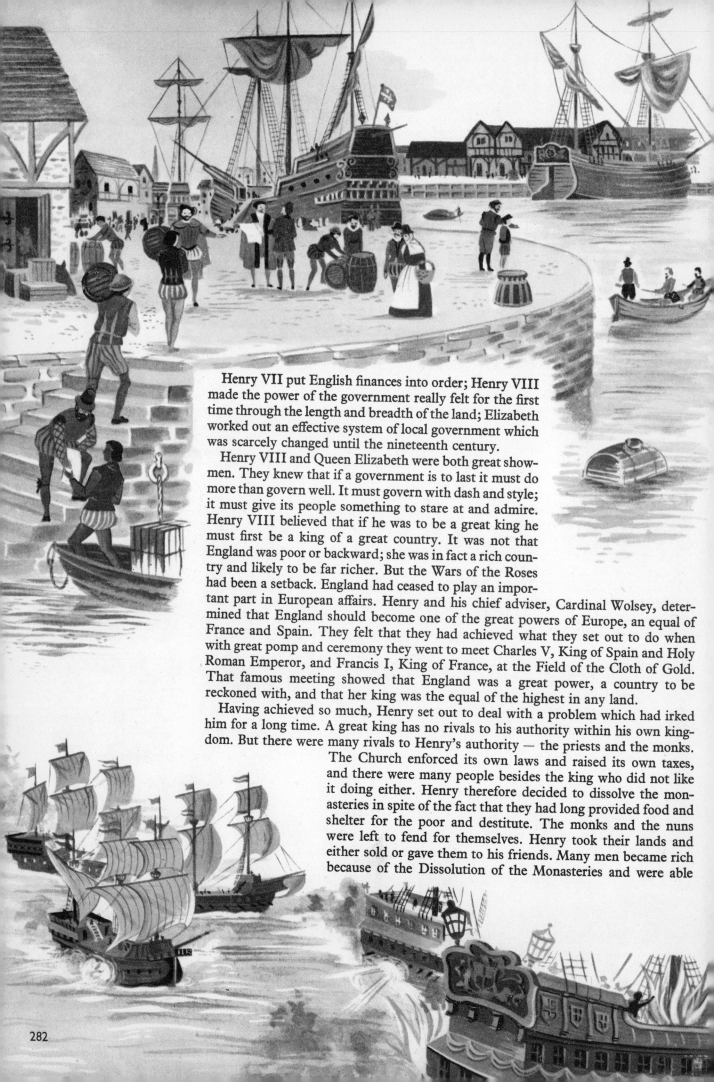

Henry VII put English finances into order; Henry VIII made the power of the government really felt for the first time through the length and breadth of the land; Elizabeth worked out an effective system of local government which was scarcely changed until the nineteenth century.

Henry VIII and Queen Elizabeth were both great showmen. They knew that if a government is to last it must do more than govern well. It must govern with dash and style; it must give its people something to stare at and admire. Henry VIII believed that if he was to be a great king he must first be a king of a great country. It was not that England was poor or backward; she was in fact a rich country and likely to be far richer. But the Wars of the Roses had been a setback. England had ceased to play an important part in European affairs. Henry and his chief adviser, Cardinal Wolsey, determined that England should become one of the great powers of Europe, an equal of France and Spain. They felt that they had achieved what they set out to do when with great pomp and ceremony they went to meet Charles V, King of Spain and Holy Roman Emperor, and Francis I, King of France, at the Field of the Cloth of Gold. That famous meeting showed that England was a great power, a country to be reckoned with, and that her king was the equal of the highest in any land.

Having achieved so much, Henry set out to deal with a problem which had irked him for a long time. A great king has no rivals to his authority within his own kingdom. But there were many rivals to Henry's authority — the priests and the monks. The Church enforced its own laws and raised its own taxes, and there were many people besides the king who did not like it doing either. Henry therefore decided to dissolve the monasteries in spite of the fact that they had long provided food and shelter for the poor and destitute. The monks and the nuns were left to fend for themselves. Henry took their lands and either sold or gave them to his friends. Many men became rich because of the Dissolution of the Monasteries and were able

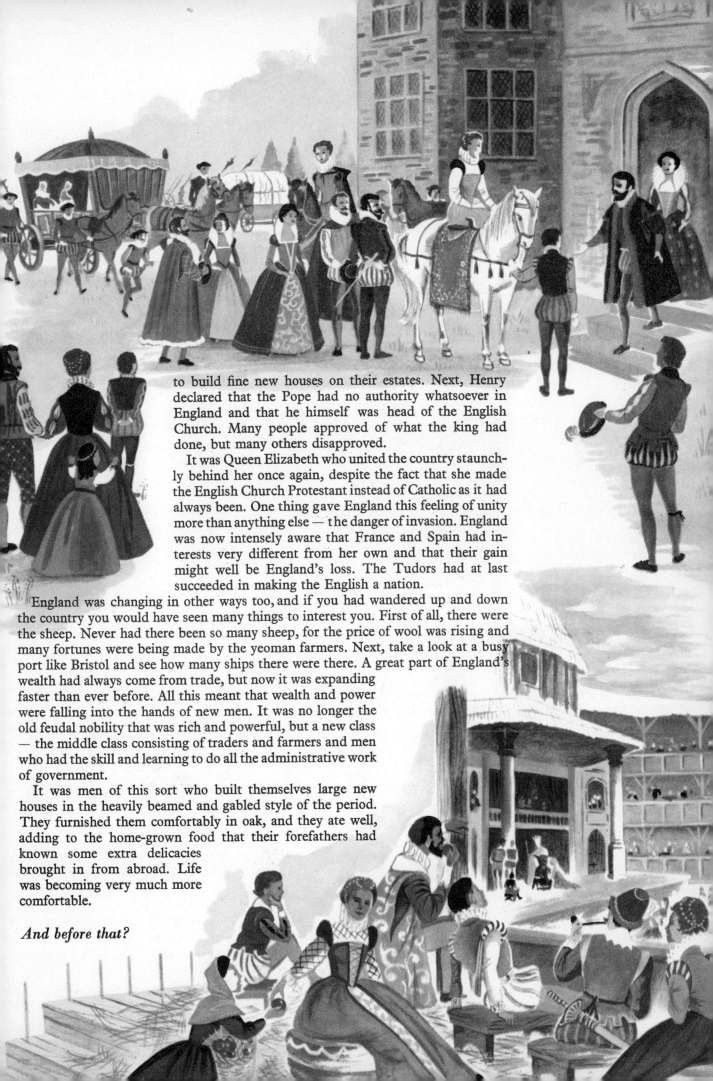

to build fine new houses on their estates. Next, Henry declared that the Pope had no authority whatsoever in England and that he himself was head of the English Church. Many people approved of what the king had done, but many others disapproved.

It was Queen Elizabeth who united the country staunchly behind her once again, despite the fact that she made the English Church Protestant instead of Catholic as it had always been. One thing gave England this feeling of unity more than anything else — the danger of invasion. England was now intensely aware that France and Spain had interests very different from her own and that their gain might well be England's loss. The Tudors had at last succeeded in making the English a nation.

England was changing in other ways too, and if you had wandered up and down the country you would have seen many things to interest you. First of all, there were the sheep. Never had there been so many sheep, for the price of wool was rising and many fortunes were being made by the yeoman farmers. Next, take a look at a busy port like Bristol and see how many ships there were there. A great part of England's wealth had always come from trade, but now it was expanding faster than ever before. All this meant that wealth and power were falling into the hands of new men. It was no longer the old feudal nobility that was rich and powerful, but a new class — the middle class consisting of traders and farmers and men who had the skill and learning to do all the administrative work of government.

It was men of this sort who built themselves large new houses in the heavily beamed and gabled style of the period. They furnished them comfortably in oak, and they ate well, adding to the home-grown food that their forefathers had known some extra delicacies brought in from abroad. Life was becoming very much more comfortable.

And before that?

The world is a very different place now. In the eighteenth and seventeenth centuries you would have found many things that seemed familiar though many others that were rather strange. But the Middle Ages were different; people lived very differently and they thought very differently. Things changed slowly even during the Middle Ages, but there are good reasons why we draw a dividing line about the year 1500 and say that modern times started then. The late fifteenth and early sixteenth centuries saw more changes in man's everyday life than had ever happened all at once before. The world we know to-day has grown up out of the past and each generation has given something to our modern way of living. But if we look carefully we find that it is the world of the sixteenth century and afterwards that has given us most, and that is probably why the Middle Ages seem so strange.

If you had been living in England in the twelfth and

thirteenth centuries you would have almost certainly been working on a farm. You would probably have been doing the same had you lived in modern times right up to the eighteenth century, but there would have been one big difference. In the first half of the Middle Ages you would have been a serf. We have been used for so long to coming and going as we please that it is a little difficult to realize exactly what serfdom must have meant. You would have had a cottage, a garden and a number of strips of land to farm, but these would not have been your own. In return for these you would have been bound to do whatever work your lord required of you. In practice this might not have been so bad as it sounded. Your lord, or rather his bailiff — a kind of farm manager employed by the lord to see that the estate was run properly — would have made you do so many days' work a year on the lord's farm. You might have had to look after the pigs or the chickens; or you

Middle Ages

said in favour of this old feudal system. It had started years back when the whole of Europe had been in turmoil and every farm and home had been liable to be plundered by enemy armies. Only a great lord with fighting men to serve him could offer protection against the dangers of the times. In return he expected service and allegiance. A soldier must fight for him and a farmer must farm his land for him.

When William the Conqueror came to England he treated the Saxons who had been living there as though they had no rights whatsoever. He proclaimed that all land everywhere in England belonged to him. Some he kept for himself, particularly the forests which became a vast game preserve where poaching was a crime punishable by death. The rest of the land he distributed to his barons and knights as a reward for their services. No baron received all his lands in one piece; he was given an estate here and another there

might have had to do so many days sowing or reaping according to the time of year. The rest of your time would have been your own and you would have spent it working on your own land. There were other dues to be paid, of course; when you wanted to grind your corn, for example, you would have had to use the lord's mill and to have paid him a proportion of the corn you had ground there. This system of doing work for your landlord instead of paying him rent could sometimes work quite well, but in other ways it was rather discouraging. If you didn't like your cottage or your land or the bailiff, you couldn't decide to move. You were bound by law to remain where you were and to serve your lord all your life. If you ran away you could be severely punished if you were caught, and it was not at all easy to find somewhere else to go where you could earn a living and not have too many questions asked.

Once there had been a lot that could be

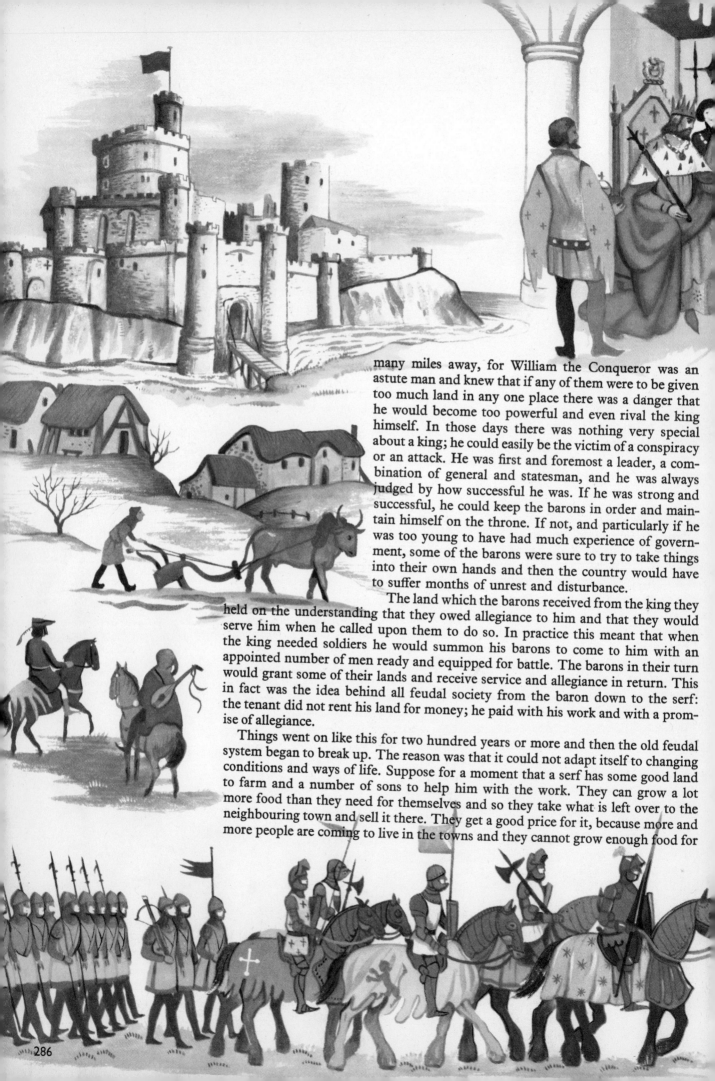

many miles away, for William the Conqueror was an astute man and knew that if any of them were to be given too much land in any one place there was a danger that he would become too powerful and even rival the king himself. In those days there was nothing very special about a king; he could easily be the victim of a conspiracy or an attack. He was first and foremost a leader, a combination of general and statesman, and he was always judged by how successful he was. If he was strong and successful, he could keep the barons in order and maintain himself on the throne. If not, and particularly if he was too young to have had much experience of government, some of the barons were sure to try to take things into their own hands and then the country would have to suffer months of unrest and disturbance.

The land which the barons received from the king they held on the understanding that they owed allegiance to him and that they would serve him when he called upon them to do so. In practice this meant that when the king needed soldiers he would summon his barons to come to him with an appointed number of men ready and equipped for battle. The barons in their turn would grant some of their lands and receive service and allegiance in return. This in fact was the idea behind all feudal society from the baron down to the serf: the tenant did not rent his land for money; he paid with his work and with a promise of allegiance.

Things went on like this for two hundred years or more and then the old feudal system began to break up. The reason was that it could not adapt itself to changing conditions and ways of life. Suppose for a moment that a serf has some good land to farm and a number of sons to help him with the work. They can grow a lot more food than they need for themselves and so they take what is left over to the neighbouring town and sell it there. They get a good price for it, because more and more people are coming to live in the towns and they cannot grow enough food for

themselves. The serf begins to feel that it would be very much more satisfactory if he did not have to spend so much time working on the lord's land. If he paid rent for his land in money he would have all the more time to grow food which he could sell for a good price in the towns. The idea appeals to the lord too, because it will mean that his estates become easier to manage and, of course, he can do what he likes with the money he receives; if he is not interested in farming he can spend it on something else. Money begins to play a more important part once everyday life becomes more settled.

England was gradually becoming a prosperous country. For one thing she was supplying Europe with most of the wool it needed, though for a long time she did not weave the wool into cloth herself. Then King Edward II persuaded some Flemish weavers to come and live in England, and from that day on England had a prosperous cloth trade and a reputation far and wide for making some of the finest cloths obtainable.

The growth of the English cloth trade was just one of the reasons why town life was developing fast. Towns were crowded and dirty in the Middle Ages, but what would probably strike us most now would be how small they were. Take London as an example. Norman London consisted of a small walled town built where the present city of London stands. The gates to this walled town had famous names which are still a part of London life: Aldgate, Moorgate, Cripplegate, Ludgate, Aldersgate, Newgate and Bishopsgate. Outside the walls to the east the Normans built the Tower of London, partly to defend the city in case of attack, and partly to remind the people of London that any attempt to rebel would be swiftly crushed. To the west an abbey and a palace were being built at Westminster. There was one bridge across the Thames at Southwark.

If we take a look at London in Tudor times, we can see how much and how little London has grown. London is no longer a walled city, because there is seldom

287

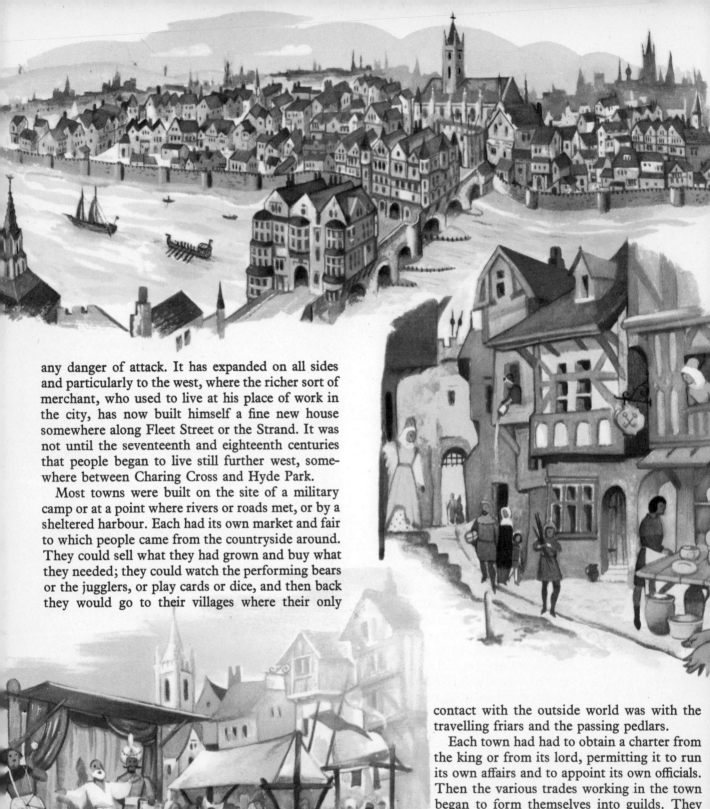

any danger of attack. It has expanded on all sides and particularly to the west, where the richer sort of merchant, who used to live at his place of work in the city, has now built himself a fine new house somewhere along Fleet Street or the Strand. It was not until the seventeenth and eighteenth centuries that people began to live still further west, somewhere between Charing Cross and Hyde Park.

Most towns were built on the site of a military camp or at a point where rivers or roads met, or by a sheltered harbour. Each had its own market and fair to which people came from the countryside around. They could sell what they had grown and buy what they needed; they could watch the performing bears or the jugglers, or play cards or dice, and then back they would go to their villages where their only

contact with the outside world was with the travelling friars and the passing pedlars.

Each town had had to obtain a charter from the king or from its lord, permitting it to run its own affairs and to appoint its own officials. Then the various trades working in the town began to form themselves into guilds. They did this in order to regulate the quality of the goods sold and the price at which they were sold. Usually the guild consisted of three types of people: the apprentice who was bound to serve his master for a number of years and to learn his trade thoroughly in that time; the journeyman who was a qualified worker at his trade; and the master who was the employer. The guilds did an immense amount of good, but like many other institutions they were unable to adapt themselves to changing conditions. Trade and industry grew too fast for the guilds to keep up with them, and in the later Middle Ages they began to lose their hold, and only the system of apprenticeship survived.

In most ways life was rather uncomfortable in the Middle Ages, or would have seemed so to us with our twentieth century standards of comfort and hygiene. Towns, we know, were crowded and dirty, with houses built close together and only an alleyway between them, very much like the old native quarter of an African or Eastern city. There was no sanitation and all the refuse was thrown out into the streets. Towns did not change a lot in this respect for a long time to come; they were still crowded and dirty in the sixteenth and even the eighteenth centuries. The Black Death killed a million people (out of a total population in those days of about three and a half millions) in the winter of 1348, but the Great Plague of 1665 and the Great Fire in the following year would not have wrought nearly so much havoc in London had the city not been so congested.

Houses, it is true, were gradually getting more comfortable during the fourteenth and fifteenth centuries. The Norman castle had been much more a place of defence than a home. Usually it was built on a rising stretch of land, and had a moat all round it and a drawbridge. Inside was a courtyard surrounded by a high wall, where you could stand and be protected by the parapet while you shot arrows at the enemy or poured molten lead on him. Beyond the courtyard was the keep, built with walls twelve feet thick and serving both as a place to live in and as a last line of defence. The keep contained everything that could be wanted for a long siege; there was a well for water and ample storerooms. Above was a great hall, the floor strewn with rushes, where everybody ate together at trestle tables. There were windows but there was no glass; when the weather was bad the windows were boarded over with planks of wood. A great fire burned in the centre of the hall on a hearthstone; there was no chimney and the smoke had to get out as best it could. Above the hall was a common dormitory.

Things gradually became more comfortable. Chimneys

were built and glass put in the windows. Rooms were panelled and furnished with tables, chests and chairs made of oak, and hung with fine woolen tapestries. Appetites, of course, were much bigger in those days. An ox or a pig would be roasted whole, and starling and lark pies would be reckoned as a delicacy.

Very few people then could read or write. Only the clergy had any sort of learning and this explains why the king's advisers were so often high dignitaries of the Church. But the reason why the Church had so strong a hold on men's minds during the Middle Ages was that people believed that if they sinned they would be punished in hell. A rich man would leave as large a sum as he could afford to the Church in his will in the hope that his sins would be forgiven. This may seem rather simple-minded to us now, but people then were genuinely and profoundly religious in their outlook. It was during the Middle Ages that the great cathedrals and parish churches were built in the incomparable architectural styles of the period: the Norman solid and square, the Early English lighter and more delicate, the Decorated rather too ornate, and the Perpendicular pleasanter and more restrained.

How full of contrast are the four centuries of the Middle Ages! There is the brutality of war and conquest, the squalor of the towns, the diseases and the plagues which spread unchecked because there was very little medical knowledge to fight them with, the ignorance and superstition which made belief in alchemy and witches possible, and the denial of personal freedom upon which the feudal system was built. But against these you must weigh the beauty of medieval architecture, the ideals of the orders of chivalry which bade every knight be the champion of the weak against the strong, and most important of all, perhaps, Magna Carta, one of the first steps towards the ideal of government by consent.

And before that?

IN ROMAN BRITAIN

they might come to accept Roman rule and not try to drive the invader out. In the north and west, where there was always trouble, the Romans had to keep an army ready for action. In the far north they built the famous Hadrian's Wall, a long defence line marking the northern frontier of the Roman Empire.

But in the south the Roman experiment worked. We have found a great many traces of the very comfortable life that people were living. There were large, well-heated villas, some with their own farms. There was a forum or market place in each town, where people met and talked or bought what they needed. There were hot baths like the famous ones at Bath, and at St Alban's there was even a theatre. We remember the Romans today because they built the only good roads that England was to have for many hundreds of years, but in those days people were grateful to them because they brought peace and security.

And before that?

When the Roman legions invaded Britain no defending army barred their way. They advanced quickly across south-east England and settled along the line of the Thames estuary. Later on they moved forward again and occupied all of southern England and the Midlands. There they stayed for the next three hundred years or so, and by and large people were happy and contented under Roman rule.

The Romans did much for Britain. They built fine roads along which troops could be moved at great speed if trouble should break out in the west or north. They built themselves comfortable villas and fine towns; Bath, St Alban's, Colchester are three of the many English towns of today which were flourishing places in Roman Britain. The Romans did all this with a purpose. They had to stay in Britain and they intended to make themselves as comfortable as possible. But more important than that, they thought that if they made life comfortable for the British

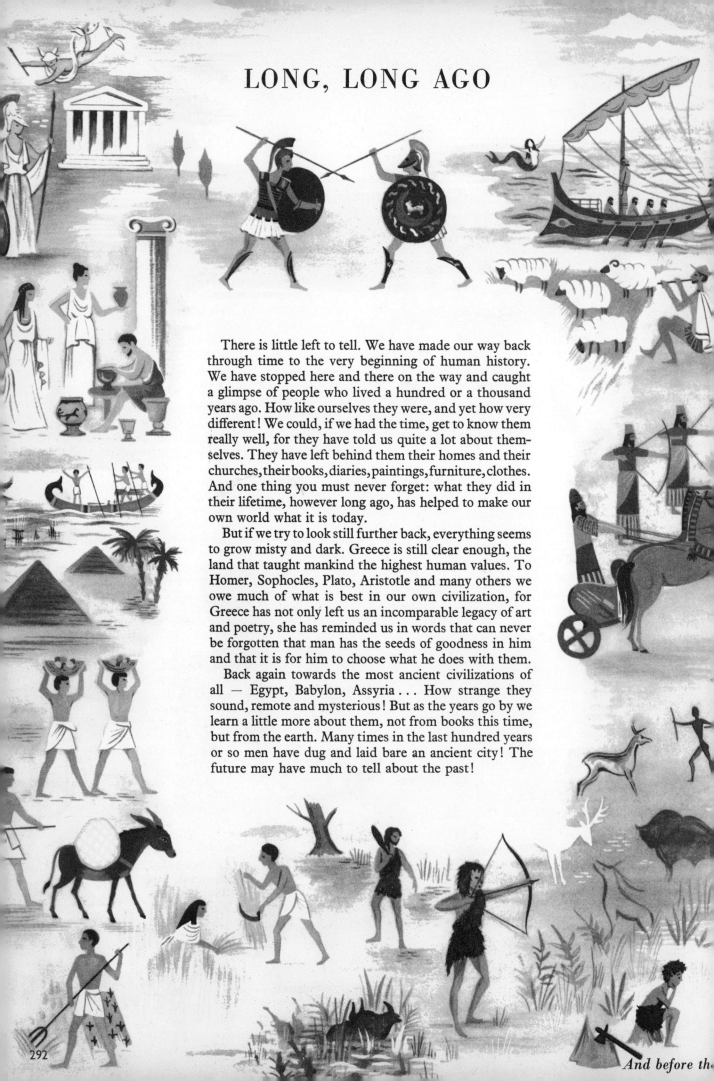

LONG, LONG AGO

There is little left to tell. We have made our way back through time to the very beginning of human history. We have stopped here and there on the way and caught a glimpse of people who lived a hundred or a thousand years ago. How like ourselves they were, and yet how very different! We could, if we had the time, get to know them really well, for they have told us quite a lot about themselves. They have left behind them their homes and their churches, their books, diaries, paintings, furniture, clothes. And one thing you must never forget: what they did in their lifetime, however long ago, has helped to make our own world what it is today.

But if we try to look still further back, everything seems to grow misty and dark. Greece is still clear enough, the land that taught mankind the highest human values. To Homer, Sophocles, Plato, Aristotle and many others we owe much of what is best in our own civilization, for Greece has not only left us an incomparable legacy of art and poetry, she has reminded us in words that can never be forgotten that man has the seeds of goodness in him and that it is for him to choose what he does with them.

Back again towards the most ancient civilizations of all — Egypt, Babylon, Assyria . . . How strange they sound, remote and mysterious! But as the years go by we learn a little more about them, not from books this time, but from the earth. Many times in the last hundred years or so men have dug and laid bare an ancient city! The future may have much to tell about the past!

292

And before th

I N D E X